PRAISE FOR *ORCHARDS OF EDEN* BY NANCY MENDENHALL

"Nancy Mendenhall has brought to life in vivid detail the birth, maturation and death of a tiny desert town. She tells the story through the eyes of one family, which sets out to create the good life for themselves and their children, pioneering as irrigation orchardists along the Columbia River in eastern Washington. Their dream lasted from 1907 through a world war and the Great Depression until the confiscation of their land for the Manhattan Project during WWII. An economic balance sheet would say that their dream failed; but the richly woven human story revealed in *Orchards of Eden*, a history that reads like a novel, tells a different tale. Through all their struggles, these White Bluffs orchardists loved their river, their farms, the town created and their lives in it for almost forty years, as few of us are gifted or privileged enough to do."

--- William Keep, college professor (ret.) and desert gardener
formerly of Yakima, Washington

"Vivid! Authentic! The life of an isolated river community before the Hanford Project ushered in the firestorm of the atomic age."

--- Helen Wheeler Hastay, educator (ret.) raised in White Bluffs

"I would recommend (this) to any reader who enjoys filling in the gaps of Pacific Northwest history...the early irrigated farming movement in the Northwest revealing all the odds against the small farmer, all the forces at work from the railroad and power monopolies to the government itself. A generation later I played in the irrigation ditches of the huge Columbia Basin project. Little did we know of the history shaping the farms, changing forever the desert lands of Washington.

The story is told mainly from the perspective of four generations of the Shaw-Wheeler family, as recorded from letters,memoirs and interviews. The family and others like it formed a small,lively community that supported them through the tough times and despite differences,created a shared vision of the Columbia valley's future. This well-researched and well-told saga based on the lives of real people deepened my understanding of the unique irrigation project that surrounded my young years. "

> --- Margaret Hamilton Wood, Ph.D., former resident
> of Columbia Basin towns, Wenatchee and Quincy

"Mendenhall does a great job of combining the rich personal history of an extended family with the history of an early irrigation project and the social/economic issues facing small farmers of that day."

> --- Susan Wheeler, descendant of 1907 White Bluffs settlers

Orchards of Eden:
White Bluffs on the Columbia, 1907-1943

by Nancy Mendenhall

Far Eastern Press
P.O. Box 9627
Seattle, WA 98109

Orchards of Eden: White Bluffs on the Columbia, 1907-1943 First Edition

Printed in the United States

Back cover photo of Hanford Reach by Rich Steele
Front cover photo of young Rose Wheeler and peach harvest from Marion Wheeler
Other photo credits are before index

Cover design by Eric Oberg and LesleyThomas
Interior design by Lesley Thomas

ISBN 0-9678842-2-5

For the Settlers of the Priest Rapids Valley, 1906-1943,
and their Descendants

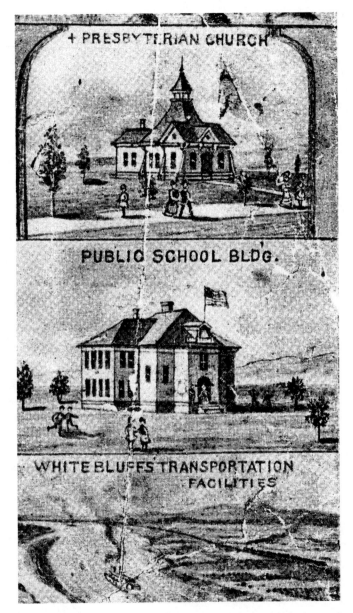

A1. Portion of land company's promotional brochure for White Bluffs

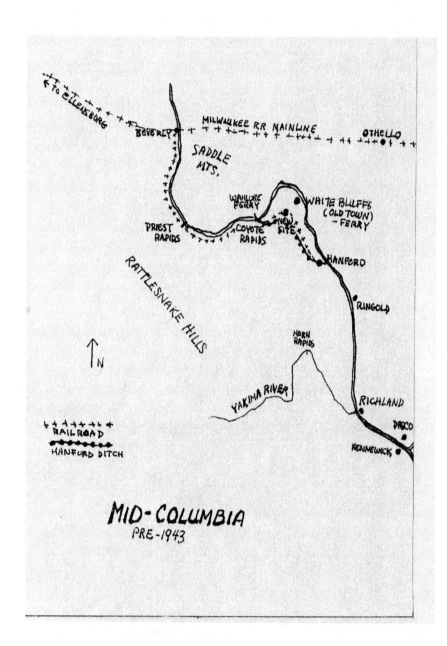

A2. Pre-1943 map of Priest Rapids Valley

A3. Portrait of Jane Niven Shaw about 1880

A4. Portrait of George Shaw about 1880

A5. Portrait of Frank M. Wheeler, about 1900

A6. Jeanie M. Shaw, graduation from normal school, 1899

A7. Jeanie Shaw Wheeler, as a farming partner

A8. George Shaw with beloved cow Nancy, named after
his mother

A9. Apple orchard in bloom

A10. Rose Wheeler with peach harvest, 1914

"What wondrous life is this I lead!
Ripe apples drop about my head;
The luscious cluster of the vine
Upon my mouth do crush their wine;
The nectarine and curious peach
Into my hand themselves do reach;
Stumbling on melons as I pass,
Ensnared with flowers, I fall on grass."

From *The Garden*
— Andrew Marvell

"Sometimes mid scenes of deepest gloom
Sometimes where Eden's bowers bloom..."

From the hymn *He Leadeth Me*
—Joseph H. Gilmore

ACKNOWLEDGEMENTS

I am indebted to the research, memoirs, letters, and other writings, of George and Jane Shaw, Frank and Jeanie Wheeler, Margaret Jean Wheeler Schuddakopf, Donald Niven Wheeler, George Shaw Wheeler, and Helen Wheeler Hastay. I was privileged to have many hours of fascinating interviews, in particular with Helen and Donald, and also with Marian Wheeler Coleman and Rollin Wheeler Morford. Marian Wheeler Burns retrieved an amazing collection of photographs from her parents' files.

From outside the family, I am especially indebted to Martha Berry Parker for her extensive research of the Priest Rapids valley, and to the White Bluff-Hanford Pioneer Association for all of the personal histories they collected and distributed. Mrs. Parker's strong sense of the value in the lives of the settlers, and the settlers' voices themselves, were important to compare with what I learned from the Shaws and Wheelers. Marthiel O'Larey, a descendant of settlers at White Bluffs, who has done an immense amount of research on the area, gave me great and continuing encouragement, as did Bill Keep. Olive Walker, a descendant of the settlers, shared memories in a letter. Bill Wiehl, another descendant, shared photos, and valuable information from the memoirs of early settlers. Annette Heriford has the gratitude of all the settlers and their families for her work in keeping the annual reunions going over decades.

Great encouragement and support came from my immediate family, especially my husband Perry, who put up with my weeks of absence each year and my mumbling, distracted answers to everyday questions. My daughter Lesley Thomas not only edited the manuscript but regularly convinced me of its value and kept me working. Far Eastern Press was an insightful, supportive publishing house to work with, and without them, of course, this book would not have been possible.

CONTENTS

INTRODUCTION

IN 1906 A LAND BOOM opened up in the Eastern Washington desert, firing the imagination of those who had missed the earlier rush for homesteads in the green strip west of the Cascades. Private land companies had procured arid land cheap from the government and the railroads and, hoping to recreate the speculation bonanza of the late 1880s, were now offering it with guaranteed water rights. The land companies' brochures flooded the country, and even Europe, describing the marvelous opportunity to become successful farmers for those with little experience. Many pages long, illustrated, and full of superlatives, the brochures were modeled on those distributed years earlier promoting homestead land for dry farming. But this time they extolled a different type of farming, a more efficient type based on irrigation.

The brochures reached the west coast cities and towns, now filled with sawmills and fish canneries, mud, and smoke. They had instant appeal. The tired myth that the West was an immense potential garden awaiting the victorious Euro-Americans soon recaptured power through the promise of harnessing irrigation science. Those curious folk who picked up a brochure in a train station or at a Chautauqua lecture read that they need not be concerned that farming ventures had turned out disastrous for families during drought years on the Great Plains. American land corporations, alone or with the government, were solving the problem. The thought of the good country life freed of its drudgery through science appealed especially to hundreds of families, non-farmers, who were dissatisfied with city-living.

The dilemma of the vast but arid West had drawn huge amounts of business energy for decades. With the remaining Native Americans now on reservations, it was unthinkable that the fortunes to be made from land speculation and development would be limited to regions east of the Mississippi and a green strip along the Pacific Coast. The government saw farther, that the settling of the arid West was not only business opportunity, but a solution to the oversupply of immigrants, unemployed workers, and impoverished tenant farmers in the East. Some economists even declared the West to be the answer to growing labor unrest. The Agrarian movement had loftier hopes. It saw irrigation as the means to fulfill the Jeffersonian ideal of a land-owning yeoman-farmer class, a class rapidly disappearing in the East, if it had ever existed. Horace Greeley had already started an experimental western community based on irrigation. John Wesley Powell believed the desert communities formed around a water district would have a common interest and have the best chance at a democratic local government, free of the corruption of the cities.

Irrigation's true believers had eloquence and passion that matched that of the Mormon settlers. Their argument was not that small farmers using irrigation could control the market—forces that would remain beyond them—but that they could overcome poor markets through the diversity in crops, efficiency, productivity, and quality that science could assure. To people with little commercial farming experience, it made sense.

Congress had already passed several pieces of legislation during the late 1800s to salvage western farming by offering public land to those who would irrigate. The legislation failed to help any but huge cattle companies who took the land through fraud, having no serious plan for irrigation systems. Desert land acts did not empty the cities of the unemployed any more than the Homestead Act had; as public policy they all failed. Few of the unemployed had the knowledge or means to move to an arid wilderness and create a sustaining farm, much less to build an irrigation system, no matter how marvelous the vision. So far, only the Mormons, a few Spanish settlers in the Southwest, and the Pueblo Indians had succeeded. But even though the desert land acts failed in their intent, they helped keep alive the myth that the West was a potential garden, an Eden waiting to be claimed and brought to fruition. Only courage and imagination were needed.

In 1902, when courage and imagination still proved not to be enough, the Progressive Republicans swallowed their dislike of federal involvement and pushed through the National Reclamation Act. It included funding for the needed dams and reservoirs at a few selected sites. Now, in the recharged enthusiasm, private land companies, some more responsible than others, put together corporations, sold stock, and set out to convince the public of the unmatched opportunity in the clean, rich desert. Some of these companies extolled the desert of Eastern Washington, through which the powerful Columbia River flowed. Though the developers didn't create the garden myth, they used it well.

In the spring of 1907, the second year of the boom, another crowd of would-be farmers boarded a Northern Pacific train to head east across the Cascades into the desert. Their destination was the Priest Rapids valley, a practically unknown district on the banks of the mid-Columbia. Among them were George and Jane Shaw from Hoquiam, a small rain forest lumber town still suffering from the 1890s depression. The Shaws had much in common with the other recruits. They were not professional farmers, yet accustomed to raising a garden and a few stock for their own use. They had moved several times already, each time farther west, until now they were turning back east. They were accustomed to a meager living, especially during the recent depression, and believed small town or farming life superior to that of the disordered cities. Now they were in their fifties, their children grown, and George, a timber cruiser, was often short of work. They soon felt at home with the others on their train, exchanging comments on the promises of the land companies.

Scattered among this mainly homogeneous group were some families who were better off, identified by their more stylish clothing and luggage. But whatever their background, none of the travelers had experience with irrigated farming. The Shaws had an advantage that would prove more important than any prior knowledge of irrigation or even of farming. They had partners in Jeanie and Frank Wheeler—their daughter and her husband—who would stake them financially during the early years of growing fruit orchards.

In addition to land lust and a spirit of excitement about harnessing science, many of the boomers shared another interest in the desert. Tuberculosis was the greatest scourge of the day; indeed, some of the adventurers were already infected and seeking a cure. Desert air was one of the few treatments available. Others were determined to protect their children by getting them out of the city, an idea the Wheelers definitely had in mind for their own toddlers.

The Priest Rapids area had yet another attraction beyond irrigated farming and healthy air: the fine potential dam site at the rapids. The idea of huge dams to power industry was just emerging. The Puget Sound area was burgeoning and already short of energy. "The greatest dam site in the world" was one of the exciting values that the land company promoted. Dams could mean electricity for farms, a rare commodity then. The brochures declared that financial backers for the big dam were in Washington D.C. lobbying. In the meantime, private irrigation systems that didn't need huge dams but could support hundreds of farms were rushing to get hooked up along the Columbia River.

Probably few of the boomers were aware of all the social arguments regarding the development of the West, but many were quite aware of the great fortunes being made in land speculation. In particular, land with guaranteed water rights was not cheap. Accepting the risks, they would look at the Priest Rapids valley and the new water system, and if it seemed close to what was advertised, they were ready to turn over their down payments and sign mortgages. They felt the risk a good one because they knew that the Priest Rapids valley, a type of desert called sagebrush-steppe land, had a great advantage in the Columbia that flowed through it. None of the large rivers of America had the gradient, the clear, pure water, and the potential power that the Columbia had. As for the climate and soil, one only had to look at the blossoming fruit trees of nearby valleys of Yakima and Wenatchee to see the possibilities.

The Priest Rapids valley was a strange sight for people from the coastal green belt. The desert fronted directly on the river with only a narrow riparian strip of willow and other brush. To the other three sides was a vast sea of sand and sagebrush, a vista broken by a few homesteads, encampments of scattered tents, and three tiny mushroomed towns. A new seventeen-mile irrigation canal had no water in it. But directly in front was the clear blue, fast-running Columbia, and across it, rising to six hundred feet, were the shimmering bluffs it had carved that gave one village its name, White Bluffs. That view was entrancing. Many of the boomers, after a few days of camping and pondering, decided to put their money down.

Ten years later, on the west bank of the Columbia and reaching out into the desert were rows and rows of bearing fruit trees and acres of gardens and alfalfa pasture, a brilliant show against the tan and sage green valley. In April the orchards blossomed as bright and fluffy as clouds. By summer they drooped heavy with fruit to be packed and shipped off to Seattle markets. Grapes, berries, melons, vegetables, and hay all were produced from the magic elixir of Columbia water poured onto volcanic desert soil. In the middle of this Eden was the town built by the orchardists and the small businesses that had followed them into the valley. Their community, isolated as it was, provided everything for comfortable country living of that day, yet was free of the narrow mindset of most small towns. Few families got rich, perhaps only those who brought wealth in with them, but many others chose to stay for the riches the valley did offer. Three separate immigrations would bring new ideas and energy to keep the community vital.

Today the farms and the town of White Bluffs, and its twin just down the river, Hanford, have disappeared from the map. No orchards or alfalfa fields exist, and there is little sign of those 1906-07 settlers or their descendants. The area is closed to the public, and nature has reclaimed the banks of what is now called the Hanford Reach, the only stretch of the Columbia left where the current still flows almost as it was meant to. At each site ruins of a concrete structure and a few rows of blackened stumps gives away the secret that something like settlements must have existed here. The rest has been swept away. In the background, across the sagebrush, are the surreal forms of what was first euphemistically known as the Hanford Engineer Works. Smoke rises from the angles of alien gray concrete that loom above the greenery of the riverbank.

In many ways the desert boomers' aspirations were little different from those that had pushed thousands of immigrants west across America. Their willingness to strike out boldly with little financing into unknown territory seems familiar. Some of the problems they could foresee, for they were the universal problems of farming, but many they couldn't imagine until that spring when they began tearing out stands of sagebrush for their baby orchards.

This early irrigators' story echoes the struggles of twentieth century small farmers everywhere to seize hold of a good living, a goal always slipping beyond reach, finally to lose out to agribusiness and industry. But in other ways their story is unique. White Bluffs became the imperfect but real life version of the small democratic communities that agrarian visionaries saw as the promise of the West for ordinary people. Hanford, just down the river, was another example. The measurement of their economic success or failure, cut short by outside forces, will always have a question mark attached. However, the success of the communities they gave birth to has ample documentation.

The four partners, the Shaws and Wheelers, and their descendants, are the personalities through which we can view how a great cause played out on a miniature stage. They were among the families that were part of the settlement from its beginning until its end, their observations being here augmented by the memories of other settler-irrigators and by the reporting of the regional newspapers of that day.

1

LAND BOOM

*"No attempt will be made to discourse in flowered strain on
the wonders that can be wrought with irrigation..."*

Land company recruitment brochure for the Priest Rapids valley, 1910.

FRANK WHEELER, a journeyman brick mason who traveled the western
states following construction jobs, was one of the hundreds of city dwellers
swept up in the excitement of the Eastern Washington land boom. Married,
and with three children, he was searching for a way to spend more time at
home. Now the promise of irrigated desert farming offered it. A few years
earlier, traveling between jobs through California, he had seen mile after
mile of lush, orderly trees crowned in clouds of blossom, a splendid sight
against the desert. That idyllic vision had remained, not quite dormant in
the back of his mind, along with a memory from his youth of the apple
orchards of upstate New York. Though good coastal farmland was beyond
his means, California had proved that technology could green the amply
available desert.

Frank Wheeler had received a classical high school education. He had
read Thoreau and Emerson, favoring Thoreau. Because rain often closed
down his construction work, he had times when he could catch up on serious

reading, more time, in fact, than he could afford. However, he didn't have to be well-read to be aware of the irrigated farming craze, for talk of it was everywhere, and as free and cheap land with good rainfall disappeared, the irrigation fad grew. Frank was sympathetic with the "back to the country" movement that had captured middle-class romantics, and agreed with the populists that saw evil emanating from the urban strongholds of capitalism. Naturally skeptical, he was not sure that rural communities were the source of public virtue either, but he was always interested in social reform and may have followed the Agrarians' arguments for federal support of small-scale, democratic, irrigated communities. The western plains and deserts he had seen were dominated by large grazing companies or corporate orchards with poor homesteaders living in their shadow.

Though Frank, the son of a Methodist minister, had never farmed, his interest in horticulture as well as his fatigue with bricklaying made him a potential, though cautious customer for a land deal. But much of the land taken from the Native Americans had transferred in no time to railroads and other private corporations through grants and fraud. The public lands still available in Washington called for dry farming of crops such as wheat, and this did not tempt him. Frank knew it was a long stretch between the concepts of the Agrarians and the realities of a farmer's life. Yet the idea did not go away; the vision of the good farming life was too powerful. He found especially appealing that an irrigated farm could sustain a family in comfort on very little acreage, and with labor so light that the whole family could join in.

The desert itself, not just farming, inspired him, a man tired of working in the damp, and of having his paycheck slashed by rainy "no work" days sitting in boarding houses. His eye may have been caught by land company brochures as he passed through a train station one day traveling to another job. One of them promoted a district on the Columbia River, highlighted by drawings of thriving fruit orchards and a pastoral little village. The misty memory of California orchards came into focus. He took sample brochures home to his fond wife Jeanie, and their new life was conceived.

Jeanie and Frank were an unusually good-looking couple, judging from portrait photographs. Margaret Wheeler, their eldest daughter, confirmed it in her writings. Of her mother she wrote, "She was small, thin, and dark complexioned, with flashing brown eyes... naturally pretty with delicate features and beautiful hands and feet." Jeanie herself boasted of her youth, "My waist was so tiny my husband could enclose it with his hands." That fetish of the times, a tightly corseted waist, somehow never ruined her health, nor slowed the hiking and biking of this young woman. Jeanie was a certified teacher before she married, teaching in one room schools in the rain forest of Grays Harbor County. She met Frank at his father's church when he came home from one of his work trips, and as she later told a daughter, "It was instant attraction, both ways!" He was a husky man of medium height with noble but friendly features, fair skin and curly brown hair. He was quiet in public, but with family he was full of dry wit accompanied by a twitch of smile and raised eyebrow. Jeanie found he loved to read, just as she did. Later his daughter Margaret wrote that as a college woman she thought her father was the best looking man by far that she had met.

After two years of colorful love letters from the traveling working man, Jeanie resigned from teaching to marry him in 1900, when she was twenty and he twenty-nine. The times were difficult for the working classes, but with wages of $160 or more a month, not nearly the bottom of the labor market, Frank made enough to sustain a household in reasonable comfort as long as his wife/household manager Jeanie could be as frugal as her mother and father. And as long as the weather cooperated for him. The Wheelers ordered a house built for them in Tacoma on a lot large enough for a cow, chickens, and garden. Frank disliked smoggy Tacoma, but it had the most active hiring hall.

Jeanie soon missed her small town freedom and friends. She was now left alone in the city while Frank traveled, working six days a week, ten hours a day. The situation was poor for a couple in love but typical for a family of a skilled craftsman in the West. She turned to a passion of her mother and many Victorians, flower gardening, while also tending their vegetable garden and chickens in Frank's absence. When they started a family with baby Margaret Jean in 1904, and then two years later, twin girls, Rose and Dorothy, Jeanie found she had more than enough to fill in her lonely days. She managed the home and finances, shopped, raised the garden and preserved its produce, cooked and baked on her wood stove, cared for the animals, sewed clothing, and raised the children, usually without help. Frank, often accompanied by his younger brother Nat, traveled up and down western Washington, sometimes working, sometimes waiting, wondering if there were a better livelihood for him.

The Wheelers were in many ways a typical western small town family for their times. They were "mainline" Protestant, lovers of nature and culture, and eager to try new "scientific" ideas and activities. But in other ways they were more unusual. They spent some of each paycheck on a library collection they were building. They were more radical than the norm in their social ideas, though not shocking for those times. From today's point of view, Frank's most unusual ideas were regarding women. From the beginning he encouraged Jeanie to develop her interests and talents, to read, and to go out in the community. When he wasn't working, he would stay home with the children so that she could. He didn't nag her about housework; in fact, he told her to put it aside and read with him. Donald Wheeler, their youngest son, says, "He was more a feminist than any of the women in the family! Where did he get such ideas? I don't know. Perhaps he just got them out of his own head." But with all the reading Frank did, he could not have missed the activities of the Suffragists, and with his family background, he knew about the earlier work of Abolitionist women. These brave activists, he must have noted, weren't all single women.

Frank's feminism was only one aspect of the philosophy he had developed by age twenty-nine. It was not just Frank's good looks and economic prospects that had attracted Jeanie in the first place, but his ideas and his ability to express them. She probably thought that he should have followed his father into preaching, as his father desired, but Frank did not feel socially outgoing enough for the responsibilities of a minister. Nor did he see that his father had felt very successful with his career.

It was one thing for Frank Wheeler to feel the same impulses that fueled the Agrarian movement, and to spend many evenings dreaming of his own family farm in a gorgeous setting, raising a healthy brood of children. It was another thing to entertain such a move seriously. How was it that a well-read, skilled craftsman at the top of the trades, with a good home in a growing town, and with a very young family, all girls, was swept up in a land boom? Frank wasn't a naive romantic. He knew perfectly well that almost all farmers lived enslaved to debt. He surely realized that irrigated farming could not entirely avoid the problems of traditional farms, and that farmers had been suffering hard times at least since the 1880s. A powerful need was driving him.

Part of his motivation could have been that he was already suffering the aches and pains of a laborer—rheumatism he called them, or neuralgia—and had no reason to believe they would get better if he continued with his occupation. He came to believe that Tacoma was not a healthy place for him or his family.

We don't know how soon Frank mentioned his plan to Jeanie, perhaps it was right away, but he soon firmed up the idea that they should buy a piece of desert land with guaranteed water rights and an irrigation system available. Then her parents, who were just making ends meet and were unencumbered by children, would go out to start up the orchards that he yearned for. He would bankroll them. Jeanie and Frank and their three little children would come out for the summer work. In a few years they would be thinning and picking and packing beautiful apples—and selling them. Before long the orchard would be producing fully, and the Wheelers could leave their smoggy city forever. We can imagine the hunger that grew in him.

Location was more important than finding free or cheap land. On the plateau east of the Columbia River there were dry-farmed homesteads that had once raised wheat and were now foreclosed, growing only dust-storms, not attractive at any price. If he must, he would pay the price that private developers asked. The one Bureau of Reclamation project in Washington, in the Yakima valley, already had its full quota of colonists. As Frank studied whatever he could find about orchardry, he may have missed the more technical discussions of American irrigation engineering of that day. Already government projects in the Snake River valley of Idaho were in serious trouble from the inadequacy of the water supply they had pledged to provide. But the brochure Frank had in hand promised that there would be no shortage of water at White Bluffs, for the mighty Columbia was not the Snake.

Today irrigation is viewed, with hindsight, as more problematic than it was at the turn of the century. There were few political or economic leaders who saw any difficulties with watering the entire West except for the technical ones of delivering the water and the cost associated. The United States had little history yet of irrigation's problems to make it leery: soil leaching, drainage, increased pests, or alkalized drinking water. Destruction of desert habitat was the least of most people's concern, while big dams had been thought of, but were a long time in the future. Yet the letters and memories of the Shaws and Wheelers show that they had true interest in nature for its own sake. They were not our stereotyped idea of Victorian extractors who saw in nature only what they could take from it. But unlike many environmentalists of today, they saw no conflict between Earth in its natural state, and what marvels they could make it produce with a little bending and shaping. Today's arguments over dams and massive irrigation and the immense problems they have caused would have been inconceivable to them. The Wheelers were bringing up their children never to throw trash on the ground, to cherish wild things around them, and whatever logically followed from those simple rules.

Frank's chances were good that with Jeanie's support he could talk his father-in-law into a partnership. George Shaw, a restless sort, was ready for a new adventure in a new place. Only his wife Jane had kept him living in his current home as long as he had. He was especially intrigued by animals, any kind of animals, so farm animals would do, along with the orchard. But Jane Shaw was a different matter; she was quite happy with her small town of Hoquiam, her friends, and the house Jeanie had helped them finance only a few years before. Yet she was a critical link. Of the four, she was the one with serious commercial farming experience as a young woman on her parents' farm in Wisconsin. More than that, she had the organizational skills that could have commanded a factory or hospital. Frank may not have known that yet, but he knew Jane's energy, that her daughter had inherited it, and believed that together the four of them could succeed as farmers. As for Jeanie Wheeler, farming's main attraction was probably that she would enjoy her husband at home more often. Much of their married relationship took place just as their courtship had, through letters.

The Wheelers, more than the Shaws, kept up with what was happening in the country, but all of them knew that the market for farm produce had been poor for decades. Only the idea of a more scientific way of farming and its increased productivity made the plan conceivable, while Frank's commitment to a continuing inflow of cash from bricklaying made it realizable.

Frank, of the four partners, would be a unique introduction to a small farming community. According to family journals, he descended from a group of Puritan Wheelers who arrived in New England in 1630. They soon demonstrated their independent attitudes by refusing to follow the colony rule that they must build their house within a half mile of the town hall, and as a result, removed to another settlement. Frank's father, also the son of a minister, seems to have had considerable influence on his eldest son's ideas. He had been raised in serious poverty for a time on the frontier. He was a typical Methodist of his day in his concern for the downtrodden and their souls, and in his dedication to evangelism. The Social Gospel movement, which combined political and social reform with its evangelistic concerns, was one of the influences on him along with the Populists. Frank Sr. was a missionary in India for twelve years, his family with him most of that time, and had returned to the States only for the sake of his family's health.

Young Frank had not been favorably impressed with the coast frontier when he climbed down from the train at Vancouver, about 1893, carrying his invalid mother and escorting three younger siblings. They were following his father and the two older girls to a new pastorship, leaving behind a beautiful rural area of New York. Later he would write in a fragment of a memoir he never finished, "We had nothing to do but go where father was...I was fairly stunned by the appearance of the country, slashing, burning, a charcoal jungle it seemed to me, and little good after the neat order of Central New York." He could have been angry as well with the church for assigning his father to such raw places as the western mill towns after his long and devoted service in India.

A young strong man could find work in Tacoma, usually in lumbering, and Frank went there to experience first hand how the lower class labored. "The RR wanted to hire us by the day--$2.25 and board yourself, very little for the hard work (I was an axeman) and expensive clothing, and I had to sue for my pay and pay most of it to the attorney." He was husky and willing, and never unemployed for long, but the conditions, as much as the pay, were poor. He needed a profession. Through family connections he worked his way into the trade of brick mason, the elite of the skilled trades, much as a lineman or an electrician is today. It was a most fortunate break for him and soon after for brother Nat as well. The country was crowded with unemployed as thousands of immigrants arrived from Europe daily.

While working in the Southwest as a new journeyman, Frank Wheeler crossed paths with members of the Western Federation of Miners, then the most activist and radical of the western unions, and dedicated to industrial rather than craft union organization. He watched and listened to arguments pro and con trade unionism, making friends with a radical unionist, Jake Andersen. Jake nursed Frank through a life-threatening bout of Rocky Mountain spotted fever and passed on his politics along with his good nursing. They became lifelong friends. By the time Frank returned to Washington he had read the publications of the Industrial Workers of the World (IWW) and other socialist arguments that explained the imbalances he saw around him: the gross excesses of the corporations, the destruction of the environment, the worsening conditions of small farmers and laborers. He accepted the concepts of class struggle and decided the socialist doctrine answered questions that populism couldn't. From then on Frank considered himself a socialist as well as a Christian. He remained much influenced by the Abolitionists for according to his letters he came to believe that the worst aspects of American culture came through the lingering influence of slavery.

Though as far as is known he never joined the IWWs, during his daily encounters he forced his natural shyness aside and began speaking up on the economy of the country and on the political scene, where the socialists were building a base. Speaking up, just as their father had done from a pulpit, seemed a duty to Frank and soon to Nat. They fought for the eight hour day, overtime rates, and safer conditions. On the coast construction jobs they were before long targeted as leftwing radicals and troublemakers.

Though craft unions were growing in strength during this period, the Bricklayers Union remained indifferent to the plight of common laborers and mill hands. Frank became increasingly dissatisfied with his union. Frank's children recall that he and Nat were so outspoken on radical working class issues that they had difficulty at times getting hired through their conservative hiring hall. That didn't stop the brothers from their conversion work. Frank saw nothing untoward in reading the socialist paper, *Appeal to Reason,* and the King James Bible in the same evening. When he was angry with the world and his inability to change it, he consoled himself with the thought that the privileged would get their due reward at Judgment Day.

None of this had much to do with tempting a man into fruit farming. But now in 1906, a husband and the father of three, Frank had to argue against his own beliefs and experience to convince himself of the sanity of his farming dream. He was aware of western land speculation and how public lands had slipped into the hands of the railroads and speculators. Liberal publications like Greeley's were screaming in outrage. Even people not well-read knew about the railroads and their land grants, and their tremendous power over the lives of western farmers. The very fact that the Priest Rapids valley used steamer transport, not railroad, was one attraction for him of that particular district.

This brick mason believed that he could learn what he needed to know about horticulture from reading such experts as Luther Burbank. To actually make a profit from farming was another matter. The land in production in the U.S. had doubled in the last thirty years, and market prices to farmers had been in a downward slide since the 1870s. The orchards he had seen in California were corporate orchards, the picking done by contract labor gangs, mainly immigrants, who moved from harvest to harvest for the barest of livings. Even in Washington agribusiness already had its beginnings in the hop fields of Yakima, where teams of Indians were hired to pick. Would small scale irrigation be able to compete with this trend? As a socialist, Frank was probably skeptical that small irrigators could overcome a risky market through irrigation's touted benefits: diversity and dependability of crops. Still, some part of him believed that though the irrigators could not win the pie, they could capture a bigger slice of it. There was only one way to find out. Hundreds of families across the Midwest and West with the same hope were pouring over the land company brochures just as the Wheelers were.

The Agrarian's dream was not just about farming but about community, and here too, the brochure Frank shared with Jeanie seemed to be directed right to them, for the Priest Rapids valley it promoted already had little boom towns with all the amenities of the times that farm living required: schools, post offices, stores, livery stables, even hotels going up. These settlers would not have to experience the misery of the Mormons' first years in the desert. The tracts were small and arranged closely around the towns, so that no one had to live isolated from neighbors and society unless one chose to. The women, in particular, would never succumb to "prairie madness".

Frank Wheeler was very much a family man, all important in how he looked at a venture in the desert. He had no interest in saloons or organized sport, or even in large social gatherings. If he wasn't working, he wanted to be with his family. His choice of diversions for Sundays (which he tried to keep though he didn't always go to church), was, in good weather, taking a launch across Puget Sound to a beach camp. In bad weather, he was happy reading and talking about what they had been reading. He liked to sketch animals in a casual way, on any scrap of paper, often with ballooned political witticisms. He loved sitting down to a good meal, then playing with his children. But he realized that his wife and her mother were social people, and that the nature of the proposed community was important to them.

Jeanie must have been surprised when Frank and Nat's after-supper visits turned from politics and shop talk to farming, but once she saw how serious her husband was in his desert dream, she knew she would soon say yes. She had roughed it as a child on a rain forest homestead and wasn't afraid of rigorous work. How could being a farm wife demand that much more than what she was already doing: raising and preserving vegetables, baking all their bread. Her interest in flower gardening would be blessed with endless sun and irrigation. She may have giggled at the romanticized illustrations in the brochures—one of them showed a woman cheerfully hoeing a small ditch, while the smiling children with her balanced small baskets of grapes—yet she too was influenced by the "back to the country" movement. She as well as Frank had the concern of many parents that even the western cities were becoming each year more crowded and disease-ridden. In the desert, her children could be outdoors all the time except when sleeping. But most important to her, once the farm could support them all, Frank would be at home with her and the children, and her mother next door.

Petite but strong like her mother, and also like her mother, never timid, Jeanie demonstrated ambition early when she sold mail-order spices door-to-door. Her 1897 diary doesn't reveal much of her inner thought—she wrote that she worried it would be read by little brothers—but reveals a girl with interests not much different from many small town girls of today. She wrote about girl and boy friends, school and church, with occasional comments about her spice business, child care jobs, and her classes, which she always excelled in. Though Jeanie had many responsibilities, her mother, described by her descendants as a rather liberal Calvinist, saw to it that the girl also had free time. She even permitted excursions with boys from respectable families the Shaws knew.

One day's diary entry gives the flavor of small town teen activities of 1897, carefully censored for curious eyes:

> July 15th: About 9 o'clock Burton came and wanted
> me to go berrying. I didn't want to very much, but at
> last I said I would go. So about 12:30 we started and
> such a crazy boat. It turned completely around several
> times. We had bad luck and didn't get hardly any
> berries. After supper I put on my cream waist and went
> down to prayer meeting. I wish I could be a better
> Christian. The meeting was very interesting about the
> "thorn in the flesh" to keep us from being too exalted.

Jeanie often comments in her diary how much she liked a certain sermon, but seemed to have few concerns about her personal state of sin; at least, this is one of the few times she mentions it. The girl had more real worries early in life. During the same period she writes, "Papa quit work again." Another time, "We finally got our bills paid off." She sometimes expresses concern about her mother and her fear that she is overworking. In order to make ends meet, Jane was taking in laundry, delivering the surplus milk from their cow, and caring for neighbors' children, as well as raising three young sons with a father often absent. Two years before, the Shaws had lost a six- month-old baby girl to childhood disease.

Jeanie was successful with her spice sales. A favorite family photo shows her posing, proud and pretty, next to the bicycle she earned, and her mother got a sewing machine. Another photo, published in the local paper, shows her and two girl friends standing on the peak of Mt. Baldy, near Lake Quinault. These young westerners had gone up in a crowd by horseback. But a good part of the year the rain poured down and kept even the most intrepid girl indoors. Then she turned to her beloved books.

After Jeanie finished the tenth grade she enrolled in a teacher-prep academy at Montesano, where she was soon first in her class in all but geometry, and in that she was second. She wrote in her diary that she yearned to go to a real college, but this would do. She graduated at seventeen and went to her first teaching assignment at the Humptulips settlement in the forest. Two of her brothers, as soon as they could work, followed her father into the woods. The third and youngest would fulfill his mother's hopes after an unstudious childhood, and not only finish college but become a state veterinarian, then a college professor of animal husbandry at Oregon State College. He set a precedent.

Jeanie had a natural flair for teaching and was popular in her one-room schools in the village communities. She was barely older than some of her boy students, who probably would have done anything for her smile. She had already paid for a house to be started for her parents when she met Frank Wheeler. Marriage in those days meant by state law that a woman could no longer teach full time, but she decided Frank was more important than her career.

The respect and friendship that grew out of the Wheelers' physical attraction carried them through long absences and difficult times. Fortunately both of them liked to write as well as read for they would get much practice at it over their lives, trying to stay in contact. It was not that unusual for a traveling man to write to his family, but Frank's letters, which he apparently never edited, were special in their wide range of topics and his free expression of personal feelings. They covered anything on his mind, running from natural history to politics, from religion to health to family concerns, always with a strong point of view. A passage from one of his later letters to his oldest daughter is typical of his style when he was angry and frustrated with "the system" that kept ordinary folk from the good life:

> The tragedy of life is to me that it would be so easily possible to put travel and good living in reach of all and yet there can be nothing but the sheerest stupid rancor. None of the potential energies of nature are touched nor the creative abilities employed. Because the U.S. chooses to construct a worse than pagan System of Exploitation of every productive thing for a few, with a more than Inquisitorial Mandate, the same old piffle of tariffs, armies, race hatreds, and all such must continue to distract and insult thinking people.

Clearly Frank was thinking about much more than slapping mortar on bricks, or what he would do on his next day off. One wonders what he would have done with his life if he had not gone into the desert venture. He had occasion many times to muse on that.

In the winter of 1906-07, the Wheelers lost one of their six-month old twins to pneumonia following an epidemic of whooping cough. Just before or after this sad time they became committed to moving to the country, the death adding fuel to their conviction that they must find a better place to raise a family. Despite the grief and guilt they suffered, they were sure they hadn't lost their baby through neglect, and blamed it at least partly on the climate and pollution of Tacoma as well the whooping cough and other regular epidemics that plagued the city. The fact that the Shaws had also lost a baby to an earlier epidemic made the concern for infant health even more urgent.

With antibiotics unknown until 1928, many people of the Wheelers' generation were convinced of the necessity of fresh food, fresh air, and outdoor exercise for good health, especially for the lungs, especially for children. We know from Frank's letters that he believed these teachings, and especially in the value of fresh, natural food. The Wheelers consulted their homeopathic family physician about their idea of desert farming. He assured them that the climate of rural Eastern Washington would be far more healthy for children, though he could not recommend the Yakima valley, where typhoid was active. Because of Frank's interest in horticulture, another influence may have been Luther Burbank, who wrote in 1907 in his "The Training of the Human Plant" that children needed to be raised in the country. But it was not just physical health that concerned Frank. He believed that Tacoma was socially and morally ill, based in part on his observations regarding construction contracts.[1]

Frank's reasons for making a risky move into a farm investment obviously had several strong influences. We don't know so much about Jeanie's early sociopolitical ideas or how they may have influenced her willingness. She had a strong role model in her mother who was a supporter of the WCTU. It was concerned for many women's issues, not just temperance. "Temperance, Moral Purity, and World Peace", its national platform, was nothing to laugh at, the moral purity part being specifically directed at the epidemic venereal diseases that were ruining families. Conservative people condescended to the organization, not because it was ridiculous, as they pretended, but because they feared it. It is safe to say that Jeanie grew up familiar with such concerns as poverty, women's suffrage, and child labor laws. But the ideas that buzzed around her may have had nothing to do with her agreeing to go farming; her personal reasons were enough. Though she was strong, we know from letters that being housebound with noisy children in poor weather exasperated her when she longed to be out in her flowers. If the Wheelers were successful orchardists, another dream could be realized. Both she and Frank, though modest in their own needs, were ambitious that all of their children be able to attend college.

For the partnership piece of the Wheelers' scheme to work, it was fortuitous that Jeanie got along well with her parents. She was the linch pin there as her husband and her father were not close friends, and were too different in temperament ever to become so. Yet she apparently believed they could be good partners with the addition of her energetic mother. Frank also tried to get Nat, his brother, to join in the desert farming venture. Nat's interest was not so much in farming as in the outdoor adventure the Columbia could provide. He would try the desert for one summer, but found he couldn't handle the heat and the rash he developed. Then, except for visits, he bowed out. That must have disappointed Frank, but the enthusiasm spread, for one of Jeanie's brothers, Win Shaw, and his wife Juliette, would soon claim a desert tract of their own.

The Wheelers, sometime during 1906 or early 1907, arrived at the Shaws' home with the land company's brochure in hand. For anyone with an interest in farming, especially those with little hard experience, it would have been difficult not to be excited by the pages of colorful description, fancy with calligraphy and illustrations, and full of superlatives that spoke to the "Myth of the Garden". Only a shred of the Wheeler's original brochure remains, but a 1910 version by Fred Weil, agent for the Columbia River Land Company, is representative in content and style of what they studied:

"No attempt will be made to discourse in flowered strain on the wonders that can be wrought by irrigation, to paint in glowing phrases the transformation of the desert into a land flowing in milk and honey..." Thus the twelve pages began, and then went on in more concrete detail about most questions a

buyer might have. "...Plenty of water, purest in the
world for drinking, excellent drainage, need not fear
for the health conditions, subsoil loose gravel, no alkali;
White Bluffs leads all other districts." More... "Climate
is White Bluffs' greatest asset from a commercial
aspect. Growing season commences three weeks earlier,
ends three weeks later [than the nearby Yakima]...The
Power Co. furnishes power at reasonable rates for both
irrigation and domestic uses."[2]

The brochure went on to proclaim that ground could be cleared and
ready to plant for $10 an acre, that a farmer could get at least four
cuttings of alfalfa, that apple trees grew six feet in a season, that destructive
frosts were almost unknown, and that settlers would experience warm days
and cool nights, little snowfall, and of rain, six or seven inches annually. The
brochure had appropriate testimonials from local business and from
government experts. "No irrigated district is the superior of the White
Bluffs country: soil, climate, vast area, irrigation possibilities, a wonderful
country!" was the accolade from the president of the Yakima Valley Bank.
And it was no wilderness; a daily steamer brought supplies and passengers up
the river.

The land company did not dwell on the problems of desert farming. The
promised "warm days and cool nights", it turned out, could in summer be hot
days and hot nights. Right then, to the two couples watching the Hoquiam
rain run down the window, the image of endless sun seemed very fine. The
statement about the "rarity of killing frosts" was not innocent error, since
the true information was available from the agricultural college, but would
be believed by those not familiar with deserts. The brochure didn't mention
the dust storms nor the insect pest problems that had already developed in
the neighboring Yakima valley. Of course it said nothing about the

depression in agriculture that had become endemic, nor did it discuss the power rates, or freight rates, or the virtual monopoly on buying enjoyed by the fruit brokerage houses in Seattle.

Regarding the irrigation system under construction, the brochure was just as optimistic: "The Hanford people have overcome all the problems and vexation incident to the starting of a great irrigation project, and the system is in very successful operation. There is no irrigation company superior to the Hanford Co. in financial strength, integrity, and responsibility". The brochure sidestepped entirely the fact that this particular stretch of the magnificent Columbia had serious problems for irrigators, and contrary to what was claimed, they had not all been solved. The engineers and the construction crews were racing to solve them before the settlers arrived.

Regarding the important matter of transportation of fruit from the remote valley to market, the brochure more modestly admitted that lack of a railroad line was a drawback, but added that the Milwaukee Road would shortly build a branch line, with two other railroads mentioned as sure to come in. This would place the district's products within six hours of the Puget Sound markets. In the meantime the growers could continue to use the river steamers, raise less perishable crops, and watch their fruit trees grow up. The steamer traffic would assure competition to the railroad, and keep shipping prices down.

The steamer connection was more than practical transport. The charming riverbank setting of White Bluffs with its daily steamer traffic on the Columbia was one of the most appealing (and true) of the brochure's enticements. Probably most of the clients of the land companies took the brochure for what it was, huckster hyperbole, and like the Shaws and Wheelers, expected to go out and look for themselves.

George and Jane Shaw, sometime during winter of 1906-7, agreed to be the vanguard of the desert orchard venture. It would be a third pioneering move for each of them, but so different from those previous that the novelty must have provided fresh energy needed, especially for Jane, who had sworn she was through with reckless migrations.

2

BREAKING GROUND

"Any one of my daughters will do what three men can."
John Niven, of Jane and her three sisters, re: their farm work, 1870s

GEORGE SHAW'S ANCESTORS had been farming in America for
generations when Jane Niven, his wife to be, arrived in America from
Paisley, near Glasgow. The Shaws had abandoned the rocky fields of New
England following the western garden myth, and they converged with the
Nivens in barely settled Waupaca County, Wisconsin in the 1870s. Jane was
a rural school teacher of twenty-four when she fell for George's charms,
with no idea it would lead her into a deeper wilderness. But George was
really by preference a woodsman and hunter more than a farmer, and
lumbering the old growth was about over in Wisconsin. The Shaws were
parents of four young children when they moved to the rain forest of
Southwest Washington where there was plenty of timber left to be cut. They
joined hundreds of other Midwesterners who were tenant farmers or had
not succeeded on their original homesteads and had the energy to try again,
homesteading the magical green country of the Pacific Northwest.

George's family story was classic American Pioneer. Before Wisconsin,
both his father and mother's sides had been farming poor ground in New

Hampshire. His grandmother on the Shaw side, Hannah Leather, was probably Native American. The Shaws were originally from Scotland. while his mother's Johnson family had come from Great Britain before the Revolution. In the mid-1800s a number of the Johnsons joined a migration of New Englanders who traveled to Kansas for better farm land. Some of them were also in hope of swinging the vote to make it a free rather than slave state like neighboring Missouri. Whether the Johnsons were active Abolitionists or simply looking for land, all Yankees were considered enemies by slave-holding Kansans. According to George's uncle, Valmer Johnson, they arrived in 1855, John and Nancy (Johnson) Shaw with them, just as the Kansas civil war broke out. Though eventually the Free-Staters would win, for a time it was a dangerous place for Yankees. Some of the Johnsons went home, but others fled north into free Wisconsin, settling at last in wild Waupaca County, soon to be joined by the Shaws.

For George, pioneering again in the Washington desert didn't present much of a problem. He already spent most of his time outdoors, both through occupation and choice. When he worked, he surveyed timber from Washington down to Northern California. At home in the off-seasons, he hunted when he wasn't doing chores, and sometimes when he should have been doing them, Jane felt. Jeanie, their eldest, said the family ate deer and elk, but more often beaver. George always had a well-loved dog or two that Jane didn't care for that went with him everywhere. Margaret, the eldest Wheeler child, who twice, at eight and at twelve, lived with the Shaws all winter, describes her grandfather in his sixties in her unpublished "Family Sketches". "He was small, compact, graceful and well-coordinated....had white hair, ruddy complexion, and piercing dark eyes." His portrait photo as a young man shows him as dark and handsome. He looked part Indian and so did his four siblings.

The Shaws didn't talk about their Indian blood. The Yakima Indian

War had been over in Washington only thirty-five years when George and his Scots wife arrived there on their latest trek west. But his interests as well as appearance favored that Shaw side of his family, for according to his daughter Jeanie, in Southwest Washington he became known to the community as "Siwash George". This apparently didn't offend him. He quickly learned to pilot a dugout and hired out first as a freighter on the small rivers to service the remote villages. He learned the Chinook jargon trade language used all over the Northwest and taught a bit of it to Jeanie.

George was reserved, partly because he was quite deaf from an early bout with typhoid, but he loved to "yarn", as he termed it in his Downeast dialect. One didn't have to hear well in order to be an entertaining yarner. These yarns, which made him popular with many people, concerned mainly his adventures with animals and life in the woods. A single preserved letter to him from his son Clarence, logging on Puget Sound, imitates this tradition. Almost the entire four page letter recounts what is happening in the woods with its creatures. The son knew what his father liked to read about. George, far more than his son-in-law Frank Wheeler, fits our conventional image of the frontiersman.[1]

Margaret Wheeler says that in temperament her grandfather was a man of unwavering moderation in almost every respect. "He might take an offered drink but was never seen drunk. He would take an offered cigar, but didn't smoke as a habit." But smoking or drinking in any amount opposed Jane's beliefs and it was a bone of contention between them; at least once she caught him imbibing in what could not be termed moderation. Frank Wheeler was another who disapproved.

George's timber surveyor's logbooks show him to be a meticulous man able to do calculations of board feet in an area, and decide what trees to cut and what to save. But the work demanded that he be constantly on the move. Another granddaughter, Helen Wheeler, remembers a ditty he recited about some timber bosses in the Wisconsin woods: "Birch, beech and maple, up hill and down; Hell and damnation for Johnson and Brown." He lived a rigorous life during the working season, but it suited him most ways. However, the long season of lay-off each winter caused much stretching of dollars for the Shaws. His journal shows that when there was nothing else available, he went out to cut firewood, one or two cords a day, at sixty cents a cord.

George's timber cruising profession got him into trouble, it turned out. The timber companies, like the big grazing companies, had great interest in acquiring ownership of public lands which were legally available only in 160 acre tracts to individuals. Frank describes in his memoir how "they would strike a deal with a hungry person for a gratuity of $500 to $1000. Then he would purchase the desired land in his own name and as soon as possible turn it over to the timber company." Part of George Shaw's surveying work required him to locate the good public sections that the companies wanted. The company would then send the "dummy entryman" to buy it.[2]

Getting involved in such schemes to steal public lands was no small deviation in professional ethics for a licensed surveyor. Yet the West was full of surveyors who had been dragged into situations exactly like this and had been caught. However, there was little serious effort on the part of the government to stop the practice by the land companies. At the time the Wheelers came to the Shaws with their farming proposal, George was under pressure to try a different occupation. Frank Wheeler would never have permitted himself to get into such a compromising position, and didn't approve it in his father-in-law. Now, it may have given him leverage in getting George to commit to a major move and a farming partnership.

George's wife, Jane Niven Shaw, came from a family of shopkeepers, not farmers, by tradition. They had given up a tea and spice shop in Glasgow and had immigrated to Wisconsin in 1870 on the advice of their physician.

Helen Wheeler says, "Grandma Niven, a McKean highlander, is never smiling in any photo. No wonder! They had lost four sons in adolescence to childhood diseases." When they had one son left and three daughters, they were advised that if they wanted to save them to get out of Glasgow and its coal dust-filled air for a better environment.

The pattern of a family moving a long way for the health of their children comes up also in Frank Wheeler's family, first when his grandparents retreated from the Wisconsin frontier for a more settled area in Wisconsin "with fruit for the children", and finally returned to New York. It happened again when his father brought his family back from India. Child mortality rates were high, improving little until the late 1930s, and were a continuous worry even for the upper classes.

Jane and her remaining siblings grew up on the Niven farm in Wisconsin and no more of them died. A family anecdote has it that when John Niven, a small man, was asked how he expected to farm successfully with an undersized son and three petite daughters, he replied, straight-faced, "Any one of my daughters will do what three men can." John and his family did become successful Wisconsin farmers. Jane and her siblings also were hired as teachers soon after becoming farmers; their public school education in Glasgow put them far ahead of their neighbors. While a teacher, Jane met George Shaw, became engaged, then pregnant, and married him. She may have regretted her infatuation with a handsome but restless woodsman, but she stuck with him. Social histories of that period and earlier report that in the rural areas pregnancy during betrothal was not unusual, which may explain why she waited three months to have the wedding—it wasn't that shocking. "I wanted to finish teaching the term", she told her sister, and then for some reason waited two more months. Perhaps George was out of town working.

There are many photos of Jane showing a small, fine-figured, dark-haired woman who kept trim all her life. She had an unusual face: a long nose, wide mouth and short chin, all dominated by large expressive blue eyes. Helen remembers Jane's natural good humor and friendliness that is not our stereotypical view of a Calvinist, but her beliefs in hard work without complaint and service to others sound very "Yankee". Jane was accomplished at all women's handicrafts except weaving. She was proud of her handwriting, could sing by note, and quote from Shakespeare. Margaret describes her grandmother as always quick moving and decisive in manner. "I marvel now that she was able to accomplish all she did." Perhaps John Niven's boast about his young daughters had formed the template for Jane's self-image, for she did indeed go on to accomplish as much as three men. Jane would soon have her chance to demonstrate her farming talents under high pressure from two households to succeed. According to her letters, she found it an enjoyable challenge; however, it was unlikely she would have put anything different in writing.

Jane told her granddaughter Helen about their migration from Wisconsin to Washington. When Jeanie, their eldest child, was only seven, George decided Wisconsin was getting altogether too crowded. "Your grandfather could see his neighbor's lamps at night," was the way Jane put it. His sister Addie and her husband called him out to Washington where there was still plenty of work for lumberjacks. George staked his claim on the Humptulips River under the dripping Spanish moss, got his cabin up, a garden started, and sent for his family. George's mother was especially heartbroken, feeling she would never see her oldest son or her favorite daughter-in-law again, and she was right. It was often the case with the westward moving families.

Jane and Jeanie and three little brothers, amid the usual tears from those left behind, departed Wisconsin for Washington on an "immigrant" train. Intended for those that couldn't afford regular cars, it had wooden benches for people to roll out their bedding on, and in each car was a toilet and a coal cook stove (also the heater) which allowed families to fix their meals as they traveled. Other cars carried their animals, or in some cases they rode with them. The Shaws were barely allowed to stay aboard for Jane didn't have the fare for Jeanie.

George was never as organized as his wife, and the funds he sent were just enough to cover Jane's ticket. Jane, who deplored cheating, would have to get Jeanie on as a free six year old, the brothers being four, two, and four months. Donald Wheeler, the youngest Wheeler son, tells this family story:

> The conductor challenged Grandma on her daughter's age, "She looks awful big for six..." Jane, head bent, rummaging in her purse, muttered, "Now where are those yalla tickets." (Jane and her family had studiously rid themselves of their Scots accents, but when upset she could slip, and "yellow" came out "yalla".) "What part a Scotland are ye from?" asked the Scots conductor, all kindness now. The result was that Grandma was allowed to ride. When they reached their destination, the fine chest of drawers from Paisley that Jane had put aboard, their clothes within, was confiscated until Grandpa could come up with his daughter's fare.

The immigrant train was better than the ship Jane had crossed the Atlantic in, the Niven men in steerage, the women and children in cabins, miserably sick a good part of the way. Jane stated that she would never board a ship again, even if it meant never to see the beloved cousins they'd left behind in Scotland. Now, after enduring the immigrant train for four days with four young children, she found herself and children being transferred to a sailboat and then to a dugout canoe—none of them could swim—finally to reach her new little cabin deep in the dripping forest.

Jane lived on the banks of the lonely Humptulips for about two years, surviving just as we picture the typical homesteading wife. She managed much of the time alone, surrounded by dependent children, tutoring Jeanie, her husband off somewhere timber cruising. One day George's sister, having drawn George out to the Humptulips, was tempting him with the idea of homesteading British Columbia. The climate was better and more land available. Another favorite family quote from Jane at this point: "I don't know where you're going, Jarge, but I'm going to Hoquiam and putting the children in school." To Hoquiam, a real town, they went.

It isn't difficult to imagine George becoming a partner for a new risky adventure. But for him to travel over to the desert alone to start up an orchard wouldn't do. Jane's mind for organization and her tireless work ethic were called for. She who had earlier said she was through with adventures, agreed to another one. Her children were grown. If her daughter was determined to take on a new pioneer escapade, as if it hadn't all been done before, then she wanted to be there to assist her. Jane's personal religion was helping others, and that had to include her husband, too, whatever she thought of his adventures and risk-taking. She knew, more than the others, the everyday slings and arrows of farming. But her father, a man who started out knowing nothing of farming, had succeeded, and her partners-to-be were all intelligent, strong people, used to hard work and doing without. They could succeed too.

The two families planned that Wheelers would finance the down payment for one of the ten acre plots with perpetual water rights offered at the new district around White Bluffs at $250 an acre. This converts to about fifteen times as much in today's dollars, quite an investment for the Wheelers. They would carry a mortgage at seven percent. The price included shares in an irrigation company to which they would pay a monthly fee for guaranteed, metered water that would be provided from an already operating system pumping directly from the river. Housing they would have to provide themselves, but the ditch construction company was leaving behind some large sturdy tent-houses that could be purchased reasonably. Just how the others got Jane past the fact of tent-living is a wonder, for she was a woman who took housekeeping seriously. But it was to be only temporary. The partners sent the land company a description of the type of acreage they wanted, and reserved some tents.

Early in the spring of 1907, George and Jane packed up their belongings, stored most of them, boarded their cow and chickens, rented out their house for the summer, leashed George's best hound, and paid what bills they could. The Wheelers came to the Longview terminal to see them off, and the partners went over their strategies one more time. Then, amid anxious and excited goodbyes, the Shaws climbed aboard the Northern Pacific and headed east.

Jane was soon aware from conversations that many in their car were land boomers, including women, and felt relieved that if it was madness it was shared. Before she had quite gotten over the stress of their departure, they passed out of their familiar fir forests and into the pines in the rain shadow of the Cascades' eastern slope. Then, abruptly, they were in the desert. In early March, it was not at its best, the sagebrush steppe stark, dry, and empty. She saw none of the desert flowers she had read about. George had to show her the brochure again.

Central/Eastern Washington was not a wilderness or even a frontier, regardless of how it looked to Jane. Before the European diseases struck, it had supported a large population of Native Americans, especially along the rivers. Parts of it had also been settled by homesteaders who drove out the Indians, then largely abandoned their places during drought years coupled with severe winters that had killed most of their cattle. Despite that, at the time of the Priest Rapids land boom, homesteading districts were still opening up on the plateau just east of the Columbia River. People were staking them intending, once more, to try to raise wheat. These homesteaders drove their wagons and stock miles to get to any water, and suffered regular dust storms, poor diet, and rattlesnakes on a daily basis. Building a community was even tougher than building the farms. They were up on the plateau instead of down by the river because it was virtually free land, requiring mainly a "proving up" residency period. As the Shaw's train rumbled on through the endless sagebrush, they may have wondered about the sanity of their irrigation dream, but they surely concluded that dry-farming the desert was completely demented.

Where the tracks crossed the Columbia at Kennewick, the Shaws transferred with their new associates from the train to the steamer, Jane fighting her qualms about boats, barely glancing at the scene around her as she avoided a look at the water. But she had committed; the paddle wheel started turning, and the boat moved out into the powerful current. The Shaws were finally on the river that would be a main force in their lives for the rest of their lives.

Though George was used to working on rivers, neither of them had been in a setting anything like that confronting them. Coming up on the new village of Richland, they saw the beginning of tall, golden-brown bluffs along the east bank. Against the expanse of the river, they were startling, nothing to calm a nervous soul. Suddenly, the steamer turned in, put its bow directly to the bank, and the crew threw down gangplanks. People rushed to get off as if they knew what they were doing. But for the Shaws, when they tore their eyes away from the bluffs and the river and looked out across the desert to the west, it was a barren sight. As far as they could see to the distant purple hills, there was nothing but buff-colored sand, an occasional hillock, and monotonous gray-green brush. Nothing in the brochure had prepared them for it; nothing looked like any farmland they had seen.

Back out in the current again, the steamer moved smoothly north, its engine throbbing, its sternwheel turning in a steady way that put Jane more at ease. Now, every few miles, they passed a homestead made of logs, sometimes with a fence, always with shade trees just budding, perched right under the great bluffs. They also came upon deserted buildings, barely shacks, with dead shade trees. But a few people were indeed farming; how successfully the travelers couldn't guess. A little boom site, Ringold, a tiny place not a town at all, appeared on the east bank. Then George pointed: a short distance up the west bank they saw the new settlement of Hanford. The bluffs now were much closer, their color shifted to a glowing gold in the late afternoon sun. They would have dwarfed the little town were they not kept at a manageable distance by the river.

At Hanford half the remaining passengers hurried to disembark with their luggage and direct their freight. They disappeared into the noise and confusion ashore, but they couldn't go far without running right into the desert. The roads between the tracts were nothing but deep sand, while the "town" buildings were false-fronted shiplap hastily thrown up, some sporting paint. The Shaws saw little sign of farming, but much tent-camping. Hanford was as basic as a place could be and still be called a town, but there was no doubt that business was taking place, and the remaining passengers were anxious to get on to the next stop, White Bluffs.

The steamer set off once more, and in a short time the Shaws saw the six hundred foot bluffs turn color yet again, this time to a gleaming cream and white that gave their new home its name. By now, they were no longer frightening, just amazing. Then, before the ferry turned in toward the shore, the would-be settlers saw promise: the geometric design of a mature orchard—the McGlothlen homestead they would later learn. Perhaps it was true that all it took was water.

How the Shaws felt when they claimed their new land, we can only imagine. The first salvaged letter from Jane that describes life in White Bluffs was written two years later. Fortunately, the regional newspapers carried much reporting of the boom, the great canal project that had started it, and other happenings of the new town. Richer personal stories of the first decade settlers were collected in the 1930s and again in the 1980s, many of them with photos, so it is not difficult to place the Shaws in the scene. [3]

George and Jane went ashore with the rest of the settlers, stowed their freight on the bank, and took a quick look around the few actual buildings for the land office. White Bluffs was even less a town than Hanford. Scattered up the sand road that led from the shore, work crews were rushing to frame in all of the businesses and services that the brochure promised: a general store, a drug store, a livery stable, a post office. Up the river a short way they spied the unmistakable two-story hip-roofed shape of a schoolhouse, and nearby what turned out to be a church under construction. New plantings of poplar shade trees bordered the riverbank. Jane's spirits lifted.

White Bluffs architecture would soon look just like that of Hanford and all the little western shiplap railroad towns that were hastily thrown up and opened for business. The plank walkways on the main road were not to keep people from mud, as in Hoquiam, but from being mired in the deep sand. Also promising were the concrete foundations for a bank building. It seemed that money was expected. But there were very few houses. Aside from two or three log homes of earlier homesteaders, the rest of White Bluffs was living in tiny shacks or white wall tents, surrounded by long rows of little branched sticks, about three feet high. If the Shaws turned away from the hypnotic river, the scene was not beautiful.

Like Hanford, the town was chaotic with noise and movement, not only from the construction crews, and from all the people disembarking with their supplies, but from the men, horses and equipment being barged out. The Hanford Irrigation Project Corp (HIPC) had constructed a canal down from Coyote Rapids, ten miles above White Bluffs, and the canal and the laterals to service the tracts were nearly completed. Two other companies were digging trenches for buried wooden pipe that they would use instead of the canal. It was tempting, imagining all the water soon to be rushing down the big canal, to consider that company's land offers.

With George doing the asking and Jane shouting the answers to him, they found out that the HIPC project was much more than a canal. Despite the impressive current in the river, they learned that the Columbia in this particular stretch did not have the gradient for a gravity-fed canal that could simply divert off the river. This explained why the district had remained un-irrigated and undeveloped until now. HIPC, a private corporation, had taken the risk with expensive construction required to solve the problem. It had constructed a diversion dam and power plant with turbines upriver at Priest Rapids, then strung power lines downriver to Coyote Rapids, above White Bluffs. There two great pumps had been installed to raise the water up the cliff to the start of the seventeen mile canal that did have the missing gradient. The engineers expected the canal, or Hanford Ditch as everyone called it, to carry enough to water all the land for sale. The cost of the project had been considerable, and there was naturally great pressure to recruit as many buyers as possible for HIPC tracts. The Shaws looked and Jane listened and called out to George the wonders of HIPC.[4]

HIPC's competitor, White Bluffs City and Orchard Tracts (WBCOT), had purchased 600 acres, partly old homestead, and partly government and railroad land, at the historic White Bluffs site. It had installed a simpler system using pumps only. A third company nearby was known locally as the "Todd Plant". Using barged coal for power, these last two pumped directly from the river into wood-stave pipe systems that the water company shareholders themselves would maintain. Jane heard the pumps humming close by. WBCOT would provide not just irrigation water but year-round piped water to businesses and town houses as well. People who bought WBCOT ten acre tracts or business sites would, as with HIPC or the Todd Plant, buy shares in that water company and pay a fee for its services. Each system, the great canal or the smaller pumping plants, assured the required "perpetual water rights". Each strategy had its merits and, it turned out, its problems.

Despite the HIPC promotional bustle, the Shaws/Wheelers were fortunate in the company they had chosen. Jane Shaw had no way to foresee the troubled times ahead for the companies, but she had made it clear before she ever left Hoquiam that she was not going back into the wilderness. That meant they should settle on a WBCOT tract, for they were right in and around the town with an attractive setting close to the river. Through a combination of luck and inspiration, it turned out that their farm-to-be was on one of the best sites available.

The Shaws had no time yet for leisurely touring of the scene. They needed to check out first hand every promise that the brochure made. Convinced that their water system could function, they went on to investigate the state of transportation. They wanted to know the steamer schedule, and if the railroad was truly coming in. The steamers were fine for crops that could stand storage, but the state agricultural college had published that the ideal specialties of the valley, because of its uniquely early spring, could be soft fruit like peaches, cherries, plums, and apricots, and also berries and grapes. These fragile crops needed express shipping. For the district to develop to its full potential, some people insisted it had to win a railroad link. Others believed the steamers could offer everything needed if the settlers kept their goals modest and stuck to the hardy crops.

The real estate brokers and the general store owner echoed what the brochures promised, that a branch line was about to be constructed, running down the valley from the Great Northern line in the north to connect with the Northern Pacific at Kennewick. Another possibility was the Milwaukee Road, which had just completed its bridge across the Columbia at Beverly Gap, about forty miles upstream. It was just a matter of time. For now, the steamers offered regular passenger and freight service.

The Shaws located their WBCOT man and went out with him to locate the staked tract they had reserved. Jane was delighted that she had gotten just what she asked for in a tract across the road from the school and the Presbyterian church, and less than a quarter of a mile from "town", close to the river. If the Shaws could get accustomed to the vistas of sagebrush and sand, the rest looked possible. That evening, before they wrapped themselves up in their quilts on their brand new land—the neighbors assured them the rattlesnakes didn't come around town—we can imagine that they walked down to the river. Jane listened to its soft swirly sound and to the coyotes yipping on the bluffs looming in the twilight. Lantern lights glowed through the tents scattered across the desert like huge fireflies, conversations drifted, and fragrant sage aroma crossed their faces in the light breeze to mingle with the river smell. White Bluffs was a remarkable place for rain forest people. George, so used to camping out, probably felt quite at ease that night, even without his great firs. Jane was lucky if she slept at all.

The next morning the Shaws completed their land purchase, signed for their shares in the water company, and made arrangements to be hooked up to the irrigation system as soon as they had their pipe laid. They picked out two large tents—one for a kitchen/living room and one for sleeping—and hired a team to drag them to their tract. Before long Jane had borrowed a broom and was sweeping out, watching for the "black widders" and scorpions as her neighbor warned her. As for snakes she might see, she was told not to worry as they were almost sure to be big but quite harmless bull snakes that fed on rats, while the rats were not rats at all, but ground squirrels. The tents were quite acceptable. Clean and roomy, with wooden roofs, sides and floors, they were intended for long-term summer living. Jane didn't suspect that they were destined to be her home year-round for nine years.

George hardly knew where to begin— so much to do, and in short order. He knew he had to set up Jane with water and kerosene right away if he wanted dinner, and after he helped her make the tent into a semblance of a home, he had to rent a team and start clearing and plowing to put in a stand of alfalfa for his dear cow he planned to bring over. He saw people using what they called a sagebrush grubber: a railroad iron dragged by four horses. He hoped he could rent one of those for a start. Then, after clearing, he had to plow ditches, lay the irrigation pipe, and tie to the WBCOT system. None of that had been necessary back in coastal country. In fact, except for clearing, there seemed to be a great deal more to do in irrigated farming. But ten acres wasn't so great a place to care for, and there would be some quieter seasons.

For now, he would have no breathing space as their trees would arrive shortly on the steamer, and he must be ready to get them into the ground, and watered. They needed also to order a fast-maturing crop to grow between the tree rows. Asparagus seemed to be a favorite, and alfalfa was another. Even more urgent than all this was to get their own vegetable garden started, for they had to eat. We can picture him looking out where his neighbors' cattle were tethered in the sagebrush, wondering what in God's name the poor animals ate, yet they seemed healthy enough. "It's the bunchgrass!", he was later informed, and it held its nutrition all winter. The desert was full of surprises.

George had one consolation in that it was easy to walk around and see just how the others were handling it all. One could see for miles. What he saw was not just sagebrush, he soon realized, but a more complex community of plants that had learned how to thrive, as he would, in a desert. In early spring not many of them were showing, but on the back of his new place were cottonwoods, their buds already about to pop. Down by the river there was a long marshy swale, full of sprouting grass, edged by budding willow. He imagined it was cover for some kind of edible birds and rabbits, while out in the brush were obvious burrows of some small animal. A Sunday walk with a shotgun would be interesting.

By the end of the day, Jane's tent house and kitchen were organized. She had a barrel full of river water that everyone seemed to use without worry, and her kerosene camp stove had a teakettle steaming. She had purchased a washtub and board, but had no intention to start taking in laundry again. George had cobbled together a makeshift table and two chairs from some crates. Their bedrolls on sage branches would do until their furniture arrived. If Jane could get her man to build an outhouse, she was set. The home and community were basic, but they were all she had to have. Until Jeanie had helped them build the house in Hoquiam, she'd never had much more. For a moment she thought of her new Hoquiam house, now rented out, then put it aside.

Later, Jane took time to walk out and to study how people were laying their irrigation pipe and ditches. George, being a surveyor, would understand better than most about slope, she knew. She gazed about to see how many people had their own cows, if there were a bull, and what opportunity she would have for selling milk and butter. Away from the river the land seemed colorless. She commented on this to her neighbor, but that woman, of a year's seniority, smiled and told her to wait to pass judgment until she saw it in early May, awash with spring flowers of every color, even the ones they considered unwanted weeds, like the bright yellow mustard. And in any case, by summer, with her water hooked up, Mrs. Shaw could have all the flowers and shrubs she wanted growing around her tent.

That evening the Shaws lit their kerosene lamp and together drew out a sketch together of how their little fruit trees should be arranged. The order, planned with the Wheelers, had a few trees each of different varieties of pears, peaches, plums and apricots, and several kinds of apples for the family orchard. For their commercial apple orchard, they'd settled on mainly Winesap and Jonathan apples and some peach and pear varieties. They had brought an assortment of vegetable seeds with them.[5]

The Shaws had hoped to observe and learn much from the more settled people, but were shocked to find that they outdid most of their neighbors in farming experience. Everyone seemed to be from somewhere other than a desert. Fortunately the two homesteads not far from town, the Craigs and McGlothlens, demonstrated much of what was possible. A month later the Shaw place was a clone of the ones around it: alfalfa and asparagus sprouting, rows of baby trees leafing out, water sparkling in the ditches, and flowers shooting up by their tents.

Out in the desert, scattered through the sagebrush were splashes of bright greasewood budding out amid a myriad of mixed smaller plants in bloom. Jane was thrilled to see each new kind and color emerge, and felt her affection for the desert bloom with them. Her neighbors could identify a few of them by name as they appeared: first the yellow bells, hiding under the sagebrush, followed by pink phlox and sunflowers and a surprising red mallow, then blue violets, wild iris, and bright pink wild roses in the swale. Farther out in the desert were brilliant yellow blooms on the prickly pear cactus and innumerable low-lying blossoms in every color. She would eventually learn the names of most. Though the desert's spring flowers turned out to be on show for only a short time while there was moisture, Jane would find that the irrigated alfalfa turned out beautiful shades of blue and lavender, and even in hot, dry August her new world was not barren, for then the rabbit brush and even the sage would bloom yellow and fragrant all around them.[6]

The Shaw tent home was now tidy and neat, as both of them liked things to be, and just as comfortable as a cabin. Jane's wood stove arrived on the steamer. George had found that firewood and wood for building a barn and chicken house was scarce, but neighbors assured him that June's high water would be bringing their year's supply of driftwood down the Columbia, and he had better be ready to catch it. He arranged with a neighbor to share a skiff; catching logs on a river was a topic that he could show them a thing or two on! On Sundays he took his dog Tip and a shotgun and went out to find cottontails or a sage hen.

The town proved to have everything else they needed except for what they could order by catalog or from downriver, and the mail and freight came daily, just as promised. Every Sunday Jane went to worship with the other churchgoers and soon was volunteering for socials and knitting caps for fund raisers in her new community. As she had hoped, the women had joined forces to reestablish all the institutions of hospitality and service they had left behind. Their homes were tents, and their fingers rough from planting, but they knew what made a community.

That October the Shaws decided they weren't quite ready to face a whole winter in tents and returned to Hoquiam to finish their affairs there. But they had no question that they would be back in the desert with the first sign of spring to do more planting. In March, Jane wrote her daughter from Hoquiam, " I have sold the chickens, I didn't want to be bothered shipping them, and we can get some at Kennewick to start with....The house is so empty I cannot bear to stay a minute. I will advertise it for rent." In a short time she and George, joined by their cow, were back in White Bluffs, now her full time home. Soon after that, Jane began her butter sales.

We wonder how soon the settlers realized that water, transportation, and market, as well as the natural world of their new home would be huge challenges and would stay that way. Their innocence was for a while a blessing. However, in one way irrigated farming was similar to all other farming: the Shaws soon discovered that the prices the Priest Rapids growers got for their famously early asparagus, hay, and strawberries were chronically poor compared to what they paid for supplies. And irrigators had extra costs in water and pipe. But if they had misgivings, they reminded themselves that soon their productivity would make up for it and more.

Since the trees would take at least four years to bear, the Shaws and their neighbors knew it was important to choose the right crops to grow in the meantime. The old-timers were glad to tell them what had worked best for each of them, but beyond that it was all a gamble, for their methods of marketing had been limited and haphazard. Most important of all, the new orchardists learned, was to take advantage of the Priest Rapids' early spring and win the race to the Seattle market.

That year the steamers coming up from Kennewick continued to be packed with land rushers. A fine hotel was finished by December, and the bank opened. Phone lines were installed the next year. If the newcomers were bored by the vast sagebrush vistas, surely they were awed by the unsurpassed river and bluffs they looked out on from their tents. Inevitably, after the settlers experienced their first dust storm, a few families packed up in disgust to board the next steamer. Only twenty miles to the east, up on the Wahluke Slope, and to the southwest on the Horse Heaven Hills, new homesteaders, ignorant of the region's history of cyclical drought, were tilling the ground for their first wheat crops. Their plowing was augmenting the dust storms.

The settlers busy at White Bluffs knew almost nothing of the history of this strange land they had come to. Many of them never would, for they would be far too engaged in plowing, planting, pruning and picking. But if they were the curious sort they would take the opportunity at a church social over a piece of berry pie to ask one of the old pioneers about the early times in the valley and how they had survived.

3

THE PRIEST RAPIDS VALLEY

"My young men will never work. Men who work can never
dream, and wisdom comes to us in dreams."
Attributed to Smohalla, Wanapum shaman, 1870s.

THOUGH THE WHITE BLUFFS/HANFORD area was swarming with human activity when the Shaws arrived, today twenty miles of the Hanford Reach—excluding the Hanford Works itself—has returned to almost its original state. A wild park has, ironically, been one product of the nation's World War II experiment with weapons of mass destruction. But putting that gross contradiction aside, if we travel to the Reach today we can actually view the scene that the Shaws encountered, with a few awe-stricken kayakers and fly-fishers at times added in. This now protected area, in the middle of which the Shaws set their tents, is revered by photographers, naturalists and scientists, as a last place to see the original shrub-steppe lands that once covered central Washington.

The Columbia River is the eastern border, its bluffs walling the valley off from the vast plateau. The other three directions are lined with distant hog-backed ridges. Saddle Mountain, a place revered by Native Americans, lies in tan and gray hues across the great bend of the river to the north. Gable Mountain, another sacred place of vision quests, shows up by itself to the west, the last ridge of the Ahtanum Hills. Farther away to the southwest are the purple-hued Rattlesnake Hills. In certain areas, in the Shaws' time, sand dunes moved across the desert with the prevailing winds from the southwest, creeping along until they reached the Columbia, dropped into it, and disappeared downstream.

The last great lava floods on earth 17 million years ago created the Columbia Plateau with layer after layer of basalt. Today these are sunk to 400 feet, covered in some places by glacial gravels and rich soils, in others by scabland. Plates thrusting up formed the hills. About 12,000 years ago, a lake 2000 feet deep, the glacial Lake Missoula, broke through its banks and poured across the Columbia Plateau toward the Pacific at about sixty-five miles per hour, leaving behind a deposit of rocks intermixed with more rich, gravelly soil. Whenever the lake built up enough pressure on its bank, it would repeat the process, so that there was not just one gigantic flood of which ancient mythologies speak, but a series. Volcanic dust blew in from the southwest periodically creating rich soil deposits in some places hundreds of feet deep. The Columbia made this geologically rich country its own, cutting through it to form the great sandstone and soft claystone bluffs on its east bank, benches above the shores, rushing rapids, and sixteen protective islands with quiet reed-bordered sloughs out of the main current. Below Priest Rapids the great swing of the river to the northeast, then south again, set the scene for waves of human history and for our story.

The valley south of those rapids, now about 400 feet above sea level, is not entirely flat. Much of it is barrens the settlers called "knolly ground" formed from the ancient glacial gravels. The expanse is also interrupted by coulees that turn green in March, sometimes with tiny springs, and even ponds where cottonwood, willow and grass can thrive all summer. These are havens for local and migratory birds, hares, mule deer, and elk. Out in the desert itself live ground squirrels, sage hens, owls, hawks, eagles, badgers, coyotes, bobcats, rattlesnakes, lizards, and more hares. But biologists estimate that about eighty-five percent of the wild fauna live in the riparian border along the river.

If we could travel there today, we, like the Shaws, would be transfixed by the river and the bluffs. But we, like they, would soon acknowledge the more subtle pastel beauty of the dry tan steppe. The major vegetation of the shrub-steppe is various kinds of sagebrush and bunchgrass. These protect a host of other species that have learned to live in an arid world. By the time the Shaws arrived the rich bunchgrass was degraded from overgrazing, and where it didn't provide cover, the sands easily joined with the wind to become sandstorms. Introduced grasses, brought in with migrating cattle herds even before the setters, were already changing the land and providing a new, inferior ground cover, along with spiny Russian olive trees and the Russian thistle that each summer created new tumbleweeds. The settlers planted Carolina poplars and black locust trees along the river for shade, and they thrived.

Today we would still see all of these, especially the sage, and an even lusher growth of willow, cottonwood and locust in the swale just upriver from the White Bluffs town site. Across from the swale is a fair-sized island, creating a slough out of the main current. Willow, rye grass, and wild roses grow in a tangle clear to the slough bank. The pastoral feeling of this stretch contrasts with what lies just out front: the living energy of the mainstream Columbia and its stark shining bluffs across. The Shaws saw the river run at a good eight knots during highwater, sweeping the beaches clean. It runs slower today, and the bluffs are sloughing from irrigated plateau farming, but the scene is almost as magnificent as when the Shaws first saw it.

The air as well as the river is full of drama from thunderheads, blizzards, whirlwinds on the bluffs, and often brilliant sunrises and sets. Each morning and evening oblique light and shadow create an always changing ambience accenting the pastel shades of the barrens below. The southwest winds send welcome rain clouds, but also dust storms. In winter, drifting snow from the north blankets the sands, broken by sudden thaws from Chinook winds. In March and April, late frosts sneak in. Then, by mid-April, there is moisture from a few rain showers, and all at once the sands and gravels are ablaze with the wildflowers that entranced Jane Shaw. This is the time to journey to this valley, for before long the heat of summer takes over, reaching 110 degrees or more in the shade. The flowers, even their foliage, disappear. The chill waters of the Columbia slow down and warm. Today the Wahluke Slope on the east side of the river is green with irrigated corporate orchards, vineyards, potatoes, and alfalfa fields. But a stretch of the Hanford Reach and its bluffs, named a National Monument in 2000, will not be watered, and will keep its own unique beauty.

The new would-be orchardists, especially those coming straight from a rain forest, needed adjustment time, but before long came to love the natural setting of the valley. White Bluffs children, especially, were not confined to town and farm. Boys, and many girls too, found time to roam the desert, the river, even the rapids upriver and the bluffs across. Their memories, seventy years later, are full of the child adventures they invented amidst the natural world that surrounded the settlement.

To fully appreciate the orchardists' history, one needs to know something of the people that came before them. The Columbia, like other great rivers, has been since ancient times a highway for travelers—Native American tribes, then gold miners, cattle and sheepmen, followed by homesteaders, then the orchardists of our story. Scientists estimate that people were on the plateau and along the river 15,000 years ago, at the time of the floods. Kennewick Man, one of the oldest and most complete skeletons found in North America, discovered just downriver, is thought to be about 9,000 years old. Near Priest Rapids is the site of ancient house pits that stretch over ten acres, one of the largest prehistoric archaeological sites in the Northwest. The Rapids was a favorable winter camp location partly because of the large supply of drift wood thrown up by the river's rapids and eddies.

At the Columbia's great bend just above White Bluffs, a natural fording spot evolved for people moving east and west, north and south. For the Wanapum, and other tribes too, it was also an excellent spot to camp and fish the annual salmon runs, then dry and store much of their winter food supply. The Columbia Plateau Indians had acquired horses from the tribes east of them and from Spaniards in California. With horses they had mobility to hunt and to move their camps large distances as needed, but kept their secure hold on a stable economy and nutrition based on the dependable salmon. But as in the rest of the West, the indigenous population was decimated by disease brought by Euro-Americans, especially malaria and small pox. By the time Lewis and Clark passed through, the huge population along the river was already greatly reduced. When the orchardists arrived, the Wanapums still living on the mid-Columbia numbered less than a hundred. Most had removed to the large Yakima Reservation just to the west, either forced by the army, or to escape the threats of the homesteaders who wanted the valley land.

S.L. Sanger reports an interview with Frank Buck, believed to be the last Wanapum to take part in the whole subsistence cycle, which his tribe had co-mingled with the Euro-American economy about the time the Shaws arrived. He remembered that the spring began with digging of roots that lay in vast beds by Soap or Moses Lake and just above Priest Rapids. In two weeks the women could dig and dry enough, mainly camas, for their year's needs. Different groups also claimed wild hemp fields where they cut their materials for rope and fish net. Moving south to White Bluffs' farms, some picked asparagus and strawberries for cash and stored their surplus food at their campsite there. Then all moved on for king and sockeye salmon, steelhead trout and whitefish on the Yakima, also to be dried and stored. Buck remembered they might stay to harvest eels for two more weeks.

In July they loaded up their buckboards and travois and left the hot valley for a three-day trip to the Cascades where they hunted deer and elk, then in August picked huckleberries, again drying food for winter. They returned back through the Yakima area in time for the hops picking there. With that cash they purchased their staples for the winter: flour, sugar, coffee, bacon, cloth and any tools needed, arriving back in White Bluffs in time for the fall salmon, sucker, and white fish runs. Their last stop was Priest Rapids, their winter home, where they lived in longhouses built from driftwood frames and woven tule reeds.

The irrigators watched the Wanapums pass through each year with their wagons full of supplies, and sometimes the children followed them up to their nearby campsite on the gravel bar of the slough. They watched them pull out their tule rush mats, canoes and other belongings from their dugout storage pits and fix the tule mats onto the frames of their houses and sweat lodge. Their horses were hobbled to graze in the swale and not wander into the nearby alfalfa pastures, though they sometimes did, creating some ill feelings among the irrigators. But they had pastured their horses there for centuries, and the new alfalfa made it even better. Wanapum men speared salmon from their cedar dugout canoes at night, using torches. The women filleted the fish, then hung them out on racks to cure in the wind, or over a smudge fire. The dried fish was stored in baskets, sometimes as meal. Winter came, allowing time for the weaving of fine basketry which became another way to bring in cash. But much of winter was spent in ceremonial gatherings. Early homesteaders had learned much of desert living by observing all these operations, and the orchardists could as well, were they able to pull themselves away from their plowing, planting, and pipe-laying.

Frank Buck recalled that in winter at Priest Rapids, "There was plenty of food." Plenty for people who had learned to live in balance with the river and desert. But it was food for a small band of Wanapum, and that was not the case on the reservations. By the time the irrigators arrived, the great salmon migrations had already been greatly reduced by the Euro-American uncontrolled salmon-wheel fishery along the lower Columbia, halted in 1905, and their huge gill net fishery near the mouth. Netting at mid-river had been outlawed. To the Columbia Indians, the shrinking runs were among the worst of the manifestations of white invasion, along with disease, alcoholism and general poverty, but the fish problem was far from the minds of the new orchardists.

The Shaws and Wheelers learned their Central/Eastern Washington history from early homesteaders nearby like the Bordens, augmented by a regional history by a retired cattleman, A. J. Splawn: *Ka-mi-akin, Last Hero of the Yakimas.* During the 1850s Washington east of the Cascades had been closed to white settlement by the territorial governor Stevens while he attempted, through a harsh treaty, to force the Indians onto reservations. The Yakamas (their spelling) and others had turned to camp raiding to halt the activities of white and Chinese miners, whom they saw as the forerunners of settlers. Splawn says the governor handled the treaty negotiations stubbornly and badly, and then was unable to keep his commitment to close settlers out of Eastern Washington for a period; he couldn't. The result was the tragic Yakima War of 1856-58 and others to follow. The Priest Rapids valley was unique in the Columbia Basin for the small quantity of blood spilled on its sands. Ironically, the Yakama chief Kamiakin, a futurist who already had introduced cattle raising and irrigating to his people, and would have been a most likely leader for a transition to farming, was outraged by the treaty. After joining the war for a time, he abandoned it as hopeless and went into exile in Canada for years.

The Wanapums, whose territory bordered the river from Priest Rapids to Pasco, chose not to join the Yakamas and other tribes in the wars. Aghast as they were over the invasion of cattlemen, miners and homesteaders onto their territory, their Dreamer religion forbade them to fight back, go to reservations, take up farming, work for cash, go to school, or in any way interact with the invaders. Their priest/shaman taught that the invaders would soon somehow be destroyed and life made right again. The Wanapum chief, Sohappy, refused to go to the infamous treaty conference. After his death, the new Wanapum leader, a charismatic shaman named Smohalla, continued to follow the Dreamer laws. He led his people on the path of isolation with Priest Rapids as their main camp. Splawn quotes him as saying about the reservation and farming path, "My young men will never work. Men who work can never dream, and wisdom comes to us in dreams."[2] Just to the north, the Salish speaking Kawatchkins, a larger tribe under another Dreamer, Chief Moses, also chose not to fight and to refuse the Yakima reservation. To the south of Pasco, the Palouse tribe had taken the same route.

Acreage was snatched up rapidly by homesteaders after Governor Stevens opened the region. Most of them believed the Indians had no rights except to the reservation lands and wanted them removed, even as far away as Oklahoma if possible. Homesteaders who came too late to get the best locations often spent their energies trying to get the reservations broken up, or simply encroached with their herds and hand-dug irrigation ditches. Even more liberal Euro-Americans like Horace Greeley, who had such enthusiasm for the prospects of small irrigators, and had promoted colonies on his own, saw no future possible for Native Americans but assimilation. His bigotry was typical of his day: "God has given this earth to those who will subdue and cultivate it, and it is vain to struggle against his righteous decree." Indians would have to learn to be farmers or disappear.

The Indian Agent Wilbur at Yakima was constantly forced to answer to rumors and angry demonstrations by homesteaders who claimed Indians were arming for war, and that therefore they too needed to be armed. But the attack on a white couple near White Bluffs in 1878 was the only killing of that valley's homesteaders recorded. It was carried out, not by Wanapums, but by a band of Umatilla Indians who had fled their reservation, been fired on by an Army gunboat at White Bluffs, lost some of their group, and were seeking revenge. However, the first homesteaders didn't make the distinction and took it as proof of their fears.

During the same period, Agent Wilbur followed a rumor of 2000 Indians gathered at White Bluffs under Chief Moses, readying to attack, only to find him with a handful of warriors wishing to negotiate a new reservation on the northern Columbia. Wilbur reported to his superiors that the purpose of the rumors by "irresponsible" whites, mainly cattlemen craving pasture, was to get an uprising incited. Their hope, he believed, was to make the situation so urgent that the Army would recommend the Yakima reservation be broken up and opened to settlement. At one point the Agent was forced to jail Chief Moses to keep him from being lynched.

Several tribes claimed rights to camping and fishing sites in the Priest Rapids valley, but none of them succeeded in formalizing them. Moses slowly negotiated what is now the Colville reservation to the north, and the Wanapum and Palouse received nothing. More Wanapums left the river for the Yakima reservation in fear of white attack and for the security that Agent Wilbur offered. But he was a missionary as well as the agent. That meant they had to abandon their Dreamer religion and become Methodists. Smohalla's Dreamer followers, hunkered down at Priest Rapids, found their numbers inevitably shrinking under pressure, some converting, some taking their religion underground. None, however, resorted to violence. Though the invaders did not disappear as Smohalla predicted, his advice was from one perspective good, in that the mid-Columbia remained uniquely peaceful.

These occurrences took place only thirty years before the Shaws and other irrigators arrived at White Bluffs. We can't know how much the Shaws/Wheelers were aware of this history at first as it is not mentioned in any of the surviving letters, but we do know that the Bordens, early homesteaders who were on good terms with the Wanapums, could have filled them in. For more of the tragic detail, the Wheelers at some point owned Splawn's book, mentioned above, and included it in their research of the valley's history.

Not far away from the Priest Rapids valley, the cattlemen/irrigators on the Yakima River pecked away at the reservation through the Dawes Act, and through outright squatting. By 1913 the government planned to cut the eighty acre individual Indian allotments on the reservation to twenty acres, then to sell the rest and use the money to build a modern irrigation system for all farmers in the area, now including Indians. The Yakamas who were now farming fought this second attempt at robbery, saying their own irrigation systems were quite good enough if the incoming Whites were not stealing water from them. Eventually, of course, the government would get its way. Through leases and sales of Indian allotments, almost all of the productive agricultural land was soon in the hands of non-Natives, who were also able to deny access to the treaty fishing sites adjacent.

Meanwhile on the Columbia the unlanded Wanapums had worked out their own means of survival. Their Dreamer teachings were liberalized to the extent that some did farm labor for needed cash. They still moved along the river between their seasonal riverbank camps and kept their winter home at Priest Rapids, a place so inaccessible that homesteaders ignored it, enduring the new influx of settlers along the river in 1906-07. Just as Smohalla predicted, despite no treaty, for generations they were able to hold onto Priest Rapids and to a few campsites.

The irrigators, like the homesteaders before them, were living on Indian ground seized by the government, then granted to the railroads, who then sold it to land developers. The irrigators had paid a high price to the developers for their acreage and considered the Indian claims terminated. How they felt about the history of their new home probably depended on how they viewed the conquering of America in general. But probably few of them gave much thought as to how this land came to be available. The despair of the survivors trying to accommodate on the reservations was out of sight. In any case, there was no spot in America where one could build a house, or plant an orchard or field, and not be on soil won through an unfair treaty.

Whatever the Wanapum thoughts on the new, much larger influx of farmers, the irrigators themselves, according to their contributions to *Family Histories for Hanford and White Bluffs, Washington* (hereafter referred to as *Family Histories)*, generally found the Wanapums they knew to be an admirable if standoffish group. They watched them quietly adapt to the new valley economy. As long as no one wanted the gravel beach by the slough where the Indians camped in season, coexistence was no problem, and indeed the Wanapums were welcome for the seasonal labor they provided. The farmers were not concerned that the Wanapums didn't send their children to school—that was their business—while the store owner at White Bluffs said they were circumspect about paying their annual bills, and he welcomed their trade. Few people complained about Indian horses in their alfalfa fields. The Wanapums did present a formal complaint when the route of the Hanford Canal was planned to pass over the grave of their chief Sohappy, their lawsuit creating delays until the grave was moved. Other times Indian graves were desecrated, but "white law", at least some of the time, pursued the guilty ones.

By the 1920s, only about thirty Wanapums—Tomanawash, Sohappy, Buck, and Hudson are names recalled by the Wheelers—made their seasonal trips through White Bluffs with their wagons and small band of horses. Helen Wheeler remembers how as a child of five her father scolded her for going over to their camp to watch them. "Don't stare at them like that, he said. They are human beings just like you! But I didn't go to stare, I just wanted someone to play with, but their kids always ran away." Her closest sibling, Donald, at nine, was already too busy much of the time to play with a little sister.

Already, by the 1850s, the White Bluffs fording spot had become a favored rendezvous for white travelers too. An Army post with twenty soldiers was opened on the east bank for gold miners' protection. Then, in the 1860s it became a transfer point for steamers bringing supplies up river from Astoria at its mouth. Because of the river's big bend and the rapids at the end of navigation, it was a perfect place for a terminal where supplies were off-loaded for hauling by horse and mule to the gold mines to the north and east. Some years a White Bluffs trading post was open. About that time, however, other Euro-Americans arrived who were not just passing through, or rather they were passing through repeatedly. These were stockmen from the lower Columbia, arriving first at the Kittitas and Yakima Valleys, then the Priest Rapids. They sold cattle to the miners, later to the stockyards to the east.

The stockmen discovered that the Indians had a marvelous range for their horses from the indigenous bunch grass. In some districts it was as high as a horse's belly, a result of the volcanic soils and the unusual short winters and early springs. The drivers discovered that the drier Priest Rapids valley, though its grasses weren't as lush as the Yakima's, had a spring even two weeks earlier. Wintering over there, the cattle required no hay-feeding at all. Generations later this bunch grass, though much degraded, still allowed poor settlers without hay to keep stock through winter.

With all the river traffic, by 1866 eastside White Bluffs had a hotel and several stores. Developers were already quoted in the press that it would be a future center of trade, even though it was not on a railroad. But the competitive route of the Army's east-west Mullen Road through Walla Walla, avoiding the loose sand to the east of the river, had stronger lobbyists. The Great Northern railroad would create the town of Wenatchee to the north and the Northern Pacific would build Kennewick/Pasco to the south. As no tracks came to White Bluffs, the ferries closed down, and the speculators drifted off. By 1870, except for Wanapum camps, White Bluffs was virtually deserted. The one remaining building from this period, identified as a blacksmith shop and now protected under the Antiquities Act, can still be seen at the eastside White Bluffs ferry landing.

The cattlemen soon found out that allowing their wintering cattle to subsist purely on the native bunchgrass had drawbacks. As first pointed out to them by the Indians, great clouds of dust were forming and blowing each summer where there had been none before. Just as in most of the West, herders were guilty of overgrazing, and the desert top soil was often thin and always fragile. The bunchgrass was no longer so lush. Weather, too, could surprise them. After years of not having to worry about winter feeding, 1861-62 brought the first of a series of extreme winters across the West that caused the stockmen to lose most of their cattle and horses. In the Yakima and Priest Rapids valleys they had not bothered to put up any wild hay. When a severe winter struck again two decades later, and yet again, many outfits were driven permanently out of business.

The cattlemen moved on to British Columbia, or turned to sheep, or became local ranchers growing fenced fields of alfalfa and rye for their cattle feed. Many dug by hand the first long irrigation systems in the territory. A handful that settled in the Priest Rapids valley and on the Wahluke Slope were before long able to buy up cheap acreage from the railroads or government and persisted with their herds. There was still a living for a few that craved the herding life, for cattle, horses, and sheep were now in demand at the close and growing markets of Puget Sound and Portland. For some small ranchers, rounding up wild and formerly Indian horses and selling them was a significant part of their income.

Now sheep flocks, able to subsist on the degraded pasture, moved into the Priest Rapids area. The drovers, English and Scot, later Basque, built lambing stations up near Saddle Mountain on the east slope of the Columbia. In later years the orchardists could see the flocks coming west by their clouds of dust on the plateau. The drovers crossed the river at White Bluffs, paying for their sheep by the head to ride the ferry, and probably paying its cost of operation for the entire year. The sheep further degraded the natural desert cover, clipping it shorter than cattle did. The homesteaders were compensated a little for the dust created, as a few stray lambs were always left behind. They took the lost lambs home to raise for their prized wool, so needed for their comforters in the bitter winters.

Homesteaders had drifted into the isolated Priest Rapids valley only after the more grassy Yakima and Kittitas land was staked. This valley was not what the railroads' homesteading brochures had promoted as ideal dry-farming country. Dry-farming requires at least fifteen inches of rain a year; this desert valley had less than eight inches. But the rain came at the right time in the spring to make wheat a possibility. The Wahluke Slope, in particular, caught just enough moisture from the west for people to believe they could succeed with a 160 acre homestead allotment. In the Othello area on the plateau just to the east of White Bluffs they endured bringing all of their household water four to ten miles by wagon, forced to reuse every scrap. The job of children each day was to herd the family stock by horseback to small ponds in coulees a good distance away. These farmers soon found their topsoil blowing in their faces, just as it had on the prairies, and disappearing off to the northeast. In the 1880s came the long drought across the West, and in a few years the plateau was littered with tiny abandoned settlements.

The plateau homesteaders had been fooled, as so many were during wet years on the Great Plains. Their 160 acre allotments were not nearly large enough for dry-farming the plateau. Though it seems laughable today, the pseudo-science of that period, promulgated by Hardy W. Campbell, and widely disseminated by land developers, claimed that the spell of good wet years had been encouraged by plowing. It loosened up the soil, which in turn had sucked more rain from the sky. The excessive deep plowing encouraged by this theory, "rain follows the plow", had helped turn the prairie dwellers' original problem of sparse rainfall to an uncorrectable one, causing massive abandonment of homesteads during drought years. The failed settlers had traveled west only to have it now happen to them again. Donald Wheeler, Frank and Jeanie's' fourth child, tells of hiking up on the Wahluke Slope as one of a Boy Scout troop and coming across deserted places with sand-filled cisterns that were mysteries to them. Raised with irrigation, the boys couldn't imagine why farmers had come to this dry hot place, or how they had survived even a season. Now it seemed only good for migrating sheep.

The homesteaders who staked claims down by the river resigned themselves to the extra labor of irrigating and fared much better. This would not be like the Snake River valley where early irrigators had bitter and unending battles in and out of court over who, and when, and how much water each farmer had a right to. Not only would the Columbia never run out of water—and it was clear, clean water—it was also transportation. The homesteaders stretched along the Columbia's banks, mainly from Hanford up to Wahluke near Coyote Rapids. They brought their supplies by difficult sand road from Yakima, and sent their crops downriver by whatever craft they could float, often drift logs lashed together. Once regular river freighting began in 1905, they brought their supplies right up from Kennewick. Since the bluffs on the east side of the river resulted in only narrow strips of bench land, the west bank at White Bluffs became the populated one with a ferry connecting them.

George and Jane Shaw learned of early riverbank farming from several homesteaders still resident, located just up river. For them it was fascinating and instructional. Mrs. Koppen now had a large well-furnished log cabin with huge shade trees, but she could tell about the difficult beginnings. As no timber grew in the valley, the homesteaders captured driftwood for their houses, fences, and fuel. They purchased canoes from the Wanapums or whipsawed logs to build skiffs, then rowed out to capture logs as they floated down each year at June's high water. They made their roofs from poles topped with reeds plastered with clay and burned the sandstone from the bluffs in kilns until the silica melted off, leaving lime for plaster. Plastering the inside walls of their cabins kept out heat and cold, insects, and most important, dust.

The Koppens copied the farming techniques of the East, adding a water wheel on the river to irrigate their garden and stock, and dug cisterns to fill from the water wheel or to catch what little rain there was. Potatoes, wheat, hay, onions, dried peas, beans and corn, apples, smoked meat—any crop where spoilage could be held off—was shipped safely down the river. Only for a short time in mid-winter did the Columbia ice over, and then, not every year.

Once the homesteaders had simple water systems created, they were able to grow almost all of their food. They told the Shaws how, with no canning equipment, they had dried it or stored it in root cellars or straw-lined trenches for winter. They boiled corncobs and mixed the syrup with melon centers for sweetener, grew hops for yeast, and ground barley for coffee. Meat and fish they dried or smoked, and everyone tried to have at least one cow as well as chickens. Keeping food cool in summer was managed with a well or deep hole that they could lower a food bucket into, and Jane was soon doing the same. Another simple technique she learned was a burlap- covered container under a slow drip-box in an irrigation ditch that kept food cool through evaporation. Some winters they cut ice from the river and hauled it up to an icehouse. Buried in sawdust from all their sawing of driftwood, ice could last most of the year.

Growing fruit was not a new idea among these homesteaders. Fruit was already highly valued by both Americans and Europeans as part of their diet, especially for the health of their children, but it was not easy to transport. If you wanted peaches you grew your own. Apple cider, often the hard version, was the staple drink on the frontier, but each apple tree had to be grafted if its fruit were to be valuable for eating. When settlers traveled across the country by wagon, later by train, they brought their fruit tree starts and grape and berry vines with them, babying them across the country far more than they did themselves. But for fruit, irrigation was a must. With that addition, the hot summers along the banks of the Columbia were perfect.

Homesteaders did need cash for things like tea, ammunition, cloth, and salt. Before the steamers made the market accessible there were four ways to get cash in the valley: freighting for the mines, trapping, harvest labor for wheat growers, and railroad construction. Then in fall came the annual trek across the desert for their supplies. All of these activities took the men away from their places for long periods, and Jane found out that homesteading women now living in some comfort were a talented, tough lot, able to carry out all operations in their spouses' absences. Women bragged or complained about how they had plowed and sawed wood when they had no brothers to do it. Now grown women, they told Jane how they and their mothers had herded on horseback, ran their homemade irrigation systems, raised almost everything they used, gave birth to children, and raised some of them. They told the marveling irrigators that when the bravest among them rebelled from loneliness and felt they must get out to visit a neighbor, they would tie logs into a raft, make a sweep oar, and float on down to the next farm. One family's women boasted of rowing and floating a skiff down to Pasco, over forty miles, to see a real town. Then, Jane supposed, the husbands must wanted them back badly enough that they found a way to fetch them.

Somehow the homesteaders found time to create a community. Mrs. Koppen wrote in her diary of 1896 of a Christmas party she hosted at her log home that brought in most of the non-Native people from the valley—over thirty. The entertainment included George Borden on accordion, and dancing. These settlers were not from highly strict denominations; only one woman, Koppen reported, was offended enough by the dancing to leave.

The successful homesteaders' numbers stayed small, and their homes remained, with few exceptions, spread in a narrow border along the riverbank. This was in part because their irrigation systems stayed small due to the lack of gradient in the district. Typical water wheels could be used only for low land close to the river, not being able to raise water more than ten feet for limited flow. Wells could be dug, but a windmill of the day was limited in its power too. Just before the Shaws arrived, some people, trying to expand, were using distillate or gasoline pumps to irrigate larger orchards. But cost and transporting of fuel ate away income. Without gravity-fed systems, the riverbank homesteads remained charming but marginal family-subsistence enterprises.

Less than a hundred miles up river in the Wenatchee valley, and closer yet in the Yakima, commercial irrigation was already bringing riches to large apple growers. The difference was the greater gradient of the rivers in those locations. Priest Rapids people had to settle for fulfilling more modest dreams, and the national promotion of irrigation as the "fulfillment of the country's democratic promise" was almost as remote from real life in the valley as it was on the reservation. For a small subsistence place, however, the riverside was close to ideal.

The greatest trial for the homesteaders, they remembered, was the dust storms. Once their alfalfa or other grain took root, and their wind-breaking trees grew larger, they were able to hold onto their own topsoil. But every so often during a drought year, the almost forgotten storms would come roaring back. When the wind stopped and the women were forced to shovel out their homes and barns and rewash all of their laundry, they probably wondered what in God's name they were doing in such a unforgiving place.

Flooding, at least, was not a regular problem on the Columbia. Although the flood of 1894 was frightening and destructive, the families were blessed with better housing from the huge new supply of logs that came down from northern forests. Enough children were now in the area that the settlers took the opportunity to build a log school building on the river's west side. The enrollment was tiny but encouraged their hopes of drawing in more families. These would then attract transport business. Their hopes came to pass. By the 1890s, commercial riverboats were hauling produce south and passengers and supplies north as far as Priest Rapids on an irregular schedule. Though families continued to come and go, a small but permanent valley community based on farming had formed. Yet, by 1906, only two families near White Bluffs, the Craigs and McGlothlens, had irrigation systems that provided enough water for commercial orchards. At the turn of the century, the valley still remained a quiet place where a few families had the energy of the great river to themselves. [2]

In 1893 the first surge of corporate land development began when

Northern Pacific Railway through its land grants developed a sizable canal and platted the site of Sunnyside on the Yakima. It was intended to be a duplicate of what had taken place in California through irrigation. Lots were sold, buildings thrown up, and quick growing shade trees planted. But it was a dire warning to projects that followed, for when the mid-1890s depression hit, this project (and hundreds of similar ones around the country) were denied continuing credit. Railroad investments overall became risky, and Northern Pacific abandoned the town site and ditch. Though Sunnyside was later restarted as a Christian colony and survived, the message was there. Desert land developers and growers were as tightly tied to the economy as any business.

Despite the problem of finding financial backers, by 1910 Washington had almost 400,000 acres under irrigation, a third of it under private water projects, the rest under the Bureau of Reclamation. Now, finally, land speculators turned to the neglected Priest Rapids valley, believing that with its even better climate, it would win a Bureau project too. But the Bureau engineer sent to study the area agreed with others before him. The poor gradient, the scabland terrain, and the cliffs below the rapids presented technical difficulties too great to recommend a project. The government took its resources elsewhere. While the Yakima blossomed, the Priest Rapids valley remained sagebrush land with a strip of riparian green, a conundrum to the engineers and speculators.

The valley of short winters was nonetheless not forgotten. According to G. Haynes in *Family Histories*, his father Manly Haynes, sometime in the 1890s, floated down the Columbia from Wenatchee's apple orchards and "became obsessed with the idea" that the same marvel could be created below Priest Rapids. Someone would figure out how to defy the lack of gradient in the river. Haynes somehow bought up thousands of acres and donated land for a town site. He caught the attention of his well-connected father-in-law, Judge Cornelius Hanford, from the Seattle-Tacoma area. The judge also saw vast potential and was able to get significant east coast backing, including General Electric. The town site became Hanford, and the water project was named the Hanford Irrigation and Power Company—HIPC.

This was not all for the love of fresh fruit, or even cider. At the time, engineers declared Priest Rapids to have the largest power producing potential in the world, hence the General Electric interest. In 1905 the news hit the press that the "Hanford Bunch" had found a solution for the Priest Rapids site. Finally the valley could be watered. The usual lavish brochures and news releases flooded the Northwest. Meanwhile two smaller land companies, the aforementioned WBCOT Co. and "Todd Plant", converged on the historic White Bluffs site and raced to get their town established as fast as Hanford. Their concept of a system of pumping directly from the river into wood stave pipe had always been available, but not promoted earlier because of the cost of fueling the pumps. Now that didn't seem to matter. The boom was on, and Frank Wheeler became one of the captivated.

The speed at which the boom grew was due to another brave venture. That same year a river pilot brought an 82 foot steamer *Jerome* down over wild Priest Rapids from Wenatchee all the way to Kennewick and began offering boomers a ride upriver. The schedule soon jumped to one or more trips a day, with many boats in service. The Oregon Steam Navigation Co. had, in its heyday, 26 boats on the river. Anything a builder or family needed could be shipped from Seattle to Kennewick on the morning train, be loaded onto a steamer, and arrive at White Bluffs by that evening.

Between 1905 and 1906 forty families from the Puget Sound area arrived by steamer with their livestock and supplies, chose tracts, set up tents, and started tearing up sagebrush. By the next spring, White Bluffs was already an encampment of about three hundred people, the Shaws among them. So eager were the first irrigators that they began putting in fruit trees even though no water system was yet operating. Families carried water from the river, some horseless families using neck yokes, as much as a mile, every evening, trip after trip. Trees took years to mature, but the irrigators believed that help was coming fast as work on the three different water systems pushed along. Meanwhile, in Washington D.C. the arguments for and against western irrigation went on, and the irrigation lobby continued to build in strength with the Bureau of Reclamation at the helm. The isolated valley was as busy as a colony of ground squirrels as each steamboat brought more boomers.

4

FROM SAGEBRUSH TO STRAWBERRIES

"You will think it is fun to see Grandpa irrigate, such a lot of little
creeks coming bubbling out of a spout at the side of the ditch."
Letter from Jane Shaw, 1909

THE ORCHARDISTS' FIRST YEAR of the project sparkled with energy
and learning, just as the water sparkled in the ditches, but almost
immediately they were hit with three serious problems. First came the dust
storms, increased from their normal pattern by so many families plowing at
once. The dried out topsoil continually blew off to the northeast. It blew into
peoples' eyes and covered everything they owned. Jane Shaw saw she would
have to lower her standards for housekeeping as she dusted for the second
time in a day. During the worst storms she, like the homesteaders before her,
would trade a broom for a shovel. New seedlings of any kind could be
smothered, and she knew that to keep up her spirits she must concentrate on
protecting her flower starts until they could withstand the onslaughts. Even
more essential , Jane had to keep the new vegetable garden alive.

Some families couldn't stand the storms and gave up. Others took
direction from the homesteaders to get their ground cover in as quickly as
possible and forget about dust-free homes for the more serious issues in extra

labor and expense for replaced crops.

Next, the promised railroad link did not materialize, while the steamship companies were rumored to be in economic difficulty. In fact, they were desperate for the produce of the settlers for their downriver run. Tied to this was the settlers' third frustration: the freighter lines, to operate at a profit, or even to survive, charged a rate that was not in balance with what the growers could get at the Seattle market. The railroads charged their usual high rates. All of the growers' cost of operation—freight, supplies, water, everything—was out of line with prices they got for their produce. This was not unusual for farming, but irrigators had more costs.

Last, and worst of all, the settlers belonging to two of the three water companies could not get the water promised. Only those belonging to WBCOT, the Shaw/Wheeler's source, were satisfied. Some families continued hauling water by hand and wagon to their new orchards and row crops, but many left, finished forever with the idea of irrigated farming. It took over a year to get the water problem partially corrected. Meanwhile the population of both White Bluffs and Hanford continued to grow as new innocents arrived, bringing fresh energy. For the survivors, it was not the beginning expected, but their faith was that with patience they could overcome all of these problems. The Shaws fortunately had Frank Wheeler's financial backup.

Mayflower Farm was the name the partners chose for their place. Named after an early peach variety, it recognized the importance of the early summer market. From the beginning, their focus was not on apples alone, unlike many of the settlers. But whatever trees the new orchardists chose, the urgent task of every family was to start some kind of fast crop to sustain them. The Shaws decided on fast-growing asparagus to go between their orchard rows. Asparagus was popular, for it would produce the second year, required no expensive supplies, and doubled as ground cover. Better yet, "grass", as they called it, would use the White Bluffs early spring to reach the Seattle market in May, right when the grower's cash jar was empty.

George and Jane soon found out that "grass" was not the magic crop. It was successful, in fact it was altogether too healthy, soon taking over the orchard as its own. It held down soil and evaporation well, but their backs ached from the stoop labor, both at planting and harvest times. After a few seasons of liniment rubbing each evening, the Shaws would decide, like many, that asparagus was fine for their own table but was not the cash crop for fifty-year-olds.

Alfalfa, in contrast, was not a labor-intensive crop in the season between the sowing and harvesting, and many settlers took that route. Alfalfa was fine for holding down the soil, made nutritious hay for the valuable cows, and was a nitrogen fixer important for the fruit trees. George soon saw that on ten acres they could not raise trees, grapes, berries, garden, and animals, and still have enough land for the alfalfa his cows needed. He would raise as much hay as possible for the small dairy herd he privately dreamed of, but saw he would soon have to lease additional irrigated pasture.

When the Shaw cow freshened, Jane had her churn and arm ready. Business people, construction workers, and teachers were her happy customers. George built a chicken yard, purchased chicks and feed, and before long Jane had extra eggs to sell too. The next thing they needed was a pig, then a horse and wagon for hauling and transportation. The cow (later cows), would provide them with a calf each a year for meat, or more cows, as the case might be. That was the basic assemblage for a farm of small acreage, and around them they saw similar spreads emerging. Later they would find the means to raise a couple sheep as well for the wool and meat. The Shaws had experience with subsistence level farming and thought they could do fine while the trees grew. They would not be begging from the

Wheelers for their day-to-day sustenance. [1]

As for their partners, Jeanie Wheeler and her children came across the mountains to White Bluffs as early as she could manage it each summer and stayed with the Shaws in their big tents. Frank came whenever possible. Although we know that the two women, especially, wrote regularly when they were separated, very few letters were preserved from those early years. Fortunately for this story, the year the Shaws arrived the *White Bluffs Spokesman*, a weekly newspaper running from four to six pages, began publication. We have a valley resident, Martha Parker, to thank for drawing on this and the other regional papers to create a year-by-year account of what went on along the river. For the Shaw/Wheeler activities, Margaret Jean Wheeler (Schuddakopf) is the person we look to most for memories of the earliest years since she was the first Wheeler to live year round, twice, at Mayflower Farm. There are also a few detailed letters from Jane Shaw and a handful of photos surviving from those days. Unfortunately faded black and white photos cannot impart the spectacle of an orchard in bloom, or leafed out and loaded with fruit in summer.

Jane Shaw spent little time directly in orchard work and avoided the berries too. There was a great deal more work to be done than there were hours for, and if a woman was willing to take on more tasks she was drafted. Some were out in the new orchards and vineyards daily; others like Jane, learned to draw the line. She concentrated on a farm woman's work: housework, cooking and baking, light gardening, food preservation, sewing, and, by the second summer, babysitting for Jeanie. She developed cottage industries she excelled at and enjoyed, and brought in needed cash. Like everyone, she would join in at planting and harvest, though her main role at those times was crew meals. But she wasn't going to chop wood, haul water, or cultivate. She in particular set the standard that her daughter wisely followed: the women didn't milk. "They have enough to do!" she declared.

Not every woman felt able to draw the line there. Most families had a cow and once the women had learned to milk, there were a hundred reasons why they ended up doing it.

Jane's bread baking, as well as butter churning, were soon well-known in the community. If a neighbor woman was too exhausted to bake, she knew she could slip over to the Shaw's and if lucky, for pennies find needed supplies for a quick supper. In the warm spring evenings, Jane seeded a border of flowers around their tents. Like her neighbors, she created a sunscreen with sunflowers, and castor beans and hops to climb the tents. Then she ordered a few ornamental shrubs too. As long as the water was flowing, she believed they could have a little more beauty, and a shade of green that wasn't the interminable muted "sage green".

With pressure to have the spring plantings in before the thermometer soared past eighty, the Shaws could have used up every ounce of energy they had. George must have counted his blessings each weekend that Jane believed in keeping the Sabbath. On other days, he himself believed in stopping work after supper, or they could have chosen to keep going until they dropped every nightfall. Unlike some families, they were wise, setting their schedule to what they knew they could endure, and this choice was supported by their partners, the Wheelers, in absentia.

That spring George also found a job surveying up the valley at Crab Creek for a few weeks. This was probably the last time he surveyed for salary, and it is from his journal of this work that we learn more of how he had occupied himself in the prior years. The bit of cash was just what he needed to start his small dairy herd. He would never have more than six cows and some calves, but that was enough for one man to care for and milk twice a day. Dairying had quickly become popular in the valley. The annual calves provided meat, something orchardists were always short of, while skim milk could be fed to pigs, and the cash crop, sour cream, was shipped down river. The alfalfa that cattle needed grew lushly, overcame the sand storms, and produced up to five cuttings, just as advertised. The cows, in return, produced fertilizer that helped the trees shoot up.

That same summer of 1907 the new community was struck with a crisis far worse than the dust storms. The Todd Plant pump house burned in August, destroying the pumps many families relied on for their irrigation. Those growers who could not tie in quickly to the WBCOT system frantically hauled water by the barrel from the river every evening and poured it to their baby trees. There was no way to save most of them. Parker says that again some families packed up, either having lost all, or sensing for the first time how fragile their survival was, decided now was the time to bail out while they still could. The company agreed eventually to pay for the lost trees but not for the season lost, and the disaster caused the first lawsuit in the valley against a land/water company.

Another group, those waiting on the HIPC Canal, had their own anxieties. When the water first flowed from Coyote Rapids through the canal it leaked so badly that over half the water was lost before it even got to White Bluffs. Three miles down the Bend, the water broke through the gravelly bank, and the canal was ordered closed down until it could be patched with cement. Those growers depending on it tried to convert to the hand-carry method but they, too, could not save all their trees. A year passed before the canal was reopened, and more families left the valley. These ruined families must have looked with envy, perhaps even anger, at WBCOT, the one remaining system operating as required. A photo from the period shows the Shaws, their tent houses, and a young pear orchard with several spaces in the rows where trees are obviously missing. Those on the lucky water system had their losses too.

Even though the settlers had known each other for only a year, they hated losing neighbors, and sight of the dead trees they left behind must have soured the relief of those who still had their orchards. Yet, the number of families arriving in response to the brochures was still greater than those leaving. This was in part through ignorance and in part through faith that a big dam at Priest Rapids was sure to be started soon.

We wonder how the Shaws and the other WBCOT shareholders viewed their fortunes as they recognized the fragility of their situation with everything depending on two pumps. But Jeanie and three children — Margaret, Rose, and baby George — had come to join the Shaws that summer, and it was hard to focus on worries as the tent and yard were filled with running feet and children's voices. Jeanie saw that her mother, in particular, had given up a settled though frugal life for something far more challenging. She couldn't tend her three little ones and still help much with the orchard, but she was quick to apply her energies and talents to the new flower and vegetable gardens and the berries. Canning and preserving were always waiting in summer. The heat in the kitchen when it was over 100 outside was her worst challenge. But she soon learned that toddlers were easily entertained with a garden hose and splashing cool water.

The annual spring trips into White Bluffs were another challenge for Jeanie and the children. They rode the Milwaukee through Ellensburg and across the river at Beverly to Taunton, a whistle stop in the desert about ten miles to the east of White Bluffs. Knowing they were coming, George Shaw hitched up the wagon, took the ferry across the river, crawled up the old homesteaders' road over the bluffs, and made his way across the desert to pick them up. It was one adventure the young children never looked forward to in the freezing spring nights. Their grandfather couldn't seem to keep the blankets around them as they jostled with each other for the warm spot. Jeanie wondered just how comfortable winters in a tent could be when even a May evening was this chilly. Though her parents were obviously energized by the adventure, she determined that she would come as soon as possible each spring to help. Frank would come as much as he could afford to, torn between supporting the project and being there to enjoy it.

The partners discovered that White Bluffs living required a combination of modern and earlier practices. Like the homesteaders, George caught drift logs for fuel, and in winter hauled their water in barrels or sawed ice. His only farm machine was their horse, and the horse usually was not pulling a wagon, but dragging a "stone sled" when doing orchard work. Jane was washing on a scrub board, and Jeanie, with many diapers facing her, made it a priority to see that she got something a little more advanced. Like the homesteaders, they expected to grow almost all their own food, buying mainly flour, coffee, tea, sugar, soda, molasses, and salt. Jeanie, regardless of the healthy desert air, wondered about raising children there year round. The "shopping center" was forty miles down the river, and White Bluffs was usually without a physician. But on the other hand, a registered nurse, Mrs. Brisco, had come in the same year as the Shaws and lived close by. Mail was regular, and mail orders from Sears came fast. Telephone and power lines were already in, if one could afford them. Jane thought the school and church were the quality one would expect in any small country town.

Jeanie saw how her mother and father had quickly made ties in the community and how the common dreams and worries drew the diverse people together. She saw that there was plenty of community for her to fit into, even during summer when everyone was concentrating on their farms. The men called on each other to help with spraying, haying, erecting buildings, repairing, herding, breeding and doctoring of animals, butchering, hauling, log-catching and ice-cutting. Women turned to each other for nursing, child-birthing and raising, and scarce supplies, and joined together to carry out the usual community betterment projects such as Sunday School and food baskets for families in difficulty. But unlike earlier days of sharing and bartering, the irrigators paid their mortgages and taxes with cash, and people who went to work at the larger farms were paid wages. Jane could take cash for her eggs and butter, and no one thought it unneighborly.

May 6, 1909, two years into farming, Jane wrote a birthday letter to Margaret who had just turned five, talking as if she expected them over again soon. Even though this was a letter to a child, it tells us much about the scene at the farm:

> My dear little Granddaughter,
>
> Today is my birthday and by the time it reaches you it will be yours. If you were here you could fill your apron with wild flowers. I was pulling some weeds out of the alfalfa and they were beautiful, blue, red, yellow, and white, but there is plenty of room for them to grow outside of the alfalfa. Yes, and you find them everywhere.
>
> Grandpa is spraying the trees this afternoon. They are growing wonderfully fast. Grandpa measured one of the branches and it was nine inches and there were 17 branches all in a bunch at the top of a cherry tree. Here is a leaf off an apple tree. A month ago they looked like sticks stuck in the ground. You will think it is fun to see Grandpa irrigate, such a lot of little creeks coming bubbling out of a spout at the side of the ditch. The chickens are laying fine, one day got 9 eggs, the next day 8. I sold two dozen to the store. They are 30 ct/doz...
>
> School is out here now and I will miss the little folks playing and the bell ringing. A little girl came to the door today selling greens. We had all we wanted for dinner for a nickel. They were turnip tops and pigweed, but tasted fine... Well, I must close now, and I am wondering how

soon you are going to be able to write me a letter. Love to
all and a kiss for brother and sister and I hope you will
have every birthday happier than another is the wish of
your loving Grandma.

We can't tell from this letter what problems the Shaws were
experiencing, but it is clear that the farm was taking shape. The school had
been let out early for the summer, indicating there was much work to be
done on the farms and extra hands needed.

By now, the water delivery from the canal was marginally under
control for those shareholders, and out-migration from White Bluffs slowed
down. During harvest time daily steamers throbbed down the river full of
produce. But though it was not yet obvious to the valley people, trouble was
coming for river freighting. The Northern Pacific had gradually absorbed
the local railroad lines and ever since 1883 had been in a rate war with the
river freight companies on the lower Columbia. This war did not get
sufficient coverage in the local press to worry up-river growers. They took
for granted the freighting down river to the transfer point with the
Northern Pacific at Kennewick, then on by rail to the Seattle commission
houses. But the small river steamer companies, losing most of their business on
the lower river to N.P., and having little paying freight for back-haul up
river, had for years been struggling to stay afloat. When the Priest Rapids
valley boomed, river freighting got a new surge and won few more years'
grace. The steamer traffic from Kennewick north grew again at such a rate
that a new ship was added to the fleet each of three years. To the Shaws
and other uninformed growers, the situation looked safe.

The Shaws realized soon upon arriving that the Columbia was the
valley's lifeline. There was no real road into the area, only wagon tracks
through the sand. If one got off the tracks and mired down in the heat of
summer, it meant serious trouble. People rarely tried to move produce that

way. In 1909 the Milwaukee Road opened its line through to the coast, but its "division point" closest to White Bluffs was Othello, on the south end of the Slope twenty miles away. Othello sprang up fast as a center with its railroad maintenance yards and mutton market, but though it was so close, little connection developed with White Bluffs/Hanford. The sand road between was almost impassable, and twenty miles might as well have been 200. A railroad link north and south along the river was far more practical. This was of special importance to Mayflower Farm, raising a significant number of soft fruit trees.

Talk of a rail link into the valley was constant, but nothing visible occurred. White Bluffs and Hanford businessmen and orchardists wanted more. Wenatchee to the north, Yakima and Ellensburg to the west, and Kennewick to the south all had developed into farming centers that shipped their produce over the tracks to both eastern and western cities. The valley businesses, more concerned with reliability than aesthetics, thought that a railroad spur was more progressive than holding onto steamer service that was forever fluctuating. Deciding to increase the public pressure for a railroad link, the businesses took up a collection of pledges of over $12,000 to encourage the Milwaukee Road to begin its construction of a spur down the valley from Beverly Gap. This action convinced some marginal growers to hold on a little longer.

Frank Wheeler, we know, had studied all the connected developments of water, power, transportation and population. A naturally skeptical man, he had earlier weighed the risks and decided it was worth the gamble that the developers, anticipating their great wealth to come, surely would find the energy, political clout, and funds to see that transportation and all the connected developments went through. But without doubt the pledges for the railroad were another blow to whatever hopes were left for water freighting.

In the meantime, as long as the steamer traffic stayed alive, the settlers felt they could manage by continuing to ship crops that could be dried or stand storage like potatoes and hay. With their express connection out of Kennewick they had proven that pears, grapes, asparagus, melons and even strawberries were possible if a shipment moved perfectly. Soon the Shaws were raising honey bees. They had to have them, they learned, or their orchard might not get properly pollinated, but honey was also another fast crop that could safely go down river.

Following their discouragement with asparagus, the Mayflower Farm partners decided on strawberries for their next major "fast crop". The profits were great if they could get the luscious but fragile berries to market in time. Beating California to market became a springtime *cause celebre*. The next preserved letter from Jane tells how the Shaws joined in:

Sept.17, 1910

Dear folks, I never would dare to try to respond to that fine long [letter] of Jeanie's but I will Frank's that came tonight...I can see nothing but strawberry plants, as we have been hard at it for four days. They got here the 14th and we have 3/4 of them set out. They are fine plants, strong and hardy. We trimmed their roots and branches and the soil is good and moist. The first day papa went down at five in the morning for them as they came late the night before. I washed that morning and that day we put in a thousand plants. Next day I put in 700 alone while papa was fixing up more ground over by the onion bed. Today we got one of the Alexander girls to help, also Mrs. Colburn trimmed for two hours. Mr. Gage said he would help us Monday, but I suppose Griffith expects papa to help him haul in his hay. The day before the plants came papa went about five miles after some posts as he wants to fence in the alfalfa for a cow pasture this fall...

The news of strawberry planting was what Frank had been waiting for. Aside from early profits, the surge of energy and care required in handling berries was good practice for what soft fruit would later demand. The Shaws were off to a good start with all that neighborly help, but they soon found out that strawberries were even worse than asparagus for the stoop labor. Again they had to resign themselves to aching backs. There were not enough younger people to hire for extra help; that is, there were a great many bachelors, young and old, but they had their own places to tend. Fruit trees seemed more attractive each week.

In the same letter about strawberries, Jane wrote not only of happenings on the farm but also of the connections she had developed in the community and the sharing that went on.

...Well, we have had some dandy sweet corn and three roosters. One makes two good meals, then some. Mrs. Brown had some nice beans. She brought over a mess twice. I gave her some onions in return. The late potatoes are the best. I think blight was the matter. Even the Klondike people [settlers who had made their stake in the Klondike Rush and become notable farmers] have poor spuds this year....

Mrs. Cornwall stopped here and we played flinch. They want to go to the Yakima fair and are talking of hitching their horses with ours and take a tent and camp near a farm as near town as we can get. I guess I might go if we can find someone to look after the cow and chickens. I got Hensley's machine but it is ancient as the hills and runs accordingly. Maybe by using coal oil and getting some of the sand out, it will do better...

Hoping the little ones are all right again, with love
as always, Mother

Much of Jane Shaw's character comes through in this letter: her appreciation of nature, her pride in all they are planning and accomplishing, and her care in what she reports (and doesn't report) about her neighbors. She seems quite pleased with their farming progress and with the community, and if she is tired of tent living we'd never guess it. There is nothing dour about her life in the way she relates it; even a game of cards is all right as long as it isn't on Sunday. The only complaint is about the "machine" she got from Hensley, a cream separator vital to the dairy business. She and George shared this process, including the weary work of washing and sterilizing it after each milking.

The good formal education of this Scottish immigrant is apparent in the letter, even though it was intended just for family. She and Jeanie both had more than most of the neighbor women. The formality of the Mr. and Mrs. titles, however, was not Jane's idea. That was what they all started with at White Bluffs and it never changed. Friends and neighbors of twenty years still used the formal address to each other, the one exception for Jeanie being her neighbor and best friend, Clara Barrett, whom she came to call "Clara" eventually.

A follow-up letter from Jane, just for Jeanie, tells the outcome of the Yakima fair holiday, and is as close as she comes to complaining in writing, and only to her daughter:

...I am alone. Papa went to the fair with Mr. O'Brien and others. Cornwall couldn't go as his last crop was ready to cut. I finished wetting down the new strawberries today as tomorrow is the last day of grace on the water line. Mrs. C. wanted me to go over there and stay nights but I didn't want to...I will be able to

send you some pictures of the ranch soon. There will be
three views. I will be glad when Papa gets back. I don't
like to do chores anymore. With love, Mother

There is a definite note of pique here, "I am alone." Perhaps no other
women were going to the fair. Most irrigator women found they did not
leave the district very often, some not at all. The Shaw chickens needed to
be tended, the water metering was coming on line the next day, and the
new strawberries needed to be wetted down, so Jane stayed home. She
forecast what her granddaughter Margaret observed for herself when she
lived with them two years later: Jane would retire from "chores", meaning
the outside work, but not entirely, not when it came to harvest time. In
1927, seventeen years later, she would write a letter telling of the boxes of
apples she had packed that week.

Those early promising days didn't last. As the railroad took more and
more of the Lower Columbia business, the upriver steamer schedule was cut
rapidly to a mere two boats a week, a great setback for berries and
vegetables, and certainly not a situation in which to plant soft fruit. Only
three years into their orchards, the Shaws and Wheelers were distraught.
They talked to their neighbors and found everyone worried. What was to
become of their farms and orchards if the boats stopped? Unlike the old
homesteaders of the area who had developed their river community roles
and alliances over the years, the new settlers were a diverse lot. Some were
still so entranced with their surroundings that they wouldn't leave, though
suspecting they should. Others had firm faith the railroad link would come
and that they could wait it out. The Shaws and Wheelers fell into this group
with Frank bankrolling the farm. Others had invested their entire savings
and had nowhere else to go, even had they wished to. Yet new hopefuls
continued to arrive, resulting in more net growth for both White Bluffs and
Hanford.

Though Mayflower Farm was soon able to grow much of its own food, and to sell its commercial crops with reasonable success, Frank found that his infusions of cash continued to be essential. As the orchard grew, so did the water bills, the biggest outlay of all. He would keep laying brick for a while longer. Jeanie would keep coming across the mountains in early spring to help. George worked to develop a respectable dairy operation in addition to caring for the orchard. Jane continued as consultant, main cook, food processor, and butter churner.

Margaret and Helen, the oldest and youngest grandchildren, had especially strong recollections of their grandparents. Their grandmother, in particular, seemed to be adept at creating a plan, putting it in place, and expecting others to help accomplish it. It was partly her upbringing and her Scots Presbyterian creed, and partly that though she didn't have perfect health, she was blessed with energy and believed that hard work, and good works for others, were what we were on earth for. Many of her neighbors, in theory at least, would have agreed. The granddaughters remember that Jane rose very early to begin her cooking routine that never varied: baking early in the day, a pot of soup simmering on the back of the stove, and excellent dinners served exactly at noon. It was inefficient to cook, serve, and clear up any other way. She had her regular customers for her butter and eggs, and was continuously processing one kind of food or another. In summer she was often babysitting with her grandchildren as well. Helen wrote later:

> When she sat down to rest a bit in the late
> afternoon, she took off her work apron and put on a
> pretty white diminity apron. That was our signal that
> she was resting. Then she picked up her knitting or
> crocheting, and opened her Bible. She could manage
> both at once, and reread her Bible through every year.

Everything she touched was tidy—her tent, her
clothing, her chicken yard, her garden, her writing.

Though the grandchildren were always welcome, Jane, as well as
George, was reserved in displays of affection. Margaret wrote later,

My grandparents doted on babies, but felt that after
about six years that too much shown emotion was
improper. Grandma would typically break down her
reserve only at arrivals and departures, when she couldn't
help tears. But when I lived with them I never felt they
didn't care for me; they were just reserved.

The Shaws treasured their days off. Margaret recalled that on Sundays
and some evenings, George strolled out to hunt sage hens, play with his dogs,
or spin yarns with the neighbor men. He soon was seen as a source of
entertainment to the settlers, who had no radios and only the small weekly
newspaper for diversion. Donald Wheeler says that his grandfather was
known as a "character" among the business men in town, and when he made
his rounds on errands, they liked to see him coming. They knew he brought
entertainment, nothing uncomfortable. Unlike Frank Wheeler, he never
presented them challenges to their conventional views and he had no
problem accepting a gift of a cigar or a shot of homebrew, to Jane's dismay.
She would have nothing of the sort in their own home.

Jane also had particular routines for Sundays. By now she had an array
of blooming flowers and brought a bouquet to church each Sunday for the
altar. Afterward, she gave it to a different family each time. Sunday
afternoons she read her Bible and church papers, then wrote letters. This
was typical of many of her neighbors. But, Margaret adds, "Grandma had
her own special Sunday activity with her trips taking charitable
offerings—cookies or bouquets—to the poor, the ill, or the neglected, often
taking me with her." Jane's generous side shone through in her constant

service to others, her handmade gifts always in progress, her typical good humor (less typical to her spouse) and her refusal to speak unkindly of her neighbors. Later, her grown grandchildren remembered her service to the community as remarkable, and felt she was not as appreciated as she should have been. "It's not that she had enemies," says Helen, "but that people just didn't realize all she did for them."

George Shaw was also a well-organized person, Margaret recalls, and probably without this the Shaws wouldn't have survived as a couple, for in so many ways they were different. He, like Jane, kept himself trim, never eating a second helping at a meal. After dinner he lay down for twenty minutes in any convenient spot, slept, then went back to work. He never was late for Jane's scheduled meals, though he carried no watch, for he could tell the time without one. Nonetheless she always called out for him (and the others) when the meal was ready, and Helen remembers that for such a tiny woman, "her voice could carry across the desert." Woe to those who came late! They would eat, but suffer her disapproving silence. Margaret adds, "But grandfather's ordered world meant that work stopped after supper, except for routine chores, and so he was considered by some who always worked in the barns, fields, and orchards until dark as less than industrious."

Jane was annoyed frequently by what didn't happen in that twilight hour after supper when her spouse was "through", but the routine chores—the wood box and water barrel—weren't filled for morning. She had to have breakfast ready at the exact hour to be happy, and it was impossible with George neglecting the kindling and slipping off in the evening to play with his dogs. So she would scold him until he lost his temper. He, like her, had so much to take care of. In addition to the garden and orchard chores, caring for his spotless barn, and eventually hand-milking five or six cows twice a day, he had all the other animals to care for too. Then there was the cream separator to wash. Jane didn't recognize this as adequate output; after all, she couldn't stop at dusk, nor did any farm wife. The difference was, some wives suffered in silence. However, despite a lot of shouting in the Shaw tents, neither ever cursed or struck the other, says Margaret. They simply weren't the adoring couple that her parents were. As a team to run Mayflower farm, they did well.

The Wheeler children in most ways loved their summers in White Bluffs, but by the time each became six it was a working vacation at least part of the day. Indoors they reported to their mother and grandmother; outdoors, in the absence of their father, to their mother and grandfather. Though the children considered their grandmother strict but humorous, the grandfather was more difficult to relate to. Deaf as he was, especially to children's high voices, communication wasn't easy for him. With children it was often shouting, and though he never laid a hand on them, they, unlike Jane, felt intimidated by his shouted orders or scoldings. George Wheeler, as the oldest boy, was the one to receive the most orders. Even though small for his age he was instructed how to milk the most docile cow at six or seven, and from then on was expected to pick up on a man's chores quickly. He made his share of errors, his patient father wasn't always there to console him, and the contrast between the two men's styles made the grandfather's impatience stand out more.

Margaret felt that their grandfather shouted when he wanted to be sure they were listening to him. It could be regarding an act beyond decency, in his mind, such as leaving the outhouse door open when they were inside. Or something dangerous, such as trying to short-cut through the young bull's pen. He had received the bull on loan from the County Extension, the intent being to improve the dairy stock in the valley, and was paid breeding fees by the customers. But the bull made the adults nervous for the children, and was a subject of regular lectures.[2]

Margaret, the obedient, got along with both her grandparents despite their reserve. She enjoyed pleasant times with them, such as when George hitched up the horse on Sunday, and they drove out together into the desert to look at the display of wild flowers. Generally, though, she saw her grandparents' only positive interaction with each other to be the economic one. It was much later when Jane was a widow, that Margaret, grown, understood how much her grandmother missed the spouse she so often berated.

As mentioned earlier, Win, one of the Shaws' sons, and his wife Juliette, were also swept up in the land boom. They arrived sometime in 1907 or 1908 to start their own place about three-fourths mile inland from his parents. Like his father, Win decided to concentrate on dairy, alfalfa, and berries while building up an apple orchard. As Juliette was a registered nurse and a midwife, her work was cut out for her. She and Win purchased one of the best construction tents, and she set up a clinic and hospital. She and the other nurse, Brisco, were always in demand. We have little information about White Bluffs as viewed by Win and Juliette Shaw. Due to bad feelings between Jeanie and Juliette, and disagreement between Win and his mother over the subject of alcohol use, this branch of the family, though not far away, was not really close. They all got together on holidays and to share equipment, and saw each other at meetings. Win sometimes snuck his father a drink.

Win and Juliette were important people in White Bluffs and well-received by the community as a whole. Juliette literally saved lives, while Donald Wheeler titles Win a factotum, involved in everything. Like many of the settlers, they were childless. They were among those who came into the district with needed skills and never had to rely entirely on their orchards or row crops for income. They could not make an entire living from any one activity, but combining them worked well for everyone. The Wheeler children admired Juliette, a California Indian, in particular for her hunting and fishing skills, something rare in women they knew. Little George marveled at how "she could shoot a squirrel through the eye." She, like Jane, was an excellent cook, and that may have been a source of envy to Jeanie, who had so much to do beside getting out a meal.

As for Frank Wheeler, most of the excitement of the early years that partner had to observe at a distance. The following portion of a letter from him, written in early May, 1911, gives the picture of the absent farmer, father, and husband trying to stay in touch, moving between worries about his crops and his family's diet, and teasing humor:

> ...Jeanie, I don't think it would hurt you (at 106 lb) or Mother or Dad (18 hr work day) or the children, to eat a chop once a month or a little hot soup at lunch. I thought there was a market there. Any asparagus in our bed? It seems to me our grapes must be slow or roots not as old as some folks or there would be lots showing up as they cant be more than a year younger than Juliette's and theirs were loaded last year. I hope the folks will get a little fruit for themselves. Apples are in bloom here. Do any show up there? There must have been a fierce frost there as even the little trees are white with bloom here. Tell Margaret that Im very pleased with that letter. Daddie will have to treasure that always as the "first fruits"—a little lamb launched on the sea of life on a school book. Yes, I know other folks have common old lambs, but this is our first—another little Jeanie. Its great isn't it, Grandma and Grandpa? With Dorothy [Rose] to make mud pies, and George Jr. to help granddad, and Margo to work letters and Marian to help mamma, I don't expect to

have to work much longer.

> How are those pear trees Jeanie? Have a good
> time, Beloved. Youv not got much rest yet, just a bit of
> change and you need quite a bit more. Love to folks
> and lambs, with all my love, Frank

Although some of Frank's odd spellings are genuine errors, many of his idiosyncrasies were an effort at spelling reform that some people were trying to effect. Always the radical, he had decided to eliminate all apostrophes, most commas, and to simplify contractions. It didn't catch hold with the others. He was a little worried in this letter, believing that four-year-old trees, and the grapes too, should have started to bear. He didn't need to have worried, at least not about trees. Margaret recalls that the next year she helped with a huge home peach canning operation.

Nineteen twelve was a most difficult year for the Shaws, especially Jane. Finally the trees were bearing, and more hands were needed at the busy times. Margaret, just eight, had been sent to live there all winter and help. When she and Jane were returning from a Sunday wagon ride, the horse suddenly made an illegal move forward just as Jane was climbing down. She caught her foot in the wheel and was thrown to the ground, her ankle broken. Margaret remembered, "Typically, grandmother's thoughts were all for me as grandfather went after the horse." Juliette set Jane's leg and cared for her in the tent hospital, also cooking dinners there for all of them. For some reason Jane's leg didn't set right. Whether there was no way to get her to Kennewick to the doctor, or she refused to go, isn't clear. The Wheelers don't recall that anyone blamed Juliette. Probably the family didn't know that the leg was setting wrong until they thought it was too late to fix it. As soon as Jane was able, she was back to her high activity, but she limped and had pain, which she didn't talk about, for the rest of her life.

The Wheelers would not have sent their eldest daughter to the Shaws two different winters, 1912 and 1916, had she not been needed at the farm. They needed her themselves, for she was a willing worker, and Jeanie's hands were full of four babies and toddlers. Margaret must have missed the more relaxed, noisy, untidy home of her own family, but understood the call to do her part for the farm. Her grandparents were reasonable, she says, putting her health and schoolwork first. She received real cooking lessons from Jane and was able to do enough of the housework after school that Jane could keep up with all her other chores and cottage industries. Much later Margaret looked back on those two years of farm life and put a philosophical perspective on the experience:

> From all of these relationships I drew a sense not
> only of extended support of the family... but buttressed
> also by the many occupations initiated by grandma,
> which provided me with the experience of children
> working with adults. In winter it was picking and
> carding wool from sheep they had reared themselves—a
> job I hated. In early summer it was harvesting berries
> and asparagus, and in late summer it was working at
> the outside table cutting up peaches and apricots for the
> big canner. Actually I'm not sure we children
> accomplished much but we were there, part of the
> team, while grandpa soldered the lids on the tin cans. In
> between, with hot spatulas, we affixed starter to frames
> for the beehives.

Neither the Shaws nor the Wheelers saw anything wrong with children working from an early age; it was what almost everyone had to do. Though Margaret didn't like some of her work, she said nothing. This wasn't just stoicism, for all around her she could see farm children doing exactly the same things. If carding wool was what she hated most of her chores, she doesn't seem to have been abused. It was simply boring and smelly.

Even though the Shaws labored hard, it is most likely they were enjoying their new home. Jane had recreated her life in Hoquiam, with less variety in diversions, but with more economic security. Never again would she need to take in other people's laundry. George, with a steady financial partner, was in a much better situation for a man of his age than he had experienced logging during the most recent depression. He was now completely justified to spend every day with his prize animals. As for Jeanie, she was bearing children every two years—Tacoma or White Bluffs made no difference—and just as she had hoped, the children were now outdoors all summer and healthy. If anyone was impatient during this period, it was Frank, waiting for those beautiful trees to produce and free him from his wage-slavery.

Finally, in 1913, the dreams of orchardists and developers alike came true as a steam engine chugged into the new White Bluffs terminal. Hanford and White Bluffs were at last linked directly to the outside world. But the railroad link brought other changes for the valley, and even as they cheered their greeting to the train, the settlers knew they were not all happy changes. White Bluffs, though it now had almost everything in convenience and service that its residents had hoped for, was never the same again.

5

THE RAILROAD ARRIVES; THE TOWN DEPARTS

"Fortunes were made again and again in the West by buying up cheap land where a railroad terminal was intended, but before that information became public."

Donald Niven Wheeler, 2000

THE MILWAUKEE BRANCH completion dovetailed with the collapse of the river transportation, and there is no doubt the connection was a close one. In the intervening years the Shaws and Wheelers had taken the risk that the steamer shipments would continue on a regular schedule to meet the N.P. express at Kennewick, or George and Jane would never had put in thousands of strawberry plants in 1910. But they weren't in the right circle to know what was coming, for it was that very year that steamer traffic began cutting back again. Soon only fast passenger and mail gas launches were operating daily. The entire economy of the valley had been at risk for three years when the Milwaukee link was finally completed.

Now the residents saw prosperity dawning over the bluffs. General Electric was a backer for more development schemes; power lines were already laid along the river. The district blossomed with new energy and new people. But there were serious shortcomings with the branch, one of which affected the whole valley: the tracks stopped at Hanford and never went farther south. Looking at the map, this at first seems inexplicable. Only another twenty-five miles of spur across flat desert was needed to connect with the east-west Northern Pacific line as it passed by the Horn of the Yakima River. Or just a forty mile link would connect with it at Kennewick. The assumption of the Milwaukee may have been that the Northern Pacific could take up its share of the spur by bringing up a joining branch from Kennewick or the Horn if it so desired. It never did. The Milwaukee Road, the more progressive of the two lines, had come on the scene too late to get land grants, and was always on the financial cliff-edge, according to Donald Wheeler. Its owners, though they would support the valley development in other ways, could not see a good reason to take their track farther. After all, they would do better assuring that all fruit in the valley had to move on Milwaukee tracks north to connect with its westward line through Ellensburg. Perhaps there were some politics between the two companies at the time that went beyond the issue in the valley. Whatever the combination of reasons, the Milwaukee's spur stopped at Hanford.

That the Northern Pacific declined to bring a connecting spur north across a flat terrain of desert is even more curious than the Milwaukee's refusal. Valley growers had considerable interest in opening up a railroad route to Portland, as Portland in those days was a more efficient port than Seattle. The common opinion was that it could move the fragile soft fruit to the east coast as much as five days faster. A connection south from Hanford to the Northern Pacific line would have allowed valley growers a competitive southern shipping route. One explanation for the NP lack of interest is that railroad investment in land development was no longer as popular as it had been. All the roads were in some trouble from over-expansion, and having trouble getting credit. In any case, NP talked about a branch into White Bluffs, but went no further.

Locally, however, businessmen knew the great potential for Priest Rapids was being throttled. Several groups worked to put together the resources to complete the link. One group, the Wenatchee Southern, went before the Interstate Commerce Commission for a permit to run a line south from Wenatchee to Beverly to connect with the Milwaukee spur, then to complete the rest of the spur from Hanford to Kennewick, finishing the link. They were turned down three times, the last time in 1920. They had put up the funds and done the survey, they had acquired almost all of the right-of-way needed, and had even built a laborers' camp at Beverly. The exact words of the denial, as quoted in the local press: "The ICC stated that the new road would not relieve car shortage...The ICC further stated that the Great Northern [at Wenatchee] was going to improve its facilities so it could move freight and passengers more rapidly. [Therefore] another road was not needed..."[1] The ICC had apparently caved to pressure from the Great Northern which controlled the north end of the state. It didn't go near the valley, hence there was no way it could "improve" services for it. Great Northern was fighting any southern link out of Wenatchee by another company. Eventually the Wenatchee Southern did prove a need and received a license, but in 1925 was unable to get financing. In 1927 they dissolved. The link to Pasco/Kennewick was never completed.

For the White Bluffs residents an even more outrageous maneuver took place with the spur line construction. Though it was not as far reaching, it was more insulting, and something the Wheelers and many others could wax furious over eighty years later. The Milwaukee, in building its branch down to Hanford, did not follow the river to pass through White Bluffs, instead laying the tracks to bypass the town, shaving off a small piece of the Bend, then curving south toward Hanford. To go on into White Bluffs, according to a map of the area, would have cost the Railroad about two to three more miles of track. Instead the White Bluffs terminal was installed a mile and a half out in the desert from the town. Some businesses in the valley were involved in this gambit.[2]

Today, such a distance isn't worth talking about; then it was significant. People used horses, boats, wagons, or walked to get about. Now the White Bluffs businesses were completely cut off from easy access to the terminal, while all the growers were forced to deliver their produce to the new terminal on sand trails across the desert. By the time the tracks reached that point people had known the route for some time and in disgust had resigned themselves to it. What happened next, however, they never did accept. No sooner was the terminal in operation than businesses felt they must move their buildings to that location.

Before long the plan emerged to move the town itself. The majority of residents, and many businesses not in on the plot, were appalled. It was soon clear who would benefit: those with lots for sale at the terminal site. For some time only the depot and a fruit packing and storage warehouse were at the new site. Then water lines were installed. The Wheelers and Shaws walked to stormy public meetings where people tried to discourage businesses from moving. For over a year, they held out; why would anyone wish to leave the riverbank site?

According to the *Yakima Herald* of October 8, 1915, the county moved the process along by a cancellation of all back taxes, and the new townsite offered free lots for those White Bluffs businesses who would move. That fueled the migration. D. Wilkinson, the telephone company owner, held out until 1915, as did J.L.Kincaid the banker, who moved only after being threatened that another branch bank would be brought into the new site. The town could not support two banks. The hotel moved, the Mercantile moved. In 1916 the Post Office was ordered to move, and that moved the newspaper office which was in the same building. Margaret wryly observed, "Unfortunately for those that wanted to move everything last thing, there was no way they could move the ferry."

For the residents, as bad as the inconvenience was, the aesthetic crime done was worse. If they hadn't become wealthy ranchers yet, at least their settlement on the riverbank had evolved into a beautiful little town with poplar and locust shade trees, serviced by a cross-river ferry and the remaining steamers. As more and more businesses gave up and followed the drift, the new White Bluffs emerged, a town with no charm at all out in the middle of the sagebrush. Those that moved quickly put in shade trees, but they could not move the river; they had only the HIPC irrigation ditch. The settlers were proud of the old town they had created and, in their view, it had been ruined. They did not let the insult die in their hearts.

Before many years passed, there were no businesses left in "Old Town" besides a plant nursery, a convenience store that sold such things as kerosene by the gallon, and the ferry. The school and church remained; they had no economic pressure. The old site was for a time allowed to keep a post office, named East White Bluffs. Then it too closed, the postmistress remarking that if all Old Town families had used it as much as the Wheelers it could have remained open. As private households joined the drift, some who had been friendly broke off relations and remained so. Donald and Helen Wheeler, growing up ten years later, remember that "moving the town" was still a regular topic of conversation. Two distinct factions still existed, the Old Towners and those at the new site, called Out Towners, maintaining a low-keyed feud that the children inherited. Later, some new families leapt over the gap. The Walkers lived in New Town, yet their children became best friends of the Wheeler youth. But Helen remembers her parents' friends were the Old Towners, and the people who had moved were viewed with at least resentment. "It all took place four years before I was born, and yet I was as conscious of it as if it had happened last year."

What happened at White Bluffs was a time-honored scam. Donald Wheeler describes it:

> Fortunes were made again and again in the West by buying up cheap land where a railroad terminal was intended, but before that information became public. Typically desert land was $2.50 an acre in the early 1900s. When a town sprang up around the terminal, lots could then be sold at tremendous profit. Sometimes the landowner was the railroad itself, while other times the railroad land had passed to a private land company... People in White Bluffs knew which individuals had manipulated the entire town for their own financial gain.

Old timers with good memories recalled a similar incident in 1885, not far away at Union Gap, where the original town of Yakima had started and then been forced to move. Northern Pacific in laying its track through the area, had decided to by-pass Union Gap and plat a town of its own four miles to the north on its own land, locating its station there. After much public protest, N.P. offered to pay the cost of moving to all who would do so. The residents still resisted. Maurice Helland says that after an angry delegation went to Washington D.C., the railroad finally offered free lots to those forced to move. The land speculators in on the White Bluffs move included a local real estate man. He became a number one object of Wheelers' and others' scorn.

To the Old Towners, the idea of anyone leaving the riverside for the desert through choice was insane. The beauty of their surroundings and the wonderful variety of activities on the river were so much of the reason to live in White Bluffs. The farming families without businesses mainly didn't move, and since the school, church and Grange all remained by the river, the most important gathering points for families remained in Old Town, providing an enclave with a permanent separate identity that drew in other families too. Helen says, "Families were always coming down to our beach or over to Barretts' Island, swimming, ice-skating, and boating. And everyone came over to the Grange dances, church, or events at the school."

The White Bluffs community never got over its bitterness, say Helen and Donald Wheeler, and its various factions were strengthened. But nobody hated the branch line, christened *Sagebrush Annie*. The growers had their one-day express for soft fruit via the link at Beverly to the coast market. During harvest season the passengers—shoppers, students, medical cases, businessmen—also had fine connections to the cities of the coast, riding in comfort all the way. During other seasons the schedule was once a week. Even though the valley's commercial produce now moved north on the Milwaukee, Kennewick continued to be the medical, legal and business center for the area. In 1914 a graveled county road opened from Kennewick through Richland north to Hanford. Trucks took over for local hauling and a stage made a scheduled run from Kennewick. Now the Wheelers could use this stage for their seasonal migrations that began before *Sagebrush Annie*'s summer schedule. For years entrepreneurs still tried to make water traffic profitable using fast gas launches. Strawberries were still going downriver in 1919. But before long river freighting was abandoned. Gas boats used much more fuel than trucks.

For Jeanie Wheeler *Sagebrush Annie* was a godsend. A trip to her girlhood home, Hoquiam, packing along her youngest offspring, was at least a possibility to plan toward. For Frank the train was his lifeline to his family when he was off working. Even if he had only two or three days between jobs, he now could make a rush trip to Mayflower Farm. The new spur connection made so much difference in the marketing of quality fruit that, for a time, the growers swallowed their irritation over the rates. Donald comments, "The freight was high, the express higher yet, but we felt it was worth it."

Though *Sagebrush Annie* became a vital part of the life of the community, the relationship with the railroads gradually reverted back to the resentment typical in the West. The residents would at least grumble and often cry loud over rates with little success. Benton County, and several other counties to a lesser extent, would later have a special battle with Northern Pacific, a large landholder. NP, during the Depression, refused to pay its property taxes that the counties relied on for road development and maintenance, claiming the land had no value. This resulted in on-going court battles, squeezed counties, and road projects that could never quite get completed. NP tax refusal was one more insult to feed the chronic animosity that farmers across the West felt for their benefactor-enemy.

The valley's isolation had been only partly solved. One side effect of this was that the valley, and each town and hamlet in it, continued to develop their distinct personalities. Within each community, residents continued to rely on themselves and their at least tolerant relations with each other for the ingredients of a good life.

In late May of 1915, Jeanie Wheeler climbed aboard the Milwaukee day coach at Tacoma and started across the mountains on her annual trek. She had in tow Margaret, now eleven, Rose—nine, George—seven, Marian—five, and Donald, just toddling at two. With the help of the older children she had managed all the preparations and transporting alone, for as usual during springtime, Frank was out working a construction job. At least this year she was not pregnant too. Jeanie was strong physically, but she was sensitive to others' opinion. Her family was unusually large for Washington, and women of her day typically did not travel that way, with so many children, alone.

We can picture her struggling up the steps of the coach, imagining onlookers to be thinking, "Why doesn't she just stay home?" or, "Doesn't she have a husband, is she a widow?" Or worse yet, "Can't they control themselves?" We know this is what went through her mind because her poor relations with her sister-in-law, the popular White Bluffs nurse Juliette, were caused by Juliette's refusal to attend Donald's birth, and her overheard remark about "people who breed like pigs". Some mothers could overlook such remarks from a woman who cared for everyone else's children but had lost all of her own. But Jeanie, who could never say such things about another woman, was humiliated and unforgiving.

The solution for her travels, of course, was to have her strong and handsome husband with her, always, and she could face any slings and arrows. But, after eight years, he found it still necessary to bankroll the farm. Cash for the farm's spring purchases, such as fertilizer, kept Frank bricklaying just when he yearned to be at White Bluffs enjoying the sights and aromas of blossom time. George Wheeler recalls that Frank during this time was working on the huge job of the Ruston smelter stack at Tacoma. Not only was it dangerous, he sprouted a cancerous growth on his hand. Though it was removed with no reoccurrence, it must have made the Wheelers all the more determined in their goal of country living.

Moving twice a year was difficult for Jeanie, but once she and her brood arrived, life went quite well. She could turn her children loose to the countryside, mainly needing to watch the thermometer and be sure that they always wore hats in the sun. Then she could turn her attention to the family venture, her flower garden, and her usual sewing projects. If it was too hot for anything else, the bank of the slough, under the now large shade trees, was a short walk away, and its waters safe and warm, its mud cool and delightful for toddlers. Only her spouse was missing. Two years after *Sagebrush Annie* began its runs, he was still laying brick. For although the railroad link had brought the orchardists almost everything they needed, it hadn't brought them the most important thing of all—a healthy market.

Frank was not oblivious to Jeanie's sacrifices for the farm, nor his in-laws'. A change had to happen for everyone, something that felt like progress. Though George Shaw's own role had worked out well for him, Jane was still housekeeping in tents year-round. Perhaps, he thought, the market needed new varieties of fruit. He studied Extension Service bulletins and ordered a wide range of experimental fruits, berries and grapes. Margaret observed he would put off buying a new pair of work boots to order another tree. But they only had ten acres to work with. Perhaps that was the problem—more acreage needed. But with what would they purchase it? Every dollar that came in went right back out.

Jeanie noticed that the farms that seemed to be doing well were those families who had come in with some cushion or had developed another business along with their farm. A cement plant, a tree nursery, a sawmill, a telephone company, the newspaper, and a convenience store were some of the enterprises families started up or took over that helped support their orchards. Others had the plums of the post office, school bus, and ferry services. Few families seemed to making their complete living from what they received from the fruit market. She looked for a way she could supplement their income. Unlike her mother, she preferred outside work, like berry picking, which she could be happy at all day. She saw an opportunity in bees. Not everyone could handle them—Jane and Frank were allergic—so those that could were in demand. Bees could be mail-ordered from Sears like just about everything.

Jeanie became a bee handler, not just for her family, but for neighbors as well. People called on her when their bees swarmed to start a new hive, or to set supers (new combs). Then she tied on her special netted hat and gloves and marched into the swarm. Jeanie's following letter about her bee work is

122

typical of those that she saved; they have some sort of "incident" in them, usually with a humorous twist. When Frank received letters with no humor, he had reason to worry.

My dear Frank, (no date, mid-teens)

Ill try to get quiet long enough to write. I did a big washing this morning, was just finishing when O'Briens sent for me to hive some bees...I also put on a super for them. I put three supers on yesterday and some of the bees aren't ready yet. One super is nearly full on the big swarm I put in last year.

...The Mayflower [peaches] aren't quite ready. I am watching them. I can get boxes from the Produce. Walter found a nest with 15 China pheasant eggs, two quail eggs and six hen eggs. Isn't that an oddity? Right up in the berry patch. Tom Brown came and wanted to know if I wanted to hire a man. Of course I didn't understand, and he went on "to keep your pig out of my alfalfa patch." Then, he said, he "wouldn't have to do it for nothing!" So Walter and Dad fixed up the fence between and she hasn't been there since, never was there very much. But now she is going up to eat all the apples at Dad's. She can easily be stopped there, too.

The bees, like berries, gave Jeanie a reason to be outdoors and some cash for her household but did not really change their overall situation. The Wheelers had to admit that so far irrigation had not overcome the market through efficiency or ingenuity. In fact they had become part of a scenario suitable for a muckraker novel. By the time the water company, railroad, commission house and bank had all taken their cuts, there was little left of their fall check to pay the waiting bills for box materials, spray, fertilizer and taxes, to say nothing of normal household needs.

Jeanie decided to try another experiment in the fall of 1916. She would not return to Tacoma at the usual time, and would stay over the winter in White Bluffs taking all of the substitute teaching she could get. Frank agreed to it; he knew she enjoyed teaching and that she needed to see progress. So did he. Her mother agreed to take care of her two grandchildren not in school, Marian and Donald, when Jeanie was called.

That fall gave Jeanie second thoughts about desert living in winter. The small cabin she was able to rent was on the other side of town. No one was ready for the winter that descended on them. One of first grader George Wheeler's least favorite memories of White Bluffs was of trudging back and forth daily, through a record freezing wind, between the rental and his grandparents' house or the school. The caps, socks and mitts their grandmother knit them could not keep out such chilling blasts. Jeanie and the two smallest rode in a wagon brought by her father while the others ran to keep warm. The rental was nothing but bare planks; they slept with bricks heated in the wood stove, then wrapped in towels.

Young George was not only introduced to school but to men's winter work. His new job was to get up and light the fire each morning (it had been laid the night before), then to thaw the ice in the basin for washing. Sawing logs for firewood was worse:

> "I remember crying while pulling on one end of a
> cross-cut saw, with Rose on the other. My fingers were
> aching with each pull, but we had to saw that wood
> before we could get warm with it in the stove. And the
> chilblains when the toes and fingers thawed were an
> excruciating ache..."

The unusually cold winter was too much, even for the valiant Jeanie—the house wasn't even as warm as her mother's tent—and she fled for Tacoma in November, leaving Margaret again with the Shaws.

The family were not alone in their suffering. Though the White Bluffs winters were short compared to neighboring districts, they were often windy and sometimes below zero. The settlers' houses or tents had no insulation, and the snow covered people's wool comforters by morning. The lucky Wheeler children always wore wool in the winter, but they remember that some of their school mates had nothing but cotton to wear year round. Though few of the settlers complain much of the summers in *Family Histories* , many recall that as children they suffered from the winters just as George describes. Wool-padded clothing would have been fine but most families had just enough sheep to make into their comforters, and perhaps a fleece-lined coat for the man.

That 1915 winter continued to set records. Snow was two feet deep, everything froze, and when temperatures dropped as far as -27 everyone knew what it would do to the more fragile soft-fruit trees. Many became firewood. Frank was proud of Margaret for the contribution she made that hard year, living with her grandparents. On May 20, 1916 he wrote her for her twelfth birthday, the first letter that we have of the long correspondence that developed between father and daughter:

> ...Well, my little lady, I should have sent you a
> birthday letter. Im very pleased to have a girl that can
> work in Mama's place and keep house too. I hope youll
> go right on growing and learning just as you have....I
> hoped to have a plot of ground in good shape so all you
> children could try for some of the [children's
> agricultural club] prizes. But I didn't get anywhere
> near doing it. But Im sure if you could you would enjoy
> it and we will hope for it for next year. I worked a full
> week on this job, the only time so far. And it rained

quite a bit too. I like the soft clean air of the sagebrush at White Bluffs. It seems to be so light even when it is hot...

Jeanie was to remark later, "1915 was our worst year." It was not just the extreme weather and poor housing. The decade 1910-1920 has been called "the Golden Age of American Agriculture". If so, it was badly tarnished by the time it reached the Columbia. Drought recently had again caused abandonment of dry farms on the Slope. The only dry farmers that seemed to make money were those who conducted wild horse and wild cattle roundups and sold them to rendering plants, or trapped coyotes, badgers and bobcats for saleable furs. Growers in the Snake valley made no net profit either, despite a government irrigation project that kept water costs low. Farmers across the entire country must have been suffering, for in 1916 the federal Farm Loan Act was passed to help them refinance mortgages they couldn't meet, and to make operational loans. Later, some farmers felt the loans made matters worse, for it encouraged them to expand, and then to face more loan payments they couldn't meet, resulting in more foreclosures. In the Priest Rapids district 1915 was a tough year but there was no widespread crisis, for the hardy apple trees mainly survived the terrible winter and went on bearing well.

Mayflower Farm had to increase production somehow, or Frank would be working for wages forever. The previous spring George Shaw had taken steps of his own, deciding to invest more energy in something he felt confident of and had more control over than the fortunes of fruit trees. He borrowed money from the White Bluffs bank to purchase more dairy herd. This gave the Shaws some independence from the fruit market and income of their own. But Jeanie's miserable experience that November made her think that other changes were necessary, not just farm expansion. For the first time she fully realized what her mother, now sixty and lame, went through each winter living in tents. She put her heart into the proposition that no matter what, the next summer Jane would move into a real house. The partners agreed.

Jane came up with a plan that each couple borrow $900 through Jane's cousin, Walter Niven, who was a banker in Wisconsin. Soon after, the Wheelers made the final payment one year early on the farm's original mortgage and received the deed. Niven's bank then carried an $1800 mortgage on Mayflower Farm, the only mortgage, and, as it turned out, not nearly so risky as one through a stranger. The Shaw's part of the loan helped to build Jane's house. She told Margaret at the time that the funds were from her Niven family, but later Jeanie told Helen the funds were from the sale of the Shaw house in Hoquiam. Probably it was both.

Some orchardists had moved out of their tents much earlier, but mainly to simple frame cabins. Very few felt they could sacrifice the time to build a log place like those of the homesteaders. Jane had waited, and now for a time the new Shaw house was one of the finest in White Bluffs. This left the big Shaw tents free for the Wheelers to move into during summers, to be right next door, close to the farm, the school, their church, and their grandmother's great cooking. Everyone must have been much happier.

The most interesting house in White Bluffs, just across the road from Shaws, had been built by the homesteader Helsom. He had copied a southwest desert design, building it partially underground so that it was always warm in winter and cool in summer. But no one imitated the design. Frank was interested, but apparently it was too radical for Jane's taste. Her house was a typical wooden construction of the time that one could have seen in any town of the Northwest. Like the other White Bluffs homes, it had no insulation, no electric lights, no plumbing, no bathroom. But it had a large screened-in porch soon covered in summer by a Virginia Creeper vine that helped to keep it cool. The porch became the most important room in the summer, used for both eating and sleeping. There was a parlor, three bedrooms, and a kitchen with a good wood cook stove and oven, and free-standing cupboards. All of the rooms had plastered walls.

Like most desert homes, in the yard was a covered cement cistern to catch rainwater. The cement basement with a partially dirt floor was just right for keeping canned food, but Helen remembers that it also provided her grandmother a perfect cool place to go on hot summer days. Here Jane did allow herself some radical design, out of view of the public, for she had her special space there in the cellar with a chair and lamp. She could be found reading or writing there when she took her afternoon rest after putting out a big dinner in the sweltering kitchen.

The next summer Frank, Win, and others rowed across the river to a spot at the bluffs where there were fine slabs of sandstone. Frank chiseled them into portable shapes, they worked them down to the beach, then hired the ferry to bring the slabs across the river. They brought back enough to make Jane something she had always wanted for her home: a stone trim across the front of the house, stone steps, and a pathway. She added more ornamental shrubs and a patch of lawn to create a front garden of colorful, moist beauty.

Jane, as she had long hoped to do, started a boarding house. Soon she won the local teachers as tenants, the school being right next door. In addition, her fine meals allowed her to steal away some of the hotel's dinner customers. The Shaws now had a small but steady income from boarding guests in addition to the sales of cream, butter, eggs, honey and produce. Even so, though they gradually acquired modern equipment--a cream separator, canning machine, and a cider maker--the accommodations were still far from what we today would call living in comfort. The kitchen had no refrigerator; the washing machine was now gas-operated, but it still had a hand-cranked wringer. A hose brought water to the house from the irrigation ditch, but in the winter the men continued to haul the water from the river in barrels. Yet, the arrangement was better than most of her neighbors had, and Jane performed in that simple house as if it had the latest in modern conveniences. Jeanie could now overcome any guilt over the conditions her mother had been living in. Except for some heirloom furniture they had stored in Hoquiam, which had then burned, Jane now had everything she had ever had, and more.

Looking for more land with their share of the loan, the Wheelers were lucky to buy the Kent Place, a small orchard just a short distance from the Shaw's house. The mature trees, on only 3/4 acre, were not a significant commercial expansion, but provided a fine shady place to set their tents. Now Jeanie could have her own flower garden while the chicken house and garden were easy to run to for meal supplies, and her mother for child care. For summer living the tents were even better than a house, for they were cooler.

Though the quality of living shot upward with improved housing, the business of making a living from fruit ranching did not. Like most Priest Rapids growers, the Wheelers/Shaws had no experience from which to guess how much a tree could yield, or what their expenses would average. The market prices did hover in a certain range, but the natural set-backs, except for jack rabbit cycles, did not occur in any predictable pattern. No one could say when the next dust storm was coming, or the next late frost that could take half the soft fruit. This was, of course, the gamble that all farmers took. Irrigation was supposed to overcome this great unknown, and indeed it did free them from dry farmers' greatest fear—drought. But so far irrigation had had little effect on the rest of the equation.

Jeanie decided she needed another cash-making venture besides substitute teaching, beekeeping and berry picking for other farms. She saw other women going to and fro the packing sheds at the larger farms where they worked for wages: Bleykers, Roberts, and Lovelands orchards were among them. These large spreads succeeded through quantity of production and their value-added activities like sausage and jam factories. Lovelands had come in the same year as the Shaws, but with their own chartered railroad car to bring all their supplies. They now boasted a showplace that realtors liked to entice their clients with. Though most of the farms stayed marginal operations, these fine places offered work, enabling their humbler neighbors to keep going. Jeanie decided it was no shame to go to the packing sheds, for so many were doing it. Soon she found she actually enjoyed the work, and not just for the money. Frank deplored that she felt forced to that, but she didn't feel forced and refused to stop.

The Shaws/Wheelers and most of the 1906-7 settlers stubbornly held on, partly because White Bluffs offered so much more than a chance to be successful farmers. The orchardists' children, many interviewed for the *Family Histories* in 1981, were delighted with White Bluffs as a place to grow up. Jack Zane speaks for them when he says, "I can't believe I could have had (and I include my sisters) a finer atmosphere to grow up in than the White Bluffs-Hanford area." Even as children they recognized the exceptional beauty of their surroundings in both the natural world and their own created orchards. Many of the older settlers nostalgically exclaim of the pride they had in what they grew, if not what it earned them. Though Frank hated bricklaying more each year, his wages earned him a wonderful place to flee to, to a different kind of work. If he had simply moved to the valley and taken up moonlighting as a farm laborer, he would have earned only thirty cents an hour. So far, irrigation technology had not lived up to the dreams they had caught from the Agrarians, but the valley itself had. The irrigators that remained, even those that did farm labor for others, felt that what they had now, marginal as it was, surpassed what they had left behind.

Just how Jeanie privately felt about farming after ten years is harder to guess. She didn't confide in her children about such things until much later. It would have been disloyal in her mind to complain to them. But we know she found many sources of pleasure in Mayflower Farm. Her flower garden continued to expand, and she soon excelled as a top fruit sorter and packer, a job she never gave up. As for Frank, his love for horticulture had not slackened.

6

ALL THE WATER WE WOULD NEED

"I am the only person left alive that knows the whole HIPC
water project story; I don't think it's written down anywhere."
Donald Wheeler, Rolling Bay, 2001

AT THE VERY TIME the settlers were clapping their hands over their
railroad link, they were wringing them over the unsolved problems of their
water systems. Water, after all, was what everything depended on. After
the mishaps of the first two years none of the farms had been completely cut
off their supply, but the users, as stockholders of the water companies, had
chronic worry. They had already lived through the worst that natural
adversaries like sandstorms and frosts could offer and so far had managed.
But water issues were more complicated and more within the realm of
humans to resolve. The settlers had paid dearly for adequate affordable
water and the perpetual right that guaranteed this, up to ten times the
normal cost for desert land. They resented the constant worry, from the
system's operation to their own water bills.

The laws governing western water rights were complex, and the valley's
legal battles had begun early when the Todd Plant burned, leading to years
of court battles. The case raised all the knotty unresolved issues. Did

perpetual mean forever? Did it mean one had a right to all the water one wanted all of the time, or just equal shares of whatever was available? What was "adequate"? Did it mean adequate water for one land holder even if it meant cutting off another? The plaintiffs in this initial case claimed that as the pumping plant was not adequate, due to wrongful representation excessive prices had been paid for the land. The court's ruling was ambiguous. It stated that the plaintiffs had a right to sue for damages due to insufficient water, but stated that "the company had no automatic responsibility to provide a continuous flow of water." This seems to mean that there was no responsibility until after the fact, after the crops were damaged, and was no doubt a different interpretation of "perpetual water rights" than the growers wanted to hear.[1]

Unlike some districts, the technical and financial problems of the Priest Rapids district water companies gave the users as many headaches as water rights issues. While the WBCOT system and the extinct Todd plant were simple operations that any mechanic could operate, they were defective in that they required coal or coal distillate to be purchased and barged up river to power the pumps. This made water the most difficult cost for the growers. In addition to the Todd Plant's early problem with the fire and subsequent lawsuits from growers, it ran into trouble again when it bought a lateral irrigation pipe from HIPC that ran out into the desert to outlying farms. Todd found that, like HIPC, it couldn't deliver due to leakage. That was the final problem, resulting in its bankruptcy. Somehow HIPC then found the means to patch the pipes and pick up those users again.

Soon after this, the private company Pacific Power and Light (PPL) laid power lines down the river and WBCOT installed 100 h.p. electric pumps. Convenience improved, but paying for the private power was no more cost-efficient. Maintenance of the buried redwood stave pipe system was also far more than expected due to wood shrinkage in the dry climate and the fondness of the townsite's shade tree roots for the pipes. After a few years, continuous digging up and replacing of pipe was required. WBCOT's shareholder/users found that its costs of maintenance and operation forced them to raise the water rates every few years. Growers often were in arrears. When WBCOT floated bonds for survival, it was in arrears on its payments as well. More burdensome, each stockholder was held personally responsible for the arrears of the company and all its members, an impossible arrangement for farms whose fruit trees hadn't yet grown a bite of fruit.

Much of the financial trouble came from the fact that the water companies were captive to Pacific Power and Light (PPL). Unlike the railroads, the power companies had no special devotion to the development of farming communities. Desert water experiments came and went, while PPL's best future was in the surging growth of Puget Sound and in the big dam coming that would provide for that. A small desert water company was simply one more customer at whatever the market could bear, and not such an important one at that. In the early years there were few if any controls on the charges private power companies chose to set.

The settlers knew the survival of their local water companies was more critical than any other piece of their operation. A fruit tree could not last a summer in the desert without water. Or if it got less than adequate water, even for just a week, it bore less fruit. Donald Wheeler remembers well the financial problems of WBCOT and says, "The folks always made sure to pay the water bill, if everything else waited." Many settlers, agreeing, would wait years to hook up their homes to the new power lines; most waited decades to install modern bathrooms, or to buy tractors or autos. The water systems had to come first. When some users could not keep up with their bills, the water company was no longer bound to deliver, and the ditch master, the manager of water usage, could close off their ditch gates, but this did not help either party. The delinquent users couldn't sprout another seed the next year without water. The water company could put a lien on the farm, but a dried up farm did not help the company to pay its own bills.

On the other hand, if the company did not deliver adequate water, whether through carelessness or technical problems, or didn't deliver a fair share to a certain location, the users could sue. Then there were court costs, and if the water company itself went bankrupt, what was there to sue? And where would the farms get their water? The stockholders of a water company had to take their responsibility seriously. In all this, the WBCOT system struggled along. Though it was not a cost-efficient system, it did manage to deliver water to its farms and businesses.

The Shaws and Wheelers were luckier than many in that they never suffered serious damage from inadequate water after the first two years, but they suffered much inconvenience. WBCOT service to the farms was turned off in winter. Then the families were forced to haul river water for their households, sometimes cutting ice. The Shaws/Wheelers endured this until 1922 when they were at last able to pay for a well to be dug for household water through the off-farm earnings of their son George.

Some families had shied away from the water companies from the start, and others dropped out of them when they saw increased problems emerging. They attempted to run their own pumping systems, using windmills, and when that failed to be adequate, gasoline. Out in the desert they pumped from wells they had dug, while those who could pumped directly from the river. This was a less stressful solution than a water company but not a cheap one either, considering the fuel they burned. Donald remembers that across the river were the sad remains of a pumping system an early settler had tried to operate from a steam boiler fueled by drift logs. A creative idea, it had not been successful for some mechanical reason and was abandoned before it ever watered a tree.

The building of the HIPC diversion dam that produced its own energy for pumping, fueled by the Columbia itself, had been the right strategy on paper. It would produce all the needed water and far more cheaply. But it failed on both counts, especially for its users at the lower end of the canal. It was an embarrassment to the irrigation lobby as well as its own corporation, and unending trouble for its users/stockholders, the majority of the irrigators in White Bluffs. The irrigators realized early on that the HIPC land developers and engineers had not resolved all their technical challenges before the land sales started. Donald Wheeler comments that had the problems been resolved in time, the three generations of irrigators that tried to bring the valley to its potential might almost have succeeded. But one must say "almost", because time was running out for the small family farm.

Donald in 2002 commented, "I am the only person left alive that knows the whole HIPC story; I don't think it's written down anywhere. I got it from the engineer at the HIPC power plant when my high school class visited in 1929." The story demonstrates the obsession that took hold among speculators infected with irrigation mania and the struggles they went through to green the desert.

In 1905 the determined Hanford Irrigation and Power Co. thought they had found the answer to the problem of the river's poor gradient in the Priest Rapids valley. Their eyes on the potential riches through opening up one million acres, they built the diversion dam with turbines at Priest Rapids, creating the power they needed. They ran power lines fifteen miles downriver through rugged terrain to Coyote Rapids just above White Bluffs where the terrain became reasonable. There they installed two great pumps that raised the water up the high bank to a canal they constructed that did have the sufficient grade. This Hanford Canal, or Ditch ran down the valley seventeen miles and emptied back into the river below the boom town Hanford. The Columbia thus powered its own pumps to create the missing gradient, an ingenious system that was being completed as the Shaws arrived at White Bluffs.

In 1908 the water started to flow down the canal to all its waiting customers who had been hand-delivering their water. Soon all could see it was leaking badly, and water wasn't getting down to the lower district users. This was due to the gravelly nature of the soil at the river bend above White Bluffs. Though the leaking sections were cemented again and again, the problem continued. The situation was not unique; American ditches typical lost half their water through evaporation, leaks and seepage. In their planning the engineers should have accounted for this, or perhaps they had, but the land sales department hadn't. The more people that came into the valley to start their alfalfa fields, vegetables, vineyards, and orchards, the more was demanded of the Ditch. Soon it was clear that the Ditch could not supply enough for the farms it served, farms which were mandated to share the water fairly according to how much they had under cultivation. Fourteen years later, over half the water coming down the ditch was still leaking out or evaporating. The growers at the lower end did get water, but not what they needed for high production and not what they had paid for.

This is not all of HIPC's sad story. Second, and more complicated, Donald explains, the power source at the diversion dam couldn't produce enough. Springtime was when most power was needed by the pumps at the ditch head, for the trees were growing their fruit then and needed the most water. Because of a peculiarity of hydraulics—the "pooling" effect at the bottom of a dam—the power generated was the least then. At low water in fall, when the harvest was finishing and less power was needed to pump less water, the amount of power generated was the greatest.[2]

HIPC's only recourse was to buy power for its heavy use period from Pacific Power and Light (PPL). This company was to become one of Frank Wheeler's Ten Most Hated for what he saw as unrelenting greed in the rates it charged small farmers. Eventually the Public Power Commission would bring PPL to task, but in 1910-20 this sort of control was far in the future. PPL conducted business as usual for a private power company, that is, HIPC was able to buy power only at top rates. But when HIPC had excess power, it was able to sell back to PPL only at "dump rates", all that PPL was willing to pay since it was buying whether it needed power or not. This cost of purchased power at top rates ate badly into HIPC's profits, and the problem was passed on in the water bills to the users. The growers were not privy to all this unless they had chatted with the engineer as Donald had. All they knew was that their power bills were much higher than they had expected, and for some, the flow in their ditches was lower.

Some valley boosters believed that the reason the valley never developed more was because the big dam at Priest Rapids did not go through. Its backers could not get the credit they needed for what was, for private corporations, a massive undertaking. Donald believes that despite the pooling problem, if HIPC had given more attention to correcting the leaks, the existing diversion dam could have covered the growers' needs of the day. Demand for industrialization and agribusiness, not small farming, he believes, was the push behind the big dam. Others say it was desire for general valley development. In any case, the early HIPC project had two inherent defects somehow overlooked by the engineers, and the third forced on it by the larger power company. Much later, massive federal projects would have the funds and clout to overcome all of this, but for now the HIPC promoters felt they had done what they could for the technical problems of water delivery. They pushed on—they had too much invested to stop—selling land that was guaranteed water rights from the canal, and talking up their vision of the gigantic full-channel dam at Priest Rapids.[3]

The reputation of the Hanford Canal spread and HIPC failed to sell as many tracts as anticipated. It filed for bankruptcy. In order to get out from under the dilemma of its money-losing irrigation system, HIPC proposed to split into two companies. It would become a profitable power company (its turbines at Priest Rapids) called the Black Rock Power and Irrigation Co. which would be uninvolved in water suits over the ditch, and a second unprofitable Consumer Ditch Co. which would be liable for failures to deliver, but being in constant danger of insolvency, would be a useless target for claims by irrigators. This gambit was fortunately denied by the courts. It was appealed. Meanwhile the court-appointed receiver raised the water rates, and the users/stockholders took the receiver to court twice the next year. It was a critical case for the farmers, and Judge Hanford, an original founder of the project and town, entered into the suit on the side of the users. Manly Haynes' grandson comments in *Family Histories* that Haynes, another original founder, entered the suit as well and exhausted all of his finances fighting the receiver. Their support undoubtedly helped; in 1922 the judge ruled in favor of the users.

Before long, WBCOT, the other water company, would go bankrupt as well, to be taken over by a users' group that in its turn would suffer the same fate. Donald's research led him to believe that there was no trouble-free western water company :

> Except for the Columbia, there was no western
> river that could supply unlimited water to all interested
> users. The Yakima and the Wenatchee couldn't. In
> most places what could be allotted per user was
> determined by how many users and what the storage
> capacity was, such as a lake. On the Columbia (pre-
> Grand Coulee dam), it was more a question of what the
> pumps and ditches could produce....More money was
> spent on water litigation than on schools.

HIPC and WBCOT and their offspring remained in receiverships most of the years, with continuing attempts by consumer coops to take over their functions ending up in new bankruptcies. Donald comments that it is a good thing that HIPC was not able to sell more tracts, for they could not have delivered the water.

Regardless of lawsuits and receiverships, the irrigators had to keep the water flowing. There were only a few actions the ordinary users could take. They had formed a water district in 1921, but with no resources could accomplish little. It would be 1928 before the court instructed the users they could prepare to take over the former HIPC. Meanwhile they could keep their monthly payments current, they could do their share of the ditch maintenance, and could and did engage in more lawsuits over water rights, delivery, and rates.

Donald remembers that as soon as he was old enough he was the errand runner who delivered the Wheeler's water payments. He describes another less pleasant chore:

> The old town's wonderful shade poplars had been planted by someone right on top of the wood stave water mains. As the trees grew, their roots went down to work apart the pipes, and with all that moisture the trees thrived, but not the pipes. I and other small boys, because of our size, had the creepy job each fall after the water was turned off—nobody asked us if we wanted to—of crawling down the mains to cut away poplar roots. It wasn't really very dangerous as the men stood by at all times, and for some reason snakes and spiders were not lying there in wait, but nonetheless it was not boys' favorite task. Then the pipes that were in worst shape had to be replaced. The town would not have dreamed of pulling out the beautiful and useful shade trees. It was better to reroute the pipes or just

keep cleaning and replacing them, so we boys looked
forward to that ceremony each year.

On the HIPC Canal the problem was not roots but windblown sand, and burrowing animals that provided holes for water to escape to nowhere. Sage rats, rabbits, beavers, even badgers the children living near the ditch were encouraged to hunt. Then, each fall when the ditch was drained, teams of canal users had to shovel out the silt. At the lower end where the flow was weak and weeds could grow and clog the current, horse teams dragged a heavy chain along the drained ditch to pull loose the weeds. All this could be hired labor when the water company was solvent, but each year more it fell to volunteer labor from the users, and was on top of what every irrigator did for maintenance of his own farm's ditches where weeds, silt, and rodents abounded. Farm ditches demanded constant vigilance, as each system was a vast network of channels going to each tree or crop row on a set schedule. If one ditch was clogged, a tree would fail to get its required water before the water was directed to the next channel.

Still, root, weed, and rodent control was easy compared to combining for organized protest on water and power rates. As a small group of shareholders in an isolated valley, their cries weren't heard. It took a nationally organized group like the Grange that spoke for all farmers, not just small western desert farmers, to have any meaningful voice. As the years passed, the valley and state Grange joined in with its national office to become an ever louder voice on the need for cheap rural power for their water systems. If one follows Parker's excerpts from the regional press, there wasn't a single disagreeing voice heard in the valley on the preeminence of this problem.

Like all irrigation systems, White Bluffs and Hanford needed to have some method of distribution that the members agreed was fair, and a way to enforce it. The ditch master, selected by the shareholders, was the water policeman. In every district, each farm was allowed so many acre feet of water per season, depending on how much was under cultivation, and paid a monthly fee based on its use. At White Bluffs it was 36 inches, a lot more generous than many places, says Donald. Others say that later the allotment was 32 inches, based on that at Yakima, and didn't take into account the sandier soil.

Donald describes the technicalities of water distribution:

The allotted flow to each farm was controlled by a wooden measuring box where the farm lateral took off from the main pipe—a box ten feet long by two feet wide by a foot deep. All the water going into that farm passed through its box, through a slot in it a foot long by an inch wide. The rate of flow for the Wheeler's acreage in the last years was set at ten inches when under eight inches of water, a pressure factor.

Obviously people could cheat. If someone fudged a little on the size of their opening and there was ample water the ditch master would ignore it, but if someone's flow was significantly over the limit he was empowered to put a wooden plug in the slot to shorten it. At White Bluffs this was likely to happen if there was a problem with the pumps, or new ditch leaks cutting down the flow. Were it not for this control by the ditch master, the people at the far end of the system wouldn't get their allotted share.

The HIPC ditch master happened to be a neighbor of the Wheelers, and each morning they saw him setting out with his horse and buggy for the little trail that ran alongside the Hanford Ditch, not knowing what trouble the day would bring from burrowing animals or cheating growers. The job was not an easy one, but was a lark compared to its counterparts in the Snake River valley where a smaller river could not keep up with the burgeoning demand. There, Annie Greenwood tells us, the ditch master carried a shotgun, while desperate farmers guarded their water gates, ready to shoot or club with their hoes anyone who tried to steal or seize the water they felt was theirs. That ditch master had the duty to adjudicate between angry groups and even close neighbors. The Priest Rapids growers were spared such violence, at least the Wheelers never heard of it. Though they were not HIPC users they heard all the valley news. But though the irrigators didn't club or shoot each other, those at the southern end of the ditch probably made the water stockholder meetings and the ditch master's life stressful.

Though Priest Rapids farms fared better than in some districts, water bills and shortages did cause families to leave. Others left the system, a solution possible only for farms that were solvent enough to afford a pump and fuel. The larger the farm, the more likely the grower was to take this route. This in turn made it difficult for the remaining users to cover the system's costs. In the late 1920s, when most of the WBCOT shareholders had abandoned that system, it finally closed. Then it was left to Frank Wheeler to figure out how to salvage what remained for himself and his neighbors to keep their orchards going. It would be 1929 before real, lasting changes came through the courts to help the irrigators on the old HIPC system, to be covered in a later chapter.

In the end, the most publicly recognized problem for the Columbia would not be water sharing but the disappearing salmon runs, but this was not a concern to the early irrigators on the middle river. To them, the fish harvest by their Wanapum neighbors looked bountiful since they had not seen it in earlier years. The possible effect of irrigation on salmon fingerlings was buried under a host of more urgent problems of their water systems, even for environmentally conscious families like the Wheelers. The battles over the water systems never ended, and no doubt anger and frustration drove some families out of the valley. Yet irrigation did keep one promise: these farmers never faced the droughts that ruined dry-farming.

7

PLANT, PRUNE, PICK, PACK

"Until all the fruit was safely on its way to the coast everyone worked ten hour days, children the same as adults. Child labor laws did not apply."

Margaret Wheeler Schuddakopf, 1966

JUST AS FRANK WHEELER had expected, there was plenty of healthy outside work for all ages at Mayflower Farm. The settlers' children discovered soon that the valley suffered from a labor shortage and that they would help fill it. Almost all of the families were much smaller than the Wheeler/Shaw group, and though growers could call on their neighbors for help, when it was time for thinning or picking apples, or cutting and stacking hay, everyone needed help at the same time.

George, the Wheeler's first son, was not unusual when he found himself drafted at seven to take on a man's work. Being small for his age couldn't excuse him with his father gone so much of the time. The work he did was not brutal—sawing wood, hauling water, feeding stock, milking one cow—but he feels his grandfather's impatience made it more onerous than necessary. The girls also had plenty to do at a tender age, but "nothing we couldn't handle" says Helen. Their complaint was more that the work was never caught up. Yet, as we shall see, all of these children managed a healthy amount of social life too. And the goal, the carrot their parents kept before them, was that the farm would make it possible for every one of them to go to college.

The 1915-16 Polk's Directory for Benton County listed 64 owner-operators in the area of White Bluffs/Cold Creek. Of these, half had no children or no sons. Margaret was able to remember nine families, including across the river and at Hanford, that had four or more children for all the labor that was needed. Some families had lost all of their children to epidemics, and some like the Shaws had grown children that weren't with them. Having purchased tracts that were typically ten acres, not huge ranches, a family or even a single man could manage the orchard work with no help during the winter. But in the spring, summer and early fall, as soon as an orchard came into bearing, the new orchardists soon saw it was impossible for one man, or a married couple, to manage everything. The larger farms hired men year round; the smaller ones could never afford that. Few professional migrant workers and very few displaced wheat farmers came to the valley, bypassing it for the more well-known Wenatchee and Yakima areas. In White Bluffs, the main source of labor had to be their neighbors, and later on, college students whom their own youth brought home for a working vacation. "During a harvest, speed was everything, and every possible hand had to be recruited," Margaret remembered. "Children even of six soon learned, to their dismay, how useful they could be." Donald adds:

> Some profitable valley crops, strawberries for one,
> were given up by families simply because they required
> too much work, even if there were people to do it.
> Weeds, fed by irrigation, went mad in a berry patch.
> And no one wanted to weed those berries, not for any

money. It was too bad, because we got the best price for them of any crop, but we couldn't take the time away from other work to deal with them. Asparagus was another early market winner we gave up as a commercial crop for the same reason. We didn't have the time.

Most of the growers found that they had to find work or business besides their farms to pay the bills. But of those that did, very few traveled back and forth as Frank did. Many hired out as day laborers to the larger farms, then went home in the evening to their own work waiting. Their absence meant additional chores for their wives, who regretted that they (or their spouses) had been attracted to the brochure's claim that most orchard work could be handled by women. One reason Frank was able to be gone so much was because he had a male partner in his father-in-law, but he depended each year more on his growing flock of children to help. The Shaws also had their son Win to call on, and he and his father did assist each other during heavy demand times, but their farms were always separate enterprises.

Aside from young Margaret's two quiet winters with the Shaws, it was May before the Wheeler tribe arrived for their working vacation. Then the tents, fields, and orchard came alive with young voices as they laughed or argued over their assigned tasks. At first it was the fun sort of work such as feeding the hens and gathering eggs, or kneading bread dough. Before long a hint of drudgery revealed itself but still it wasn't too bad—carrying feed to a calf, bringing in kindling, setting a table. Soon, however, the girls took over much of the "dishes" routine; while the boys were carrying pails of water and bringing in wood, and both were mopping floors, and clearing out the encroaching sand. Some, fortunately, found work they liked to do. Margaret discovered she liked cooking and could do some of her share that way, relieving Jeanie for duties she preferred, or at least a change. Rose decided she was not a younger version of Margaret and tried to trade for outdoor work with brother George. He was glad to have her. Donald remembers:

> My first job, at five, was showing teams of school
> children where the peach pits lay in abandoned
> orchards near us. Peach pits made the very best
> charcoal to go inside the gas masks of WWI soldiers.
> Even though my folks were neutralists, they didn't want
> anyone gassed, so I went proudly out to show the
> volunteer gatherers the big treasure.

All the steps that went into feeding the woodstove were probably the dreariest tasks for farm boys, unending as they were. Hauling, sawing, chopping and carrying, and cleaning out ashes were nothing like today's flip of a switch. The job girls least loved was wash day, with its tedious processes we skip past today—sorting, scrubbing, boiling, bluing, starching, hanging out, collecting, sprinkling, heating the flat iron on the wood stove, then ironing and folding— all by hand labor, all so they could look clean and neat at church or at a public social. George Wheeler, in his memoirs, recalls his mother at the weekly process:

> ...She chugged back and forth on a wooden washing
> machine, hand powered by way of a spindle that stuck
> up from the tub, that swished back and forth against
> spring action. While she did that she taught me to read.
> Later I got my turn at the machine, and it was hard
> work, but she insisted that it was a great step up from a
> washboard.

For young boys, and some girls, running errands, especially if by horseback, was one of the best work assignments. George says that when less than a hundred pounds himself, he learned to hoist and balance a hundred pound sack of feed on the back of a horse. Children who lived along the irrigation ditch where lush rye grass had caught hold were assigned to herd their livestock when they weren't in school. Log catching was best of all, being work, adventure, and trophies rolled together, and all children along the river looked forward to it. In fact, it was dangerous and difficult, regarded as challenge more than chore.

George Shaw, and then young George, and finally six-year-old Donald were the milkers. Frank usually kept at least one cow, but even when he was home, he was not a good milker. Donald remembers Frank liked his cows, but he was slow. "At thirteen I took a quarter of the time dad did." Perhaps Frank had tendinitis from his bricklaying and didn't want to say anything. He was not inclined to complain of his ailments, Margaret remembers, and no one knew what repetitive motion syndrome was in those days, though surely milkers suffered from it. In his letters he does mention "neuralgia" in his arms bothering him on the job and at night. In any case, Donald remembers that his father could not get the right motion for a fast milking. The Wheeler girls never milked, for Jeanie had passed on Jane's advice never to learn, and on this one topic, even Rose, her most rebellious child, listened.

Traditional girls' work was more indoors than out, but that made it less, not more pleasant a good part of the year. A woodstove made for a sweltering kitchen when it was over eighty degrees outside, so families used kerosene "camp" stoves as much as possible, or better yet, a fireless cooker, which was simply an insulated box to hold hot food. Rather like the crock pots of today, but with no heat source, it relied solely on insulation to finish the cooking. The delicious beans, split peas and stew dishes that emerged from the cooker were a regular part of the Wheeler diet. But no matter how hot the weather, eventually the family would cry for bread if not cake, so the women and older girls were forced to enter the kitchen and fire up the wood stoves to bake in the very early morning. If a massive canning operation was scheduled, invariably when it was hot, that again required the stove and unavoidable misery.

Annie Greenwood, speaking of her Idaho irrigated wheat farm, says that the worst job for the women by far was not clothes washing but cooking full dinners in a terribly hot kitchen for threshing crews of as many as thirty people, then cleaning up to start on their supper. Orchardist women avoided this hell, expecting their crew, who didn't come from far away, to bring their own lunches and to go home for supper. But for fruit growers as for all farmers, staying cool enough to eat and sleep well in between work sessions was important for maintaining their strength.

Preventing food from spoiling in the summer heat was the same challenge that the homesteaders had struggled with and was solved in much the same ways. People still lowered butter and milk down the well in a bucket, or kept food in a burlap bag under a drip for evaporation. But now most families also had an ice box of some kind, and until the icehouse ran out of its winter supply from the river, they could at least for special occasions have a block of ice. To get some escape from the heat of harvest time, people took their dinner break at midday to eat and relax on their shaded, screened porches. They slept there as well, with mosquito nets over the beds, or hauled their beds out to the orchard. When the heat was greatest, before sleeping they soaked their sheets, wrung them out, and lay under them. Most youth tried to get to the river or Hanford Ditch once a day to cool off. A careful mother and father watched their young crew closely to be sure they didn't get overheated or overworked.

If there were no sons at home, the women were obliged to release their girls to do outside work while they managed most of the indoor chores alone, and then were called for the outdoors too. Margaret remembered well:

> Inevitably women took on a good deal of work in
> addition to their regular jobs... they irrigated, milked,

thinned, sorted, packed fruit, and in rarer cases herded on horseback, drove spray wagons or hayed. Some of them bore children. Some women stayed out of the orchards, but few women in that valley sat on porches and rocked at any time.

Jeanie, looking at her increasing brood and the unending list of chores for a farm woman, decided that if she were going to take on more, she would get paid in currency, not gratitude. When she became a star packer, she was in demand at the big farms. That meant that if her family came home hungry at noon, Jane was cook, or they had to do something about it themselves. Only if they were lucky were there some leftovers.

Young people, too, liked the cash they got for working for a neighbor. Young George says that his first work off the farm was picking up pears off the ground at a neighbor's orchard when he was ten, for ten cents an hour, and remembers that Margaret and Rose were picking with him. When he was eleven he got his first big salary. He was hired for a brief stint herding sheep ten miles across the desert. The Basque drover passing through couldn't get his flock to leave the river for the lambing grounds on Gable Mt. where lush grass awaited them. He called on boys for help. George, agreeing to go immediately, rushed home and started throwing a camping outfit together. Donald tells the rest of this story:

> "But who will milk while you're gone?", asked our mother. My brother hesitated one second, "Don can."
> "But he doesn't know how." "I'll show him."
>
> I was six. He got the cow and took me out to the barn, showed me how to grab the teat and pull down on it. I tried. No milk. "Try again!" I tried, no luck. "Now you try again and you get milk this time!" he said, with a definite threat in his voice I had learned to respect. I

tried again and got a squirt. He rushed back to our mother, "Don knows how to milk! I'll see you in three days!"

George and the other boys were paid off at ten dollars a day, "A princely sum!" Donald comments that from then on George Sr. and Jr. gradually introduced him to all the farm work. "At seven I could completely hitch Win Shaw's big Percheron team. I had to stand on a box to get the collars on." His brother from then searched out cash jobs at the larger spreads. One of the first things he bought was a bike so he could get around to even more jobs as well as fun. That same year, he tried to organize some asparagus workers when the boss attempted to reneg on the original deal:

> [The boss said] ..he could only pay 25 cents an hour, but if the price went above a certain point he would pay us 30 cents. I watched the market and when the price went above the mark, I asked that he pay us as promised. He refused and so, after work, I tried to get the boys to strike. They agreed... [but later] they were all back at work.

George was betrayed. The boss knew how to get around the pint-sized labor organizer; he was accused of stealing, and fired. "It was a good lesson for me."

George's money wasn't spent only on himself. Like other boys, his income was at least in part considered family income. Working for a well-digger and thinning fruit in neighbors' orchards at fourteen was what earned him the funds to pay for the well, and for electricity to be wired into the Wheeler home. He was rightly proud of his effort. With so many readers in the family, keeping three kerosene lamps clean, trimmed, and fueled was a lot of fuss. Now a tired worker could come in, wash up, flip a switch, and grab a book. "Even so, we all read under one light bulb," says Helen.

"Pacific Power rates forbade anything more."

All of the children helped with the orchard work, but Frank also expected all of them to help with the housework; a boy could have a mop handed to him as easily as a girl. He wasn't loathe to demonstrate how a mop was properly used. His colorful way of getting his feminist attitudes across come through in this letter to Donald who was staying elsewhere with Margaret for his first high school year and planning a camping trip:

> ...Now Donald look out for your teeth and let
> Margaret teach you to make good griddle cakes, and
> wash your clothes so you can enjoy camp and be neither
> calf pest or a boob cheapskate. One rainy day you can
> learn to make a pudding or biscuits and soups are
> almost all made on stock. Most baking powder stuff is
> alike—four or five things are the formation. A man
> just simply can't grow up to be a bull calf and sponge on
> the girls and women.

His children remember that Frank practiced what he preached. When he was home, he not only mopped, he frequently made bread or cooked the breakfast or supper. The reason he did it, whether he enjoyed it or not, was that it allowed Jeanie a change, to get out of the house. We can imagine that few of his neighbor men took sympathy that far. They, like their wives, could argue, "The men have enough to do!"

The men's work was barely mechanized and had all the extra labor required by irrigation. The routine care of the animals and garden and the more basic orchard tasks, such as keeping the ditches clear, they passed off to children as soon as possible, so they could concentrate on the heavier or more technical tasks such as haying, plowing, or thinning fruit. Before long, boys, and sometimes girls, were drawn into the men's most responsible, even dangerous duties such as driving a team, pruning and picking on high ladders, and spraying. Donald remembers, at seven, driving the spray wagon in the orchard for his grandfather and taking a corner too sharp, putting the front wheel into the ditch:

> Grandpa came striding back, furious, grabbed my
> leg hard, but then went and got another cross tree,
> hitched it to the back of the wagon, brought the horses
> around and pulled the wagon out. Then he rehitched
> the horses, and did the right thing: he let me steer the
> corner again on my own.

Margaret remembers how she and others hated the job of stacking the acres of prunings after the men cut them, but for Donald, one of the worst jobs for young boys was the one already described, cleaning out the roots that grew into the water mains. For George the least favorite job, and starting early in life, was cleaning out the privy at Shaw's place. It was arranged so that the contents were in a box that could be removed. "...it held about five wheelbarrow loads...it was my job to spread out over the orchard. I considered myself a martyr whenever I performed this task; fertilizer was one item we were often short of cash to cover." We can't know how many other families felt forced to use human waste, but since the growers had so few animals, providing adequate fertilizer was one of their chronic problems, not just that they couldn't afford it but that there was none to buy. By the time Donald took over as chief chore man the partners must have given up this practice, for he doesn't mention it.

Frank himself had few tasks he would not do, but one he simply could not do was to butcher his animals. No matter how he avoided it, he inevitably became fond of them. Except for poultry, which he could manage, whenever possible he brought someone in to do the brutal work. Donald says, "One day when I was a teenager he told me I would have to kill the pig. Oh, I hated it. I resisted. It was a pet; they all became pets, even if

154

you knew the sad end. But I did it; I knew he couldn't." We might question
how Frank thought it was easier for the boy. Possibly his idea was for his boy
to overcome any tendency he had to the soft heart of his father, a definite
disadvantage for a farmer.

Plowing was another task that Frank avoided, for he had an abdominal
hernia that the jerking strained. He tried to find someone else to plow, and
used a hoe for the lighter work. Thinning peaches was another job he hated,
as he had a terrible reaction to the fuzz, but he didn't excuse himself from
it. He loved peaches; he was determined to grow them. Margaret writes,
"He didn't complain in the peach orchard, but I would know he was
suffering for he would get very quiet."

All jobs were exceeded in misery and hazards by the spraying operation.
Everyone hated spraying and knew it was dangerous as the County Agent
lectured on it regularly. Since it took more than one person, the youth ended
up in the orchard, exposed to toxins as they drove the wagon for the man
handling the sprayer. Of the Wheelers, only Margaret, because she was
afraid to drive horses, and Helen, because she was the youngest, were
exempt from the spray operation. In order to reach all the branches, the
spray was pressurized by a pump on the wagon. A converted Model T engine
supplied more power in later years. Donald looks glum as he tells of how
impossible it was in the heat to follow the County Agent's safety instructions:

> He told us we must wear masks but no one did that
> I know of. It was so hot already! Sometimes already
> getting up to 100 degrees. I tried a mask once and had
> to take it off right away; I would have fainted.
> Eventually, when I was fourteen and Dad was gone all
> spring, I had to take over the whole operation. I
> ordered the materials, mixed them, brought the wagon
> up and set up the sprayer, and then did the spraying

while Marian drove the team.

All of these seasonal labors were nothing to what was demanded by the harvest season. Then everyone from seven years on up joined in picking and packing; cherries, beans, or berries, everyone focused on that one operation. The pace was frantic, the heat intense as the fruit ripened by the minute and had to make the express railroad connection or be ruined. George writes, " I remember picking at Loveland's for 30 cents an hour when it was 110 in the shade. What made it possible was the very low humidity." It must have been more than that; it must have been the beauty and aroma of the fruit itself that kept them going, and the sense that now, finally, the reward was close in sight.

Margaret wrote later:

> When it was the home garden or fruit, a whole line of small people would be assembled at an outside table to sort, cut, and pack into jars or tins, while an older person operated the canner and cooker. When it was the commercial crop, one crew, including hired labor, would be out in the field or orchard. Kids that were too small to go up the ladders were picking on the ground..Not a few men with orchards just coming into bearing, or a crop failure the previous season and with a family to support, undertook to work a ten hour day for others in addition to operating their own places.
>
> The other crew was in the packing shed. Boys while quite young hammered up the boxes and hauled them to the packing crew. Teens and adults, men and women, packed. Men and older boys nailed the filled boxes shut, then moved them to be hauled to the railway terminal. Until all the fruit was safely on its way to the coast,

everyone worked ten hour days, children the same as
adults. Child labor laws did not apply, so although
children might be excused by their own parents to go for
a dip in the river, if they were working for neighbors,
they had to follow their schedule.

The packing sheds were the cooler though not necessarily easier place to
work. Those that were fast enough could win that envied location. The
actual packing, since it paid the best of the shed work, was competitive.
George describes it further:

"...[it] involved not just sorting out any defect...
but also, for apples and peaches, sizing and wrapping
each fruit separately in tissue paper. It had to be
"faced" just so, and it would look nice when the box was
opened. One had to know just the right amount of fruit
per box to keep it from shaking if too little fruit, or
crushing if too much...the fruit had to be of even size to
make the patterns come out right and have the correct
bulge on the box...Mater loved packing partly because
she was so expert in sizing by sight, and wrapping so
elegantly that she got a premium price for packing--
seven cents a box--when those packing the mechanically
presorted were paid only five cents per box...[later it
was fifteen]... Mater commonly packed 100 boxes in a
ten hour day, or 11,300 apples, for a wage of $7....

The fruit] was packed in wooden boxes...the
bottom had two thin boards (so thin they could bulge
and hold the fruit firmly in the box) held by cleats on
each end with four nails to a cleat and four nails on
each end of the two sides, 24 nails to the box. Another

eight nails went into the cleated lid. For making the
box we were paid one cent. One summer I made 27,000
apple boxes for Mr. Loveland and about 3000 apple
and peach boxes for us...I was never very fast, around
375 boxes in a ten-hour day. Some men could do more
than twice that, but they often had someone to stack for
them...The money I made went for college tuition which
was $150 [a year at private college] when I started.

Margaret says that her mother liked packing for the money but also for
the camaraderie, the excitement of the rush, the skill required, and the
recognition. "Mother thrived on all of this." Yet there were many women
working in the sheds with husbands that never helped them in the house.
This was the busiest season, but one wonders how quiet life ever was for
irrigator women, and how they found the hours in the day or the energy for
all they did. Jeanie later admitted to a personal fault, one her teenaged
daughters sometimes took her to task for. She put housecleaning the absolute
last, whereas some of their friends came from immaculate homes. Reflecting
on her years of farming later, she wrote to Margaret, "Most women sat
down for a little sewing or writing letters in the afternoon after everything
else was done. I must admit I liked to do these in the morning!" Helen,
reading this, adds, "Yes, before she was so tired she would simply fall asleep if
she sat down. I remember once I came home and found her actually lying
down. I was shocked. I had never seen her lie down until bedtime. I fussed
over her until thoroughly awake, she said, 'What's the use?' and got up."

The work the Wheeler women remember seems rigorous if not
exhausting. Yet many of the things that Jeanie had to do, she also enjoyed
doing. She was an expert seamstress and took pleasure in making all of her
own and the girls' clothes and the boys' shirts. Every woman had to sew, but
some of them turned that task into art, through the design of the garment or

the embroidery or crocheting that went on it. Though not every woman was as creative as Jeanie, what Helen describes was at least partly true of others:

> Mother was so artistic. She could refashion
> beautiful new looking clothes from old ones, and never
> had to buy a pattern, made her own from newspaper. I
> remember my senior year that the ball was coming, we
> hadn't a cent, and I had been in gloom for weeks over a
> boy. Mom went up in the attic and got an ancient dress,
> took it apart and secretly refashioned it into something
> stylish with a beautiful sash...I put it on— I was
> transformed. I went to the ball without a partner and
> danced every dance. My cloud of months vanished. I
> took that dress to college and wore it many times,
> always with compliments. That's what Mom did with
> clothes, all the time. It was a form of art for her, like
> her flower garden.

Most of the women took pleasure in crafts and turning out pies, bread, and preserves that people raved about. They were usually displayed at some kind of social gathering or Grange exhibit. Such work wasn't drudgery for Jeanie, but cleaning was. The tidy housekeepers were probably those who, like Jane, did "no outside work", or may have taken on less public service. Helen remembers grumbling on one occasion about the messy condition of their home. Her mother's answer, which she later acknowledged to be true: "Never mind, later on it's the picnics you'll remember, not the mess!"

Though Jeanie and others liked the pressure work in the packing sheds, the orchard had enjoyable off-season jobs for those who loved peace and quiet. Margaret says she knows her father liked irrigating and hoeing around his trees. Hoeing was peaceful and low stress; it gave him the chance to get to know his trees, to see how they were thriving individually. He could check the fruit for ripeness, the branches for pruning needs. He could do a graft of one variety onto another, something he became proficient at. Except for a dip in the slough during the hot season, it was as close to recreation as he got during the work day. "He always had a smile when he brought samples of his new fruit varieties to the dinner table." Even pruning, heavy as it was, had an art to it, and certainly planting new trees gave growers pleasure. Margaret remembers how her grandfather enjoyed talking and singing to his cows and how as a child she decided he liked animals better than people. If so, he had plenty of pleasure from his dairy operation.

From the parents' point of view, finding ways to turn their kids' work into fun was the best possible way to entertain them. Bringing home bum lambs left behind by the sheepherders was a kids' specialty. Perhaps the adults, even though they badly needed and wanted the lambs, thought it an undignified pastime, too much like scavenging. Margaret writes:

> Enterprising children, no older than ten or eleven, attracted by the terrific din when a flock of sheep arrived on the ferry, would rush to the landing. The flocks, often driven by Basques, accompanied by dozens of sheep dogs, might stay overnight at a sheep camp near the river. Amid the barking of dogs and the shouts and whistles of the herders rose the terrific din of the bells on the bellwethers. Sometimes a herder would give a child a stray "bum" at this point. Generally, however, the strays were located the next morning after the herd had vanished into the sagebrush toward the west. Sometimes the children would have to follow several miles to find a stray; the very persistent and lucky might find several, all to

become pets fed with a nipple. When the parents
decided it was time to butcher a now thriving pet, the
child regretted the whole enterprise.

Catching and raising stray lambs was fun but important, comments
Donald. There weren't any commercial stock growers residing at White
Bluffs, and families couldn't simply go out and buy a cow, pig, or sheep when
they wanted one. The Wheelers were never able to have more than three
sheep at a time, much as they valued them, so each one was a prize. The
mutton was considered a treat, the wool most likely became batting for
comforters since by this time settler women did not spin or weave. As Jane
said, "They have enough to do!" But cleaning and carding the wool fell to
the youngest, their price for the earlier fun, and if Margaret speaks for
them, they found it a dreary pastime.

She continues about livelier adventures she did not take part in but
heard about from her siblings:

Another favorite way for youth to escape the
home routine was to go out and herd stock on the
desert. On one occasion three girls, one not yet in her
teens, herded cattle all summer on horseback, miles
west of town proper. Boys sometimes went even farther,
working for stock outfits...Some parents kept a tighter
rein on their children than did others. Every parent,
however, was compelled to allow a fairly wide latitude
to a boy who was expected, in the course of the day, to
turn in a man's work, to perform the same way, day
after day, and never to complain. Most of the youth,
including as many of the girls as were permitted,
accepted such duties without murmur.

For many of the younger set the best work of all was wood-catching on the river. George Wheeler writes:

> The trick was to know the eddies, a huge one of
> which formed right in front of the ferry landing, but
> with many smaller ones along the shore in different
> spots. If we spotted a log coming down, we tried to get
> above the other boats and cut out into the current,
> quickly pike the log to the boat, drive a dog into the log,
> with a rope from the dog to the stern of the boat. This
> had to be done fast because there was a big riffle
> downstream that swept one back out into the main
> current. If that happened you could not get back up on
> the White Bluffs side, you had to row across and then
> work back upstream before attempting it back across,
> a couple miles of rowing.

Searching the 1910-1930 letters of the Wheelers to discover how they felt at the time about their herculean labors, we find "work" mentioned in terms of their accomplishments not their suffering: "We packed 200 boxes..." and "We have a fine raft of logs now..." without dwelling on how tired they were. The work Frank complains of in his letters is bricklaying; all he wants is to get back to his orchard. His son George's memoirs gives a picture of a heroic, not terrible time. After the description of the chilblains he suffered at seven sawing firewood, he moves from one exciting work adventure to another. Donald's letters to his sisters talk of his personal adventures or in terms of Mayflower Farm's production, never complaining. Though Frank and Margaret often write each other about the need for Jeanie to get a break, it is for her morale, not her physical health that they worry, and though Frank regularly worries about his children's health, it is in fear they aren't eating right, not that they are exerting themselves too much.

Margaret later saw it more objectively, often writing to her family, "Don't work so hard, dear people, it's no use!" But Helen observes, "She was never there during the more quiet times. She always came for the harvests, so she saw it at its most hectic." Helen remembers that Margaret and her brothers, in particular, did work very hard, but still found time for recreation, while her own role, as the youngest, was not a difficult one.

The *Family Histories*, looking back after fifty years, frequently recall the disappointment in the season-end payment from the commission house but do not emphasize the exhausting work the irrigators performed. When the second and third generations describe their work as youth, it is to commend it, that it taught them to respect work, to admire their parents, and to value the projects they shared with their neighbors. From the distance of many years reflected in memoirs and interviews, those children, now elders, all felt later that they did work very hard compared to children today, or city youth then. But the demands on them, as Donald Wheeler says, were the community norm, and they accepted it at the time. Of course time fades pain, and the "golden age" effect takes over. But the work/fun adventures they describe were not rare or exaggerated ones; they were part of the life.

As for the adult view of the labor required in fruit farming, one settler commented, "There was twice as much work as on a wheat farm!" Unquestionably some families left as soon as they could after figuring this out. Others had no other farming experience to compare it with, but soon found out it was no Eden. Why did so many stay? Was it because ten acres of fruit trees in blossom against the river and bluffs were more uplifting, more satisfying than ten miles of ripe wheat? Or was it because of the community they had built around those orchards? That, even more than trees and crops, would be so difficult to replace.

ILLUSTRATIONS

B1. Wanapum lodges of tule reeds at Priest Rapids

B2. An early White Bluffs irrigation system with young
orchard, about 1907

B3. White Bluffs ferry

B4. George and Jane Shaw with tent house and new pear
orchard, about 1909

B5. White Bluffs elementary school, built 1906

B6. Maypole dancers at the White Bluffs school

B7. Priest Rapids power plant, before 1943

B8. George Shaw in orchard, about 1915

B9. A collection of drift logs, 1909

B10. Building log rafts at the Rapids

B11. Work party in apple orchard

B12. Spray crew

B13. Shaw house, built 1916

B14. Margaret in winter orchard, about 1916

8

A TOWN WITH A HEART

"Women who in town would not have had much in common in a town joined forces where every body counted."
Margaret Wheeler Schuddakopf, 1966

EARLY WHITE BLUFFS was nothing like a text book or movie version of a western frontier town. Nor was it, except for its location, merely a continuing and expanding of the early homesteads scattered along the Columbia. White Bluffs, and Hanford too, evolved as such socially rich communities in part because they were more like the hamlets along eastern American rivers. The land had been offered in small tracts clustered along the river, the platted towns, the Hanford ditch, and eventually near the railroad terminal. Everybody could walk or row to their neighbors or even to town. Even the families on the east side of the river were not isolated. They came across by ferry on demand, and older children rowed across to school daily except at high water. Exceptions were a few families farther out in the desert who had chosen that land because of its cheaper price per acre, and had paid to have a well dug, or were hauling water, hoping that they could at some point get tied to the Hanford ditch. Even for them, a ride to town was not a major undertaking.

The physical compression of the two communities was an effect of being tied to, and totally dependent on, communal water systems. The unfortunate moving of the White Bluffs townsite did not change that. Later there would be more farms farther out using wells, and some that broke off to run irrigation pumps of their own from the river, but by then the towns' social characters had been established. Very likely none of the residents had heard of John Wesley Powell's concept of saving the West for ordinary people. He believed they could establish economically thriving, yet democratic communities based on the sociopolitical skills they would have to learn in order to maintain their water systems for fair distribution. But at White Bluffs and Hanford, whether they knew it or not, and although they had no government support, they were carrying out a real life version of his dream.

The effect of the closely formed, cooperating water communities carried over into all aspects of life. Because the women were not isolated from each other on distant ranches, they were able to channel their energies to a critical mass. Jane Shaw stepped into the White Bluffs scene just it was blossoming with a church, new school, livery stable, good hotel, regular freight and mail, and downtown shopping. For any further developments in the community, volunteers were required. As everywhere in rural America, the women were the ones who provided the social timber and hammers while the men concentrated on getting seed or trees into the ground. For most of the women, their goal was to replicate the institutions of the communities they had come from—the clubs, the cultural and recreational events, and the public services. Women would also try to do this on spread-out dry farms, of course, but it was far more difficult.

The men's social involvement was more dependent on the season. A few of the men attended church regularly—George Shaw and Frank went occasionally—and after a Grange unit was established many attended that. Freemasons and other lodges had been popular in their home towns, and like the women, men brought their social alliances with them. The lodges were social and benevolent associations who concerned themselves with their own, yet tended to cross class lines and helped to bind White Bluffs early into a close community. But Margaret, Donald, and Helen Wheeler agree that it was the activist women who crossed all groups with their projects and made the community bloom, along with its orchards, even when it suffered economic blight. Annie Greenwood's book describes the same dynamic in the Snake River valley, she being one of those activist women.

Margaret observes:

> Women who in a town environment would not have had much in common joined forces where every body counted. The Ladies' Aid membership, in particular, reached out to women far beyond the community church that sponsored it. The same broad reach happened in time with the Grange, and later the PTA. The local branch of the Women's Club was more a professional women's affair that drew in some farm wives.

A couple dozen women, Jeanie included, tried to be active in all of them. How they found the time to get to the regular meetings and carry out projects or large events when they had farms or businesses to run, and no modern bathrooms, refrigerators or powered washing machines, will remain a marvel to those of us who never had to do it.[1]

The irrigator wives thrived on their community-building, just as John Wesley Powell had dreamed they would. Instead of farm husbands wondering what to do with their weeping, lonesome wives, they were more likely to wonder when their wives were ever going to stay home. This social wealth explains partly why so many settlers chose to endure their relative poverty rather than flee back to a city, and why, if we need any more reasons, people were so furious at the railroad for causing the town to move out in the desert. By 1913 they had already achieved so much.

Despite all the promotion of the valley, the net growth of White Bluffs and Hanford was slow, for as newcomers moved in, others were moving out, finding that they couldn't afford to live in this promised paradise. The newcomers were sometimes able to salvage the abandoned orchards, sometimes not, but they could use the buildings. The 1910 U.S. Census reported the White Bluffs-Cold Creek population at 323, including the two Shaw households. By 1920 it was at 387 for a net gain of sixty-four, eight of these being the Wheelers, but less than half of the households were from the 1906 migration or earlier. The valley was like the rest of the West; it was no longer a frontier, but people were still moving frequently.

According to the *Family Histories*, people left for various reasons: illness or aging, more work or experience required than expected, the heat in summer, the cold in winter, or too small a reserve to start with. Some left for school. For most, the gap between income and expenses was a major cause. Some families with no other income but their farm found they couldn't wait out the years for the trees to mature. New families took their places. Land company promotion was part of the push, but behind this lay the strength of the "Garden" myth that was beyond any salesman's tactics. Margaret writes that the newcomers continued to be older than typical pioneers and tended to be people who wanted to try something different. They, like the first settlers, included a few people born in Northern Europe and several from Canada. Most were from the West or Midwest, some from New York and Pennsylvania. In the Polk directory they gave every kind of occupation aside from farming. This lack of farming background influenced how long it would take them to operate at capacity. It also meant that many had a trade to go back to somewhere else if they decided the whole idea was a mistake. But their innocence of agriculture may have worked, in some cases, to allow more staying power, and they took comfort in that they were suffering their problems together. Not even the few "gentlemen farmers" among them could rise above such things as freight rates, and everyone cried out together about the poor prices for their lovingly grown fruit.

Jane and Jeanie were among the women who worked on every project that promoted their community. They were instrumental over the years in the start-up and operation of the traveling well-baby clinic, school health program, immunization program, free school lunches, and both a school and traveling town library. The two women saw their work for the clinic as particularly important, with the public library another favorite. Even if most families were not the avid readers the Wheelers were, with no television or radio to compete, the library projects had broad support.

The men went to the College Extension Service sponsored meetings to learn more about scientific farming, and to eat the pie provided, at a price, by their wives. It was a chance to socialize a little over fertilizer content and method, spraying, plowing and dust control, irrigating, diversifying crops, and was probably more acceptable than the saloon or pool hall to their wives. Donald remembers that the men listened politely and asked questions. Some would try out the new ideas, others scorned what an outsider tried to foist on them, and the agent sometimes found himself up against economic questions he wished to avoid. Other public involvement for men could be to work on a popular project like the building of a ball field, and a dedicated group, including Frank Wheeler, took care of maintenance on public buildings.

On the other hand, there were some men and women who never socialized beyond their families and close friends, usually bachelors or couples without children to draw them into school or club activities. Some of them had chosen their tracts out in the desert, not convenient to the town. Most of these settlers were short of funds for water rights, but others obviously had come to the desert to get away from human institutions, not create new ones. Still others were like Jeanie's best friend, the homesteader Clara Barrett, who was a generous hostess at her own farm, and might go visiting, but didn't turn out for community meetings and projects. Helen remembers:

> Though Dad enjoyed hosting people for a meal in his home, he was not one of the joiners. He was gone a great deal, but even when he was in White Bluffs he deplored going out to meetings and gatherings, and could only occasionally be dragged by Mom to local Grange meetings, though it was the local organization he thought most of. He preferred County Grange, Pomona, at Kennewick, for that was where political issues were discussed and action taken. But normally Dad's contribution to the community at large was more on an individual basis. He gave fruit away to people he thought could use it—widows, single parent families, and Wanapums camped nearby. He would ask them to come in and pick what they wanted from a tree he would turn over to them.

Many men were similar to Frank in sharing fruit and in their level of community activism. But there were others, not so much the full time farmers, who were able to donate more time. The most famous of the men for community service was Fred English, the druggist, who led the White Bluffs marching band for many years. Other men could always be recruited to help with ball games. Men could even cajoled into serving as stage crew for a play during the quieter seasons, especially if their own children or wives were performing. A few men sang, and some sang well, Helen remembers, at local concerts.

The White Bluffs activists knew they must give special attention to young people through Sunday Schools, sewing clubs, sports clubs, and soon, 4-H. Donald says that his Boy Scout leader, a junior high teacher, truly enriched his life, introducing him to the wonders of the area's natural history through hiking and camping. Organized sports were a big draw for most. By the 1920s local baseball was immensely popular across the country, in White Bluffs taking the place of the rodeos in cattle-ranching communities. Once the high school was built in 1922, basketball drew out even more energy.

In all of this, White Bluffs seems like a typical small American town of its day, just more successful, probably, in the percentage of families it drew into its activities. Its Ladies Aid could have been found anywhere in rural America. The White Bluffs branch of the Federated National Women's Clubs, however, does not fit our stereotyped notion of rural women's pastimes. Its printed programs list discussion topics like women's suffrage, Bible reading in the public school, modern Irish writers, and personal and property rights of women. Book reviews, musical performances, plays, even an art show, were all planned months in advance. It was not intended to be a service club, but a serious effort to imitate urban culture. Jeanie's accounts as secretary-treasurer show an impressive budget, reflecting that at least in White Bluffs the Women's Club did much in the way of service too, ranging from scholarships to direct charity. Later a Junior Women's Club was also formed whose activities were largely social. [2]

The Women's Club, Helen remembers, was not without its frustrations for her mother and grandmother. "Although there were many interesting committees to serve on, they were always appointed to the cemetery committee!" She thought possibly some of the members were envious of Jane's and Jeanie's formal education. But by 1926 Jeanie would work her way up to become the president for the year. In the meantime, the leaders were quite willing to use her writing and arithmetic skills, and she was frequently the secretary-treasurer. Still, the club caused her some pain, for every so often an issue would come up that disturbed her, such as world peace, and she was torn between her desire to speak up and her desire for friends.

In order to sponsor all their activities, the clubs were continually fund raising. The Ladies Aid collectively created at least one quilt a year to be auctioned off, and published the usual local cookbook for sale. Most of their fund-raising was through preparing food and selling it at public events and the Grange dances. Women with little cash could find or borrow the ingredients for a pie or cake. From all these collections the women would cover their share of the clinic's needs, send a basket to a family in difficulty, or send youth off to a special competition.

Margaret (somewhat an outside observer since after eighth grade she was gone except during summer) thought in retrospect that White Bluffs people could easily find a useful community role to play if they wished. The original homesteaders had their circle, but it was merging with others more each year. The Wheeler siblings remember the Old Town-Out Town schism rather than division by income, religion, ethnicity, political affiliation or length of residency. New residents coming in helped to diffuse that feud, and most people treated each other as neighbors with common interest most of the time. One wonders if White Bluffs would have survived even a decade had the activists not understood the magic ingredients that make a community, and how little they depend on wealth.

Helen, however, recalls more about the dynamics of White Bluffs society, partly from her own observations, partly because her father had a lot to say from a pro-labor point of view.

> The businessmen were the ones that really ran White Bluffs. It wasn't an incorporated city; there was no council to make decisions. The only government" was the deputy sheriff, who spent his days playing cards with

his cronies. It was the businessmen who decided on what
important things were going to happen in town, and
Dad was right—of all of them, it was the Freemasons
who ran White Bluffs as a town.

The Masonic businessmen were active in many of the promotional
activities to improve the town and district, and to bring new people in, but it
did not save them in Frank's opinion. He may have inherited negative
feelings from his minister father, but Frank's poor opinion went beyond that.
He had objected to Masonic cronyism on construction projects in Tacoma,
and now in White Bluffs, he unexpectedly found himself in a stronghold of
Masonry. And his father-in-law was one; so was Win, his brother-in-law.
But Frank didn't care about what went on in their lodge meetings. Helen
goes on:

What outraged him was the way local Masons
controlled the key County jobs, such as school janitor, or
road maintenance. Aside from poorly paid seasonal
farm labor, these jobs were often the only wage labor
available. He saw that farmers who really needed work
went without, and lodge brothers got the jobs.

Frank even believed that Win Shaw got a plush job as an equipment
operator on the road due to his Masonic connections, though his son Donald
points out it was also because Win had a team of draft horses they wanted to
hire.

Another group the Wheelers already detested was the American Legion.
They were not overjoyed when county and local units were formed in 1921,
soon to boast 100 percent membership from veterans in the valley. Though
the local Legion was active in promotion of many White Bluffs and district
civic projects, it was famous nationally and in Western Washington for its
anti-labor and other ultra-conservative positions. In the period of World

War I and just after, it was the outspoken enemy of neutralists like the Wheelers. Helen remembers that it did not improve the Wheeler opinion that the first local Legion Commander chosen was a real estate developer whom they believed had bought up land along the Milwaukee right of way before the tracks went in and thus profited when the town was forced to move.

The Grange was the organization the Wheelers felt especially positive about. It was another strong group, with ten halls and over a thousand members in the county in the early 1920s, about one hundred of them being in the White Bluffs lodge. Like the other lodges, it was a national organization, had its secret rituals, and accepted members by ballot. But unlike the others, women in the Grange had equal status and were not shunted off into separate auxiliaries. Although they did not often get into officer positions, it did happen, and women certainly could and did speak at meetings. The National Grange supported a great range of issues and programs such as improved farm home design, free rural postal delivery, marketing and farm supply associations, and women's suffrage. It stood not for efficiency as the goal of farming, but "the greatest good for the greatest number"; in other words, it valued the small family farm highest. The state and county Grange also had political platforms, while the local Grange became a focal point for the social life of the town through its public dances. Margaret writes, "These dances, always to local live bands, were usually the most exciting action on Saturday night at any of the villages in the valley."

In addition to all of the civic, service, and social groups, there were usually three active churches in White Bluffs, sometimes more, and each had a Sunday school and perhaps other associations. In addition to the water users' associations, during some periods farmer belonged to marketing associations. It almost seems that White Bluffs was over-organized, but we have to consider that there was no television nor even radio to take up people's time, the newspaper was a weekly, and magazine subscription offers were not by the hundreds as they are today.

It was difficult for Jeanie to stand up for her radical beliefs and yet remain socially popular, but that was the price she paid for a rural life. In any city the Wheelers could have found ample left-of-center groups and families to visit with. But for all the negative feelings the Wheelers had for certain factions, Jeanie as well as Jane remained among the most actively involved. Since they had good friends attending these groups, and most of the activities were worthy in their opinion, they tried to put aside their differences and personal slights experienced. They tried not to think about the Old Town-Out Town feud or the politics of their neighbors as they planned a tea honoring their young ladies, or organized the schedule for the traveling clinic.

With no City Council, the County Seat being a long ride away, and the Deputy Sheriff being known mainly for his skill at poker, there was almost no local government at White Bluffs or Hanford. How can one see these communities as being even rough examples of what Powell had envisioned? Despite the importance of the Freemasons in being able to control county jobs—later many of them formed into a Chamber of Commerce— it seems an exaggeration of Frank's to claim they "ran White Bluffs". They ran certain important aspects of White Bluffs, but all of the Wheelers agree that the women's service groups were another vital factor in the community's functioning, Donald claiming that they got more done than any of the men. Everyone agrees on the importance, also, of the Grange. The truth seems to be that White Bluffs—and we might guess, Hanford as well—flourished through a loose interlocking of a wide variety of associations that served the role of government as needed.

Even youth seemed to have a respected say in how the community should behave. George Wheeler remembers an incident of uproar at the high school that students managed to straighten out appropriately. The high school boys had watched a film about venereal disease, and George and a friend had seen such symptoms on one of the boys in the school shower. The principal was too fearful to take action since the boy was from a leading family. George and friend then took it to the school board and asked that the young man be suspended until he could bring a good report from a doctor. When the school board denied the possibility, the boys declared, then you must inspect him yourselves, at which point the board agreed to suspend the boy until he brought the doctor's report. We can sense Frank's moral outrage behind George's brave stance, but nonetheless, it was students who took action.

About five years later a larger rebellion took place at the high school. The juniors, against rules, decided they would join the seniors on senior skip day. The principal was so irate he canceled their credits for the year, meaning they would not be able to graduate the next year. The juniors thought the punishment too severe and talked their parents into letting them go to Hanford high school. One of the parents drove them in his truck the seven miles twice a day. Helen, a freshman, was allowed to go with them, even though she was not being disciplined, and enjoyed greatly the year as a celebrity. Donald took the opportunity to go to a Seattle high school, which turned out well for him too.

Partly because of the small population, and partly because the residents all had to work together first to manage their water systems, and then later to build such popular improvements as a ball field, a hard division into rich and poor did not emerge at White Bluffs. Regardless of income, everyone wanted White Bluffs to thrive as a town and the Priest Rapids valley to thrive as a district. Although the wealthier families did have social gatherings among their own crowd, they also were part of clubs and lodges that included the poorer families. Their fine orchards were admired by the others for their beauty, and they were a place to earn money when there were few other options. Helen writes of the "show places" that emerged among the farms:

> There were several places that were well-established and beautiful by the time I came along, especially to the north of us, like Lovelands, Clarks, and Roberts, where Mom often went to pack. The Koppens, early homesteaders, also had a lovely place, full of art work. At the "Klondike" the ex-gold miners had created some fine orchards and homes to go with them, even with indoor plumbing. Across the river were more people who had started with funds from the Goldrush, Young and Thum. Mrs. Thum kept her own house in town too, so she could be in town when the river was too high to get across. Wiehls, early homesteaders, had another fine place over there, and also a house in town, which allowed him to be on the school board. Andersons had a big place, and they started the movie house. He drove the school bus, so he must have been a Mason.
>
> South of White Bluffs there was the Taylor's fine place. Mrs. Taylor, a cultured lady from England, was a friend of Mom's. At In-B-Tween there were two other big orchards. That was about the extent of the big farms during the late Twenties. Some of the business people also had orchards, but that didn't mean they were necessarily rich. The O'Lareys owned and operated the newspaper and had an orchard, but they were certainly not wealthy, though eventually they were able to build a big fine home at the new site.

Other large places mentioned in land company promotions were Bleakely's eighty acres and and Von Herberg's 400 acres of alfalfa and cattle ranch up near Vernita. Martha Parker comments that none of these families arrived poor to end wealthy from their earnings in the valley. People who came in with little ended up with little. She may have missed a couple exceptions, but this is also the way the Wheelers and others remember it. The other possibility, people who came in with money and left with nothing was too often the case during the Depression as we shall see.

Although the Wheelers were not among the wealthy farmers, they were not among the poor either. Rollin Morford, Rose (Wheeler's) son, says that while visiting at the White Bluffs-Hanford annual picnics in the 1970s he had his perceptions changed, for while he remembered only the Depression years when everyone was poor, he found out that prior to that the Wheeler kids were the envy of many. "It was because Dad worked," Rose explained. Helen's childhood impressions of having the best rowboat, the best victrola, one of the best swimming beaches, one of the best horses, one of the best home libraries, even the best dance tent (their home) confirm this perception. Frank chose not to put all his extra cash into trees for the future, but a good portion into quality of life in the present. There were farms far larger and more productive, but their children didn't necessarily have what the Wheeler children had. And there were some families with no farms at all, but all could get work, at least during harvest, at the large ones.

Aside from population size, water management, and the local need for sharing labor, another explanation for the cohesiveness of White Bluffs was that its residents were almost all native-born citizens of northern European and British stock, later to include two related families from Czech stock. The draft registration of 1917 listed only one alien. Margaret Wheeler comments that White Bluffs residents had little ethnic or cultural suspicion of each other to fuel strife. Helen says, "I don't recall any friction between the Catholics and Protestants beside what the Ku Klux Klan briefly tried to stir up with no success. There may have been some anti-Masonic feeling other than Dad's, but I don't recall hearing of it." Overall, the community seems socially liberal for a small rural town. It was not strict in its regulation of proper conduct, even bootlegging, and church attendance was by individual choice.

The feelings of the settlers toward their Wanapum neighbors seem to have been individual by family, as judged from their remarks in the *Family Histories*. Some remembered that as children they found Indians "scarey", others, like the Wheelers, found them admirable, even friendly. Others didn't remember them. But they were mainly separate from the White Bluffs community. One settler comments in *Family Histories* that his family considered the Japanese farming families across the river at Ringold to be their friends and mentors, and were unhappy to see them evacuated during WW II.

Margaret Wheeler comments that if there had been more cultural diversity at White Bluffs it would have been less peaceful but more interesting. Later, Helen and Donald saw smaller Hanford with its Italian and Jewish families as more modern and sophisticated. "They drank more and were wittier. That impressed us as teenagers." The odd fact that White Bluffs and Hanford were only seven miles apart probably added to the success of both towns, for there was just enough difference between the two to provide novelty. They enjoyed rivalry in sports and scholastic competition, gossip material, and possible courtships, while doing nothing to undermine each other economically.

In acceptance of political differences, White Bluffs again seems more liberal than one would expect from a western hamlet. If anyone was seen as different at White Bluffs it was Frank Wheeler, since he made it a point not conceal his views on anything. As usual, he practiced what he preached, and Helen recalls with chagrin some of her and her sisters' own snobbishness, and the difficulty they had sometimes following his model:

> We resented it when he would invite the most poor, not even respectable squatter family on the river to dinner. The father was gone, probably for some legal problem, and the mother of the family was struggling alone. "She is a nice little woman," he told us when we girls grumbled, "you will treat her with courtesy." Another person who was a frequent dinner guest was an ex-convict (homicide) who had won a pardon through a local family's intercession and came to live at White Bluffs. As for our bachelor neighbors who drank too much and played poker for money, Frank and other more sober people simply tolerated them. "Chucky and His Boozum Buddies", he named them.

One of White Bluffs' and Hanford's greatest civic problems that touched everyone, and that was never overcome, was the frequent burning of public and business buildings during the dry season. The economic and social cost incurred as they were forever rebuilding was one more burden on communities where there was little surplus. Helen says she doesn't recall a single private residence burning (after 1925, when she would have remembered) but the papers reported the larger fires. Consider how disruptive this partial list of major fires must have been, starting with the aforementioned Todd Plant pump house in 1908: 1910—the entire Hanford business district; 1912—a business block in White Bluffs; 1913—the fine White Bluffs Hotel (and the saloon). Then there is quite a jump to 1930—the Hanford Warehouse, and Community Center; 1936—Hanford High School; 1939—a range fire of 30,000 acres; 1942—White

Bluffs High School (built in 1922) and the new White Bluffs Hotel.

Despite the river being close to many of these buildings, and pumps being available, there was no serious organization of firefighting until 1930. Then a hydrant was installed and equipment purchased. But obviously the buildings were dry tinder. The bright side was the lack of deaths; the low buildings were quick to escape from. Early on, two young men had been found guilty of arson, and some people suspected arson in later cases, but there were no charges made. During the Depression, job creation through rebuilding from fires was seen by some as an act of God.

Though the residents of the valley suffered from these fires, they were spared in other ways. From what we can glean from the newspapers, the *Family Histories* and the Wheelers, almost no felony crime, aside from bootlegging, occurred around White Bluffs or Hanford in their thirty-six year history. A double homicide by an "outsider" hitchhiker who killed visitors during a robbery, was the shocker of the 1920s. Also remembered is the failed burglary of the White Bluffs bank in 1922 by three young local men. Those, along with the early arson case, seem to be the extent of known serious crime, a small list indeed for thirty-six years.

White Bluffs had its minor tradition of youthful pranks and naughtiness, such as the aforementioned "junior sneak", but the mischief was kept quiet or confined to special times like Halloween, and was never in the classroom. School in White Bluffs was orderly if we can believe Helen when she says she was one of the biggest problems for the teacher, with her inability to stop talking in class. "Earlier there had been some pretty rough young fellows in White Bluffs." says Helen. "All that had passed over by the time I got into school." Community-minded people wanted to be sure that sort of behavior didn't catch on again, and they were successful.

Stealing was so rare that in White Bluffs people who locked their homes were considered peculiar. "I remember that when Grandma wanted to take a trip to Wisconsin for a few weeks to see her relatives, we realized there was no key to her house." Yet, a bitter crime for the Wheelers was the disappearance of their fine Morgan horse, Ribbon. Even those Shaws/Wheelers who didn't ride were greatly attached to her. When Donald was a teenager, Ribbon and her bridle, simply disappeared one day. The family advertised with no results. Though Donald scoured the hills for days on a borrowed horse, even following a band of wild horses for a time, Ribbon was never found. Later her bridle was discovered hidden under a bush out in the desert. Someone had stolen her and then, worried for the consequences, had turned her free, or sold her out of the district. The Wheelers thought they knew the young culprit, but couldn't prove it. The valley was large; she could have gone anywhere and become a fine catch for someone.

Ribbon was not only a favorite, but, aside from George's bicycle and their rowboat, their only transportation. In a valley with so little crime, the family felt victimized as well as grief stricken. Then one day two strange horses appeared in their orchard. Though Donald advertised for the owner, no one ever came forward. The horses stayed. One died later, but the other, a bay mare they named Molly, was an ideal all-purpose horse. She was not the beauty Ribbon was, but fast, willing, and perfect with children. Donald says: " Later I realized Molly must have belonged to Tomanawash, the chief. Her brand that looked like an anchor I saw was a "Rocking T". He was camped just a short distance from our place, and was aware where she was without doubt. Knowing we had lost Ribbon, he let it go." Molly lived in the family eighteen years, and plowed many fields, hauled many stoneboats, and even took second prize in racing at the Indian rodeo one year, while a whole third generation learned from her the fine art of bareback horsemanship.

Of course there must also have been crimes that went unreported in those days. Everyone knew about two cases of child abuse, for it became the subject of meetings, but "No one ever spoke of a rape to me," muses Helen. As a social teen she would certainly have been the recipient of village gossip, even if her family did disapprove. Some things didn't get gossiped about, or the terms used, or attitudes, were different. People referred to "fast crowds", men were accused of "taking advantage" of a girl, or girls were blamed for being in situations where they "shouldn't have been". Girls did get pregnant out of wedlock, and almost always they were soon married. Helen remembers how her grandmother scolded when she caught the Wheeler girls gossiping about a pregnant classmate. "She glared at us, 'Well! You're young aren't you! Here...now, take these to her!' And she handed me her latest crocheted baby items."

Of the lesser crimes and reprehensible behavior, the Wheeler youth observed people who fought on Saturday nights when they'd had too much, and later when there were cars, a few drove drunk. George tells of shenanigans by his junior high cohorts, but no real vandalism. The only widespread, publicly acknowledged illegal activity in the valley was bootlegging. Prohibition had started in the county in 1911, and was statewide by 1916. Then grape growers who were barely making ends meet with grapes selling at two cents a pound fought a powerful temptation, some not too vigorously. But hiding a still was difficult in the desert. Donald says:

> The simple way to bootleg was to make hard cider,
> about five percent alcohol. Most people made cider
> anyway from apples they couldn't sell, and it was easy
> to let some of it get hard. If anyone came around
> asking, well, it was just cider in the process of becoming
> vinegar which everyone used for pickling. People could
> get drunk on hard cider if they worked at it. Our
> neighbor did quite a business in it, and sometimes we
> watched people staggering away from his place. As for

the Wheelers, we drank our cider sweet.

The valley was following a strong American tradition when it chose to continue its cider drinking, legal or not. For many, if not most families, the low-alcohol drink was probably not even considered liquor, but they appreciated the buzz as well as the vitamins.

Underlying feuds could also erupt at times, like the one within the Community church over doctrine, but these were not the norm. Aside from all the activities public-spirited residents tried to provide, just how White Bluffs managed to stay so orderly is not clear. Probably there was a natural siphoning-off to the larger towns for individuals who wanted a more daring time. Helen believes that Frank and Jeanie's idea of avoiding trouble and bad behavior was to assure that people had plenty of work and recreation going on, and this seems to have been the town's consensus. The churches also had their influence, though not nearly so much as in earlier times. No one was called up before the congregation to confess sins at the Community Church. The various lodges probably played a role of social control among their own members. The valley was still a backwater, nothing to attract organized crime. Helen believes that during her teens the closest house of ill-repute was forty miles down river in Kennewick. Her big sister Rose was amused to find them accommodations there one night when, after a medical visit, they were stuck in Kennewick with no place to sleep. "That was the kind of naughtiness she enjoyed." Helen and Donald don't remember any activity around cannabis, which grew wild in the valley, but Parker found a mid-1920s newspaper announcement of a valley workshop being held regarding its evils. Apparently the exposure to the fast life of the cities, even in the Roaring Twenties, was limited mainly to what the college students brought back with them.

Like other tiny rural communities, a major means to keep valley behavior in line was no doubt through gossip. Since White Bluffs homes were mainly so close together, spreading the news was an easy task. Helen says she and her sisters, as teens, did their share of gossiping, but were always a little ashamed. Neither their grandmother nor their mother engaged in it, and Frank's spoken criticisms of his neighbors typically dealt with their public deeds, not their private lives. For this reason many things going on in the adult community probably never made it to the ears of the Wheeler young until they were young men and women. But for some families, no such strictness would have prevailed, and people could be assured that nothing they did would stay secret for long.

The telephone came early, in 1910, and was a socializing influence for those that could afford it, but mainly it was thought of as an instrument for serious affairs, not chatting, much less gossiping. The Wilkinsons operated the company, keeping the lines open until nine pm. After that one could call, but it was for emergencies only. During the day it was for business, emergencies, and the so essential weather reports. The party line was large. Often neighbors shared a phone, the Wheelers and Shaws sharing one for years. Donald remembers how he broke the rule just once when their phone was new to chat, and was told by a neighbor to get off the line. His mother then got on and scolded the neighbor for making Donald get off. "This doesn't sound like a business call to me, Mr. T." she broke in. When indignant enough, Jeanie didn't worry about her popularity, but Donald was embarrassed and cured of phone misuse.

Whether the adults personally agreed with the practice of gossip or not, they would hear plenty of it when they went to their club meetings. It livened meetings of the Ladies Aid that members learned whose kids had a cider party at Black Sand Bar, or whose girl needed to get married. Positive measures would be taken, leaving the deputy sheriff uninterrupted at poker.

Even during the Roaring Twenties, even after the early Forties, when the local roads finally connected to the state highway system, the towns' personalities evolved but stayed intact. If the communal water systems had broken down entirely, turning everyone loose to make it on their own, the social cohesion could have suffered. This threatened, but never quite happened. Meanwhile the Depression moved in early, as it did all over rural America, causing economic gloom for farms, but drawing the survivors and their associations together even more. After all the other Wheeler children had left for school and college, Helen, the youngest and still at home, always an interested and amused social observer, grew up feeling welcomed and proud of her home town.

9

SPEAKING UP

"...it seems to be a world of meat and little mind. Power, Worldy Power always seems to be in apostate hands...out the stinking cat pops in a dozen places."

Frank Wheeler, from a letter to daughter Margaret, 1924.

WAR IN EUROPE burst the valley out of its economic stagnation. Besieged Europeans needed American farm products, the market was robust, and for a time financial worries less fierce. Frank, at least, if not all the farmers, suspected it wouldn't last. Sure enough, by 1921, the market was wavering, then sliding. More acreage again seemed essential. But it had to be convenient to their farm, and a water system, and they would have to find financing. While the partners looked for acreage, to keep hope and energy up, they decided to try something bold that farms in the Priest Rapids Valley Fruit Growers Association had started. Value-added products is the term used now. One way to squeeze more profit from a peach was to try to market direct to the retailers. The idea was exciting; anything that could possibly work was exciting. The Shaws already had a small canner, and they all knew how fine home-canned tree-ripened peaches tasted. Jeanie designed their own colorful labels, and about 1916 Mayflower Farm sent out its flyer:

Do you want to enjoy the most delicious
peaches this summer?
PEACHES FROM THE FAMOUS
COLUMBIA RIVER VALLEY
White Bluffs, Washington
Following the new and increasingly popular methods of
marketing "direct from producer to consumer" we are
offering fine, tree-ripened fruit shipped by express,
subject to your approval.

The Carman ripens first, a delicate, white dessert
peach with rosy cheek, followed by the popular Early
Crawford and Elberta, both fine for eating and
canning, and in October, the Salway.

We are sure you would delight in this fruit—send us
an order on a postal card. Deduct express and 5 cents
per box from your local retail price and remit us the
balance. Join in with a couple neighbors, better yet.

Yours respectfully, ···

Another sheet to go in the envelope explained how customers could also
ask for this tree-ripened fruit from certain retailers.

The excitement anticipation was shortlived. The family located a
curious Seattle retailer. When he tasted one of their canned tree-ripened
peaches, something he couldn't get from a commercial cannery, he was
happy indeed to give their label a try. Soon the family heard from him that
sales went well, and a month later expected to get more orders. Then they
heard from the unhappy grocer. "I'm very sorry but when the Libby man
came around he asked me where that label came from. I told him and he
said, 'Then get your citrus fruit from them too.'"

The same thing happened to the other valley association. Pacific Fruit and Produce Co. told those farmers that if they continued their independent marketing they could forget sending to Pacific Fruit and Produce, their main source of income. The threats nipped the custom canning ventures when they had barely blossomed as the growers saw the experience would simply be repeated whenever the big buyers and canners discovered their new competition. The largest farms in the valley were able to put out enough quantity to capture a niche of the market in jellies or other specialities, but the rest saw they didn't have the power to enter the game. Mayflower Farm turned back to its normal business, and Frank went on with his bricklaying.

The Wheelers turned to another idea to boost their income. It was an even bolder plan, especially for Jeanie. They could say goodbye to Tacoma and move entirely to White Bluffs. Then they could rent out their Tacoma place. They could also sell their two extra lots next to it. Together that would give them cash for a down payment on new, good land with water rights. But where would they live? A windy shack such as Jeanie and the children had endured in fall of 1915 was not an option. The Shaw tents were now fifteen years old, and would never hold them all through the winter. Luck came their way when Win and Juliette Shaw decided to leave White Bluffs for a year of travel, hiring someone to manage their farm. Childless, they were free to ramble. They offered to sell the Wheelers their tents, both larger and better than the tents they had been using summers. After the usual late night discussions, Jeanie agreed to living in a tent year-round with six children, Helen being just a half-year old. Probably she thought that if her mother could survive tent living year round for nine years, she could manage for one or two until they found good housing.

There was another piece to this decision. Donald and Helen Wheeler believe the repressive atmosphere in Tacoma influenced their parents' decision to finally leave the town when they did. When war in Europe had erupted, the Wheelers found themselves for once in the majority politically. During the first part of the war, while the U.S. remained neutral, the various socialist groups were in agreement. For them this was a fight between greedy multi-national interests, nothing else, and Americans as a whole supported non-involvement. But in 1917 President Wilson abandoned his attempt to stay neutral, the U.S. declared war on Germany, and a Selective Service Act was passed. This meant a massive reeducation campaign was necessary to unite and organize American industry, to mobilize support for the draft, and to ready the country for battle.

The Socialists, led by Eugene Debs, had a growing party, garnering a million votes for him in the most recent presidential election. When they held tough to their neutralist position, they were seen by the government as unpatriotic, and a national security threat. The Espionage Act was passed in 1917, aimed at people like Frank who were speaking out against the draft and involvement in the war. While defiantly speaking against the draft at a public meeting, Debs was arrested and went to prison. The Wheelers supported Debs publicly and for this were labeled pro-German by the Tacoma community, though Frank explained to his children, "Im just against capitalist wars fought for profits or territory."

Debs had considerable support from left-of-center. Running for president from his jail cell at the next election, he was still able to win a million votes. But now, being socialist was no longer simply a topic for debates or a statement at the ballot box. The patriotic fervor reached the union halls and the public schools. Marian Wheeler remembers being chastised before the class in first grade by her teacher, who called her unpatriotic for not bringing her money for defense stamps. Marian wasn't sure why she didn't have her dime with her, but she knew she was being publicly humiliated. George, two years older, recalls that in childhood games the boys always made him play the German spy, the "Hun".

The Wheelers didn't like their children being harassed, but sometimes Frank pushed the issue. He shocked the school principal by requesting that Margaret be allowed to study German as her foreign language; he lost and she studied French. When Frank continued to oppose involvement in the war at his union meetings, he was in risky territory. Donald says, "Dad told us that one evening at a meeting, after he had made one of his comments, he noticed two union thugs sit down, one on each side of him. He understood the message: "Shut up, Wheeler."

Then the Russian Revolution shook the capitalist world. The world powers wondered if it would spread, even to American shores. Now American radicals like the Wheelers were living in even more frightening times, with western Washington, an IWW stronghold, especially volatile.

Yet another circumstance made the Wheelers ready to leave Tacoma. A few months before, at Helen's birth, Jeanie had nearly died of pupereal (childbed) fever and had been bedridden for months. The strep-caused fever was not widely understood at the time, but people knew it could be related to lack of cleanliness. Frank blamed the visiting nurse. This event, on top of losing their twin baby years before, reminded him again of what an unhealthy place Tacoma was compared to the desert. Then, in the middle of wartime turmoil, the Spanish Flu epidemic hit the west coast. The Wheelers had been building up the farm for eleven years, waiting for the right time to move there. Now that they had the big tents, it seemed a very good time.

Frank and Jeanie packed up their necessities, stored some furniture and other items in the basement, rented the house, put the lots up for sale, and moved to White Bluffs. It must have been a worrisome move for Jeanie. But installed in the spacious tents on their shady 3/4 acre at the "Kent Place"orchard, not far from Shaws and the school, she would make it work. Sometime that year they were able to sell the two Tacoma lots. They didn't plan to sell the house itself, knowing that one day they might need an urban residence again. In later years Frank would write wistfully about needing a "city roost". But they had trouble with the renters and found maintaining a rental at a distance was difficult. Before long they sold the house as well. Now there was no turning back. Regardless of where Frank was working, they were first and foremost farmers, and like Jane and George before them, tent-dwelling desert people.

The war years continued to be good ones for American farmers, even if full of worry if a family had a young man in the military like the Shaws. (Their youngest, Jim, was now a veterinarian taking care of horse units in France.) They grew almost everything they needed for food and were hardly affected by war rationing. The better wartime fruit prices must have given

Frank, if not every grower, some bitterness along with pleasure, for their first respectable prices were being paid for by European farmers' misery. Then, as the war ended, growers wondered what was in store for them next at the market. So many of them had expanded and now had larger mortgages.

The Wheelers nonetheless decided to keep on with the expansion plan they had committed to. Adjacent to their original tract was the abandoned eleven acre "Hensley place" right on the river, with Barrett's Island directly across. They located the owner and in 1920 had their new acreage, including waterfront and water rights, for $1516. They put down $1100, using the funds from the sale of their Tacoma house and lots, and carried a note for the remainder, to be paid in a year. Now they had not only the land they needed for the expanded orchard, but as a bonus, a fine beach close at hand. For Frank and Jeanie it must have seemed like a whole new start, but knowing a great deal more about orchardry than they had in 1907. [1]

More difficult changes took place however. During that same period, just before or just after the land purchase George Shaw and Frank Wheeler decided to break up the partnership. No one today can say why with certainty. Helen assumes their philosophical differences had a part in it, but the men already knew they had differences, so some event had brought this to the surface. The needs of the families had started to diverge, and Frank and Jeanie realized it more clearly now that they were living on the farm year round. While the Wheeler family was growing and needing more resources as toddlers became youth, the Shaws were quite comfortable as they were. George was content to operate a small dairy and small apple orchard. Jane had a nice home now, her boarding house, and cottage industries. They may have been presented with the Wheeler's idea of expansion and all the additional work and risk and said no. For them it made no sense. Or perhaps more soft fruit trees didn't make sense to them, and more alfalfa did. Margaret writes that Jane at one point commented to her that Frank was "fickle" and Margaret, now a young woman, challenged her; what did she mean by that—fickle? Jane explained, "I mean changeable." Possibly Jane saw Frank's continuing horticultural experiments as disruptive.

The Shaws took five acres of Winesaps as their share of the orchards, while the Wheelers took five acres of mainly soft fruit. No explosion took place, and the children didn't really know it had happened until they saw the new fence. Jeanie and Jane made sure that personal relationships continued much as before with the usual sharing of meals and social activity. George came over for personal visits with his daughter, preferring to catch her when Frank wasn't there. Though the Wheelers carried out their expansion, the Shaws never did change their operation. Although they had three sons, none took an interest in working the place with them, so they continued as they had been.

Margaret named the new Wheeler place Willowbank Farm. Frank

and Jeanie now plunged into a new rush of orchard development: clearing, plowing, installing irrigation pipe, and buying and planting new trees. A small house was on the new property, but they decided to stay in their tents, which were actually larger, and let it continue as rental income for a time. Frank went on bricklaying to raise more cash for the expansion. He should have been home more often for all this but he couldn't be. His children remember a few calls he got for local fireplaces, using the fine cobblestones from the riverbank. Having him work close to home for a little time was a treat.

Though Frank could give more year-round attention to the farm, how much actual time he gained there is unclear. Now he had to rely on his brother Nat to alert him immediately if jobs came up in the Tacoma hiring hall, and according to his letters, Nat didn't always do it in a timely way. Frank would sometimes find out he had needlessly missed a good job and was upset. Margaret's life changed as well. She had just spent the winter with her grandparents and was graduating from eighth grade, but there was no high school yet in White Bluffs. Her parents made arrangements for her to go to Tacoma's Stadium High, and board with a family, doing housework and child care for her keep. This was not an unusual arrangement for isolated farm children, and at least she was in their old neighborhood where she knew students and could go to their old church.

The other choice for the girl would have been tiny Hanford High. But boarding her at Hanford didn't make sense, when Stadium High had a fine reputation and Hanford High had none. That difference would mean a lot for college scholarship eligibility. Margaret went back to Tacoma, and from then on lived at White Bluffs only in the summers, as from high school she went right into college. Thus she helped begin a trend that became a tradition, and not just for the Wheeler children but for many valley youth.

The younger children were delighted with the permanent move to the farm. They joined the ranks of those who remembered the valley later as a "perfect place to have a childhood". By now they were adapted to the hard work of summer. What they gained was a year-round life of fun well-laced with work. For Jane Shaw, having her daughter and grandchildren nearby all the time must have been the greatest gift she could imagine. There would never be anymore need for a lonely evening while her husband gave his attention to his animals or told a yarn to a visitor, a yarn she'd heard many times.

The Wheelers would live in their tents in the orchard for about four years. Donald had been born in a Shaw tent, and now he started school living in grander ones. Helen, called "Jewel Baby" by her parents, remembers tent living as great fun. Everyone, even Jeanie, found the tents comfortable most of the time, although the older children, who slept in the unheated smaller one and had to brush the snow off on winter mornings, may not have been quite so fond. Yet it wasn't much colder than the farm houses were by early morning, and in summer a good deal cooler and more pleasant than a house. The big tent was far roomier than most of the neighboring homes, making it easy to invite other children over.

Being at the farm in early spring meant the Wheelers could grow a better vegetable garden. Donald remembers that the beans, peas, corn, squash, and melons were especially fine. Having the school right across the road was a great convenience, and when a substitute teacher was needed, Jeanie could quickly arrange babysitting with her mother. All they needed to do now was to bring the new orchard to maturity, and in a few years Frank could be a full time farmer.

After the family left Tacoma the political turmoil continued with the Seattle General Strike of 1919, and the 1920 Centralia Massacre. Repression of radicals continued as Attorney General Palmer began the infamous "Palmer Raids" of 1919-20. Thousands of people of leftist persuasion, mainly immigrants, were arrested, and the Socialist movement went into retreat. The Wheelers did not; they registered as Socialists for the next election, no doubt creating a stir in their new town. But there was no fear on either side; they were already well-known. Frank, having given up any hope of influencing his union, thought that at least in a small community, even with no union at all, he could be heard. Since each registered political party was required to have a worker at the polls, Jeanie applied for a position on the election board to represent the Socialists, and was, of course, accepted. All the better, the work carried a small stipend.

With the war over, political interest in the valley returned to local and regional issues, and the growers' outcries over freight and power rates rose up again. Now the Wheelers would find themselves again with the majority, as the need for affordable power for rural people was becoming as least as important an issue for the Grange as fair freight rates. At the time, only a small percent of American farms had power. The growth of irrigated districts helped it to become a priority concern. Dry farms operated with various sources of fuel from animal dung to coal, but for irrigation, dams and reservoirs were the only answer. Electric power from dams could then produce cheap power for everyone. Still, despite the efforts of the Grange and other farmer associations, the cause wasn't winning enough support in Congress. The Bureau of Reclamation did sponsor a few western dam projects but continued to reject the Priest Rapids site.

Farmers across the country should have been able to unite for rural power, but they had no real party. The populist movement, strong in the Northwest two decades earlier, had subsided. At its peak of popularity, Populist party candidates had won almost twenty-two percent of the Washington popular vote but no electoral votes. Benton County, with the rest of Eastern Washington, voted Progressive Republican. So did all four Shaws. The western Progressives supported public power, but had not sold their entire party on that notion. Their more conservative colleagues believed that any long-term government involvement in the lives of communities would undermine healthy rural people as they idealized them. The Democrats were more realistic about the lives of the poor, but were focused on urban issues. The public power movement was stalemated.

Turning to the state government for support to public power or any other aid to farmers was of no use. Similar to other states, Washington through the 1920s operated on a very small revenue structure. The counties operated largely on property taxes, but the rural counties like Benton often had trouble collecting them. Thus, though the state and the county governments wanted to see the Priest Rapids district continue to develop, neither had the resources for big irrigation projects involving dams.

A related cause with wide-ranging support was to boost the valley's growth and development. The residents felt, that without growth they would never get the services they wanted, such as a high school for White Bluffs. The Wheelers were among many families strong for higher education. The upper county leaders increasingly worried about the abandonment of farms and other out-migration. Something had to be done about the growers' balance books or the valley would remain a backwater on the powerful river. But the issue of economic development circled right back to the issues of the freight and power rates. New local businesses could not succeed unless their customers succeeded.

After all of the excited promotion a decade earlier, with no assistance forthcoming from government, the development of the Priest Rapids valley leveled off. Meanwhile, by 1921 European agriculture was recovering. The U.S. wheat market, always the barometer for farm prices, crashed in response, dragging the fruit market along. This downward cycle was beginning as farmers nationwide, including the Wheelers, had just committed themselves to expansion and for most, larger mortgages.

The majority of the valley farmers were like George Shaw, essentially indifferent to politics beyond local issues. (Margaret says she never saw her grandfather read anything more challenging than *Hoard's Dairyman*.) The Grange worked to improve that, drawing the rural people together to study and express themselves on farmers' national concerns. In Eastern Washington the Grange was the only voice for small farmers. Socialists, Democrats and Progressive Republicans joined together at the Grange Halls. Jeanie and Frank joined soon after moving full time to White Bluffs. Though considered radical by some, the national Grange drew the line at taking any position which could be labeled unpatriotic, and the Wheelers never expected it to take truly radical positions. In 1918, just as they were moving to their farm, this was confirmed when the chairman-elect of the State Grange, named Bouck, got attention as a public neutralist/socialist. When the State Grange converged at Walla Walla for his installation ceremony, vigilante mobs broke up the meeting. Bouck was forced to withdraw his candidacy. The State Grange had its charter withdrawn for a time for even considering such a candidate. It would be more careful in the future.

The post-war time was discouraging for everyone, but especially for pro-labor people like Frank. The movement toward industrial unions that had blossomed before the war now seemed dead, unions in general thrashed. Any chance for socialism had lost ground with the intense reaction that had set in after the Russian revolution. For Frank, White Bluffs had its drawbacks for lively discourse. With no brother Nat nearby to turn to, and his in-laws and neighbors not interested, Frank gradually increased the political discourse at his supper table. As it often centered on what was taking place around them, the growing children found it engaging. They learned early the art of shocking the neighbors. His son George remembers that at nine, during the war, he was observing the neighbors feeding high quality bran to their pig.

He commented, (and it was reported back to Jeanie), "That's what we put in our pancakes for breakfast, and you will too if this war continues!"

The Wheelers sensed the community pressures on children to conform and how outrageous Frank's more radical airings were to his neighbors. Donald says they explored the issues with the children, and then let them take their own positions as they saw fit. Determined that they not to be intellectually hampered by lack of a newsstand or a real public library in White Bluffs, the Wheelers subscribed to *New York Times, Seattle Union Record,* Deb's *Appeal to Reason*, and later the Farmer-Labor Party paper. The postmaster must have been impressed with their mail. Frank's knowledge of world events, and from a uniquely wide perspective, allowed him to initiate discussions never before heard in White Bluffs. Donald says, "George Shaw entertained people, and Win Shaw had some radical ideas of his own, but he kept his mouth shut in public and got along with everyone. But Dad threatened the businessmen Out Town." Helen adds that her father was soon christened by some as "The Red Down by the River". He wouldn't have protested that title, though his wife probably had mixed feelings.

It was hard to be a man so outraged by social injustices and to be able to affect so little change, even on the local issues staring him in the face. It was hard also to be his wife and support his views, which Jeanie did, and at the same time be an accepted player on the women's volunteer teams, alongside the wives of the very men he was angry with. Frank and Jeanie had given up the comfort of a philosophically agreeable community they could have found in almost any large town.

The Wheelers' arrival in White Bluffs did not greatly change the political activity there. Rather, they joined it, and shaped it when they could. During winter there was time for such that they had never had as summer residents. Still, Frank found that after a few efforts, he would never be an enthusiastic meeting-goer. Helen remembers her mother, hoping to lure him to Grange, saying, "Frank, there is a clean shirt on the bed for you if you want to change, but you don't have to. Just come with me." Donald remembers Win Shaw coming to the house and begging Frank to come to the Grange meetings more. "You are the smartest man around, and we need you," argued Win, the Republican. He had little luck.

Frank preferred speaking out when he when he could visit with someone at the post office, or on the road, or best of all, invite them to dinner. He could always find someone of a populist persuasion to agree with him at least about the the rotten deal small farmers got in the economy. Even in the isolation of the desert, however, he could not confine himself to domestic issues. True to his Protestant upbringing, he perceived the power of the Vatican, Christian Science, or Freemasonry behind most evil trends. He may have gotten some head nodding on these topics from his largely Protestant neighbors, but when he waxed forth on the cruel deeds of the British Empire and other institutions of Northern European supremacy, always taking the side of the miserable colonials, he left his neighbors puzzled, if not suspicious.

Local issues could be touchy. In a portion of a letter to his daughter Margaret he holds forth on the irritating problem of cronyism in county jobs hiring. But it is not just the Masons he inveighs against, it is all of the businessmen/local leaders:

> In our little microcosm W.B. look! In the
> spring—Kincaid-Presbyterians 100%, O'Larey for the
> Allard [Catholic] contingent, and Loveland for the
> Stonyhearted Scientists. Meet. Put wages at 30 cents
> per hr for labor or cause the County Commissioners to
> do it. Result—when 6 mos working season is over, every
> man who works and has a wife and children is a
> pauper, actually, and those in places [jobs] peons or serfs

proper only removed by the picking of their teeth, and
all of us in jeopardy. X it and you have the Chamber of
Comm. of USA intent on plunder.

Then, as he reflects on the evils of his world, he adds a calming note for
himself as well as his daughter, "Why be disappointed. I believe the Holy
Spirit not evil men will rule and enlist every noble purpose. In due time
something lovely enough to really hope for." That hope echoes the dream he
nursed for his dear orchard. The minister's son turned socialist needed
something beyond fruit to hope for, and with political and social solutions
forever being betrayed by one power group or another, he turned to what
still seemed solid. But whether he thought it could come on earth, or only in
the hereafter, is not clear.

Frank's letters appear totally unedited; he lets his thoughts flow as they
will. Whereas Jane's, and many of Jeanie's letters are planned for structure
and turn of phrase, his adjectives and metaphors tumble out. Usually they
strike to the heart, sometimes they miss. But if he had edited them they
would have lost their verve, and perhaps he knew that. The humor of the
metaphors saves the bitterness. His neighbors, some of them good friends of
Jeanie and their children, fortunately never read these letters. But he found
at least one other area of agreement with some of his neighbors who would
have applauded this excerpt of a 1925 letter, again to his daughter, on the
disregard for prohibition laws:

It seems a world of meat and little mind. Power,
Worldly Power always seems to be in apostate
hands...out the stinking cat pops in a dozen places. In
Tacoma, the Kiwanians open up with a big wet ball in
the new hotel. Aberdeen and a dozen towns are kicking
out Mayors who enforce the law. No one anywhere but
the merchants mostly, profits from drink, commercial

vulgarity and lewdness. They hold the torch, their wives work the bellows, keep up a front of respectability so the daily news items justify them more and more. Its just a thread in the same bolt of cloth.

Not every "populist" cause failed. Donald believes that Prohibition did significant good in small towns if their own community was an example. Though more affluent people could continue to buy and serve liquor whenever they wanted, as an observant teenager he saw "the consumption among the residents as a whole was cut way down." His own father adhered to the law to the point of removing "spirits" from their medicine cabinet. But however the Wheelers felt about moonshining by their neighbors, they made no personal effort to interfere with them and remove their income, and apparently most people followed that principle.

Frank did not spend his energy on criticism alone. He was always investigating new possibilities of social and economic organization. He was curious about the cooperative movement; he was interested in educational reform like Montessori and thought Jeanie should look into it. But his neighbors were not interested in supporting a private preschool, and in their experience coops and marketing associations always failed. He soon saw that the popular issues in White Bluffs would be the bread and butter issues of farmers everywhere.

Frank's need to speak out could have resulted in even more harassment than the family had faced in Tacoma, but though they were doubtless the subject of gossip, the Wheelers were never ostracized in White Bluffs. Just the opposite, they were included. The Wheeler youth were accepted partly because of their involvement in the youth groups like 4-H, Boy Scouts, and Sunday School. Their being almost all honor students didn't hurt. Even so, the fact that not one of the six children reports feeling snubbed at White Bluffs seems remarkable. Helen and Donald credit this to their mother and grandmother, who gave so much energy to community issues and projects that everyone cared about. It would have been difficult to isolate the Wheelers for the peculiarity of voting the Socialist ticket, or for Frank's unusual discourses, when the women contributed so unstintingly. Donald comments:

> "Grandma (and mother too) disliked and declined to participate in the Politics of Blowing Steam, which was a favorite indoor pastime of our father, Nat, George and Win Shaw, and an awful lot of other menfolk, including just possibly D.N.W.[himself]. But on the actual grass roots political issues of the community, the women did more than any dozen of the Steam-Blowers.

Though Frank was not a banner-waving leader or a meeting-goer, he was not just a steam blower, Don hastens to add, that part being recreational:

> Dad could move when he thought it was needed. During the period of the Espionage Act, a son of the only other socialist family in White Bluffs came for a visit. When the word got out that there was an unpatriotic neutralist in town, worse yet, a Wobbly, there were rumblings about taking action that got back to the young fellow. He came to Dad and told him he was afraid. Dad's advice was, "Do your folks own a shot gun?" "Yes." "Go down to the store and buy four boxes of shells. Don't do anything with them, just buy them." The fellow did so, and word traveled fast; there was no more talk of taking action.

Jeanie, now in the valley full time, missed her former connections but found that living in a very small town had its advantage in that an individual could have measurable influence. She and her mother could see real results from campaigns they were active in, such as the well-baby clinic, and were rewarded with appreciation even if it wasn't directed to them personally. But both women also experienced painful setbacks, such as within their church. There the disadvantage of a small town was obvious, for there was no other choice of church for them. Jane was drawn into a debate on church doctrine regarding graven images—she was against pictures of Jesus— and won, but lost on a more important issue of leadership. She could be liberal or conservative, depending on the issue (whereas the Wheelers always took the liberal position) and through her dedication and organizational skills rose up in the 1920s to the position of Sunday School Superintendent, next to the pastor in importance. But after a few years of intra-church struggle, she lost the position to a member of the conservative faction, never to regain it.

Jeanie, of the liberal faction, wasn't involved in the doctrinal issues. Her goal was for the church to be stimulating and useful. Helen remembers her as the only Sunday School teacher who could hold girls' interest, no boys attending by that time. During this same period, Jeanie and Frank supported a young liberal acting-pastor whom the conservatives were trying to push out. To help his cause, Jeanie ran for the board of elders and won. The conservative leader was outraged that a woman, a "card-player and a dancer" no less, would have the gall to be an elder, calling her a "snake in the grass". She kept her seat, but the minister was still sent on his way. Donald remembers that when the power of the liberals and the conservatives was more or less balanced, the church was lively. When the conservatives finally won total control, the church was never so vital a place again and eventually it closed from lack of attendance.

Jeanie experienced more personal defeat when she ran for school board in 1927 at Frank's prodding. He wanted her to receive recognition for her good ideas as well as her work at the school. But she was defeated and only hurt by the rejection at the polls. Unlike Frank, who always stood unflinching on his high moral pinnacle, she couldn't brush off the arrows of her neighbors. Donald feels bad about that. "Dad should have known she would lose, and that it would humiliate her. How could a socialist win a seat on the school board?" But neither Jeanie nor her mother considered deserting their community work. They patched their wounds and kept going, winning enough times to make their battles worthwhile.

The turbulent 1920s ushered in other movements that in the Wheeler opinion were unhealthy. With the economy teetering, "Nativists" were able to pass the National Origins Act of 1921 that put quotas on the number of immigrants the U.S. would receive from various countries. The number of new Asian immigrants permitted was zero. Anti-Asian sentiment, especially against their holding real estate, was strongest on the west coast and even crept into remote, heretofore tolerant Priest Rapids valley. The only imagined ethnic threat to the district's Euro-American economic power was, absurdly, at tiny Ringold, eight miles away and across the river, where Japanese farmers were raising truck produce. At Wapato, near Yakima, was another successful Japanese farming community. A faction in the valley decided to whip up the threat of economic takeover.

Though Frank Wheeler on occasion could rail against Irish Catholics, Scandinavians and "Cockneys", when he observed they were not good union men or displayed other social shortcomings, and could even invect against Scots when he was irritated with his mother-in-law, he always took the side of people of color. Now, as farmers felt their political power weaken along with their economic power, the Wheelers were alarmed to find out that the Ku Klux Klan had crept into White Bluffs.

While the Klan never took over politics in Washington, in the early

1920s it dominated the Oregon Legislature and several Oregon towns not far from the Priest Rapids valley. Its main targets were Roman Catholics, including their private schools, and Asians. Donald and Helen Wheeler remember two separate instances of burning crosses in the White Bluffs area. As Donald and friends came out of the White Bluffs theater house after the showing of a "pro-Catholic" film, they saw a huge cross burning on Gable Mountain, several miles across the desert. There was a Catholic church in White Bluffs, and the O'Lareys were a leading family, the newspaper publishers, and friends of the Wheelers. Were O'Lareys the target, or Catholics in general? Helen says she never heard anyone, aside from her father, make openly anti-Catholic (in his case anti-clerical) remarks. Whatever the intent, this effort to make an ugly scene fizzled. Acceptance of Catholics was even more assured by 1927, for then the large and popular Irish Catholic family mentioned earlier, the Walkers, arrived.

The overt Klan activity Helen recalled had worse effects. A local family had accepted a young Jewish man from outside the community to live with them as son-in-law. Somebody in the desert town didn't want him. Helen, about six, was one evening terrified to see a cross burning right in the family's yard, not far from their own. This family didn't have the clout the Walkers and O'Lareys had, and the young couple left town.

White Bluffs, with its usual tolerance, did nothing about the local Klan publicly, pro or con. Though the group couldn't get up enough interest for another pyre right away, it did burn another cross down near Hanford in 1928, according to the local press. Thus the Klan continued to smolder and encouraged the more bigoted elements within the valley's American Legion. The Legion within a year took on the important task of maintaining racial purity in the Priest Rapids valley. It declared publicly that it would assure that no "Orientals" moved in. At this very time, the State of Washington decided to initiate a "Soldier-Settler" colonization project at White Bluffs.

The State then aligned itself with the Benton County American Legion, declaring in the fine print of its recruitment brochure that the Legion would "help see that no Orientals would live around White Bluffs/Hanford". (See Chpt. 13.)

Despite Frank's radical positions, in only one incident does Helen recall her father being threatened, and it was not for political views, but for moral courage. She was in high school in the early 1930s when a community meeting was held to decide what to do about a school janitor who was found sexually abusing children. Frank spoke up at the meeting that it wasn't enough to ask the man to leave town, that they were sending the problem to another community, and declared that the man should be charged. Helen tells:

> One day soon after, I saw a carload of the man's lodge brothers come driving into our yard. I watched Dad go out to talk to them, then come back in the house. I saw how he was struggling to control himself, he was so furious. Later he told us that the men had told him to back off or else, that the offender was leaving town.

Frank was in this, as in many of his positions, ahead of his times. In an ironic twist to the incident, the man was the only other socialist voter in town, and Frank was the one who insisted he should be charged, but lost.

Settlers writing in the *Family Histories* frequently comment about how much their community was "like one big family", tolerating differences in philosophy and life style as long as people were reasonably law-abiding, moonshining excepted. The first irrigators had been welcomed by the homesteaders, the soldiers-settlers of 1922 (to be described later) were welcomed by the irrigators, and in the late 1930s, a Mormon contingent arriving would also be welcomed. The anti-Asian movement, the brief surfacing of the Klan, and the pillaging of Indian graves reveals a negative undercurrent that was not at all the predominant social mood of White Bluffs, but was there, just enough to keep everyone from really being the "one big happy family" that some settlers remember. Rather, it was a family, but a slightly dysfunctional one. This caused Jeanie and Jane more trouble than the others, for the men like George Shaw largely ignored it, or in Frank's case, growled about it, while the young people rose above it. But the women could not ignore it as they had to relate to all of the women, whatever their prejudices, in the women's associations.

Fortunately, other more healthy social energies were also stirring in the 1920s. The victory won by rural people with Prohibition encouraged populist feeling, and farmers continued to try to rebuild their power. In 1920 the Farmer-Labor Party formed in the Midwest, and was able to get several candidates on the ballot in Washington in 1922 and again in 1924. For a time the two party system was opened up to a broader and livelier sociopolitical debate. The Farmer's Union became a force in the Midwest, and the Grange continued to grow in Washington.

In 1924, Robert LaFollette ran for U.S. President on the Farmer-Labor Party ticket. He drew people of many political stripes together, including Republicans like the Shaws. It was the last serious try at a national farmer's party, but it was a powerful one. Among the platform planks were some Frank Wheeler would have been proud to initiate: recognition of collective bargaining, farm relief, public-owned railways, and public water power. Excitement was high in the valley. George Wheeler remembers that it was his first big campaign, and how he biked around the district with hundreds of leaflets. Donald, who was eleven, recalls, "...LaFollette had a very good program. Grandpa and grandma were strong supporters of LaFollette, as of course were dad and mother. He carried both White Bluffs and Hanford [Parker says the whole county] against Coolidge."

Despite LaFollette's tremendous popularity, and although Farmer-Labor stayed strong in the Midwest, it was another case of a third party not lasting long nationally. For Frank Wheeler, it must have been frustrating that just as his own bricklayer's union had never seen beyond itself to the cause of industrial unionism, the farmers of his valley could not commit themselves for long to a farmer-labor party. They slipped back into their traditional Republican habit until 1932, when three years of an even worse economy would cause them to swing to the Democrats and Franklin D. Roosevelt. Meanwhile, eight more years of eastern Republican control meant eight years with no chance of winning federal support of public power.

MAGIC CURRENTS

"I don't believe any family was on the river as much as our own."
Helen Wheeler Hastay, 2001

THE SETTLERS SURVIVED the frustrations of desert farming partly because when they weren't picking and packing they were likely to be having fun. When they recreated their clubs and associations from their past communities, they also introduced all the amusements those groups sponsored from ice cream socials to horse races. They found that talent shows, ball games and barn dances were not that difficult to organize in the valley, certainly easier than than it would have been in a district of vast wheat ranches. Their choice of public amusements was much like those one could have found in any small western town of that day. What was different at White Bluffs, and something they couldn't have predicted, was all the adventure and entertainment that the desert, bluffs and river themselves provided, without any help from humans at all. Most of the year the climate was fine for outdoor fun, and the exotic setting right at hand. In poor weather, the homes were close enough that, barring a blizzard or a heat wave, even young children could run over to visit their friends.

White Bluffs, within a few years of the settlers' arrival, offered something for everyone, for whatever amount of free time they allowed themselves. The Wheelers describe box socials, ice cream socials, district and county fairs, Fourth of July picnics, children's Christmas programs, sewing circles, Grange dances, community dinners, church programs, literary events and teas at the Women's Club, baseball, family birthday parties, marching bands, traveling music groups and camp meetings, and that universal desert event, rabbit drives—all of these created from American small town tradition. The teenage hangout south of town on the river would later be joined by a soda fountain and movie house in downtown White Bluffs. Eventually auto touring, motorboat racing, and even golfing on the sands would be introduced for local gentry.

Other alternative amusements weren't intended for families and probably did less in the way of community building but still were a break from work for the men: poker parties, cock fighting, varmint hunting, a pool hall, and of course, moonshining. Helen recalls:

> Some years, when the county voted 'wet', there was a local saloon. During dry years, it was transported across the river to Franklin county and it was an easy enough task to row across to it. How the customers rowed home safely is a puzzle, but it seems that they always survived. Then, during the quiet seasons some of the older bachelors, not just the deputy sheriff, seemed to do nothing except play poker all day.

The first movies in White Bluffs, silent flicks, were brought in by an imaginative grade school principal who rented "good films", usually comedies, and offered them free to the public. When the talkies came out, a local entrepreneur, Anderson, opened a movie house. His films cost ten cents, the most expensive entertainment in town. When he played a movie at White Bluffs on Friday, he played it at Hanford on Saturday; if you missed it one place you could catch it at the next. The Grange dance with live music on Saturday night was still the first choice for all ages until the completion of the high school with a gymnasium in 1922. Then basketball took off, but never stopped the popularity of the dances, simply provided more choices. White Bluffs' marching band added zest to whatever was going on.

Except for races and baseball, much of this fun could take place even in winter by moving it indoors. A problem in many rural areas would have been lighting for long winter nights. But power had been brought down the valley in 1910 from the Priest Rapids plant, providing electricity to all the public buildings. Lighting was a problem at home, however, for the many families like the Wheelers who could not afford to hook up to power for fourteen years. Even with the busy schedule of social events there were bound to be winter evenings when families were confined to what could be done at home by kerosene lamp. Though the valley's winter was short, that didn't change the route of the sun, and it was dark by five, the cows milked, the orchards asleep. Valley women sewed and men did repairs by dim light surrounded by children at their homework or various crafts. Parlor games were popular, and the titles are familiar: "Twenty Questions", "Going to Jerusalem".

For the Wheelers, children included, reading was the favorite indoor recreation. The work Jane and Jeanie did to develop the local public and school libraries was not pure altruism but also for personal survival. It was Jeanie's special goal to have all of of her children reading early, preferably by five years, so that she could attend to her own reading. Frank was in complete agreement, putting aside his need for more trees for the equally important need for more books. The children also had a subscription to *The Children's Hour*, and Margaret remembers the fights that erupted when it arrived over who would get to savor it first. Even more special, Helen recalls:

> We had a set of gorgeously illustrated classics,
> really an inspiration on the part of our folks. The art
> work was just as much a part of the experience as the

story and guaranteed we would read them: *Robinson Crusoe, Hiawatha, Arabian Nights, Van Loon's History of Mankind,* and *History of the Bible.* We read and studied the paintings for hours.

No wonder that, even with no museum or art teacher, the Wheeler children developed an interest in art. We can picture the family on an evening with Frank home, all of them huddled together, he and Jeanie reading aloud from the classics, the illustrations glowing like Dutch masters in the lamplight.

Along with these treasures Margaret remembers their shelves carried the popular rural/romantic themes: *Dr. Livingstone's African Adventures, Riders of the Purple Sage, The Virginian, Girl of the Limberlost, Trail of the Lonesome Pine.* Even Jane thought novels not beyond the pale; she had a whole set of popular "Waverlies". Jeanie and Jane, both teachers, didn't want books only for their own family but for the whole community, and ranked their efforts to bring in traveling and school libraries as some of their most important public service.

Quite a few valley homes owned musical instruments, and it was a popular pastime to join in with the neighbors who had a piano. If they didn't have instruments, they sang anyway. Donald says, "We sang at home often, and Dad would join in sometimes; he knew how to harmonize." Helen remembers the music in their home:

> One year when we were still living in the tents,
> Mom's oldest brother brought us a wind-up victrola and
> a set of records that included opera, Negro spirituals,
> waltzes, and foxtrots. We enjoyed it so much that when
> Rose, Marian and George were teens, the folks indulged
> in a real luxury, ordering a cabinet-sized victrola for
> $100, a small fortune then. The kids used their own

earnings to order dance records and bring in their
friends to dance. Then our big tent became not just a
home but a social center for several years, managed by
my older sisters. Our guests must have behaved
themselves within reason, for I don't remember our
folks ever having to close them down. I hated it when
we moved to the cramped little green house about 1922
or 23. We had to give up the open space and on-going
party of the tent house. We still had parties, but it
could never be the same.

A more unique pastime for the Wheelers was art. Rose and Marian
both followed their father in loving to sketch, and though they never had art
supplies they could always find a scrap of paper and a pencil, and plotted
how some day they would get real art lessons.

For years all of this indoor activity took place without electric lights,
and with considerable fussing to keep adequate kerosene lamps burning
properly for so many students and readers. Those lovers of reading, Frank
and Jeanie, were adding another to their club each year. Donald says he
believes Marian read every Shakespeare play by the time she was ten.

During the less busy seasons some families made it a regular pastime to
drop in at the neighbors. Though Frank didn't go visiting much, Jeanie built
a friendship that lasted a lifetime with Clara Barrett on the nearby island.
To reach each other they rowed the short distance across the slough, while
picnics on Barrett's Island were a part of every summer. Helen tells of her
grandmother's special parties:

She had her special Scot friends that she got
together with over tea and cookies, conversing for their
own amusement in "highlander" dialect and laughing
uproariously. Another of Grandma's favorite visitors

was a woman who was born in the old country, and had apparently brought a custom with her of a springtime walkabout. She would just start out in fine weather walking around the valley and would stop at a house in time for the evening meal and stay overnight. Then on to the next house. She picked up all the news along the way, and was welcome for what tidbits she brought. It must have been an old custom. Grandma was always amused by her visits. Generally, though, Mom and Grandma saved their visiting for the Ladies Aid meetings. Grandpa considered that his yarns provided enough purpose for a visit. Dad's favored socializing was to have people come to our house for dinner.

One of the grandchildren remembers that pinned on the wall by the table was a Hottentot call Frank must have found in a *National Geographic:* "We have meat! Who will eat!"

If we judge from the quantity of reports in the weekly newspaper, the most popular recreation had to be ice cream socials, basketball, and Grange dances. The socials won their prize for their heavenly chilled combination of fresh cream and natural fruit flavors, and because they could be pleasant when it was too hot for anything else. Basketball could be played all winter when people had more time and fed the energizing rivalry that developed between Hanford and White Bluffs youth, only seven miles apart. The rivalry grew to be "practically lethal" says Donald, though he and Helen don't remember anyone actually getting hurt, and provided everyone a rare acceptable setting to go wild. But in the Wheeler opinion, nothing equaled the Grange dances as an outlet for all ages, from babies through grandparents. The live music was by local people, in the early years a string band supplied by a homesteader family, the red-headed McGlothlens.

Margaret writes of the early days:

> There were printed programs and rules about which dances you had to dance with your partner and which ones the stag line could step in on. If your partner was too drunk to dance, which was not infrequent, you could go sit down, but you couldn't dance that number with someone else. The drinking, by law and custom, was done outside the hall, and one could choose to be wicked or not. The square dances that were mixed in with the waltzes and two-steps were dominated by the homesteader families who knew how to do them properly and didn't want to be interrupted to explain a figure. This frustrated the girls who wanted to learn, but fortunately anyone could be dragged through a Circle Two-Step.

> People who worked all day in an orchard or packing house, thought nothing of washing up and heading for the dance to stay until daylight, hurrying home to catch three hours sleep, only to rise up and stumble out to the orchard or packing house again.

Helen continues the later culture of the dances:

> In the late 1920s the McGlothlens retired, but the Holecek/Mikol family arrived with their extended family dance band. They were always in demand, and there were no such rules anymore; you could dance with whomever and however you pleased. And the Ladies Aid through all the years sold good food at the break time.

Normally the settlers traveled out of the valley only for medical or school reasons, or to make an extended visit to long-missed relatives. But there was one yearly exception, a mix of business and fun that drew people from across the county to Kennewick. It began in 1911 as the annual Grape Festival. This was during the time when growers still thought their fine grapes could become the money crop of the valley and were trying hard for publicity. The festivals, grand as they were, did not conjure a solution for marketing. By the 1920s the Festival evolved into an annual County Fair at Prosser or Kennewick. The Fair, similar in theme to county fairs everywhere in the West, called for quite an excursion by wagon and an overnight stay. Even when autos became common, it was still a major effort to organize all the bodies, clothes, quilts, food, and especially the produce for the exhibits. All displays had to arrive looking fresh and luscious, ideally better than anyone else's. The excitement of the preparations for the Fair could build for weeks for the truly dedicated.

As with any county fair, the Grange was a main organizer and supporter, with the local clubs going all out to display their fruits and vegetables in gorgeous geometric arrangements for the sake of blue ribbons. Those locals that won prizes then had a new challenge of preparing for the State Fair. People could boast a little with their home crafts and culinary arts as well, and make some deals in stock-breeding or equipment loaning. Just as today, the vendors of the latest labor-saving farming devices were promoting their wonders, from sprayers to washing machines (later on came tractors), pressuring people to dig in their pockets and be relieved of back-ache forever, trading it for more debt. People found old friends they never saw the rest of the year, met new friends, marveled at how children had grown up and what new babies had arrived. Many shared a gallon of cider, played some baseball, even did a little courting.

Donald recalls another almost annual event until the 1940s, "... the Indian rodeo held out near Black Sand Bar, but few White Bluffs folks attended, although Indians came from all over. There was some fine horsemanship, well worth my ticket." Apparently most of the settlers felt out of place at an all-Indian event, but Donald, like his father, was interested in other cultures.

The Wheelers took part in almost all of the activities mentioned so far, not every time to every event, but on a regular basis. They held fast to their original idea that life, even in the busy summers, must include fun. One simply could not keep working until the work was done, as it was never going to be. Thus, except for harvest times, the keeping of the Sabbath was a perfect way to enforce a work stoppage. For Frank it was as much for family's sake as for religion. Margaret observed that her father and grandfather, though so different in many ways, were in agreement on this. George Shaw never had followed this style, while Frank, already on a heavy schedule of "six tens" with his bricklaying work, came home intending to take time for his family. If he had simply worked on through Sunday like so many men, and left his family to go on outings without him, the picnics wouldn't have been very jolly. Everyone, children included, would have had the image of him sweating in the orchard as they floated in the idyllic waters of the slough. But Frank stuck to his rule as much as he could, and that gave everyone else their break too.

In contrast to the town's busy recreation schedule, the diversions that nature offered required very little or no organizing by anyone. Each spring began with the burst of millions of blossoms on the fruit trees, all nursed by humans, a beauty that problems with the market couldn't diminish. But even more exciting, because more brief and fragile, and of infinite variety, were the spring wild flowers blooming just a short walk out into the desert. Helen remembers, "In late April every year the teachers took their classes out, and the children would race to see who could find the very first of the first flowers out, the yellow bells. After those first days, the rule was, 'Enjoy them where they are, don't pick!'"

Spring was also the best season for excursions up the river, by horse or afoot, and of course by boat except at high water. The bluffs, coulees, blooming desert, and river provided an unequaled terrain for romantic rambling or the more serious study of natural history. For people like Donald this time out away from town was far more important than all the organized amusements. He was bewildered by youth who didn't agree. "I would be so angry on a fine spring day when I wanted a chum to go rowing across the river or into the desert by horseback and couldn't find one. They were all at the baseball diamond! But I was no good at baseball at all."

During the too busy summertimes, Frank and Jeanie found the perfect rest that they could enjoy together at the river, with picnics combined with swimming or wading, boating, and cool mud offering something for all ages. Other families often joined them, for Barrett's Island, just across the slough, had one of the most popular sand beaches. Helen remembers:

> Several beaches along the slough warmed up in
> sequence during the spring, so we could choose the one
> that was just right for the week, until finally, by mid-
> summer, it was possible to swim right in the main
> current. It was just marvelous to be so close to the river.
> I don't believe any White Bluffs family was on the river
> as much as our own.

Like the other social functions, picnics were work for the women, but perhaps no more work than usual. The shade and slight breeze by the water, with a cool dip beckoning, surely beat fly-patrol in a hot kitchen. And any baby fretting with the heat was bound to be soothed by the ambience of the river.

All of the Wheelers swam, Jeanie learning at forty, though never Jane.

Frank and George Shaw were almost the only older men that Helen recalls swimming in the river, something that always puzzled her. An explanation is possibly that the other men had no proper garments for mixed bathing, "proper" meaning, for the early settlers, almost fully covered. Other settlers recall the men and boys swimming nude at their own enclaves, no doubt more pleasant. But the Shaw and Wheeler men joined the mixed family company with some kind of suit. The idea of the boys going off with him to exclude the women would have been unacceptable to Frank and Jeanie. Frank's other special pleasure was rowing, always with a crew of children, of course.

The river especially blessed irrigators on the worst days in the orchards when the temperature hovered around 100 degrees, too hot to be comfortable, not quite hot enough to say "Stop work!" When the Wheelers were working in their own orchard, the swimming beach was a short walk away. Pickers could easily have a quick dip before heading for the house for dinner. Working elsewhere meant waiting until they got home, and it could be a long wait. Other families based farther from the river tell of what a fine time they had swimming in the Hanford Ditch as children, or, down near Hanford, in a drainage pond off the ditch. To the Wheelers, the Ditch was a poor substitute. It was cold and hard to climb out of, and Helen says she couldn't understand why more people didn't come down to the river. Perhaps their fathers were those who never stopped working, and the river seemed too far for children to hike in the heat. Perhaps the idea of their children down at the river alone made mothers nervous. But there were few children, once they could swim, who didn't spend a lot of their life in either the ditch or the river.

Quality of life on the river shot up again with the arrival of the *Ho Eliza,* a well-designed rowboat brought by Frank's brother Nat. "It had two sets of oars, and was the fastest rowboat in White Bluffs," claims Helen. The river's main current was so swift that to row across to the east side demanded a trim boat and strong oarsmen rowing with all their might, angling upstream. Coming home, the same strategy applied. To travel directly upstream one could row the eddies that ran along the shores; traveling downstream was faster but meant a hard haul back. Once all this piloting was mastered, the *Ho Eliza* took people upriver for many camping trips to uninhabited Locke's Island, or across for exploring on the bluffs. At one point below the bluffs a bench had formed, creating a lush green park ideal for a summer destination. In later years the *Ho Eliza* sported a sail and rudder. The prevailing winds from the southwest helped her sail nicely upstream along either bank. George Wheeler writes, "Of all the activities possible at White Bluffs, for me sailing the *Ho Eliza* was the very best."

When the Wheeler youth were in their teens, a man first swam across the river to the bluffs, about half a mile. Rose then declared that if he could, she could, and proved it. From then on that was a new bold pastime, although a rowboat always went along. Yet some of the young people from "Out Town" never learned to swim. It might have been in part simple fear. If you didn't get to know the river, you couldn't manage in or on it.

Teens, like teens everywhere, wanted a little time and space organized just for themselves. A far more private hangout than the town soda fountain was at Black Sand Bar, another swimming spot. It was just far enough south of town to escape the eyes of parents and town elders. George remembers that the gathering of the picnic supplies was half the fun as they were preferably through raids: chicken yards culled, corn and melon patches thinned, cider jugs shorted. The main dish at the fire pit was not hot dogs but the teens' own "mulligan stew".

Summer and early fall were subsumed by harvest, and a day off could be too hot for anything other than swimming. Still, the moment the temperature dropped a bit, some restless teen might suggest a row across the river, and a hike up and across the blazing bluffs pursuing rattlesnakes. Though they never bothered the orchardists they were exciting prey. George admits that later he was mortified, remembering this bloody pastime.

When summer eased into fall, fishing took priority for many families, including Win and Juliette Shaw. Donald says he sometimes went along with them but never had the patience to learn their special knack for enticing the introduced bass. Still, Donald and George both remember spearing and bringing home the introduced carp that spawned by the thousands in the swale at high water; this took no particular talent. When the cooks saw them coming with their strings of muddy tasting fish, they were not overjoyed. They would feel obligated to prepare them, knowing no one was really going to enjoy the results. Usually the catch became valuable orchard fertilizer. Jeanie and Frank learned to catch white fish years later, and it seemed so easy they wondered why they had neglected this source of protein earlier when they were often short of meat.

Later in fall the real hunting season began for the men and boys, and a few women too. The settlers, not content with sage hens and rabbits, had introduced quail, pheasants, and grouse. Hawks and coyotes were, like rattlesnakes, traditional enemies of farmers whether they deserved it or not, and provided more entertainment. But the serious hunting tradition of the Shaws and Nat Wheeler did not pass down to the Wheeler boys, probably because their own father did not care for it. "We boys would go after game birds with a .22 once in while," says Donald, "but that was all. We didn't kill animals we didn't eat." No one thought of eating the ground squirrels, apparently, though they were edible.

One form of wildlife that had few defenders was black-tailed jack rabbits. They did terrible damage to crops, especially at the height of their cycles, and weren't even good to eat. People believed, furthermore, that they had driven off the population of tasty "whitetails" that the homesteaders had often subsisted on. Community jack rabbit drives, common across the West, were not considered a sport as much as a necessity, but they offered another opportunity for festivities. Recruiting enough people to make a drive successful required a host who was willing to provide the space for a potluck and even a live band to finish off the bloody day. Since the rabbit migrations usually came from the east, crossing the frozen river in winter, the parties were held at farms on the east bank. The revelers were expected to arrive with clubs and a long net and to form an army for slaughter if they wanted to eat and play later. Rabbit drives were ugly to many people but they felt obligated to do their share. Donald believes they were necessary, but the Wheelers, the women in particular, did not attend. Frank never went again after his first one. "My father couldn't kill a jack rabbit," laughs Helen, "I can't imagine him at a rabbit drive."

Winter, even though it didn't last long, sometimes brought the bitter cold winds that George Wheeler describes. Then reading and games near the wood stove had to serve for amusement. But when it was calm and the river, or at least the slough, froze over, ice skating was the outdoor favorite, always with a bonfire on the beach. Once again, the Wheelers, near the river, had the advantage. "Marian was the best girl skater," Helen reminisces. "When she and Bob Barrett waltzed on the ice it was something to see."

White Bluffs flourished quietly in a recreational paradise known only to its residents, with one exception: the annual Speedboat Regatta begun in the mid-1920s. This one-day intense action in the big eddy was a modern version of canoe races held there by the Indians earlier. It began partly as one more community-boosting effort promoted by the civic groups, and partly as a merchant-inspired idea to bring cash into town. As its fame spread, the gradually improved road from Kennewick brought in an annual crowd of about 1,000 enthusiasts to take over the tiny town for a day of racing on the river and all the chaos that went with it. As many as thirty speedboats might be entered, starting with a heat for twelve horsepower and on up. But few of the locals had speedboats, if we can believe that the *Ho Eliza* was the envied local water craft. The visitors spent enough money to keep the local businesses happy, while some farmers probably didn't care at all about the noise, confusion, and garbage remaining from a twenty-five cent admission.

The quintessential high risk water sport at White Bluffs attracted only a few, and it is just as well, for it was shooting the rapids with log rafts. This, not speedboat racing, is the subject of Wheeler tales when they reminisce about the Columbia. In years when not enough essential driftwood was coming down at high water to capture for the family log booms, the solution was to go up river to search out beached drift logs and timbers. Crews of young men collected enough to make up rafts and floated them down to town. The farther up river they went, the more fresh drift. Soon, venturing above Coyote Rapids and bringing the rafts down through treacherous waters made an interesting job thrilling. They had to know just how to measure the water—not too low, not too swift—and how to steer with a handmade sweep oar. The crew tied a skiff to the raft in case it should break up when it hit the rapids.

When that stretch of white water had become routine, Donald convinced his friend Gilbert Walker one year to go upriver even farther, up past the much larger, more treacherous Priest Rapids. We wonder if the parents had any idea what was planned, if they had even seen Priest Rapids. Now the young men were in virgin territory for drift logs, finding a great quantity piled up near the eddy. But they were also in truly perilous waters. Their log raft would have to hold up against the pitching and swirling of great whirlpools, and they would have to be able to make decisions very fast. Rarely did any kind of craft attempt Priest Rapids, for white water rafting was not yet a sport. Donald and Gilbert survived the challenge, and their huge raft beached in front of town for all to see was a manly and virtuous display. Now a new challenge had been set for the young men in the area. Not many took it up, and Gilbert and Donald were the heroes of the rafting fleet for several years.

White Bluffs, and without doubt Hanford too, seemed to never run out of amusements. Perhaps that wasn't so much true for the families who lived away from the river and towns, who remember riding or driving their wagons to get to important occasions. But this meant five or eight miles, not twenty or thirty, as it could be for the dry farmers up on the Slope, who might once a year travel for over a day to get the the Fourth of July celebration at Moses Lake. Or, as another contrast, Annie Greenwood writes of her Idaho wheat ranch life, that even though the awesome Snake River Canyon was easy driving distance from their farm they went there infrequently. Annie would have loved more time in the canyon, but finding anyone with time to take her and all her children was the problem. Though the Wheeler siblings have their individual perspectives on what made life in White Bluffs special, they all agree that it was the Columbia at the heart of the magic.

The contributors to the *Family Histories* also agree that "nothing to do" was never a problem for the youth in that isolated valley. However, they admit it was not the same for their parents, that is, they had plenty to do but far less recreation. The men and women who went on the group "auto tours" of the 1920s, stopping to lunch together at the hotel at White Bluffs or Hanford, were not the fulltime irrigators. Margaret recalls:

> If it hadn't been for the Fourth of July and the
> County Fair, some men might have left their orchards
> and fields during summer only to eat and sleep. Our
> father and grandfather were more the exception than
> the rule.

The cultural entertainment at White Bluffs did not provide everything for everyone. Jeanie, and no doubt a few other members of the Women's Club, missed the concerts and lectures they would have enjoyed in a city. Jeanie did the next best thing. Though she didn't dance herself, she was ever willing to go along as a chaperone to youth dances. In fact, her daughters comment, they felt at the time that she went altogether too often. But she went to enjoy herself and listen to the live music, not to glower at the youth, and so she was called on frequently. But she would have done this anywhere she lived. Jeanie's real gift from the desert—the irrigated desert—was the chance to create a magnificent flower garden, and many of her neighbors enjoyed this same pleasure. They relished the time spent among their flowers and flowering shrubs that created shade, moisture and sweet aromas around their houses. Though Jane settled mainly for flowering shrubs and other perennials, Jeanie's garden was a special sight, for she raised a great range of annuals as well. If she was irritated by events or needed to get out of the hot house, it was only a few steps to a little paradise she had created herself, kept lush with a hose from an irrigation ditch, and full of bees and butterflies.[1]

Reading continued to be the ultimate indoor recreation for both Jeanie and Frank; desert living didn't change that. Although there is no way to gauge how common reading for pleasure was, there is a suggestion in the Women's Club strong push for a local library. Another quiet form of relaxation for most women and some men, but unlike basketball never to be reported in the local papers, was letter writing. For Jeanie it was a treasured daily pastime except during a rush harvest. Helen says, "After we were put on a rural mail route, our red flag for mail pick-up was always up. Mom would search for the last penny in the house to get that letter mailed." The reward was guaranteed; if one sent out five letters one could expect at least two back. Those correspondents are what made this story possible.

11

THE HEALTHY LIFE

"I hated being stuck at home. I could figure out how to travel
with three little children, but I knew I couldn't make it with four.
My goose was cooked; I was staying home."

Jeanie Wheeler, to her daughter Marian as an adult

WHEN THE WHEELERS became full time residents at White Bluffs they
had already spent eleven summers there and felt confident of one thing: if
they never became successful farmers, they had been right in their choice of
a healthy place to raise a family. They could look not only at their own
condition but at how the other settlers fared. The school was quick to send
word if any epidemics threatened. If they didn't hear of an accident or
illness from the children, they could hear it at the store, church, or post
office. Even though the mortality records from the early years burned in a
courthouse fire, we have much evidence of how the settlers fared. Martha
Parker's research of the regional papers and the *Family Histories* accounts
are enriched with Wheeler letters that reported the family health news.

The valley was full of hazards, so it is intriguing that fatal accidents
were so few. People from an early age were going barefoot, riding horses, on
or in the river, climbing the bluffs, and working under a blazing sun on
ladders. People allergic to bees were hiving them. Valley residents left their

houses unlocked. Rabid coyotes at rare times ran through the village, and the valley was quarantined for rabies starting in 1915. People drank river water without boiling it and had primitive means to keep food chilled. The number of deaths from all of these obvious dangers is remarkably low, though it is more difficult to say how many were injured and survived intact.

Not one of our sources mentions anyone in the irrigated area being bitten by a rattlesnake. Helen remembers reports of three fatalities up on the plateau, and she herself was almost bitten when out on a desert picnic as a child. But rattlesnakes did not come into the orchards. In contrast, up on the Plateau, Laura Lage tells of how by the time she was twelve she had learned how to kill every rattler she saw with a stick. No one died of bee shock, either, although twice the Wheelers sat for long hours with Rose's husband, then with Donald, each in coma from a bee sting. No one died of rabies; the two neighbors of the Wheelers that were bitten by a coyote went to the county hospital and were given the Pasteur treatment. One man died from a fall from a horse near Hanford, one died from a bull-goring at White Bluffs, another from a malfunction of his heater at his whiskey still hidden in a well house. One professional well digger died in a cave-in, and one youth in a one-car accident. One man was suspected to have perished from the lead-arsenate spray in use, but there was no proof of this. A small list indeed for farming accidents.

Most amazing was the survival on water, considering how much of the time young people, in particular, spent on the river. In thirty-seven years no one drowned in the Hanford Ditch, and only four on the swift, cold river. One was the ferry master, and two were boys from out of the area. In contrast, Annie Greenwood reports that a child drowned nearly every year in the ditch that ran near her Idaho farm, including a close call for one of her own.

Few valley children were overprotected. But if the Wheelers are a fair example, their children remember being lectured regularly about certain dangers and especially about the river. Helen remembers there were specific activities that were forbidden until they could prove they were strong swimmers, and older children were always to watch the younger ones. Younger ones were not to float on logs. Yet like kids everywhere they could disobey, and Helen and Donald both admit that at about five years, each of them got in over their heads and were pulled out by older swimmers. Helen remembers at six going out in the boat with another small child to catch a log and falling in. Somehow she was able to climb back out. She remembers being an inattentive babysitter and allowing three small children to sneak out onto the log boom—the worst memory she has of White Bluffs—but she was able to keep her wits and coax them slowly back to safety. Marian Wheeler, a strong swimmer, in two instances brought back non-swimmers who got out too far.

The only explanation for the survival rate of youth on the river and Ditch is a combination of respect, good instruction, and a lot of luck. One wonders if it is more evidence, too, of the general intelligence of the valley people, and the fact that although many men drank, usually it was not while in boats. The exception to that was during the "dry" years when men rowed to and from the saloon on the east side of the river. Their good luck is unexplainable.

The rate of non-mortal injury is harder to uncover. The Wheelers do not remember men with missing limbs—there wasn't that much machinery—nor broken backs or necks from horse falls. One man mangled his arm in the gears of his spray pump, but the arm was saved. Overheated people did fall off high ladders in the orchards. Margaret remembers seeing her father fall off one and watching him get up to resume picking. The hernia rate was high, we know, from the rejection rate at Selective Service. (Frank's untreated hernia was caused from a pitchfork handle jab to the abdomen when riding a jerking hay wagon). Within the family, the most serious injury aside from that was Jane's broken ankle. There was another "horse injury", a grandchild's broken arm, and that was the extent of broken bones in four generations of Shaw/Wheelers at White Bluffs. That seems unbelievable until one remembers the rarity of autos and trucks until the 1930s, and then, their limited speed.

More escapes from accidents have to be attributed to parents' vigilance. Donald and Helen remember the regular lectures about Shaw's bull, about care with tools, especially since they all went barefoot all summer, and about not getting too much sun. They were under strict orders to wear straw hats when working. The heat in summer was, along with the river, the most obvious hazard. People were aware of the seriousness of sunstroke and knew that heat exhaustion, though less serious, had to be watched out for, especially among work crews. Juliette Shaw and Mrs. Brisco, the two registered nurses, were often called to treat people with heat exhaustion, but the Wheelers don't remember anyone dying from the heat. When we recall George Wheeler's words about picking fruit at 110 degrees at the neighbor's, and that the Wheelers commonly worked until the thermometer reached 100 in the shade, this survival rate seems almost as remarkable as that on the river. Again we have to credit the growers with good sense, though some seem to have been pushing the limit at 110.

The Wheelers always had salted water available in the orchard. Frank believed in hot green tea as a coolant, based on his father's experience in India. Whether it was true or not, that was what they had at noon, and cherry juice if available. They took work breaks for a dip in the river as much as reasonable, but were careful after seeing Frank collapse once when he entered the cold water too fast after being overheated. Despite all this care, Marian Wheeler and Rose's oldest child did succumb to the heat on outings and after that could not be in White Bluffs during hot weather.

One more hazard, in particular for orchardists, has already been described: the uses of toxic sprays, and without the recommended masks. The residual effects of lead, for example, were not fully public knowledge until years later. The man at the sprayer was at constant risk of having spray blown back on his bare arms. This did happen to Frank one day and he was in agony by the time he got to the house. A neighbor woman hearing of his plight knew how to use raw potato slices to stop the burning. But no answers are provided for the ongoing and increasing problem of long term toxic effects, especially on youth. It is puzzling how a man so concerned with his family's health as Frank Wheeler endured assigning his children to the spray wagon, a part of orchardry he had been totally unprepared for.

Animals were also at risk from spray. People had to muzzle their horses to keep them from snatching mouthfuls of sprayed grass as they worked in the orchard. The poison would otherwise build up in their system until it was lethal, and Donald remembers people losing horses from it. The Wheelers grieved for their valuable colt when it got through the fence and into the sprayed orchard. When the wind suddenly shifted, whole apiaries of honey bees hived nearby were sometimes lost. The distress over the spraying problems continued to build over the years without solution.

With the two glaring exceptions of the spraying and to a lesser extent the heat, the valley seems to have turned out as the settlers hoped, a place for a healthy life. The real test came during the Depression when there was so much less money available for medical help, and people had only their neighbor nurses to turn to. Then people who had gardens and orchards were far better off. Marian worried that they weren't getting enough meat. What she meant was that they missed beef, for their diet even in the worst times included adequate protein in chicken, eggs, and (too many) dried peas and beans. Despite the benefits of irrigation, during those years some families did not have adequate gardens. Even the Wheeler's did not always cover all their needs, says Donald, through a late frost or some other mishap. There were also families who did not own garden land, and unless they were given produce, they suffered. Vitamin pills were known by the 1920s but rarely in use; few could afford them. Yet compared to unemployed people in the cities, or to dry farming ranches with inadequate gardens, most of the valley dwellers ate well. Local families even organized a food donation program so that the school children could have a free hot lunch.

The tradition of families caring for their own health was still accepted routine when the irrigators arrived in the valley and it was to their benefit. Although they always did have a nurse available, sometimes a doctor, and instigated the traveling well-baby clinic, families expected to care for their ill members, their elderly, and their children mainly on their own, and to know when outside help was needed. This expectation is obvious in the letters of the Wheelers. Helen remembers their diagnostic and nursing skills:

> Mom knew to send a urine sample to the hospital
> in Kennewick on the stage, and she suspected the
> "inward" goiter in Margaret, and was able to get other
> problems diagnosed in her children. She and Dad knew
> enough to send Rose to a specialist in Tacoma in the
> middle of the Depression when a train fare was a large
> problem. Grandma was the one who diagnosed my
> early TB.[1]

The settlers came to the desert in part to escape children's epidemics, and in that they were mainly successful. "Too successful", says Helen, "Except for me, our bunch all had to suffer through measles, chicken pox and mumps as adults living elsewhere." Though typhoid broke out among some homesteader families near Richland earlier, it didn't come to White Buffs/Hanford. Helen also caught whooping cough and rheumatic fever; she was the youngest and by then the valley was less isolated. She doesn't remember polio being a special concern.She and Donald would have remembered deaths of school chums as traumatic. Apparently there were five or less. They remember that one boy died from tetanus, one from rheumatic fever, and one small girl from diphtheria. As teens, they would not have known so much about babies' deaths, but other people remember five childhood deaths. This seem a small number for three decades in a town of 300 to 600, in pre-antibiotic days.

Especially important, the Spanish influenza seemed to have largely spent itself by the time it arrived in still isolated White Bluffs. Although not far away at Pullman over forty inducted men died at a training center and the valley was quarantined for school and public meetings, the Wheelers don't remember death as an outcome for anyone. In the family only Donald, five, caught that terrible flu and recovered in three days.

But isolation, space, nutrition, and climate, important as they were, don't get all the credit for the good health of White Bluffs children. The work of the Women's Club to organize the volunteer staffing for the traveling well-baby clinic was vital. "I can't prove it, but I know that clinic saved lives," says Helen. One positive outcome of the war was the recognition that more attention was needed to youths' health, and school medical exams were begun across the country.

The exceptions to the valley's fine bill of physical health were four. hernia, goiter, deutch disease and .tuberculosis. TB, the very plague people came to the desert to escape, followed them there. Several valley families lost young adults during an outbreak in the late 1920s-early 1930s. The Wheelers worried constantly over it and were sure that the "flapper" fad of slimness and the dieting that went with it were a factor in the deaths from tuberculosis of two of Rose's high school classmates. Rose starved herself but did not catch it. Another widespread problem was goiter. The Wheelers remember the deaths of two women with "inward" goiters, untreated until too late. Margaret and Rose both had thyroid imbalance. The most widespread problem was dental disease. There may have been a common factor in the last two problems, for although everyone was proud of the purity of the Columbia in that district, it was too pure, too lacking in minerals.

Dental care was an ongoing issue for the Wheeler family, reaching the point of havoc during the Depression. Treatment was put off when everything seemingly more urgent had to come first. Though children were given iodine pills at school, fluoride pills were not yet available, and even when a dentist was in town, the cash may not have been there. One thing we do know—all the abscesses and lost teeth in the valley can't be blamed on rare soda pop and candy. Children would have had a better start in the 1920-30s if the medical profession had encouraged breast feeding, but it was out of fashion.

Today Americans feel they should to be able to get to an emergency room and doctor as needed, but at White Bluffs this usually meant arranging a trip to Kennewick. A few families report in the *Family Histories* that they left the valley because of illness, death, or fear that they could not get help in time. Without doubt, there were decided risks in living so isolated, but in turn the isolation spared them from other risks—many epidemics, and especially from the social illnesses of cities.

Jeanie Wheeler, despite all the pressures on her, turned out to have the best health in the family. She said it came from all the beaver meat she had eaten as a child, but in truth she inherited the Niven constitution from her mother's side, those tiny girls, any one of whom could "do what three men could." Longevity came with it. All Niven women seemed to live into their eighties or nineties, and Jeanie herself to 104, so she can not be used as a gauge of the typical area health.

Frank needed to worry about his own health more than that of his wife and children, but still he would live to be eighty. He had the problems that typically plague working men. He neither drank nor smoked and was spared lung disease and alcoholism. But in addition to chronic dental problems, he suffered with bunions, rheumatism, neuralgia, and lumbago that all started, not in White Bluffs, but with outdoor work in the wind and rain of Puget Sound. He suffered arsenic burns and skin cancer from work in the smelters. Even in balmy June his joints could bother him: "My rheumatism is 50% better. Iv had a fierce week as I did not care to quit....it would be a dismal vacation if I fall flat....

Frank referred to his "home doctor book" when he said, "What I must do is to go on a vegetarian diet but I dont. I get fruit enough but to simply add it is not enough in my case." He loved good food, Margaret remembers, and couldn't refuse it. He struggled with his weight, especially after he was less active, and finally in his old age, arteriosclerosis. The debate over cholesterol had not begun. Everyone believed in the high value of their butter and eggs, including the *Home Physician,* and would not have listened to anything else. Many people also believed that their rheumatism was related to their bad teeth.

Frank's only health problem brought on by farming was the aforementioned hernia. We wonder if it was just lack of funds that caused him, and so many men, to postpone the operation. Donald thinks not. "Corrective surgery for hernia was not all that advanced then, and he apparently chose not to risk it." The Wheelers knew at least two people who had died from complications during operations. This must have left the family believing that surgery was the very last resort. However, for many families in the valley, lack of cash would also have been a consideration. Health insurance was unknown.

We can't know for sure what went on in Frank's mind about his hernia.

Unlike today, in many families too much talk about one's health was in bad taste if not taboo. Donald says that the matter of his father's hernia and truss was too personal to bring up to him. This went along with the general reserve in those days about personal matters. Unfortunately, because of this, there are areas of health, like chronic disease or mental health, where we will never know how the ideal "small irrigators' community" worked out in real life. People tended to endure such things as rheumatism as best they could. If it became too much, they had to move to town where they could get more treatment. Several of the Wheelers, for example, suffered from migraine, and there was little they could do for it. None of the health problems the Wheeler children had seem related to the valley environment or to the rigorous work they did.

As for mental health at White Bluffs, Helen remembers two cases of women who suffered "nervous breakdowns" and were sent to the state hospital. Jeanie wrote of one resident who committed suicide after his wife died, and people suspected another suicide. Helen remembers that one family had small graves in their backyard that no one talked about. People wouldn't be aware of the proportion of their neighbors who suffered quietly from personal losses, depression, or sense of social ostracism., so we can't know. We would say today that the reserve on such topics went too far to be healthy. Marian Wheeler, for example, says that she was grown up before her mother told her that the reason Juliette and Win Shaw had no children was that all of their babies had died before or after birth.

Marian adds:

> And here Juliette was, always going out to help
> other women give birth. If we had only known that, we
> would have understood her better, why she acted as if
> she didn't like Mom, and said such bitter things to her
> about her babies. Like her refusing to be midwife for

Mom, and her comment on Don's birth that 'some
people breed like pigs.' Why didn't Mom tell us?

But Jane and Jeanie didn't talk about other people's personal business
with the children. Another concern—pregnancies and birth
control—affected most women, and Jeanie's problem of too frequent births
was a common one. Again, she couldn't talk to anyone about it except her
husband. Some women could not have done that. Later, more relaxed on
such topics, she admitted that pregnancies every other year for the first four
(living) children had affected her morale. When Marian, the fourth, came
along she was angry. Later she explained to Marian, "I hated being stuck at
home, and I could figure out how to travel with three little children, but I
knew I couldn't make it with four. My goose was cooked; I was staying
home." Jeanie apparently got a second wind, but Marian feels she suffered
emotional neglect. Fortunately, Frank was very fetched with her and gave
her ample attention when he was home, Helen and Donald noticed. Every
one of them was vying for his attention as little children; he just wasn't home
enough.

Still later, Margaret questioned her mother on related topics too
personal for earlier times. Why hadn't Jeanie tried to get contraception?
Jeanie told her that she had indeed finally gotten up her nerve to ask a
doctor for something, and he had refused her. She didn't try again, too
embarrassed by his response to a request so inappropriate and illegal.
Contraceptives were legal only if to prevent disease. Frank apparently could
not take any such humiliating steps either. Jeanie went on to bear two more
children, her "goose cooked". Helen was the seventh and last Wheeler baby;
Margaret Sanger won her battle for legal birth control just after Helen was
born. After that Frank and Jeanie must have figured out a means of birth
control. At least raising such a large brood surely was easier in White Bluffs
than in Tacoma. "We saved a lot in shoe leather," Helen remembers, "going

barefoot all summer."

Even with such a good quantity of civic and social life in White Bluffs there obviously were private stresses and tragedies that people in general, but especially women, had to endure. White Bluffs families had mortgages just like farm families everywhere. The U.S. Dept. of Agriculture 1916 Yearbook even felt it had to be mentioned, "More midland farmers' wives died of mortgage than of TB and cancer together. ..."

Since the *Family Histories* are based on children's perceptions, and they speak of family hardships with the typical restraint, we are fortunate to have Annie Greenwood's unusually open reflections on the life of wheat irrigators. She felt there was relentless stress on the women in particular, whereas the men got some breaks in the off-seasons from their crops. She comments that these laboring women could all expect to bear a child every two years, and that they could expect to lose some of them. Annie mentions women "going crazy", and including herself, twice. But these were women on isolated ranches.

Of the Wheelers, Jeanie and Rose personified how full-time valley life didn't measure up for everyone. Starting with Margaret's first departure for school, the rest of the youth were coming and going, fairly freely, from an early age. That is, no one forced them to stay on the farm when they had a good excuse to be venturing forth. The idea in Frank's mind for Jeanie was that she would have a vacation away from White Bluffs every year, and he made every effort to hold to that. She went to the World's Fair in Chicago with Helen; she went to see the Queen of Rumania when the Maryhill Museum was dedicated at Sunnyvale; she went many times to Hoquiam and Seattle, though usually taking the youngest child or two. Sometimes her annual vacations didn't happen for financial reasons. Then she lost her spirit, and her letters showed it.

After Rose married a local farmer she had a farm woman's typical responsibilities that kept her home. Her first three babies were every two years, and she had a husband who was gone ten hours a day, every day, working for others and trying to build up his farm. Helen remembers that from a fun-loving tomboy and teen, Rose gradually became a reclusive housewife, not feeling well, taking little interest in anything but her children but some days too depressed even for them, and Helen would go to help. Aside from thyroid imbalance, her problems were that of many young farm wives trapped in a role of boring routines with no extra cash. Yet she must have suffered more than others for she had been so active and adventurous to start with, never a domestic flower. There was nothing very exciting for her in the community activities available to the farm wives. Her parents understood that she had chosen a road that didn't allow her creative spirit and artistic talent any outlet. We assume that there were other White Bluffs women who felt similarly trapped but resigned themselves to it or simply left the valley. By the time Jeanie and Frank had a crop of teenagers, they realized that what was a grand life for young children might not be the answer for every young adult.

We also can't know the amount of domestic violence in the little community. Even though Helen says no one ever mentioned rape by that name to her, that none ever occurred doesn't seem likely, considering the fair amount of drinking that took place. As for other domestic problems, Helen says, "The only spouse beating I recall hearing about was a woman who badly beat up her husband with a heavy skillet!" That was news. The corollary, a man beating his wife, apparently wasn't. When it came to abuse of children, we know the community didn't tolerate sexual abuse if they heard of it. In contrast, since it was still the accepted fashion to beat children, especially boys, who didn't behave, that activity wasn't important news. Nor was it likely to be news that a family was working their youth too hard. If certain youth were not allowed to come to public functions, or kept home from school more than usual, that would get community notice. Probably some of this happened, but the overriding memory of the Wheelers, corroborated by the *Family Histories*, is that of happy childhood.

As the community aged, the health and care of the original settlers of the first decade inevitably became problems. These grandparents now required a return on the care that they had earlier given to others. But this came to pass as the community was entering the hardest times of the Great Depression. These were times when the government, usually the county, gave assistance only to the totally destitute, and there was no social security or other federal aid until the late 1930s. Jane and most of her neighbors, were physically active into their early eighties or longer, which may have influenced their living to a healthy advanced age. As the brochures had promised, there was plenty of light labor for everyone, even ninety-year-olds.

The health of precious animals was sometimes more worrisome than their own for the settlers. The death of one cow could be a catastrophe for a family, totally different from that same loss for a cattle herder. Vigilance in fence repair was important, and Margaret remembers that the Shaw/Wheeler fences were not always in top shape. She describes one of the children rushing in to tell Jeanie that the cow had broken through the fence and was down. "Mother found her lowing with pain, bloating in the fresh alfalfa. No men were around; she had to run and grab the trocar, the special curved knife, rush to the cow, and before she could worry too much about a wrong move, plunge it into the cow's belly to release the gases." That cow, and Jeanie, survived the trauma, but one of their jersey heifers killed itself in an accident.

Worst of all was the loss of Ribbon, their fine Morgan mare. Her only two colts were also lost—the first from breaking through the fence and getting into the orchard spray, and the second from a broken leg due to slipping on ice in the yard. Frank was not there and was terribly upset over the carelessness of his team. Ribbon could never be bred again—the only stallion had left the valley— and finally she was stolen. These events, and of course there were others, point out how difficult it was for small orchardists to find and keep even a modest number of animals, and how the smallest bit of carelessness or bad luck, just as with orchardry, could lead to great, and in the case of Ribbon, practically tragic loss. The Wheelers had better luck with their human family. Aside from the inevitable effects of aging, the valley turned out to be, in terms of the settlers' health, exactly what they had hoped for. The illness they couldn't beat back was in the economy.

12

MY DEAR JEANIE

"I'll try to get quiet long enough to write. I did a big washing this morning, was just finishing when O'Briens sent for me to hive some bees....Then I came home and made three pairs of bloomers..."
Jeanie Wheeler, letter to her husband, 1922

THE WHEELER'S NEW ORCHARD was timed to begin bearing by the time George graduated from high school, when they would face the expense of three children out at college. The farm debt was not excessive, and Walter Niven kindly agreed to wait a few years for payback on his loans. The family need only keep up the interest payments. But the timing was off due to the necessary time for trees to mature. The postwar market had already begun its downward slide as the new trees were being shipped from the nursery. Jeanie, with a larger farm to operate, and with her partner still absent, had to keep her thoughts positive, away from her account books.

The Wheelers were now people of the valley and with their neighbors had built a community of beauty. No matter what the market, where else would Jeanie find the incredible bluffs to gaze at each evening, or blossoming orchards backed by desert wild flowers each spring morning? Nowhere else could she step out the door into her own paradise of flowers, or feast each day on fresh fruit, berries, and melons they had grown themselves, or sit down to a table with a center piece of fragrant honeycomb. Nowhere else could she be so free from worry about her children.

It was so important for her to hold onto all this as she faced each morning an unending list of important tasks, and tried to muster enthusiasm in her youthful team, who didn't take it all nearly as serious as she thought they should. Nor would it do any good to pass on her worries to them. Frank tried as usual to do his part in decision-making and giving moral support through correspondence. The pressure he felt is obvious in the testiness of the letter following, where he talks about their new acreage and about another small loan. Fortunately his partner/wife didn't get too many letters like this one, with nary an interesting metaphor:

> (no date) My dear Jeanie,
>
> I really thot I was as clear as could be that I wish the pipe in, not half in. I ordered 1000 ft. The end section is the best patch we have. A lot in the middle is hardly practical as I showed you. But the water has to go clear over this section. Please get John back and finish as it is foolish to run the water so far and stop. And there is no reason not to try some peaches. Please don't leave it that way. Of course we want alfalfa. I wished all this to go in one note at the bank. It simply has to go. That would be the limit to leave 140 by 350 feet deep dry when it is level and cleared, over an acre. I can't imagine what I wrote to cause you to stop there. And ask Charley about our house water.... And eat some more chickens quick. I'm sending MJ [Margaret Jean] ten and you the balance. But don't worry when I have the work..... I hope Geo

has it in his bean somewhere so that nothing can drive
it out. We can plan where [where he would go to
college] later. With all my love, sincerely, Frank

If Frank had kept this letter a day and reread it, he surely would have
tempered it a little, knowing what burdens she had, but that was not his
style. It got stamped and went out in the next mail. No doubt her answer
started as so many of hers did, "I will sit down and take a few minutes to
write something." Behind her we can imagine the scene: It is eight pm, the
supper dishes are stacked up waiting for a dishrag; a pile of clothes is
waiting while the laundry water heats on the wood stove; another pile,
vegetables, is on the kitchen table, waiting to be cut up for the canning jars,
that water also heating. As long as water must be heated, better all at once.
It is eighty degrees outside, closer to ninety in the kitchen, but soon it will be
cooling off. The Grange meeting has been postponed, alas. George is out
milking. Margaret is away at high school. The rest of the gang is nowhere to
be found.

Jeanie was not happy with her success developing her work crew.
During her spouse's long absences, she wrote him regularly of the chores
undone or accompanied by altogether too much horseplay. She was
exasperated with the older children—Rose, George and Marian—now
already teens or soon to be. She had, consciously or unconsciously, tried to
create a replacement for the absent Margaret in Rose and had failed. Rose,
fifteen, detested both housework and authority and had no intention of
becoming a second Margaret, much as she admired her. George, at thirteen
a good worker handling most of the outside chores, loved scrapping with his
fond Rose, and she felt the same enthusiasm. Their racket drove Jeanie to
tears.

Eleven-year-old Marian, though she would help out with the
housework, resented that her older sister preferred being off with George,

not helping her. She had a sassy tongue her mother and grandmother despaired of—no doubt her only defense—and was often embattled with her siblings. She says they teased her constantly, and she admits she teased the next in line, Donald, now eight, and already taking over much of George's work. Though Helen believed that Marian was her daddy's darling, Marian remembers how jealous she was of Donald. Donald says that he in turn was eaten alive by jealousy of "Jewel Baby" Helen, now four. Though neither he nor Helen rebelled so much against parental suggestions, Helen says that Donald teased her incessantly in clever ways that wouldn't be noticed by others. A typical approach was, "Some folks say there are rabid coyotes living over in those willows, but I don't think so, do you, Helen?" But she wouldn't tell on him, as she adored him. Helen adored the world.

Jeanie had her own adventurous side but had always been dutiful, and never rowdy or sassy to her mother and father. She didn't understand children, especially girls, who didn't behave the same way. Margaret had followed in the dutiful tradition, which made it hard to understand where the model had failed. Her crew could have done all the work quickly, in her opinion, if they had simply settled down to their tasks. She had no trouble in the classroom commanding the troops, so why did she fail at home? The children were well-fed and cared for, and knew what was proper, of course. To Jeanie, the problem had to be that the children needed their father. Those children admit that until much later, they didn't recognize the trials they put their mother through even though she told them often enough.

When Frank returned for a time, the "Father of Many Wildcats" as he had dubbed himself after his initials "FMW", calmed their boisterous behavior to a semblance of a peaceful home. His presence was an occasion for special food, recognition of achievements, humor, and less scolding from their mother. His table was a place of hospitality, but also a place to practice manners or get thumped on the head by his annoyed thumb. When guests were present, and the menu happened to be enticing to the young, they had to be especially careful. Frank had a code phrase he uttered as he saw his children reaching for the serving dish as it passed. "FHB", he would signal them, "Family Hold Back" They knew to listen. Behavior changed not only at table. Frank didn't allow his children to be disrespectful to their mother at any time, so if they felt the urge to be sassy, they had to wait until their father was at least out of hearing, if not out of town. When he left again, Jeanie missed her husband in many ways.

The parents had important rules for their own behavior as well, one being an understanding that they would never quarrel on personal issues in front of their children. Donald says, " I heard them argue over farming matters, as partners, but nothing personal." Reading Frank and Jeanie's exchanges of irritated letters during those years, Helen shakes her head, "I don't recognize those parents, I didn't know them." Whether all that public self control seems healthy depends on the culture one is coming from, but it was their culture, and it added to Jeanie's pressure over the squabbling of her offspring.

That fall Rose, like Margaret, needed to get out to a real high school, and they made arrangements for her to stay one year with Jeanie's brother Jim, and one year with Frank's sister Rohilla. Her letter reporting her train trip offers a window on her mischievous sense of humor:

> Dear Mother, Janet and I enjoyed our trip over.
> We had from about 1:30 to 8:15 at Beverly to wait
> [for the Milwaukee mainline]. We walked clear out on
> the r.r. bridge and the wind was blowing so hard we
> absolutely could not stand up without holding to the
> railing. Janet's glasses blew off but luckily fell where she

could rescue them. Then we went to call on a lady
called Mrs. Penn. We didn't know her name before
that. The school teacher at Beverly got $150 per month
last year for teaching five kids. The Beverly Hotel is the
dirtiest hangout I ever saw. A very important railroad
man helped us on and off the trains. I believe every
hobo in Beverly winked at us. We talked a lot to that
cute little fellow I told you about that I first saw on the
bluffs. By the way there was a woman who was having
hysterics over us. Thought we ought to telegraph, etc.
She fairly raved. I will tell you of the visit with aunt
Rohilla in the second installment. Your daughter, Rose.

Aunt Rohilla had special fondness for Rose, so the move worked well for
her, while for Jeanie one less child to argue with may have made it easier.
But she was not the only one with dissatisfactions. Though Frank avoided
serious bickering with his wife or children, we have seen that he was often
exasperated with his neighbors. Yet, he did not give up on the idea that
partnerships were beneficial, and now with George Shaw on his own, Frank
had the larger spread that could use another team member. Donald says,
"Over the years my father made several efforts to bring in others on various
ventures, but none of these schemes materialized, and perhaps it was just as
well." Frank exempted whole races and classes from his bite, but individuals
who charged his patience weren't so lucky. Knowing how much he wished to
travel, but not just to job sites, Margaret wrote him at least once to
encourage him to go with Jeanie on a trip, but the letter caught him on one
of his darker days. He answered with a sweep of satire that covered the
neighborhood, including his mother-in-law:

> If visit anyplace why not Scotland, the modern Holy
> Land? Well Iv had mine. Is not Mrs. Brown flanking me

> on South, Mrs Shaw just as friendly on the West, and did
> I not have Edward of the same austere mind on the East,
> McFee and the other rodents on the North. Now do you
> think Im crazy to travel? As for Sweden, I've had enough
> of that right here too.

Such sardonic remarks, if passed in face-to-face conversation with his family, with the typical quirk of an eyebrow and hint of smile, or even on paper to Margaret alone, came across as humorous, but could have been hard on a partnership. Frank was feeling the shrinking of the spirit suffered in small town life. The pettiness that White Bluffs society could be guilty of didn't surprise him. But its own division into the haves and have-nots, the generous and the overly pious, the crude and the sweet, was here so obvious, even if nothing like the British Empire, even if gentler than Tacoma. Now free of his partnership, Frank's times in his orchard, alone, were probably a happy relief from neighbors and relatives who disappointed him. And recognizing more the shortcomings of rural life would help him to cope with the departure of his children that would inevitably come to pass.

When Frank stayed home, life was calmer, and Jeanie got the support she needed, but then they ran short of funds, and she soon urged him to return to the hiring hall. Her letters to him during the next few years, and his to her, continue the tone of frustration and fatigue.

> (no date, early summer) My dear Frank,
> I'll try to get quiet long enough to write. I did a big
> washing this morning, was just finishing when O'Briens
> sent for me to hive some bees. I also put on a super [a
> new hive start] for them. Then I came home and made
> three pairs of bloomers—to the accompaniment of such
> fighting and quarreling and teasing as I never heard. I
> cannot stop them. I quiver from head to foot. But what's

the use? You'll just tell me how much worse somebody
else's are. One day George knocked the lens out of Rose's
glasses. I thought he had put her eye out. She was only
trying to get him to go with her after the cows. He acts
just like Dad. Begins to tell me how I always take the
girls' part and never listen to him! I would just die if it
wasn't for Margaret....Your $3.50 arrived safely, also
$2.00...

Bricklaying allowed the mind to wander a little, and no doubt Frank
felt badly enough about their situation, to say nothing of his aching bones,
without receiving such desperate letters. But he did his best to try to raise
her spirits with his answer. He started by trying to turn her around on
everything she had said about the children she could no longer manage, but
then realized in time his beloved needed something else. The last part of the
letter any woman would treasure:

My Own Dear Jeanie,

Well, Beloved, Ill bore you a bit about the
children. Now Marian you remember Jeanie she was
just yesterday a very much petted baby—a mighty
resolute little lady at that—but all children are
stubborn at that age as I remember. George will do
very well when Im home Im sure....Rose, will you
remember, was who went back to look for the baby
when the tent was afire and fought with George the
first time to get him out. Youv got lots of annoying things
to contend with, not my wishing, but because iv not
brought you comfort you deserve. I honestly dont know
what you would do if you had sick or deformed children
to care for....Im not trying to lecture Beloved or arouse

you to say "it is just because your slack and dont care." Every woman I know delights to tell her hubby that he is to be blamed because the children dont mind. Every woman and every womans mother. I dont know if they believe it or not...I dont know what to think sometimes. I dont believe that all the annoyances that children inflict is as much as what older people try to load others up with needlessly every day just out of wanton spite.

Im glad we never got where we enjoy quarreling. I think I remember every rough word I ever spoke to you Jeanie, and if I could take them back and put in My Own girl, or My Own Lovely Lady or Beloved, or Heart of Me, or The best and finest of them all, the sum of them, scolding locks and all,—Jeanie—and to a degree Id wish the children to remember me as a kind fair generous man than to tell how exact or severe or remembered by some selfish tricks.

Life is too short—twenty years and I look to them for satisfaction and a little longer I hope for what? Just an Eternity of Mercy and Kindness. Others can seek what they wish: Id like your Love, to understand your feeling and thoughts and feel the real thing possessed. To grow into it, not distant and hard. And if you delight and charm me with your tenderness and satisfy me, and the childrens hearts turn back home with real longing, isnt that the beginning of a better World? Id love to get out of the fret and worry Jeanie. We'll do our best but I wish this first. I like to feel that when you lay aside the trouble and you drop asleep that I would

fain wrap you up in the comfort of my love and feel
your blood run right through my heart, warm and
young and sweet. Frank

What frustration this husband and father must have felt that he could not somehow bring his tribe to that oasis of economic security that forever retreated out across the sage and sand.

Within two years Jeanie decided that she might feel a sense of economic progress if she at least moved from the tents to a real house. Frank agreed. The "green house" was not such a great step forward. It was far too small for the family, smaller than the tents, only half the place her mother had, even with the good porch they built onto it. But how could she ever invite her club women over to a "temporary" tent, having now farmed for almost two decades? But other improvements came with the house. This was when fifteen-year-old George stepped forward with his off-farm earnings that paid for a well and electric power. Telephone installation at the Shaw house came about the same time. But the phone was only for business, and the lights were purely for pleasure. Now they all read together in the living room, uninterrupted by wick trimming and flame adjustments, though still crowded under the one light bulb allowed.

A letter from late spring, 1924, tells that Jeanie's dreams of playing hostess to the club inevitably added to her worries. Helen had been ill at home with whooping cough and relapse for months. Every day Jane came to spend two hours with her so that Jeanie could get outside a bit, or at least get some project finished. Now finally Jeanie had gotten organized to have the ladies over for a tea party, and a horde of bedbugs attacked. They had just driven off Jane's boarding teachers, only to arrive at Jeanie's house; it meant social humiliation with that important group, the Women's Club:

My dearest,

I'll take precious daylight to write you—was going

257

·

to Friday, but fumigated and didn't have the light. Monday, fumigated again. Friday, used sulfur candles—three in living room, that just pepped the b.b. all up— evidently the strength of the sulfur was gone. Yesterday we bought 5 formaldehyde fumigators and laboriously stuffed door and window cracks. Left closed for seven hours. This so rejuvenated the bbs that they are fairly cakewalking all over the place in squads of three and four. All other pestilences fade into the background—wind, heat, flies, mice, turkeys, chickens, my loving neighbor, my dying flowers, inconvenient water—believe me the ancient Egyptian with his plagues had nothing on me! Out of it I expect to achieve either a case of nervous breakdown or a highly developed sense of humor—haven't quite decided which. You notice I didn't mention any big worries like frozen crop, lack of money, absence of better half, etc. I have to think hard and frequently of M.J.'s scholarship, George's success [graduating at sixteen] and of Helen's "recovery"... Thirteen weeks of nothing at all is a long time for such an active little person.

There will be 25 or 35 boxes of Carmans, and 150 or 200 boxes of Elbertas. I'll need today's money for May water bill., I took last week's for April water, and next week is for 1/2 taxes. I don't dare let it go. The club meets here tomorrow. I am most desperate for fear of bedbugs greeting the eyes of Mrs Taylor or Mrs McFee. It was 121 on back porch for three days—all flowers in bed succumbed. It was 97 on front porch.

Lots of love, Jeanie

Under the black humor one can sense that she is stretched to the limit of her endurance, only to lose her beloved flowers too. And no discreet way to steer the Club to another meeting place. It is impossible today to imagine trying to entertain in temperatures over 100 in any case. When one compares Jeanie's letters to Annie Greenwood's view of a farm woman's existence, we appreciate better Jeanie's tremendous physical and mental strength. Annie, writing her version of farm economics, says, "The cost of wheat, to be just, must take into consideration the world's greatest as yet unfreed slave, the farm woman." If Jeanie thought that, she never said it.

Jane's close-by support was surely vital to her daughter as she wondered why she had ever given up being a housewife in Tacoma, now to run a farm twice as big as before, her father with a separate spread, and her husband still gone most of the time. Yet, right next door was that tiny pillar of energy, dedication, and encouragement, plus an invitation to dinner when her daughter succumbed to a few tears. Instead of giving in to despair, Jeanie fled the confusion of her household for her mother's, or the peace of the packing house, her flower garden, a good book, or correspondence with a little dry humor thrown in. When the mood struck, she left the dinner dishes, took off her apron, and walked down the road to one of her service clubs.

Margaret, years later and now a trained counselor, commented that her mother had more understanding than any of them of how to keep one's mental and physical health while turning out an amazing load of work:

> ...At the time, like all other youngsters, I did not
> appreciate all the qualities of my mother. Did not
> realize at what cost she coaxed roses out of the sand,
> party dresses from old trunks, white sheets out of the old
> hand wringer, and appetizing meals out of a sometimes

skimpy larder. But I did, very young, appreciate the ardorousness of her labor, the intrepid way she could plunge a trocar knife into the belly of a bloated cow, pour cascara down a sick pig, hive the newly swarmed bees and take off the supers, all this while my father was gone working in other parts of the country.

I did appreciate her heavy responsibilities of running a farm, never neglecting her duties. She walked miles through the heat to pick berries for some cash, she cared for other people's kids and was ingenious at figuring ways to get children clad, to a doctor, back and forth to the coast, always to school and picnics—girls in whites, embroidered, boys in homemade shirts. No emergency was not met.

...She substituted at the school, tutored many children, taught Sunday School, worked away from home many hours a day in season at the fruit packing sheds... Gradually her interest in flowers and shrubs became a passion. She never bought herself a garment if she could buy a rosebush.

From Margaret and Helen, her oldest and her youngest, we understand that it was beauty as well as friends and family that gave this woman her strength. In the love of beauty she and her husband were in perfect accord. By the time Jeanie was seventy, every one of her grandchildren and later most of her great granddaughters had a hooked rag rug from her. Her flower garden would expand in size and variety until it was a showpiece.

Jeanie was not the only mother beside herself with the younger generation, and was indeed one of the most liberal. The restlessness of the

Roaring Twenties had reached the Priest Rapids valley, no place being too isolated. The valley youth distanced themselves as much as possible from the worries of their elders to embrace the new freedom and explore what they could afford of the new consumerism. The Wheeler girls and their chums, used to hard work and doing without, got a mere whiff of the luxuries of the new decade, but knew how to create their own copies. If the mothers refused their orders for the new style of dresses, White Bluffs flappers remodeled their own (and their diets) to emerge suddenly thin and flat-chested. Their parents screamed or stared speechless. Rose came home from the coast with her hair "bobbed like a boy" and complimented Jeanie for saying not a word. She couldn't.

The girls saved their picking and packing money to order the latest dance records and played them at lawn parties on crank-up victrolas. Their boy friends begged the use of the family Model Ts for unheard of freedoms. These sturdy autos remodeled into trucks worked all day hauling feed and milk, to emerge at dusk as sin mobiles tearing along the sand roads at 25 mph in search of a home brew party, or at least a Charlie Chaplin comedy at the movie house. The boys were the drivers and even the mechanics for the auto-trucks every long work day, so it was tough to refuse them. A Grange dance or two was going somewhere in the valley, and the autos and a little gas made it possible, if the roads allowed, to make them all. The parents shook their heads at the new wildness, but many of them continued to enjoy hard cider out in the Grange parking lot on Saturday night.

Real moonshine turned out to be the best way to make money in the valley during Prohibition if you didn't mind a little cops-and-robbers action. But the valley did not become a den of wickedness. There still was little need for law enforcement. "Revenuers" did come through, being fully aware there was only one way to make money from the vineyards on every farm. The Law provided amusement for White Bluffs residents as they watched the lights flashing across the river: lawmen tramping the bluffs searching out the abandoned cisterns where stashes of jugs were hidden. One settler writing in *Family Histories* tells of a truck crossing over on the ferry, then miring in the sand as it tried to crawl up the bluff road, making a spectacle for all as the entrepreneurs unloaded the sacks of sugar in broad daylight.

Charismatic evangelists increased their attention to the valley to offer a contrasting spectacle. They set up their great tents in the city park by the river and may have provided the most exciting evening entertainment of all, nothing like the routine Sunday services droning out somber hymns and hearing the scriptures recited in monotone. Liberal as he was, at that point Frank put his foot down. Helen says that though Wheeler girls could go to dances, they were forbidden to go to the revivals, with no explanation provided. Frank was bored with the prudishness of the Presbyterians, but no doubt liked the emotionalism of the Pentacostals even less. Donald, however, was allowed to go. Perhaps his father saw him as already so skeptical that he could trust him to keep a cool distance.

Frank and Jeanie wondered where they stood on the new outlandishness of the era, but it was decided for them in a happy way through the popularity of their victrola. Jane Shaw, though she wasn't against proper dancing, openly expressed her dismay at the shimmy and at the shocking new bathing suits adorning the beach front. Even modest women could get in enough trouble. But she was ignored along with the rest of her generation.

There were nighttime forays Frank and Jeanie knew nothing of. George remembers:

> There was not much smoking and no drugs at our
> parties. Not much money changed hands—we didn't
> have much. About the only alcohol was hard cider in

season. Not many who graduated from high school were still virgins, male or female. Many of the high school sweethearts remained mated and and married for life.

Oblivious to all this, Frank and Jeanie let their teens go out on more legitimate dates. Frank, if he was home, asked to meet the young gentlemen before they left the yard and put on a fierce face under bushy brows when he shook their hands and established the hour he expected their return. It was half-teasing. The Wheelers trusted their children to use their heads, since they felt they had brought them up that way. They may not have known about the shenanigans or may have known and chose to ignore them. It was a small, a very small town. Donald admits to going to "a few parties" at Black Sand Bar in the late 1920s and wondering just how he made it home.

From today's perspective, Frank and Jeanie seem naive about the pressures young people in the Roaring Twenties were subject to. Yet, whatever skating on thin ice the Wheeler youth may have done, they didn't tend to break through. Helen says, "The folk's greatest worry in all this [or at least the worry she, as a child, was permitted to listen in on] was their fear that my teenaged sisters wouldn't eat and sleep enough, and catch tuberculosis." An epidemic was sweeping the valley. Margaret, on visits home, was taller and thinner each year no matter what she ate. Rose was in love and couldn't eat ; a new young settler had captured her heart..

The youth weren't the only ones to jump into the spirit of the times. The farmers themselves were not immune, especially to the rush for the new mechanized products and easier credit. Suddenly they could have what they needed by simply by setting up charge accounts. The first tractors appeared in White Bluffs, along with equipment for them to pull, certainly not luxuries from any perspective, but the beginning of the credit trap. The valley upper class, such as it was, introduced pure frivolousness with the local auto-touring club. Soon the concern for better county roads—that is, gravel, not sand—swelled the club's numbers.

Frank Wheeler, so radical in his political philosophy, was conservative when it came to the new consumerism. The victrola purchase earlier did not mean he was an easy target. A gas-driven washing machine he had agreed to, and he would think hard about a refrigerator. But he did not rush for a radio, let alone a tractor. Jeanie wasn't that much more enthusiastic. What she really needed was less formidable than a refrigerator: sewing material, new wall paper, some nice dress gloves, but most of all—more flowering plants. Privately she thought an auto wouldn't be so bad. It would be nice to get a around the county a little more in the evening and on Sunday. At least she could get a view of other women's flower gardens even if Frank didn't want to stop and chat.

13

SOLDIER-SETTLERS

"...This time the prospective client didn't have to imagine what an orchard or vineyard would look like; he had only to go out and observe."
Margaret Wheeler Schuddakopf, 1966

BY THE MID-1920S, with the poor farm prices and easier credit, many if not most valley farmers would second-mortgage their farms in order to make their loan payments or pay property taxes on their expanded farms. Many would soon also mortgage their equipment, livestock, and even their crops. The Shaws and Wheelers now found out how fortunate they were that they had switched their loan to their Niven cousin. Donald says, "His loyalty and his understanding of our situation—he had a farm of his own—helped to save both the farms while all around us families of much more means would soon sink themselves."

Though land speculation was a craze throughout the U.S. during and just after the World War, acreage expansion had not been a thoughtless move in the Priest Rapids valley where the original 1907 tracts had been only ten acres. Now, however, the situation looked very different with all the extra fruit of improved quality on the market. Rebuilt European farms were growing their own fruit again, while Americans were not buying enough peaches and cherries. There were now so many other choices to buy in prepared foods and other fashionable and exotic items for the table. But the economy was more imbalanced than it had ever been. By the mid-1920s sixty percent of American families earned less than $2,000 a year, an income economists considered to be the minimum for a family of four to live in modest comfort.

As a laboring man himself, Frank Wheeler well knew that wages were at the prewar level. The labor unions, healthy before WWI, had been thrashed during the reaction that took place during and after the War and they hadn't recovered yet. As for farmers, better marketing through associations had been tried several times and would be tried again, but always succumbed to the competition of the large wholesale commission houses. Of course ordinary Americans could have gladly used all the fine Washington fruit—it didn't need to go to Europe—but other things had to come first. The Grange protested, as they always did, the imbalance between farmers' costs and revenues, but the main help they could give the situation was to start farm supply coops that at least kept some growers' costs down. Free market economists said the problem was overproduction, and that the market would self-adjust.

The new acreage under tillage wasn't the only reason for the "overproduction". Though improved roads were still mainly talk for the Priest Rapids valley, across the country road transportation had much improved. U.S. farmers were less dependent on railroads, and were beginning to truck their produce, faster and cheaper, into the cities. Advancing technology was another ever-increasing pressure. When farmers expanded their acreage, they needed more equipment to manage it. Then, being bound to new equipment loans, they were forced to produce more yet, resulting in more "overproduction".

Mechanization was not yet a big trend for orchardists. Donald remembers, "We still did our pruning and thinning by hand, and pickers still hauled their ladders and carried their bags on their shoulders. Packers still packed each fruit by hand, and most of the growers plowed with a horse or two, and hauled with a sled." But fruit growers were beneficiaries of another trend. In the valley, as elsewhere, the County Agent brought a host of new information on care of land, animal breeding, and horticulture to meetings in the Grange halls. Donald remembers that the meetings were well attended, though not everyone followed the Agent's advice. Some were still outright suspicious of outsider knowledge. But overall the new science succeeded in making the farmers even more productive.

In 1921, 271 railroad cars of fruit were shipped out of the Priest Rapids valley, and that was just one small district. There was no stopping the ever-increasing flood of fruit from the irrigated western states. Paying farmers to take land out of production was, as yet, unheard of, and in any case, how did one take a fruit tree out of production except to kill it? That was the last thing any orchardist would do, they thought. A few years later, they would have to think again, and end up taking steps that were sickening to them.

As if they didn't have bruises enough, about 1923 the orchardists took another blow when all of the fresh fruit commission houses on the West Coast (in defiance of anti-trust laws) raised their handling rates from ten percent to fifteen. Since they couldn't get their prices from the public, they would get them from their growers. Though raising the rates was an industry-wide action, the natural reaction was to personalize it. Donald Wheeler remembers how upsetting it was:

> It was up and down the entire coast, fifteen
> percent. The growers were angry and they stayed
> angry. Some of them turned on the commission men
> that came out to the farms to make deals each year.

But a commission man was just a salaried agent. There was nothing he could do about it; he was just a handy target. It was very tough on everyone. Before this the combined rates of the railroad and the commission house had been half of what the fruit would sell for on the wholesale market. Now the profit margin was even less.

Over the years each grower had developed a seemingly friendly relationship with one or more brokers, while the brokers cultivated their particular growers as steady sources of quality produce for their buyers. The Wheelers/Shaws had a broker named Schroeder they almost always used, an agent of Walter Bowen Co., who did important favors for them. As was customary, he loaned them funds in spring for box materials, fertilizer, or spray. He also arranged with the Milwaukee RR station master to let them place a box of private fruit on top of their shipment to ride freight-free into Seattle for a friend or relative. But the relationship was more than that. When Schroeder came to White Bluffs to recruit growers, he boarded at Jane Shaw's, and often ate with the Wheelers. Donald says, "Dad did not blame Schroeder personally for the rate increase; he knew better. But some people did point at the brokers, and their relationship soured."

Inexplicably, while one group of economists was crying "overproduction", another group, pressured by land speculators, argued to the government once more that a way to help unemployment in the cities was to send more people out to become farmers. Conservationists joined in, with that era's view of conservation, arguing that Dustbowl farmers driven out by drought could move farther west to try irrigation. Again this movement was successful. Through the Bureau of Reclamation, thousands more acres of Western lands were opened up to irrigation projects. More vegetables, and in a short time more fruit would be on the way to the cities.

This would only drive prices further down.

The Depression, for small fruit farmers, started early and would last a long time—almost twenty years. The idea of cheap and plentiful water and power through a big dam remained at the level of myth and kept the valley's version of the Garden at a modest size that assured the continuity of the riverbank villages as villages. Columbia Basin agribusiness, a world and culture the Wheelers wouldn't have recognized, was put on hold. That twenty years could have meant stagnation for White Bluffs were it not for an odd opportunity that the town fathers seized.

In 1922 the Wheelers and their neighbors were intrigued to see several hundred new people arrive in the White Bluffs area with all they owned. They had answered a call like a replay of 1906, this time put out by the State. Like the boomers before them, they were there to try their hands at orchardry. Even though the valley boosters knew about overproduction, they had lobbied hard to win the "Soldier-Settlers Project". They hadn't had luck getting a dam, and their water lawsuits dragged on, but this time they won. In 1919, the State had appropriated the funds to its Department of Conservation, then had gone looking for an appropriate desert location. Two districts were the finalists, one at White Bluffs, the other at the Grosscup Ranch, close to Richland. How White Bluffs won the project is another story involving Fred Weil, land developer. Mary Powell Harris, a White Bluffs teacher/observer, gives one popular version of how it happened:

> Major Weil telephoned the White Bluffs
> businessmen and told them to get busy and find out
> something about the Grosscup place to discredit it. One
> of them who had been a tax assessor recalled that Mr.
> Grosscup had gone to the tax office at the county seat
> and put in a request to have his taxes reduced because

> quite a large piece of his land had become alkaline. The
> men went to Prosser to verify it, and found the request
> was on record. Then the state...was let know that they
> would go public with the information if necessary.

The project went to White Bluffs. Fifty-eight tracts of desert of twenty acres each, some from college lands, some from Northern Pacific, and some belonging to the County through foreclosure, all with potential water (none through the infamous HIPC), were offered for sale in 1921. The brochure was similar to those of 1910, but revised to include statements of a patriotic nature. It was addressed to veterans who were of the highest moral quality, the cream of American manhood, specifically excluding "Orientals" as described earlier.[1] The new brochure was rich with production statistics, testimonials, and photos of lush farms. Margaret Wheeler observes:

> This time the prospective client didn't have to
> imagine what an orchard or vineyard would look like;
> he had only to go out and observe. The brochure,
> drawing from figures set out by the best known and
> most prosperous farmers, quoted the returns from these
> men by acre, crop, and year, and also the types of cash
> work he could find to supplement his farm.

Not only were there showcase farms like the Lovelands and Roberts for prospective growers to visit, there were more average spreads, like the Shaw/Wheeler enclave with its new and mature orchards and vineyards, the Shaw's simple but attractive house surrounded by flower garden and shade trees, immaculate barn, alfalfa field, and George's dairy herd. It would have looked modestly prosperous to anyone who didn't have access to Jeanie Wheeler's balance sheet, and who didn't know that Frank still worked out of the county most of the year, while Jeanie packed fruit for wages, and Jane took in boarders.

No doubt the Soldier-Settler Project had been planned while the commodity market still had hope. Why the Project wasn't halted, even though funded, is curious since overproduction was publicly acknowledged by the time recruitment for settlers began. But all this was buried for a time. When the soldier-settlers came chugging into town, other people hoping to start new businesses followed along, and the valley had its second boom.

The soldier-settlers drew lots for which tracts they would get. They were offered a reasonable deal if the declining market prices for fruit and the price of power and freight were laid aside, and if they were wise enough to choose the right fast crops until the orchards could bear. For $5450 with a down payment of $600 each settler would receive twenty acres of uncleared (sagebrush) land, a new rather small unpainted house, outbuildings, a drilled well and irrigation equipment. A livestock loan was available. As with the 1906 project, few of the unemployed or foreclosed could afford this deal. To prevent speculation, the buyer could not sell or barter his place until developed. He was required to occupy the house eight months of the year. There were also strict rules about the choices, care, and disposal of livestock. [2]

Once again, a big attraction to families was that these tracts were not out in the middle of nowhere, but attached to an already developed community with all the accoutrements of healthy rural living of that day. And more were on the horizon. The brochure went into detail about the great Priest Rapids Dam project that was sure to be funded soon. Then the troubling power rates would come down. Though the settlement area was near the HIPC ditch, its problems were too well-known. The new people would not have to rely on it or any other water company, for each tract had its drilled well. The new settlers would receive technical assistance from the County Agent, as well as much tested advice from their neighbors, about care of their topsoil and cover crops. They could learn about the advantage of the valley's early spring and shipping to the early market. They could compare the popularity of apples to the less competitive market in soft fruit and make their choice.

Though the Wheelers and other experienced White Bluffs growers may have been skeptical of the project's soundness, everyone wanted it to succeed. The population of the valley was in retreat, and here came new, young energy. We can imagine Jane and Jeanie's delight at seeing new faces in their service clubs and at church, and the children home from school hopping with excitement. In such a small community the most exciting thing to happen could easily be new neighbors. The only negative remark in the *Family Histories* directed at the soldier-settlers is that the plowing of so much new ground in a short time created a new onslaught of dust storms to be endured until ground cover was established. Despite the downward sliding market, the offer for new settlers went out again in 1924. The brochure was essentially the same.

The project turned out to be of special interest to the Wheelers when Rose, seventeen, began going with one of the soldier-settlers, Wilbur Morford. He was twenty-four, from the coast, with a little farming experience, but with much energy and some business school background that proved useful to the community. He was typical of the new settlers when he started with fast-growing asparagus, berries, and truck vegetables. Soon he decided he would not put in an orchard. Perhaps he could never get ahead enough financially to do it, or perhaps he saw the higher risk in the fruit market. The new settlers discovered that even if their wells produced enough water, the power bills involved in pumping it, and thus the long term investment before a tree could bear, was more than some of them could manage. In the *Family Histories* from these later settlers the excessive cost of power is mentioned more than any other problem.

Within a few years many of the soldier-settlers were, like the earlier settlers, far in debt to Pacific Power and Light, and struggling to make their mortgage payments to the state. Some switched to crops requiring less water. Some tried to switch partially to wind power, but found that though the wind seemed to be blowing dust all the time, the generators of that day still could not produce enough. Most of the men were soon scouring the district for extra cash work. The Wheelers and Shaws, observing the plight of these young families, felt much sympathy.

ILLUSTRATIONS

C1. The Shaws and the Wheelers, 1920

C2. Hay crew

C3. Donald Wheeler; he covered "outside" work at 13

C4. Helen Wheeler in eighth grade graduation dress by Jeanie, 1928

C5. New Town, White Bluffs

C6. The saloon; it opened across the river whenever the
county voted dry

C7. George Wheeler, a climb on the bluffs around 1926

C8. Apples ready to pick

C9. Neighbor boys; fruit hauling Model T

C10. College students, George and Donald Wheeler

C11. Sunday swimmers near ferry landing

C12. Jane Shaw in her late seventies, with grandchild

C13. Wheelers with grandchildren, 1941

C14. Frank with "Ho Eliza" and grandkids at slough, 1941

C15. Margaret Wheeler, a last swim, 1942

C16. Frank and Jeanie Wheeler, among the evicted, 1943

14

FROM FARMERS TO SCHOLARS

"...I hope you may get to see the British Museum a bit even if it is fruit of the most colossal barefaced robberies and oppressions..."
Frank Wheeler to his daughter, 1924

THE WHEELERS, with their dream of college-bound children, knew they were taking a risk with a small country school system. They were relieved that Margaret had no problem passing the state entrance exam for high school, nor did the others following her. Of course they hadn't left their children's education entirely to the school. Wheeler children encountered the world of learning everywhere they turned, with their mother substituting at the school and the teachers boarding with their grandparents. The Wheelers read to their toddlers, and Jeanie taught every one of them to read before they first walked across the road to their classrooms. The parents assumed that they would all do well at school, and if they did not (math being a common pitfall) great consternation reigned in the Wheeler household.

The Wheelers stayed in close contact with the local school and believed that most years it was quite acceptable for a small town, improving as the years went by. The *Family Histories* contain many mentions of the schools at Hanford and White Bluffs, almost all positive with regard to both the teaching and the behavior of the students. Helen remembers the Hanford students as more rambunctious the year that she, as a sophomore, transferred down there with some disgruntled friends. Though she enjoyed greatly the chaos their influx created, she transferred back to the more sedate White Bluffs classrooms the next year. She comments that by the time she graduated, if she wasn't prepared for college it was no one's fault but her own.

Today we can only marvel how tiny school districts with limited resources produced such good programs that even critics like the Wheelers were mainly satisfied. Actually the quality of the valley schools was probably much like rural schools everywhere in being quite dependent on who answered the vacancy ads that year. Teachers often didn't stay long in isolated, rural appointments. But Hanford and White Bluffs had a real advantage in that they could offer their teachers a community life that few hamlets had, and their reputation spread.

The majority of the citizenry supported the schools whatever particular factions they belonged to. The students knew that their parents expected them to behave and to perform. Most parents, even though farmers, were not people to pull their youth out of school for a whim, though they might have to for a harvest. In White Bluffs, insolent or lazy students—and the Wheelers remember very few—were not admired by their peers as role models. Margaret thought it was the attitude of the community just as much as the various qualities of the teachers that made the schools successful.

The schools did have their problems, mostly in getting enough funding from the county. They could not offer every subject people wanted. Of special concern for the families was that the high schools receive and keep their accreditation, for without that graduates would have a difficult time to win scholarships to colleges. Both Hanford and White Bluffs high schools (the latter opened in 1921) had barely enough enrollment to keep accreditation once they gained it. This was one more reason the residents kept striving for more population; it was not simply boosterism.

The schools were much more than halls of learning. Typical of rural schools, they were the center of much of the towns' social activity. People were naturally dedicated to the survival and success of their local institution that produced not only scholars but plays, contests, talent shows, concerts, spelling bees, and finally, when the high school gym was completed, that epitome of all small town entertainment, basketball.

Though the settlers at White Bluffs and Hanford had created themselves as irrigator-farmers, that was their generation's adventure and not necessarily what they expected from their children. So far, the orchards had not turned out to be the way to riches or even comfort except for a few. As the Depression came early to farmers it must have seemed even more urgent that their youth get another sort of training. By the mid-1920s, just as the youth had almost reached their years of adult productivity, many were disappearing off to the west on *Sagebrush Annie* for city high school, then college. Their parents paid the costs in their lost farm labor as well as tuition. Fortunately, summer was the busiest time in the orchards, and this was when most of the youth could return home, often bringing friends with them to work.

Margaret Wheeler had set the precedent for her family and perhaps for others too when she left the valley for a city high school. Now in the fall of 1922, she set another as she and a neighbor girl, Annie O'Larey, headed for Reed College in Portland. In a short time there would be valley youth going every direction. The Wheelers were not the only family with the maturing of so many college-bound children. Several had three, even five youth planning on college, a new dilemma with shrinking crop incomes.

Margaret's letters show that she suffered from being gone from home and family nine months of every year for eight years. But it worked well for history through the weekly messages that went back and forth and Jeanie's habit of saving them. The other children wrote home, but none as regularly as Margaret. It was she that became, aside from Jeanie, Frank's main correspondent when he was gone from home. Her reports give a colorful picture of a girl raised on an unconventional intellectual diet that would now be put to the test.

Margaret got little help with college costs from her parents, not nearly what they had expected to provide. Just as she had done in high school, she worked her way doing housework, later work on campus, supplemented by the clothing made by her mother and by ten dollars from her father whenever he could send it. Food shipments to her were regular; the Wheelers had started the custom when she was in high school. Later, during the Depression, these shipments were to become life-savers for city dwellers, of far more value than on the market. Twenty pound boxes of fruit, vegetables and baked goods could go by post to the students for twenty-four cents in two days and were a hit with the families they boarded with and their friends too. The fresh produce took on a symbolic as well as nutritional value for the sojourners: *We are here, we are thinking of you as we packed these.*

The 1920s saw a huge increase of female college enrollment and Margaret swept in on the flood, surrounded mainly by students from wealthy families. Most of the valley's scholars enrolled at the low-tuition state colleges or at business schools. Office training had joined teaching and education as careers where women were accepted. But the Wheelers liked Reed's reputation for serious scholarship. Donald comments that contrary to the reputation for radical thought that Reed gained, it was a socially conservative and safe place for families to send their girls.

Studies were the least of Margaret's problems. Her host mother was hypercritical of her housekeeping skills, and made her miserable at first with her criticism. The girl had health problems, but also suffered from her "inordinate interest in fine clothing" she couldn't afford, as she herself put it. The financial prospects for her second year were poor. She at one point wrote, "Since there is no tuition money, I should transfer to the state college and take up study of farm management." Her parents thought that idea absurd; they saw her as a potential college professor. Fortunately Reed administration agreed and found a scholarship for her next year.

Margaret adored Reed for the social life and culture as much as the academics. She fell in love with opera her first semester, young men the second. Though her grades were generally fine—she bombed physics and Greek—they did not take up much space in her letters. She devoted herself to her parents' idea that all of her siblings would have the same opportunity for a quality college time. But few families expected to have to support three children in college all at the same time, and that was what the Wheelers saw looming. As Margaret became a junior, Rose and George would be entering, and two years later, Marian. That had been part of the reason for the expanded orchard. The goal was daunting but not impossible if every piece fell in place. The Wheelers did not see it being in conflict with the farm. If the farm, no financial success so far, could provide them at least enough to cover the six children through higher education, that was justification for all the years invested.

Rose had decided early on that what she really wanted was not Reed, but a private art school, the posh Cornish in Seattle. But now, unexpectedly, George was due to graduate high school early. As the White Bluffs school board had feared, they were already in danger of losing accreditation due to out-migration. As proof of how serious valley families were about school, the principal convinced the entire junior class to double-up and take all of their senior classes as well so they could graduate early from an accredited high school and keep their scholarship chances. Thus George graduated the year Rose did. The Wheeler's problem burgeoned. How could they possibly support three youngsters at private schools? For Margaret was determined that George attend Reed; nothing else would do.

Helen says that all of Margaret's siblings, as well as her parents, considered the girl to be a model of courage, achievement, and devotion. She would have laughed, and in her letters she refers to herself as quite selfish, but she did set a standard that was important for her and their later lives, refusing to let her not-robust health, poverty, or other people's opinions dominate her attention. During her first spring at Reed, Margaret found a special young man to talk to, and her letters to her mother were filled with this new experience. She was beautiful, and despite her quiet nature was bound to attract men. But her feminist attitudes stood their first serious test with these associations. One side of her was the romantic who loved opera, dance, and poetry, while the other side was the fierce moralist for any exploited group, and the first group was women, the first example herself.

Donald says, "She didn't get her feminist ideas from Reed; she already had them, from Dad." But it was to her mother she addressed these new concerns, along with requests for clothing, which her mother still custom-made. Jeanie thought her daughter carried her feminism too far when she refused to let her most serious boy friend pay her way to events, but Margaret would not be swayed, and this was more and more the case:

> ...Now Mama, on top of all this and especially your
> good advice in your last letter, I must confess that I
> don't see how I can follow it, have not in fact. How can
> I live a lie? How can I go on, as I have, pretending to be
> dependent and admiring? I don't feel so, and when I am

convinced I am right, how is a change to be accomplished? Concretely, I objected to having my fare paid...You did not go so many places with daddy, and you control the finance now, so you can't imagine how false and humiliating it is...(and from a following letter) There is no such thing at present as equality. It's a lie to deceive women. Don't you think so--en masse, I mean, not in our case, but we are exceptions. I hate to be taken places, tho I like to go with someone. I consider myself as economically provident as most men. The fact that they get pleasure out of my company means nothing to me. I would not go with them unless I received pleasure too. This is the remnant of a medieval idea which I am not going to submit to any longer. Moreover, I assure you this is not "college talk". Most girls here are quite willing just to "look cute".

One can imagine Jeanie fretting over these letters. She wanted her girl to stand up for what was right, and she wanted her to be accepted and have a good time, carrying on Jeanie's own conflicts. Instead she had a daughter so like Frank. Though the letters were written to her mother, they were always forwarded to her father. He contemplated the influence of his feminist ideas on his oldest daughter, and apparently decided at this point to stay out of the dialogue. A letter from Margaret's second year gives a glimpse of how she viewed her parents' relationship: "I think I was never in such confusion of ideas, personal and public on all points. But I do say one thing, not very cleverly, I hope you will appreciate. You and daddy , I have come to believe, have made a singular success of your family...."

Margaret's ivory tower musings had received a shock just the month before when her beloved father saw the opportunity to catch a ride from his nearby construction job and arrived on campus without warning. It was his first visit. Here she had been showing off the handsome, groomed man's photo on her dresser, and he was suddenly before her in his cement-covered working clothes with his socks sticking through cracks in his boots. She did much soul-searching in the next months, not only about the sacrifices her father made for her, but about the personal demands she had been making on her mother for clothing and what it cost the rest of the family:

March 36, 1923 Dear Mama,

First, the lovely crunchy apples arrived, but the cake did not. I am very disappointed...I don't know why Daddy thot I was too serious or how any one can doubt my happiness. I guess what made me feel bad was because I realized suddenly how horribly disagreeable bricklaying is, though I always knew it was hard, and here I am doing nothing unpleasant....Don't bother much with my dress. I had much rather that you made a blouse for yourself. Don't do any embroidery either. I would rather you'd do it for Helen so she'll have lots of cute things when she comes to visit. This is the time of year I hate to be away from home.... Love to all,

Margaret

Only two months later she received an even ruder shock from the hard world and wrote to Jeanie, who was at Tillamook visiting her brother Jim:

5/1/23 Dear Mama,

Don't be alarmed, nothing is the matter with Daddy. But a horrible accident occurred. The scaffolding gave way beneath them and five men were killed outright. How he escaped he didn't explain. He

said he was very near, but how near I don't know. Ye
Gods! Never let him work again. I'll quit college sooner.
$11.00 a day is not enuf. I can't even write straight. I
nearly fainted when I got the letter. Did he write
you?... Don't let this spoil your visit. Love to the family,
Margo

By the end of Margaret's second college year, her letters dealt less and less with what was intriguing her at the moment on campus, and more with her concerns for her family, and especially with plans for her brothers and sisters. Then, as her sophomore year ended, and as the Wheelers were wrestling with what to do about Rose's and George's tuitions, Margaret wrote that she and a classmate had been chosen to be government exchange students on scholarship to France. "Of course you must go!" was her father's immediate reply. Willowbank Farm was not the world. All his life he had longed for more travel, immersed himself in *National Geographics* and Dr. Livingstone's adventures, and now his daughter had the chance he had missed. He had no idea how to pay for her train ticket to New York, but soon got another surprise. A professor in the Reed English Department offered Margaret an interest-free loan of $200. Dr. Cerf became practically a patron saint for the Wheeler youth, for the $200 became just what he hoped, a revolving scholarship. It surfaces several times in this history.

That year, 1924-25, was a turning point for the Wheelers as their children began making heavy decisions for themselves. Margaret had not even told them she had applied for the travel scholarship. Before the year was over the fledglings would sprout even more wing feathers, but for now, finally, the Wheelers could turn their thoughts a little away from farm and financial troubles. Their own daughter in Europe!

France was a lasting adventure for Margaret, a favorite topic in later times. For Frank, it was so special to have his daughter in Europe that he wrote regularly, those letters shedding more light on the man as he traveled through her eyes. She had been in France a little over a month and was just settling into life in a French girl's school when she got the first installment from him:

October 20, 1924

Margaret, I should have had a letter waiting you. I hope you will know by this time about real black bread, cheese and red cabbage and the first taste of French as is. I hope youll draw your chair right up and sit in, and not miss the old humdrum and learn to love and enjoy a bit of the Universe as exhibited abroad, and lay the foundation for other expeditions. So you found there was a reason for an extra dime or two...Is wine taboo? Or can you elect your course relative to personal matters. Shed your American notions and view things from that side when you can get perspective.

If it can be we shall hope you can return by another route and see some of England... I wish you could see Grandma's folk in Paisley [Scotland]...The Trip ought to be a common thing, a part of High School. But that would stop the ferment of propaganda in feeble minds. 90% of the plebs are bored to death by time they are 35, so enlarge on your friendships, Margaret, and set your claim stakes as wide as a miners discovery filing, to take a universal interest in good big issues and things...With very much love most sure, Daddy

Frank now had a fine opportunity to lecture on the papacy and the French colonial empire but let it go. His family background provided him more information and outrage toward the British colonists' misdeeds; he didn't know in such detail of the exploitation of Indochinese and Algerians. As for French Catholicism, it had a healthy anti-clerical stream, and there were Rousseau, Voltaire, and Robespierre. Margaret should be open to the best that France could offer, so he held his satire. Their regular letters were a push and pull between him wanting to see France through her, and her wanting to stay in touch with events at home. Frank tried to reassure her continually that they were not starving, that she should concern herself with her own menu, her own health, and her purpose in France.

Margaret and her classmate soon found their classes dull, but they were not restricted like the French girls, and once they thought their spoken French was adequate, they went about freely in their off-hours, bound only by their pocketbooks. They took trains to different cities, walking between villages, visiting every cathedral, every museum, recording it all in journals. Margaret's letters home, more private than her journal, show her discomfort to be having too much fun. It turned out that the fall harvest hadn't done well. Her fiance, a fellow student, wasn't writing her, and letters took three weeks each way. By Christmas she was full of guilt for the extra cash demands her side trips put on the family. Letters such as the following made her smile but did not relieve her worries:

> December (?), 1924
>
> My Dear Margaret, Just how does it feel to be down to your last centime in France, no jam pot to share at lunch and music lessons unpaid... Im glad you are to get an insight into other things where the ideas of the Damn Yank do not hold sway. A country that has given rise to Joan de Arc and the Cleansing Revolution holds much for our Golden Calf besot minds if we only will believe it. I think the errors of Protestantism are

run to seed as the Inquisition did, and the millions in
what we think "darkness" are a needed resistance, as
needed as salt in the sea. ...Take a sip for me and a good
bite of black bread.

Meanwhile Margaret was studying more than architecture and
art:

Just wait till I get home, won't I prove to my little
bros and sisters what wonderful food they enjoy and
what excellent cooks grandma, mama and myself are.
Every day these school children eat food that ours
wouldn't look at. There is never any sugar, pepper,
butter or milk on the table for the French girls. And the
same thing over and over again—beans, boiled rice,
boiled potatoes, boiled lentils, boiled peas, boiled.
Chocolate (watery) and bread for breakfast... For
growing girls it is a horrible diet. But do they complain?
Never. On the contrary, this noon some of them who
remember war times were telling about the rations of
bread they used to have, how it was green-black. Lots of
people don't know how fortunate they are...

By spring she was talking about her return. Though her parents urged
her to stay longer, and visit more countries, they had no way to help. George
and Jane Shaw somehow came to the rescue with sixty dollars to assure a
trip to Scotland to see Jane's long-missed relatives. Then, another surprise,
another gift of funds arrived from Professor Cerf. Frank wrote to reassure
her:

Easter, 1925 My dear Margaret,
It would have been hard to write if Grandma had
not been ready to help you glimpse "ye bonnie

braes"...[She] would be bitterly hurt if you could not go, and I hope that you may get to see the British Museum a bit even if it is fruit of the most colossal barefaced robberies and oppressions, the Gift of Empire, ever laid at the feet of any people. For the Second Beast that came up was no better than the First.

We have good health Margaret and have not been out a shoelace from your trip yet, for which I'm sorry as it would have helped us all to really skimp...Id say don't hurry home. Light has been ambling a million years from some vast orb to meet the earth. Opportunity saunters about just as loath to reward Hope. This is Easter. I played Methodist. Mamma says that our [orchard] is a glory of bloom. I hope you'll get to taste the fatness thereof....With very much love, sincerely, Daddy

The trip north turned out well. The Scots cousins were the ultimate in hospitality and small gifts of cash, even though they disapproved the American cousin's thinness and her rambling alone. With their help, she had enough money left to go for another short tour around England, Northern France, and Belgium. Though overall the year was a success, Margaret's eagerness to be home was a constant theme, "I'll be there in time for the peaches, Mama!"

We can imagine Frank sitting in a boarding house after work somewhere, turning out these epistles for his own entertainment as well as his daughter's, and wonder where she would find a husband to measure up.

A letter from Jeanie, one of the few that passed her self-censoring for history, tried for cheer, first with good farm news, then with consoling words regarding Margaret's teetering engagement, finally with optimism about the coming year. The second paragraph shows Jeanie's ability to write in high style when she took the time, and expresses a philosophy she tried to hold onto for herself:

> May 25, 1925 My dear daughter,
>
> I know you feel relieved about [your fiance]. Even the knowledge of his sickness is better than uncertainty....The crop is coming along beautifully. It seems so good not to have to worry about it anymore. George is thinning at Lovelands. Rose and Esther go to Bleakley's tomorrow. Marian earned $10 picking berries at Keal's and is as proud as punch. The boys have caught enough wood to do us. It is a big boom and George has it pretty well fastened...It was wonderful of Dr. Cerf to send you more money. You have had a difficult year, through the fault neither of yourself nor anyone else, but just a queer trick of fate. When the wind was blowing a gale the other day, I went down to the river. It was terribly ruffled, but still flowed majestically on, its depths undisturbed, bearing away alike the flotsam that marred its surface and the waves that the wind lashed up. There you are. Whatever your decision may be, you may think you will regret, but in the fullness of time, all will be well. All hard and painful things pass. We never know how we can endure anything till we have to...
>
> I certainly think you did wonderfully well on your short trip to London, to get in so many things. Won't it be splendid for you and C. to have a class at Reed [as teaching assistants]? I shall take great pride in saying, "Oh, yes, she has a class at Reed this year!" Don't worry

about your "long and expensive" education. You know
yourself that Daddy and I derive more satisfaction from
that than we would from owning the finest car ever
driven...

Lots of love, Mama

Margaret returned home to jubilation on all sides, ready to plunge into the work of the harvest, then on to her last year of college. But instead of the welcome farm routines, she found Willowbank in turmoil. The Wheelers had found out early on that the rest of their children wouldn't be as amenable to their ideas for them as Margaret had been. Now as the younger siblings confronted their parents with their own plans, the Wheelers found out that White Bluffs High, for all its virtues, had not worked out well for Rose and Marian. Rose had returned there to finish high school and had been uninspired. Now Marian had completed her freshman year at White Bluffs and was equally dissatisfied. Both girls' main interest was in the fine arts, no instruction being available in White Bluffs, and the family believed they had ample talent to succeed.

In June, just before Margaret arrived home from France, Rose graduated. But instead of preparing for art school and living with her aunt Rohilla again as the Wheelers had planned, she eloped to California with Wilbur (Wib) Morford. They were still gone. The Wheelers were disappointed, knowing Rose had talent just waiting to be directed, but they liked Wib, thought him the best catch around, if that was what the girl wanted. Yet they couldn't imagine their romantic daughter settled down to a farm wife role. Except for the wealthy, and the most domestic, her friends were either off to the state college with its low tuition, or to a business school.

George presented his own problem. He had turned sixteen just after he graduated and being so small for his age, it made sense for him to stay home a year, working off the farm for wages and saving for college while Donald, now eleven, took over much of the farm work at home. That year George devoted himself to his McFadden body-building course with increased fervor. Farm work, McFadden, and his biological clock answered the need for pounds and inches, for by the time Margaret returned from France he had sprouted, was accepted at Reed, and would be able to enter that fall as a normally-sized young man. It turned out that academically George hadn't suffered seriously from his three years at a rural high school, but he had no tuition scholarship. The family had given what they could spare to Margaret. Their college plan for their offspring was falling down, a threat more depressing to them than any harvest failure.

Margaret, however, even before she left France for home, had worked out how to finance her brother, and told them the news. She had not only secured a teaching assistantship in French at Reed, she had planned her enrollment as a half-time student for her final courses for only half tuition, and had already enrolled in inexpensive correspondence courses for high school teaching certification in Washington. The Wheeler funds, whatever there were, would be freed up for George. She would also be giving him installments from the "Dr. Cerf fund" as soon as she had a job. We can imagine how upset her parents were with her independent moves. Public school teachers, especially women, made poor salaries, and they had assumed she would want to go on to graduate school. But they had no alternative to offer.

Marian, now fifteen, observed that Margaret had gone to a high school with fine art courses, then to a prestigious college, while Rose had turned down her chance to go to Cornish, and George would soon be off for Reed. She felt frustrated and it showed. Frank, perhaps a little amazed that he had so many teenagers all at once, had earlier written Margaret regarding Marian, "...Setting down in a little place like WB is not stimulating to thot." The consequences of rural location were suddenly more obvious, and it was not just his problem, it was his wife's, and now his children's. The home so fine for them as young ones now was missing the stimulation he had yearned for in his own teens.

Someone came up with an idea. Would Rohilla, wanting to do something for Frank's children, accept Marian instead of Rose to live with her at Seattle? The girl could go to a good urban high school and prestigious Cornish both. The young woman was in raptures when Rohilla agreed. George and Margaret packed up for Reed, Marian proudly for Seattle. She attended Garfield High School during the day, taking all the art courses it had along with her academic studies, and attended Cornish in the evenings, everything just as she had dreamed. She recalls, "I was the only woman in some of the Cornish classes. One of those was a life class with nudes, and Aunt Rohilla would go with me and sit outside the lab waiting. She didn't want any men making passes at me."

For a while it all worked out. After Rohilla left town to teach, Marian was able to find another home to board at and was able to continue on with both her schools. George, happily engaged at Reed, working for his board, never was forced to drop out. Frank kept laying brick, sending them ten dollars when he could. Jeanie kept sewing the girls' dresses and making over old coats for the boys. The scholarship from Dr. Cerf kept rotating and even growing. The farm's contribution continued to be food— a weekly box out on the stage or train.

Margaret, now back at Reed, had expected to rejoin her fiance and settle all problems with him. In a few weeks she was home again, distraught from a broken engagement that she never discussed with anyone. Swallowing her grief and humiliation, she went back to campus and threw herself into her teaching assistantship. The next spring, degreed in Language and Literature and certified to teach high school, she was out job-hunting.

Despite all these successful maneuvers by the three students, showing that they could make do for themselves and leave the farm mainly to support itself, the fall was an especially tough one for the family. When the successful apple harvest was over, despite the college expenses, Frank for the first time stayed home all winter on the farm. It was not for his enjoyment. He had been called upon to do an unusual service for Rohilla. Her husband, Edward Phillips, was discovered to be dying of stomach cancer, and this was part of the arrangement that involved Marian's schooling. While Rohilla provided a place for Marian to go to school, and meanwhile took classes to prepare herself as a widow to teach, Frank would provide a hospice for Edward at Willowbank Farm. Helen remembers:

> Dad fixed up a separate living quarters for him in a cabin near the house so that he could endure his agony without feeling too humiliated by his burden on us. He ate with us until he couldn't anymore. The obvious suffering that went on was dreadful, but we all liked Ned, a man with a degree from Dublin University, and the folks considered the aid we gave as normal for a family.
>
> Until November, Dad took care of him in every way, administering larger and larger doses of morphine, until, toward the end, he was unable to get enough. Then Ned's brother Freemasons found more, and gave other comfort. Finally he died and was buried at White Bluffs. It was a very difficult time, and it mellowed Dad's feelings toward the Masons.

Yet in a month another worse tragedy struck the family. George Shaw had been miserable with prostate trouble for some time and finally decided he would submit to surgery. Just before Christmas he was about to be discharged from the hospital at Ellensburg after a successful operation. Jane had gone up to bring him home, when two hours before he was to be released, he suddenly died of a blood clot. The shock was enormous, for aside from the prostate he had been a healthy active man of seventy. Not only did Jeanie lose her father and the children their grandfather, Margaret writes, "Our grandmother was stricken with grief from which she never completely recovered to her normal activity. Then I finally realized how much she had cared for the man she so frequently berated."

All of these changes happened within four months. Despite what the loss of George Shaw meant for his own farm, there was no thought of having young George drop out of college. Frank, Jeanie, Jane and Donald operated both orchards, and Jane gave the dairy herd to her son Win. A letter from Jeanie to a friend, the only letter we could find from that year, and so terse as to be unrecognizable as Jeanie's, gives a feeling for what the mood must have been, in what it doesn't say:

> December 30, 1925 Dear Mary,
>
> ...How the time does fly and we don't seem to be
> able to keep in touch as we'd love to. This was a sad
> Christmas for us—my father passed away December
> 13th, a month after an operation for bladder trouble.
> It is the first break in our family circle—we shall miss
> him coming and going all the time. Rose was married
> last Decoration Day and is living this winter in Fresno.
> Her husband was almost killed in a shaft in a raisin
> factory. They have a ranch here and will be back in
> the spring. Margaret is teaching French at Reed
> College this year. George is a freshman there. They are
> home for the holidays. Marian is in Seattle with
> Rohilla, who is a widow now. She, Marian, is doing fine
> work in sketching and craftwork. Frank is at home this

year because we had good crops last summer.

Lots of love, Jeanie Wheeler

With Frank at home most of that sad year, the coffers were depleted. It was essential for Margaret to find work the next fall, and she did. To the amazement of her family, she won her first teaching position through her willingness to teach women's physical education. They had all considered her the least athletic among them. It didn't matter, she could do what she determined to do. At Woodland, a small Washington town near Portland, she turned the gym classes into dance classes, from folk to modern. She was finally working, away from the scene of her broken engagement, and hoping to be able to return to her siblings some of the resources that had been scraped together for her. She soon found out that on $145 a month there was very little left to mail her family, not even enough for the new pair of shoes she yearned for. She was now playing the role that her father had for years, and appreciated even more the ten dollars he used to stick in an envelope for her.

15

THE ROAD GETS ROCKIER

"After I visited Margaret Jean at Reed there was nothing short of a deluge that could have kept me out. There were several obstacles: I'd never studied hard, no money, no skills. The list could be longer...I nearly perished, but I survived."

Helen Wheeler Hastay, 2001

WITH GEORGE GOING OFF to college, Frank and Jeanie felt a major shift in the value of their farm. For tuition funds it had done poorly, not at all what they had planned. But at least, it could serve as a base from which their children could safely venture forth and return, always assured of a meal and a bed for the summer, and boxes of food all winter. The next fall Frank, feeling he had to do better than that, made a decision he suffered from and traveled all the way to New York to find steady employment. He planned to stay the entire year. His other sister, Faye, had written that many skyscrapers were going up and that he could very likely be hired and work regularly. Frank, as a young man, had always loved New York City. He knew that on Sundays he would head right for the parks and museums. Living with his sister's family, he could save rent.

But could Donald, only thirteen, manage or arrange for all of the farm's heavy outside work, with his mother and grandmother there for consultation? Letter exchange would at very best take a week, not much help for the problems that could arise. The idea now seems preposterous; we don't expect such things of thirteen-year-olds. But Frank had been working with Donald all the previous year and felt that under Jeanie's supervision, he would manage.

Donald says, "I don't think I was unique in the amount of work I took on that year, but there were few boys my age who had such a wide range of responsibilities." What George had been able to do at fourteen and fifteen, with his father coming back every few weeks to do catch up, and his grandfather there to correct him if he went wrong, Donald would do alone, though with plenty of advice. Although he wonders now at all he accomplished, he doesn't think in retrospect that he felt victimized. Since he was the errand runner, he knew all about the bill payments that had to go out. He also accepted his brother's absence during summers, for George was able to find jobs as a camp counselor and forest lookout. "George had to work for others. He needed the cash for college, and we needed his cash too." The whole family would have to work together, not just to build the farm now, but the keep the college students in their classes.

Donald's eighth grade studies, fortunately, were not difficult for him. "From September until the next July when Dad came home, I did all the orchard work myself, or arranged to have it done for payment—the pruning, fertilizing, cultivating, spraying, and thinning. I used Win Shaw's team to do the cultivating. Mother and Grandma helped with the irrigating and the animals." He, of course, did the milking. And he did it all without grumbling, Helen says. He may not have been in awe, as he was later, of all his mother and grandmother daily undertook, but he recognized it.

Jeanie got her usual instructional letters from her spouse, telling her sometimes vaguely, sometimes specifically, what had to be done. When Frank heard that Don was cultivating the orchard with a team, he wrote back immediately:

...Get Don off the disk. George ruined dozens of young
trees. It is hard to check good intentions but a disk has to
be straightened up and kept away from the end trees.
Donald cant do it, it is hard for a man...The pipe must
be tarred up on the inside. Wib could do it all in two
days, and it certainly is important. Im glad you got any
berries. After disking, the rows must be trenched. Please
get Wib down and get the water in use...

This kind of letter was what a foreman needed, but a wife and partner
needed a little more diplomacy. Donald says that Frank's comment about
the disking wasn't fair. "I was doing all that a man could do and doing it
well. I may have plowed too close at the corners, but if I did, it was a family
decision, not a whim of mine." He and the two women were running the
farm together. Yet he was just a boy. Excerpts from his letter to Margaret
show how he balanced the two lives he led and decided what should be
reported:

November 16, 1926 Dear M.J.,

I have received two copies of "Nature" magazine,
and I know it is fine....Eight of us boys have passed our
second class Scout tests, the first in W.B. and
Hanford...All the boys who tried passed and that
entitled us to second class badges...We had over 100
packed boxes of Winesaps. Grandma had 2,000 packed
(total of different apples). Mother packed 1700 boxes
in three weeks at Heideman's...

The young man was too modest about all the farm work that he, not just
his mother, was doing. His little sister Helen had less onerous jobs. She
babysat for Rose, a job she loved, and every evening after supper she went up
to spend the evening and the night with her grandmother, who wanted to be

in her own home but didn't want to be alone. "It was my job for a few years, and I enjoyed it. Grandma was patient with me, and often witty and fun. Later, as a teenager I wasn't sassy, but I could be moody, and she put up with it."

New York wasn't nearly as interesting as Frank remembered it. By November he would write, "New York is very beautiful, but any city is like a pretty woman in whom you have no interest. I couldn't like a town if I owned it." Though he did get to the parks, museums and lectures he had looked forward to, he found the stress and commotion of bricklaying more difficult each year, and longed for the serenity of his orchard, alone with his thoughts and his trees. He wrote to Margaret that Jeanie, working in the packing shed, "is happy over the fruits of her amazing drudgery. No one ever loved to work in a crowd so. I simply can't. Id rather set myself to any real task alone, and I never can escape the prison of jostling workmen worse than a cell."

Depressed or irritated letters from Jeanie fueled his feeling of being in the wrong place. When he had opted for New York for the whole year, he had not taken enough into account her growing fatigue with her lot. Though he, Donald and Margaret all were having hard years, and he wasn't sure how happy Rose was with her new role of farm wife, Jeanie's problems were the ones that troubled him most. The previous year, he had stayed home, and they had suffered financially for it by spring. Now he was gone, sending money home, and that was no good either. He wrote to Margaret that he was "damned if I did and damned if I didn't". He couldn't seem to find the right balance and turned to Margaret as a place to sort it out: "I made a poor year of it. But we had one summer together and hope we can enjoy more. I simply dont like to be away and hope you children will always feel that way yourself. Mater thinks I rob her of my wages every time I fail to go out and earn...."

We don't have Jeanie's side of this conversation. But from Frank's letters to her, which she would never burn, and his to Margaret, it is clear that Jeanie's were full of distressing issues, and to him, some non-issues. He felt she was too concerned about their physical poverty, even though he was himself. He wanted his children to get an education, to travel, to go to concerts, yet somehow not to worry about material things, in fact, to welcome a little privation. He felt he had to infuse more funds into their ever more demanding household, and jobs were getting harder to find. Yet his idea to be gone a whole year already showed its hard price.

Frank realized that a change of scene was in order for his overworked wife and partner. She had missed her annual vacation during the previous tumultuous year. Only a few weeks into what promised to be a long winter, he wrote again to Margaret :

> October 17, 1926...Can you plan a visit for Mater?
> Make her do your cooking for 10 days or two weeks and
> break up her blues. If we had been down to pea soup
> and calico for years it would not be more an obsession.
> And I'm sure that is what all of us need. Lots of the hard
> common things and no icing. Hard to get the right
> proportion, Margaret..

The problem wasn't just their poverty. In his absences, Jeanie allowed the petty side of White Bluffs society to torment her. Social as she was, she had to get out with people, but then could not separate herself from community opinion as her husband could. Without him there to give her balance, she brooded over uproar or gossip in her organizations. Frank, who took pride in being different from the herd and in shocking those he wanted to shock, thought her far superior to those whose opinions she worried about, including her own mother's. Now she was president of the Women's Club for a year, with the added pressure. He wrote the next as a P.S. to the letter above:

> I think Mater simply sticks her nose into too many things and uses up every bit of her strength for nothing, then feels cheated... every time one has enthusiasm and helpfulness, it gets well squandered by others and leads to blues. That is one thing about science. It compels people to sit still and think, if it is in them, once in a while.

Apparently the vacation for Jeanie didn't materialize, for in December, the same struggle by correspondence went on. How indeed could she leave the farm to her still mourning mother and a thirteen year old? Frank didn't want her to stay home and clean house, but if she was involved in groups she would feel pressure to compete socially (and we recall the bedbug episode). He felt she had to have a break:

> December 14, 1926 ...I hope Mater will do what Iv tried to have her do, but she wouldn't until the money was spent, then got increasingly resentful over the farm. It is better to get out to clubs and meet people than elect to be a she-ass and scrub the bottom of stove lids at home. But after having chosen, it is folly to begin to grind your teeth because another type had more to show in the stupid way. Mater is too influenced by an element Id not let Ribbon wipe her feet on if I had it to say. And really there is twice as much there for her as in a big expensive place. I wish no overcoat to pack around if I can help it. I'd rather have a 25-30 hen house..."Except God build the house, they labor in vain that build the house." Oh yes, you have to get Mater down [to Portland] and to the naughtiest show you can find so she

can thumb nose at Fanning.

"Fanning" referred to the church elder who had called Jeanie a snake in the grass. Whether she got a trip to Portland that year we don't know, but Frank had done all he could to arrange it. Meanwhile he suffered the "jostling of crude workmen" and kept sending money. Being so far from home, and unhappy living at his sister's, his correspondence with Margaret was a welcome diversion. It involved no scolding and ran the usual wide range of practical concerns, personal regrets, and philosophy, flavored by the biblical quotes and rich metaphor that must have been as precious as ever to his daughter, struggling as a first year teacher:

> (no date), 1926
>
> Margaret, I'll have to drop a line for we be the Sojourners....I hope you will go to Portland to a concert and visit, not avoid it. I know the evil of aloofness. Mix in. It is a world of people, not of things and Iv always suffered in every way from being so awkward socially, and it kills physically. Better a visit and a long talk than sleep....Can you get good library books? Well, my daughter, you are brave enough. I hope we can have another summer vacation together, and a crop of more than liabilities. Cast thy bread--ye shall find it after many days. So very lovely with truth.

Thus he tried to encourage his daughter, full of regret that she had not gone on to graduate school. And they were as usual worried for her still problematic health. But he wanted her to know that working with young people was not the worst place to be:

> 4/19/27 My Dear Margaret,
>
> You know Christ had to teach in parables Margaret, so you cant always teach just as you would,

there are too many "Mrs H.s" who will tell and print and enjoy as clever any damn lie on any subject and these hate with the ferocity of jaguars any lover of vital truth. How a mind gets such a twist is hard to see. I think there is just one test. Is a thing or thot lovely? If not, it is not right in itself or in its relation. Old grave cloths are not the proper raiment of a mind. There is enough rubbish and superstition and ugliness in this New World to sink the continent now--in a hundred years? I hope the young folks will get so out of hand they won't stand to be saddled and ridden and hamstrung...Without ideals, life is nothing but a nightmare–at best. Keep in touch with George all you can, Margaret. It is horrid to miss home warmth for often it is the main stalk of life.

Woodland was not New York City, and Margaret was frustrated with her lack of cultural outlets as well as with her colleagues and students, who didn't seem to hunger for higher learning. Portland and her brother George, so close by bus, were still not easy to work into her schedule, for like all English teachers she was swamped with homework. Her father fed her intellectual hunger and moral courage and kept her laughing too.

It was a second tough year in a row for the Wheelers, except for the fortunate George and Marian, entrenched in classes, in love with learning. Donald comments that the year was not a financial failure, however. "Dad sent quite a bit of money home". Indeed he sent too much, for in July, when he had been in New York City ten months and the humidity was making him ill, he decided he must go home, and right away. He had to ask Jeanie to borrow money from their commission man to wire for his ticket. How glad everyone must have been when the father and husband finally made it back to the farm. But, aside from what Frank shared with Margaret, the friction the couple had suffered that year they had kept to themselves. "I never heard her complain at all," says Helen, who was ten at the time. "She must have saved it all for the letters."

Back home in White Bluffs, Frank took up his hoe and strode with relief into his beloved orchard. But that fall the final settlements from the commission house were worse than ever. Then, despite continuing warnings about overproduction, the state inexplicably decided to promote farming again. Another call went out for the Soldier-Settler project, this time inviting the general public. To make it more enticing, this time a whole page was devoted to the industrial potential of the valley. The envisioned dam at Priest Rapids was, of course, the key. General Electric had been granted a "holding concern" by the federal government in hopes that enough financial interest could been drawn in. Along with the dam, locks would allow shipping to go on up river. Priest Rapids would be a major port, a city of 20,000, with jobs for people who didn't want to farm. Six million had already been invested in the planning. For now, the immediate need was more farmers.

But later that same year, the state decided the Soldier-Settler project was a bad idea. Not only had it not attracted as many people as desired, the state now questioned that it wanted more farmers at all! Furthermore, the project which had a short time earlier been a patriotic boon to veterans was now denounced as socialistic in some circles and undermining of the moral fiber. The settlers complained they had gotten a poor deal. The state was advised to get out of it and did so. The foreclosed tracts were auctioned off, fifty titles awarded to settlers who had made the most progress, and "other settlements with veterans made".

In the *Family Histories*, Nellie Tomson relates that soldier-settler families complained to the state that the original offer had been misrepresented by the promoters (not the first time, one recalls) regarding the economic feasibility of the farms. This was why the titles were awarded early, payments canceled, "and other settlements made". Government social planning was typically labeled socialistic once the urgent need was no longer seen, but the threat to the moral fiber of the settlers does not seem to have been a problem. The surviving soldier-settlers had established themselves well in the community while suffering the same economic problems as small farmers across the country, and making the same efforts to expand, at whatever cost.

The next year, Frank wisely went out to work very little and made sure that Jeanie did take some trips out of the valley. He also decided to make it up to Donald for the previous hard year of running the farm. When Margaret suggested that the boy should, like the others, have his experience at a different town and high school, Frank agreed in his colorful way:

> "Then he would be with you and study has not been obsolete
> with you and help would not be entirely fictitious and
> perfunctory as it is with a parent, off whose minds the petals
> speedily drop or are yanked, and the wrinkly oft wormy nut
> alone remains to baffle the youthful dolt. Selah."

Jeanie didn't like the plan, Donald remembers. "Mother asked who would be at the farm then? 'I'll be here, I'll stay home', Dad said. That was why he had worked all year in New York, so he could take another year off. She was still against it, knowing what that meant for finances." Donald listened to the argument, and this time she lost. Donald went to Woodland and Frank stayed home almost all of that year. He was gone on at least one job, for there are two letters of October, 1927, one simply describing his work, and one from Jeanie telling of an endurance trip, via a neighbor's auto, to visit him in Tacoma. She found him in sad condition and reported it to Margaret:

> We had a great trip to the coast. Left here Fri at 3
> and didn't get to Tacoma till 8:30 next morning. The
> battery went dead and we had to pull up beside the
> road from 2 until daylight. It wasn't any too warm
> trying to curl up on auto seats. Got back here Sunday.
> Daddy was certainly a surprised man when we walked
> in on him. He was miserable with rheumatism in his
> chest and shoulder, also a bad tooth had swelled his face
> all up. So he was a wreck. Nat not much better, back so
> bad with lumbago...

The fortunes of working men and the pleasures of auto travel could not
engage the dry humor of her earlier letters regarding misbehaving pigs and
bedbug wars. Frank's and Nat's declining vigor, as years of outside work in
the elements took their toll, was nothing to joke about. In particular,
Frank's abscessed teeth come up in several letters over a long stretch of time.
As with his hernia, he couldn't or wouldn't put his own problems first on his
list of "urgent fixing needed" and they continued to drain his vitality. His
children's teeth were more important. His trees' health suffered too, when
he couldn't buy fertilizer, Donald remembers. Having run the farm a year,
the boy was too aware of every deficiency.

As the fruit market continued its now chronic slide, nature continued to
provide its own challenges. In April the valley experienced what had become
all too familiar: late killing frost. But Frank was home, and though there
wasn't much he could do about it, Jeanie was better able to put a brave face
on it with him there by her side. A portion of one of her letters to Margaret
that passed her own censorship follows:

> ...Well, Jack Frost made a mighty pass at us, but we
> are still sitting pretty. Easter morning, for the third

time in history, 22 degrees hit the Elbertas and Bings
[peaches and cherries] pretty hard, but there's still
plenty of peaches. Cherries pretty shy. It didn't do any
good to smudge last year, and was a needless expense the
two years before. But when our cherries get a little
bigger we're going to have a circle of heaters round
each tree. The main reason we didn't heat this year is
that we didn't like to borrow money for it, as we'll have
to borrow for water and spray anyway...Anyway there
are tons of fruit, tons of it, if we get no further
frost....no dam has burst on us, nor has the Mississippi
flood been equaled here, nor cyclone nor
tornado—what's a little freeze? There is still enough to
send a little pie to Donald. Love to all, Mother

Donald himself decided something radical had to be done about frosts.
The next spring, 1928, he was home again, and when the phone company
put out a warning that a major cold front with heavy frost was headed
down the river, the Wheelers were ready. The traditional way to deal with
frost, with smudge pots, created a haze over the orchard after a freeze. The
blossoms would thaw slowly the next morning and direct sun wouldn't kill
them. But now they had the new technology, orchard heaters, and Donald
had the first chance to try them. Later he wrote about the outcome:

We had been one of the first valley families to
purchase heaters, a significant investment. It was $1 a
heater and we had ordered two hundred, then had to
buy the coal briquettes and kerosene. Now, here came a
big frost, and the new heaters would have a chance to
show their stuff. I went to town and bought extra
briquettes and prepared kindling to start 100 little fires.

The idea was to keep the orchard warm during the coldest hours—usually just before dawn.

The cold front swept in early; by supper time it was already freezing, but the heaters were out in the orchard with the fuel in them, ready to be lit. They were shaped like cones and had draft holes in them. You put 12 briquettes in them, a handful of cedar kindling, and added a half cup of kerosene. About 8 pm I ran down the orchard rows firing them up. At midnight I had to refuel, and at sunrise they were still burning. They put out the heat all right, but the temperature kept dropping and dropping. Then, the next day out came the sun. We saved only 24 boxes of soft fruit that year. That was it.

Twenty-four boxes. After twenty-two years of farming. Donald despaired when he saw how their expensive plan, so carefully carried out by him, had failed. Yet the financial condition of the Wheelers in 1928 was better than most of the growers. They still had no idea what they were on the cusp of.

Margaret, aware of her parents' growing discouragement, decided on her own radical project to bring a little more fun into their lives. She proposed to make a down payment on a used $200 Model T for them if Frank would learn to drive. We can imagine he did not want to at all, saw no reason for it, but also saw what she was getting at. Wouldn't this be just the thing for Jeanie, who loved a chance to flee the farm and the endless household tasks? So he agreed. But alas, the Model T barely made its first track in the yard before minor disaster struck. Frank, struggling through an early driving lesson, ran over and killed his best game cock that had been dusting in the road. He parked the car and never drove another foot in his life. Donald happily became the driver as well as the mechanic for the family whenever he was home, both talents serving him well in later life. But Jeanie was to be disappointed again, for the men soon saw the real virtue of the Model T through its conversion into a small truck for hauling. This was not what Margaret had intended but efficiency ruled.

Meanwhile Margaret had been delighted to have the company of her much younger brother for a year at Woodland, and they formed a friendship that lasted a lifetime. She was glad to be working, but sorely missed the intellectual stimulation of Reed. As a teacher, she also had less social freedom. Donald's coming to stay for a year was a coup for her as much as for him, and perhaps Frank had known that. Donald was already learning to hold his own on social and political issues, to say nothing of being able to analyze technical problems at Willowbank Farm. Apparently he also did learn to study, if this, as his father had joked, had ever been a problem. Margaret plotted her brother's academic career with their parents:

> It's just idle that Don can't get into college sooner. He'd enjoy it so much more than high school. Then, too, he wouldn't get into those bad habits of not having to study that I did, on account of being "too young to go to high". Remember when I took the state eighth grade exams but was "too young"? The teachers who didn't promote him [advanced promotion] were dumb. Should be entering college now.

That year Margaret saved up enough money and nerve for a long-needed operation for her "inward goiter", that plague of the valley women. Once recovered, she plunged into her sponsorship of dance exhibitions and dramas with new energy. That summer, back at the farm, she insisted that her mother take a vacation, and right then, during harvest time. It was unheard of, but when Margaret argued strongly, she could get her mother to obey. Jeanie packed her bag and caught the train to her old haunts at Hoquiam, this time with no children along to spoil her rest.

Now the road to higher learning got rockier yet. That year Marian, having worked her way through three years of art school combined with high school, was awarded a college loan from the White Bluffs Women's Club. She and her fiance left for the state college at Pullman together. Sadly, his funds ran out after only one semester. Marian was able to make it through the year, working for her room and board, writing letters home telling what a thrill every class was, and getting top marks. Then she had used up her loan. She was unable to find summer work except in the orchards and had nowhere to turn but her family for a second year. They couldn't help; the rotating fund from Dr. Cerf had already gone to George, and Margaret, who as a working sister normally could have helped, had paid for one operation and feared she probably needed another. Marian spent the winter on the farm and in the spring returned to Seattle. She was lucky to find work as a clerk. It was an infamous year—1929.

How frustrated Jeanie and Frank must have been with this outcome for their artistic daughters. First Rose, now Marian not in college. Frank couldn't know yet all that was in store for the country when he wrote, "Marian has dived to the bottom at Sears and hasn't resurfaced." But there were no good jobs in the art world, or any world, for a young woman. He didn't need to feel he and Jeanie had personally failed. Indeed, her job at Sears was soon the envy of others with years of experience and degrees too.

16

THREE-HEADED BEAST

"For the Second Beast that came up was no better than the First."
Frank Wheeler, letter to his daughter, 1925

TWENTY YEARS INTO FARMING, the Priest Rapids irrigators were again receiving year-end accounts on the minus side from their commission houses. They must have wondered how they had chosen this road, for the trials of small farmers had not been secret. The railroads had ruled the West for decades; why should other private schemes like private power and private dams have proved different? A three-headed beast—the railroads, the power companies, and the market—was tearing larger and larger chunks from the farmers across America all through the 1920s. Irrigation technology could not overcome the inevitable phenomenon that every time the market went up, thousands of people rushed into farming, created an overabundance of commodities in a few years, and lo, the market went down. The "back to the country" movement never stopped, nor did the retreat to the city. The government deliberately promoted the first to rid the city of the unemployed and did nothing directly to halt the last.

George Wheeler, home on visits from his classes in economics and "western civ", could see with a broader vision the dilemma they were in, hostages to his father's Beast. His evening chats with his parents couldn't have been cheery ones unless they stayed away from the topic of farming. They were all caught in the jaws, for while the market at least did go up and down, affording a little drama, a little teasing hope, the freight, commission and power rates, all monopolist forces, as George put it, only went up. Some years the beast bit a big chunk, other years they might escape with a nip. The growers almost all scratched for cash work somewhere.

Margaret, too, though she learned from literature and history more than economics, saw the futility of their gigantic labors. But the seed had been well-sprouted in her and her siblings; one way or another they would manage on their own. Donald, a high schooler, listened. He, too, would have to find his own way through Reed. The Wheeler youth did not talk to their parents about getting out of farming. They knew their father loved his trees, that he hated bricklaying, his only other choice, and that their mother loved her community, her flower garden, even the packing sheds. They didn't want their parents to feel themselves failures if they took it a little easier. Jeanie was the harder to convince, being more tuned to the season's bills than economic theory or the history of agriculture. How could they "take it easier?" One of her letters mentions another problem: new stricter tariffs on their fruit in Europe as its fruit farmers sought to protect themselves from the same conditions. The Wheeler orchard expansion had made little difference in the stack of bills on Jeanie's dresser; neither had the move into soft fruit. Frank added a postscript to her letter, "Apples are hellbent for the bottom, like wheat."

The Priest Rapids valley people longed for the services of the great railroad and power corporations, and used them well when they got them, but the merciless rates they paid for the services left them bitter. They did not blow up tracks or transformers; they weren't given to romantic gestures. But they had learned to be good orchardists, and it didn't matter. There is no way to know how many families left the valley over these issues. They were too churned up with the other issues of living. What was obvious to the Wheelers was the growing number of vacant places around them, foreclosed by the County for unpaid taxes, or by the bank for an unpaid mortgage. There could be a number of causes for each family who left the valley, but according to the *Family Histories*, Martha Parker, and the Wheelers, the poor market (relieved briefly in WWI) and the high freight and power rates were the huge and universal problems up until 1929. Then national economic collapse eclipsed everything else.

One can't say exactly when the small irrigators knew they weren't going to succeed, that the "Golden Age" was over. But certainly they knew early on where their problems lay and who their adversaries were; everyone did. The plight of the farmers was exposed regularly in the regional newspapers and the more liberal national press. The battle of western farmers with the railroads was a simple and constant one, weighted entirely in the railroads' favor. They would charge as high a freight rate as possible and the farmers, having no choice, would pay it. When some farmers were bankrupted, others would take their places. If whole districts collapsed, other districts along the tracks would open up.

During some decades the railroads suffered from their own greed and went bankrupt themselves, probably accompanied by cheers from the farmers, unless they happened to be ones losing vital services. It is not correct to say that the government did absolutely nothing to help farmers, for since 1866 the Interstate Commerce Commission had borne the duty of reviewing requests by the railroads for rate increases and had sometimes denied them. But this did nothing to change significantly the balance of the conflict.

When the first private power line was installed down the Priest Rapids valley in 1910, there were more rates to deal with. A power commission would soon be created to attempt to control similar greed as the beast, instead of a single head, now had two, with the private power companies like the railroads, collecting hostages. Donald says, "The Benton County Grangers traveled regularly to commission hearings to protest their debilitating power rates, but their victories were small. At best they might beat back a proposed increase." Pacific Power and Light and other large power companies were not wringing their hands over the bankruptcies of small farmers and water companies, for they were expanding in leaps in the cities. The orchardists remembered with cynicism that irrigation was supposed to overcome these monoliths through efficiency and productivity.

As for the third head of the beast—the market—the fruit growers, especially those in soft fruit, were in an impossible situation. Once a peach was picked and moved to a Seattle warehouse, they could not reject the offered price and take such perishable produce back. Later, dumping of produce to protest prices actually took place in some regions, but no one recalls this in the valley. Indeed, it is difficult to picture any orchardist dumping fruit so carefully picked.

Thus commission houses held the valley growers hostage, as much as did the railroad and power companies, until the opening of the White Bluffs Cold Storage in the early 1920s by local entrepreneurs. That finally did give apple and pear growers some power. Donald remembers what an innovation the Cold Storage was, with the insulation provided by cork shipped from Portugal. Now, for a storage fee, apples and even pears could be held for many months waiting for improved prices. The Cold Storage also sold ice for the Milwaukee's refrigerator cars, which helped pay for its other services. For fragile soft fruit, however, cold storage was not an option, so there was no bargaining power or market timing possible. Yet, the Extension Service continued to encourage farms toward soft fruit. "And they were right," says Donald. "The apple market was overloaded and too competitive with established districts. Still, the majority of the growers felt safest with apples."

The struggle with their local water companies never abated either. HIPC for twenty years tried to divest itself of its albatross, the water company portion of its operation, PRID. The government continued to disallow it. HIPC remained in continuous receiverships, still unable to deliver adequate water to the orchards at the south end of the Ditch. Then, in the mid-1920s the other system, WBCOT, as mentioned earlier, also went bankrupt. The Wheelers and others formed a local users' coop to try to maintain and operate it. Soon the coop found it, too, could not carry out the increasing repairs, pay the power bills, and make ends meet. In order to salvage the aging system the members would have to mortgage their own places and put up a bond. Unwilling or unable to do that, shareholders began to drop out. Donald remembers it as another demoralizing trend:

> More people began to buy their own pumps and pump directly from the river. It was an expensive choice but made more sense to them than trying to maintain WBCOT with the old wooden pipes rotting out and collapsing. When the largest grower, Helsom, pulled out, the coop no longer had enough support, and was forced to disband.

For the Old Towners this was the end of the dream of Powell, Greeley, and the other Agrarians who had based their model of a democratic farming community on the essential communal sharing and maintaining of an irrigation system. Now it would be every farm for itself, an impossible burden for the smaller places. Frank Wheeler make a heavy decision. Donald continues:

> Dad borrowed money, purchased a new pump, and organized the labor to resurrect the old WBCOT system for the remaining users. I and some others built a cement pump house. It was quite a risk, physically as

well as financially, as Dad was not a good mechanic, and when I was gone it was up to him to keep the pump running, and I could make some bad mechanical decisions too. But once when I was gone a whole year, he got through it intact, doing his own repairs, and proudly teased me about it later.

The new business was a non-profit, Helen recalls:

Dad agreed to deliver water to neighboring farms, including Riders, Browns, Montgomerys and Briscos that I remember, and also the school and Presbyterian church nearby, using some of the abandoned ditches. But he wouldn't charge the school or church, both having financial problems of their own, nor widows like Grandma, Mrs. Brisco, or Mrs. Montgomery, so only a few customers were paying, and it was no money-maker, but a public service.

Donald agrees it was no moneymaker, but adds that the neighbors who could pay did so, and everyone appreciated the service. Though Frank could do nothing to solve the greater problem, he was at least able to help a few neighbors as well as his own farm.

The federal government gradually recognized that irrigation projects that could grow to support themselves would require at least initial government support. Dams and reservoirs required investments of millions, much more than the private diversion dams without reservoirs at Priest Rapids and Rock Island had cost. But the Bureau of Reclamation continued to pass the valley by, as there were now new issues. The Priest Rapids lobby was battling those who favored the Grand Coulee site with its larger reservoir potential, and another group who favored a gravity-flow ditch from far to the east.

By 1925, Northwest promoters, Democrats and Republicans alike, saw federal support for a dam somewhere on the Columbia as a top priority legislative battle. Priest Rapids developers again put out a flyer to entice new investment to the valley. This time, the idea was to attract not just farmers but industry and city-builders. The flyer declared:

> Not only will it be the biggest dam in the world, in addition to agriculture it will provide the basis for an electro-chemical (fertilizer) and electro-metallurgical (aluminum) industry surpassed by none. In times of threatened war, the location is ideally isolated and protected. The fertilizer would be converted to munition, the aluminum could go into aircraft.

One wonders what the valley residents thought of all this promotion. The state had just abandoned the earlier brainstorm, the Soldier-Settler project, as impractical. On the federal level, there was still too much skepticism about the benefits of rural electrification for the country as a whole, and not yet enough demand in cities for expensive dams and reservoirs. Moving coal around was still cheaper. The Grange championed the cause, but again no dam was authorized. The valley continued to suffer private power rates completely out of line with farm revenues.

Discouraged with their lack of political gains, the orchardists went back to their pruners and hoes, something they had control over. They took more seriously the diversification that the County Agent pushed. Desperation forced more changes. One that had definite success was quality grading. Introduced during World War I, grading was at first voluntary, later mandatory. The growers did their own grading in the packing house with an inspector coming through unannounced every so often. Jeanie became an expert grader and taught it to her daughters. Though another burden to the packers, Donald believes it was the most important marketing tool they had:

> Grading was one more chore added to the already too long list, but I believe it did what it was supposed to do in building up a stronger market for fine fruit. I was walking in Paris one day in the 1930s and I saw something I thought I recognized from a hundred feet away. Sure enough, it was Washington extra fancy Winesaps. They could have been from our own farm! It was the "extra fancy" label that made it possible to market them in Paris. Since what we sold was mainly extra fancy, it definitely helped our income.[1]

Marketing associations were another approach the growers revived. The intention was to get around the commission houses or other large markets. Associations or coops kept overhead down through their non-profit status and by doing their own marketing. They could offer farm supplies to members at a discount. They also intended to keep the produce prices up by stopping underselling by individual farmers. Earlier such efforts had wilted before long.

In the late 1920s the Kennewick-Richland Growers Union attempted this strategy again. Once a certain percent of the growers had signed five year contracts with the Union they were legally obligated to sell through it at the prices it was able to get. But competing with large commission houses was high risk. The valley associations didn't have the resources to get into prolonged price wars, and they also had to cover a heavy demand for spring loans by the farmers. Their intent was good, but in reality they could not compete with the commission houses and were frequently forming and dissolving, and going into receivership. The Wheelers apparently didn't think switching from one kind of broker to another would make that much difference, and continued to sell mainly to Walter Bowen Co.

Jane Shaw did belong to a coop. Samples of her 1926-27 receipts tell how that effort succeeded. Their stock, originally worth $900 on paper, had been quite an investment. It gave members the opportunity to buy box and spray materials cheaper, while handling charges were ten percent instead of fifteen. Shaw sales for the two years totaled $1582, but the net from the coop— after commission and storage fees and box supplies— was, incredibly, only $134. Since the commission was lower than usual, any sales to another broker could have netted even less. And she still owed for labor, water and freight, with no way to pay. The Shaw five acres of apples was a small orchard, but if one triples that output, it is obvious that in 1927 a grower, even though selling through an association, even doing most of his/her own labor, and with outstanding luck, would net very little, if anything.

A note in longhand on the receipt says, "Fifty boxes were missing from the shipment". We can only hope that they were found and that Jane had a little more than $134 for her two years' work, minus labor, water, and freight costs. Another letter at that time tells that she wished to sell her shares in the association—small wonder. She would have to, to pay her bills. The manager wrote back that she was free to sell, but that at this point, "They are worth very little." The good times, such as they were, had flown off like the topsoil on the abandoned places.

The soldier-settlers were having as tough a time as any, waiting on their trees to mature. Wib Morford found that he not only could get a quick return on truck gardening, he enjoyed it, and it became a lifelong passion. Yet he couldn't make an entire living at it. He and most of the soldier-settlers found they had to find outside work. In addition to raising his fine vegetables and melons, Wib hired out as a laborer to large growers and developed skills at a variety of crafts he could assist neighbors with. For a time he worked at the Cold Storage, and later was a prime mover in the White Bluffs Canning Coop and did its bookkeeping. Even though he was allergic to bees, he became a beekeeper for a large farm, then a carpenter. Rollin, his third child, recalls that years later his father still worked ten hour days, then came home to care for his own place—not our romantic notion of the good country life. Though he had received a new little house as part of the project, it was out in the desert, too far from the river, too far from town and from Rose's own family for her to walk with babies. Soon they gave up their place, probably at the time the state closed down the project, and move back near the river to the Wheeler house while the Wheelers moved in with Jane Shaw.

Most of the foreclosed families packed up and caught the train never to look back. A few that lost their farms stayed on as tenants, although in the valley the term "tenant farming" wasn't used. They called it "renting a place". In many parts of the country tenant farming was the status of a growing majority of farmers as corporate farming took over. Not far away on the Snake, Annie Greenwood, totally disillusioned with the mystical power of land, envied the displaced tenant farmers who migrated in from Arkansas. She, like Jeanie Wheeler, worked for cash, but not in a packing shed or at the apiaries. She wrote "letters" about farm life from a rare woman's viewpoint, without sentimentality, indeed just the opposite, and sold them to the *Atlantic*. The tenant farmers were poor people, but to her the landed small farmer with a mortgage was the most abject form of life in America. She vented her rage on their Extension Agent, who taught them how to make curtains and underwear from flour sacks. Annie snorted that of course they already did that, and why wasn't he helping with their marketing?

She wrote that tenants rented abandoned places that had been bought up by absentee landholders and didn't worry themselves over mortgages. They drove cars she couldn't afford and fixed up their rented houses with furnishings, like curtains, that she had long since abandoned. She saw them as good farmers and homemakers who were more carefree, had more parties and dances with their own live music, all in contrast to her own homesteading group who seemed to slip backward, each year more exhausted and morose. If things didn't work out for tenants, they could simply move on. The dry-farming homesteaders had left in numbers when drought years hit before WWI. Irrigating wheat farmers now followed them. Annie wrote that she was glad when her family went bankrupt in 1928. That struggle was over. Tough as things were, the Priest Rapids irrigators were the best off of the three groups. They could grow almost all of their own food, an advantage that would soon be even more important.

Despite the ever increasing economic stress of the 1920s, life in White Bluffs never became a glum scene, Helen emphasizes. The free fun on the river never stopped, and social life went on much as before, not being dependent on wealth but on long-ingrained volunteerism, with the new soldier-settler blood in town giving it fresh vigor. Regardless of the dangers of "moral corruption" in the Project, the brochures had again attracted every sort of people. One large family, such as the Walkers, arriving in 1927, could change the ambience in a small community. Their arrival Helen counts as a milestone in her social life. Though they were Irish Catholic, her father did not extend his feeling about the papacy to his children's friendships. Mr. Walker was a construction contractor, and Mrs. Walker raised a huge family garden in addition to all her children. In a short time they had the magnitude of impact that the large Wheeler migration had brought a decade earlier. Oblivious of embedded factions, the Walkers welcomed all the youth, Old Towners and Out Towners alike, as visitors to their household. Gilbert Walker was Donald's partner on many boating and rafting trips. Helen counted Louise as her best friend, later to be her bridesmaid, and describes in her memoirs how this one new family made life in White Bluffs so much richer:

> The Walkers had energy and charm and were
> masters of hospitality. The kids were the most popular
> in town soon after they got there...excellent athletes
> and dancers. They were a large family like us and lived
> in a four room house—the boys slept out in the barn
> loft. Many times I stayed over when there were three of
> us girls to a bed. What they had was enthusiasm!

The new settlers, with their young energy and abilities, were soon as determined as the originals that the area develop. Many joined the Grange. Some joined the boosters lobbying the legislature for improved roads. The junior section of the Women's Club promoted more public entertainment involving local talent. The popular White Bluffs marching band opened its ranks to women, bringing in high school girls. By 1930 the census counted 670 people at White Bluffs, but that was the peak. The Depression was now official, and before long another out-migration would take place. It would include the abandonment of many soldier-settler tracts and departure of those hopeful younger families. Wib Morford was among those that stayed. The Walkers, too, stayed and continued to do their part to keep White Bluffs lively. And there was always that third group, those out at school, who kept one foot on the farm, the other in the city, unable to move forward in the valley, unable to forget it.

Margaret Wheeler, missing much of this, taught in Woodland three years, lonesome, not satisfied with her success at engaging youth in the excitement of learning. Assignments that had worked fine with her could fall flat with her students, who were largely from farming and laboring families, but not exactly like her own. Her senior colleagues offered too much advice and were ignorant on issues important to her. Worse, she was able to contribute little to the farm or to George's college expenses. In 1928, with two years' teaching experience on her resume, she sent out applications for a more lively location. The market for teachers was weaker than she expected. The next year she had better luck and landed a position east of the mountains, closer to White Bluffs. Walla Walla was a pretty river town in the desert with much more "culture" than Woodland, and the pay was better. But her parents wondered what Walla Walla would do for her career as a scholar. Couldn't she find a way to get into graduate school, or couldn't she travel abroad again if she felt stifled? No, no more self-indulgence, she declared, then thought about that more.

With the job secured, for the first time Margaret tore herself away from summer harvest duty and pleasure at the farm, and headed instead for the real cultural center, Seattle, and summer courses at the University. Perhaps she had been talking to Marian, and comparing their locations. She was thirsty for academia again, but more, she had in her heart not given up on the idea of marriage and a family, and for that she needed new hunting grounds.

That summer, before she even got to Walla Walla, all of Margaret's careful planning took a radical turn. Almost as if she knew it would happen, in Seattle she was swept away by a romantic, hardworking, very tall and handsome, but poor young man, an immigrant from Norway she met at a ballroom. Torvald Danielson, a sheet metal worker who had abandoned the fishing life of his forefathers, didn't make a high salary. He had no interest in farming, politics, religion, or unions, but he had worked successfully to perfect his English, was a fine craftsman, hiker, and an enthusiastic ballroom dancer. He could be a good father. Tor and Margaret were a showpiece on the dance floor, and didn't mind it a bit when the others stopped to watch.

According to her letters home, she knew how shocked her parents were, but she didn't listen to their polite suggestions that she not rush things. She had made her choice: marriage and children would come before further financial infusions to the farm or tuitions. She and Torvald were married at the courthouse after six weeks' acquaintance. She had to keep it secret. In Washington, marriage for a female teacher meant suspension. Once she was found out, she would be able to teach as a substitute only, but she was prepared to do that. In two weeks she was on the train for Walla Walla alone. After school was underway she made a quick weekend trip to the Bluffs. She felt defensive about the suddenness and the choice, but she had warned her parents of her mind set for marriage and children. From Walla Walla, she wrote:

> September, 1929 Dear folks,
>
>   ...It was certainly good to get home again and get some fruit and some flowers....I think I told you Torvald made $140; he makes $160 [a month], but since Daddy made more by comparison starting out, I expect to remain quite poor. However, since in comparison I have collected less worldly goods than he, I'll say nothing of that. He's interested in what I know and how I look, not what have you. And I was so interested in raving, and washing the dishes, that I didn't have a chance to look at the orchard or see the river or anything. Six hours was too short..

She ended her letter with her now constant advice. "Don't work too hard, people, there's no use."

Margaret had surely been bewitched by her new romance, not even to look at her beloved orchard or river. Sometime that summer the Wheelers had met Torvald and were still in shock—or she was—from her decision, for a month later she was still defending herself:

October 1929 Dear Folks,

[I know] you were expecting me to bring home someone so very different from what I am. You will agree, however, that at least he is very amiable and not at all dogmatic, to let me come to Walla Walla when he'd really much rather that I'd stay in Seattle. Of course he knows it's for the best. (At least it seems so at present. I have no job in Seattle and won't have one very soon.) I meet lots of intellectual men, but they seem not to be well-balanced, or else they're physically attenuated, unfit to be fathers (After all, children are my main object in getting married) or else... so gloomy or eccentric they're unendurable...I know enuf about the seriousness of life to know you'll go crazy if you begin without any gaiety... If you don't have a child by the time you're 27, it's very much the worse for you when you do. [Such was the belief of those times, and she was twenty-five]...Now mama, don't work so hard. What is the use? Donald is strong.

With much love, Margaret Jean

Regardless of their misgivings, the Wheelers welcomed Torvald warmly. Helen says that they did so with every friend or fiance their children brought home. But a serious issue faced them, Margaret hinting at it with her mention of Tor's wages, but waving it off. She had been for three years playing an economic role in the family. In a few months that would be over. Her parents knew her well enough that they didn't expect her to become a full time housewife, but just what would she do for work she would need, starting out so poor? The choices were limited. Working women were clerks, secretaries, nurses, teachers, domestic servants, or writers, unless they had a family business to go into. Yet the Wheelers hadn't wanted their daughter to be a spinster teacher, or even a spinster professor forever. The new situation was complex, but it was a *fait accompli*, and of course she had a right to it.

Their son George dropped the next surprise on them nine months later, marrying his fiancee, Eleanor Mitchell, a fellow student, the day after he graduated with his degree in Economics. He was just turning twenty-one. Now the Wheelers were doubly upset. How in the world these couples would manage in the shrinking job market, they couldn't guess. To Frank and Jeanie, marriage meant children. Rose had her third already. Too well the Wheelers remembered their early struggles and a new baby every two years. Their concern was timely; in a few months the country would go into a tailspin.

Margaret finished her year at Walla Walla, resigned, announced her marriage publicly, and rushed to her honeymoon home in Seattle to find Torvald threatened with layoff daily. She had thought she could get substitute teaching jobs in Seattle, but it turned out not so. She was at the bottom of a long list of married women wishing to teach. No matter, she proposed to teach French or English to those who could teach her and Torvald music. Meanwhile she would make the most of her romance and drink in every bit of culture the great city offered that they could afford. Her sister Marian, the working woman, moved into a small porch room they had and helped with the house payments.

Despite the Wheelers' worries, neither of the newlywed couples had children until 1936. The Great Depression held up many plans for families. But in Margaret's case, the waiting was not intentional. She intended to get pregnant as fast as possible, her only justification for her reckless move. But she didn't. A doctor informed her she must have a cyst removed; she did so immediately, using up the rest of her savings. And still she didn't get pregnant. She looked for work and saw only more layoffs. The Wheelers sent more boxes of food.

One gloomy day in 1929, Margaret's father scratched off to her a most despairing letter:

> ...My hide hangs in strips not folds over the question of living in the country. I seem to forget about some of the Nectar and Ambrosia forced on us in early days. Devouring anxiety as how to keep the old wolf off the ranch clouds my memory, but to me town is a treadmill without any toehold...

That whole spring Frank's letters had a wistful, melancholy tinge to them, even questioning one of his most fond beliefs, the superior life in the country. To have given this cause twenty-three years, now to wonder; trickling anguish was merging to a stream. Partly it was physical fatigue and the pain of rheumatism that plagued him. At thirty-three, working construction to develop the farm was fine. Now at fifty-six, his bones, muscles and teeth cried out with every brick he set in place. This may have been the first time he felt in those bones that the venture wasn't going to work out.

Partly his mood was from seeing his children go off. Right then the focus was on George. Frank loved the desert and regretted that he could not entice his oldest son back to the farm in the summers. George, seeing even more clearly than his father the way the economy was going, had chosen to stick with his summer job with the Forest Service, not to return to White Bluffs for the harvest. Now he was married. Frank tried to accept it in a letter the same month to Jeanie:

> ...I can see it as a Honeymoon eyrie, one of the fire

stations, and if George is to collect sticks for the nest so be it. Does Eleanor graduate too? Ill not try to pester George. Id think the River alone worth all that whole country and all the chance to work both could ask.

Why hide out under the leaves or hemlock brush?

He wondered why George, about to go off to graduate school on a fellowship, couldn't become a homeopathic physician so he could continue to live on the Columbia. But George's head was elsewhere—on his new wife, and studies in the East in their chosen fields.

Frank's wistful need to be near his own wife was his other clear theme. Jeanie, in perfect physical health at forty-seven, could be up and ready for another day's work each morning and still had a hard time understanding how he could wish to stay home on the farm more, while she, their bookkeeper, saw each year go by with nothing to show but more trees, berries, and flowers. She may have felt they still had a chance if they could focus a little more, try a little harder.

Frank tried to focus on his children's successes, but a letter to Margaret the same month ended on a note of self-pity. "...Iv loafed all this time. I was a Dolt. Never in thirty years has winter been any good [for jobs] but it irks Mater to have me stay on top of the stove, so I scramble out, I wish to Timbuctoo or some other rock pile in the Lord's Vineyard."

Frank well knew what Jeanie's problem was, and he blamed himself somewhat. He wrote to Margaret that he wanted to buy a lot in Seattle and build a house large enough that Margaret and her husband could live there, but everyone would have a place to stay when they visited the city. Then Jeanie, with only train fare to manage, could travel back and forth more freely. His daughter had to reply with the sad truth that there was no way that all of them together could finance the building of a house in Seattle, even if all the labor were volunteered.

Frank and Jeanie had accomplished more than either could acknowledge. They had raised their children in the healthy environment they had dreamed of. They had supported them every way they could to higher education, and were proud of the results. He was simply exhausted. But for his next letter to Jeanie, he turned from vinegar to honey. No more lists of chores for her to do, or to supervise others to do. It is almost as if he sensed the change for everyone coming:

> ...I wish now Id come back from California and known you 3 or 4 years sooner. It is just life lost....This is a most lovely morning except I woke up and Jeanie was not there where she belongs....We have our plans to work out. Id like to work it out with due regard to seeing you at times. One night a year leaves a lot to wish about. Think so sweetheart?...Well, Iv work for next week mostly. Nothing big in sight. But it isn't $150 between hugs now. Well, I'm on my way to the Baptist kirk so must adjourn. You sweetheart will be my text in thought if not in arms. With many wishes to have you with me, and a very near and dear close "with", and all my love...

By that fall the whole world changed. Frank was home to stay. Taking the train to seek work was a waste of time, the coast workers being worse off than he. Finally he could take time he wished for family and farm, and Jeanie had her man at home—as it turned out, for the rest of his life. As the Great Depression locked its grip, she had no more concern about how her tea table measured up to those of the other matrons as they all suffered empty cupboards together. The Wheeler couple finally had the year-round mellow relationship Helen remembers. The Depression, oddly enough, brought their romance, marriage and partnership a new grace.

17

THE MAN WITH A HOE

"When they had no money for anything else he would order a tree;
then my mother in turn would order flower seed."
Margaret Wheeler Schuddakopf, 1968

IT IS EASY TO BECOME so engrossed in the economic struggles of the
orchardists that we forget their original challenge: to transform a desert.
Though most of them did not see that as a battle most of the time, in the
middle of a jack rabbit migration, or later a codling moth invasion, they
could have easily used that term. But they the irrigators were the invaders.
Whatever their particular beliefs about nature, to carry out their plans
they had to tamper with it in a major way. Unlike the Native Americans
who had long-standing general rules about how to live in nature, each settler
family had arrived with their own level of respect for the environment they
were intruding on. They needed to study their strange new home and try out
their own ideas of stewardship. But they also had to agree to some common
principles in order to operate their irrigation systems. Community norms
gradually developed, not so much to preserve the nature around them as to
preserve themselves. Dust storms were only their first warning that they
would have to become conservationists if they would survive. The success they

had at tuning their farming needs to the rhythms of the ecosystem they were invading is of special interest, for today irrigation is associated with huge, bountiful agribusiness, but also with ruined lands.

Those 1906-07 settlers would today be viewed as innocents. This doesn't mean that the dangers in irrigation weren't known. Vast areas of Eurasia had already been leached beyond repair. Knowledgeable people did testify to Congress about their concern that irrigation in large tracts could go out of control. But almost all believed that small tract family farms coupled with science could avoid such disasters. They probably did not concern themselves at all with how irrigation would affect sagebrush or coyotes or salmon.

As we have seen, the nineteenth century homesteaders up on the Wahluke Slope had largely failed. But those homesteaders scattered along the Columbia and Cold Creek banks mainly survived, disturbing the ecosystem only a little. There were thousands of acres of desert habitat in all directions, and they could irrigate only a narrow strip along the river. From Harris' information and the *Family Histories,* it appears that there were never more than about fifteen homesteads along the river at any one time from Priest Rapids to Hanford. Large production for a distant market didn't and couldn't take place. Once they had overcome the Indian claim to the land, the worst trouble for the riverbank homesteaders, aside from their isolation, was the dust storms. But their storms were nothing like those on the plateau where stubborn wheat farmers had disturbed miles of topsoil. If valley homesteaders didn't grow wheat and kept their herds at numbers they could care for through winter, using the essential bunch grass and perhaps a few acres of alfalfa, the storms were manageable. Their cattle did trample the riparian border, but migrating sheep flocks that passed through did more extensive damage.

Aside from the dust, which the homesteaders felt comfortable blaming on wheat and sheepmen, they saw little change but for the better in the valley. They were probably unaware of the importance of the trampled hemp, camas and other root grounds to the Indians. If they knew, probably few cared. They saw those people as rightly or wrongly doomed. They saw the valuable bunch grass declining, but perhaps it would come back if the huge sheep flocks stayed away. They saw the exotic plants stake their claims: the Russian olive, and the beginnings of Russian thistle that turned to tumbleweed. The insidious cheat grass had yet to show its true power, while the wild rye and pigweed coming in were a benefit. Their alfalfa could make up the loss of bunch grass for small herds. As for the native animals, the number of wild horses, deer, coyotes, badgers and wildcats the homesteaders hunted for a little cash were quickly replenished, and the rabbits all too quickly. No one knows who introduced the carp or why, but the homesteaders were probably the first to see their value as fertilizer. No doubt some of the early homesteaders had wished to expand their irrigation, (which would have increased their impact), but with gravity-flow ditches impossible in the district, they couldn't afford expansion.

The irrigators arriving with the Shaws were a different story. Their whole intent was to convert the desert to commercial farmland using irrigation entirely. Now humans were definitely impacting the fragile desert. But at that time the Emersonian view of nature prevailed: if properly in harness for mankind, Nature would flourish. Watering a desert could not be wrong; not watering it was a waste, and to some, immoral. A few people did have more knowledge of history than that. In parts of the West, intensive large irrigation had caused soil saturation to the point where a whole system of drainage ditches was required to go with the irrigation ditches. Alkalization (excessive mineral deposits from irrigation) had ruined entire farms, even districts, permanently.

Neither drainage nor alkalization was a problem at White Bluffs during those years, Donald remembers, something few districts could boast.

The soil was gravelly, making for good drainage, and there was no close upriver farming district draining and leaching minerals down to them. However, though White Bluffs/Hanford at the head of the valley escaped these problems, there were drainage ponds not far downriver near Richland. They were so large that someone had stocked them with tasty "mudcats" that they fished as children. Harris talks about alkalization that had developed at the Grosscup Ranch outside Richland by the early 1920s. The valley obviously was not exempt from such problems of irrigation; just those farms in the upper valley were. We can't know how much the problem would have expanded if irrigation had continued at the scale it was in the early 1940s.

The worst damage being done to the Columbia's habitat was to the anadromous fish stock. The Indians first, and then the biologists, saw the dangerous decline well on its way before the orchardists arrived, to the point where only a small fraction were caught from the fall run. Nets and wheels had been barred on the middle and upper river since 1910, leaving no economic incentive for busy farmers to gear up for fishing. The Wheelers admired the fishing skills of their Wanapum neighbors and appreciated the gift of a fish for dinner, and had no inkling of the impending salmon crisis. Perhaps the rows of drying salmon along the bank looked bountiful. If farmers did find out about the decline they could blame it on lumbering and commercial fishing, not on fingerlings being sucked into diversion ditches.

After the Extension Service started emphasizing conservation, farmers learned to plant vetch, a cheap fast-growing ground cover useful in orchards, and like alfalfa, a nitrogen fixer badly needed in a district where there was never enough fertilizer. "We always planted vetch in the orchard," Donald Wheeler remembers. "The shortage of local fertilizers was one of those things the developers never thought of." But each time a tract was abandoned, the ground cover quickly dried up, and there was little the adjoining farms could do to stop the flyaway topsoil.

The truth about that useful ground cover, cheat grass, emerged. More powerful than the nutritious bunchgrass, cheat grass overtook it, and prevented its comeback. Cheat grass sprouted lush and green each spring but dried off quickly to a useless stubble by summer and, unlike bunchgrass, was no forage at all for winter. Donald remembers that its little hooks were misery to the humans who got them in their socks and were worse yet for livestock. Horses in particular didn't like cheat grass but would eat it when hungry enough. Then it hooked its way into their gums, creating sores that could get infected. Once it got into an alfalfa field there was really no way to get it out. It had one saving grace; it was ground cover. The introduced wild rye, on the other hand, was fine pasture. But it was not so fine in an asparagus or strawberry field. Strangely, there was no native locoweed right around White Bluffs to bother the settlers' precious few cattle or sheep, and it didn't migrate in.

All of the exotic weeds had arrived before the irrigators, brought in by migrating herds, but now irrigation entirely changed the flora around the settlements. The settlers didn't see it as a problem, as there was room for both. Not many of that generation would have argued that an acre of sagebrush was more valuable than an acre of potatoes, when there was so much sagebrush, and the world needed potatoes. But we know that the orchardists did appreciate the beauty of the natural desert, as so many mention it in *Family Histories*. With a combined population around Hanford and White Bluffs that never went over 1100, and no big dam to bring in another rush, they were possibly right that they could have continued to have both wild nature and their orchards. Today biologists say the uninhabited area is remarkably free of invasive species.

Though in other areas of the West the Euro-Americans often saw nature as adversary, the valley mainly lived up to the promise of the brochures of being friendly to human habitation. The green strips of willow and grass along the canal provided cover for the game birds that the settlers introduced. The orchards brought in larks, orioles, and bluebirds and did not create trouble for the desert birds who had their own milieu. In some stretches, muskrats and beavers moved in along the canal and provided furs for extra cash. Though their burrows were an annoyance, they were not a serious danger to the system as long as they were attended to. In some stretches pond weed in the canals became a problem, but at White Bluffs the canal current was strong enough that herbicide was never used. After some years, the riparian border damaged earlier by the big herds began to recover. How much damage the carp or bass did to the native fish during that period is unknown but had to be minute compared to what the big dams did later. The introduced poplar and locust shade trees' roots did tear up the irrigation pipes, but they did no harm to the desert flora as they could not spread beyond the river bank or irrigated area.

The "varmints" that plagued the dry farmers were not such a nuisance to the orchardists. A coyote was rarely seen near the orchards, rattlesnakes never. With the exception of the jack rabbits, varmints (ground squirrels, badgers, hawks, coyotes) seem to have been mainly an excuse to go hunting for men that craved a break in the routine. People left alone the huge bull snakes in the orchards that preyed on small animals like ground squirrels but did no harm to large ones. Some people talked about the losses in poultry from coyotes, but Donald is skeptical, saying they could be heard on the bluffs but only came into the settlement if they were rabid. "We lost chickens, but they were to the neighbors' dogs running loose, and our tall trees usually protected the chickens from hawks. Dad never used a gun, didn't feel he had to." Farmers farther out would have disagreed.

Earlier, wild horses (many of them had been Indian horses) had competed for the valuable bunch grass, but they had mainly been killed off;

Donald saw a herd only once. At White Bluffs there were none of the prairie dogs,(*cynomys*), that destroyed farms in other districts, and the "sage rats"(ground squirrels, *citellus*) were simply a nuisance for the Wheelers. They never poisoned them, simply watched closely. But a 1936 varmint hunt offering awards by the Kennewick Sportsman's Club reportedly brought in 10,000 kills of wildlife (horses were spared), demonstrating that many farmers did not follow Frank's philosophy.

Much more destructive to the settlers than those above were the native hares, the black-tailed jack rabbits. Their natural reproduction was greatly increased through improved nutrition provided by the farms. Several settlers mention in their histories that there had been "white-tailed" rabbits when they arrived, and that they had at least been good eating. No one knows for sure, but it seemed that the unpalatable "blacktails" had driven them off. The people who hunted coyotes for sport, Margaret points out, also helped the jack rabbit explosion along, but it was irrigation that brought them in from the desert. Donald remembers alfalfa fields where the jacks had passed through looking as if they had been mowed; they would return later to eat the haystacks. If a farmer could, on his own, reportedly kill a hundred in a night, one can picture what he faced. The Wheelers found out the worst when they lost a whole new apricot orchard to jacks one winter in the early 1940s. The battle with hares is one of the best examples of where co-existence did not work out for the settlers.

Even hares were not the worst headache for orchardists. The most destructive problem from the natural world was, in the early years, the late frosts in the valley. These took place every few springs, and there was no real remedy. We recall the year the Wheelers were able to save only twenty-four boxes of soft fruit. Soon, however, insects became the chief adversary. The valley was home to several indigenous and imported insects. Ticks, native and introduced flies, and mosquitoes, all encouraged by the moisture of irrigation, were miserable nuisances. Bedbugs must have come in with humans and were the scourge of all desert settlements; there was hardly any escaping. Flies required a constant battle if one hoped to enjoy an indoor meal. George describes the big flytrap that sat in the Wheeler kitchen. These sorts of pests could cause temporary fits in the people trying to avoid them, but were not lethal to humans or their enterprises. Malaria, once deadly on the lower river, never moved in; equine encephalitis came only once as an epidemic.

The insects that attacked the crops, however, were a grim story indeed. When early Yakima fruit growers brought in their favorite varieties from their home states, the pests from home arrived with them: San Jose scale, woolly aphids, backslider bugs, fungi, and on and on, and then what was to be the ultimate destroyer of crops—the codling moth. It wasn't much of a challenge for the moth to find its way into the Priest Rapids valley from the Yakima. Just how much this pest information was available to the inexperienced orchardists when they first arrived is not clear. The state agricultural college at Pullman had reports available to those who knew where to write and what questions to ask. The average settler probably didn't know that, but a trip to the Yakima to ask around would have told them the truth. The pests at home there would very soon be at the Columbia. Yet such facts would not have quelled the excitement over the magic of water applied to desert lands.

Before long, however, the settlers noticed that each year the insect pests were worse, requiring more exhausting, hot, dangerous work. Donald, looking at the spraying from sixty years' perspective, is angry:

> The government knew what we were offering to the
> public to eat was deadly to their health. All that
> research was going on about sprays, never any
> alternatives offered from the County Agent except—

spray more, spray more! Till it was twelve in a season on the apples. The big chemical companies were making their millions off these toxins, and they had their powerful lobbyists. The government was unwilling to take them on. No one did anything about it until Rachel Carson came along with *Silent Spring* in the late fifties. I shudder now to think of our apples that went into kids' lunch boxes. Sure, we tried to wash them carefully, but you know there was bound to be some residue on them. Twelve sprays! Unlike the other fruit, for the codling moth the last sprays had to go not just on the blossoms but right on the apples themselves.

No one knew either what the long-range health effects were on the orchardists applying the spray, and without the unusable masks. The codling moth in particular, with the deadly lead arsenate spray, was an influence in the direction the Wheeler's orchard took, away from apples to soft fruit. This is the one instance in which the Priest Rapids growers gave unconditional surrender to their adversaries when, in the late 1930s, many began to cut down their apple trees. The one aspect of their orchard venture that the living Wheelers question more than any other was the spraying, a problem never resolved. Donald, in the 1990s, stopped using any kind of sprays on his small subsistence orchard, but the results on his fruit were not good.

The Wanapum view of the changes in the valley had to be quite different from the settlers. Gable Mountain was sacred ground to them. We know from Relander's and other interviews that they complained about losing their horse pastures and their root grounds. And even though they weren't farming, they had to be aware of the battles on the Yakima as their relatives struggled to become successful irrigators. There, irrigation ditches were going dry each August as more settlers, often squatters, moved in. But the greater concern for them was the ever-reducing salmon runs and the loss of their fishing rights. The Wanapums still on the Columbia must have resented the orchards and pastures that required irrigation and were therefore one of arguments for big dams. But their feelings came out, not at White Bluffs but later, at protest fish-ins at the lower river's closed fisheries. Celilo Falls, the greatest Native American salmon harvesting site of all, was the first eliminated for a dam.

The small irrigators missed the significance of these encroachments. Donald shakes his head, "We were all for the big dams at the time. When one of the Reed professors told us students that the dams would destroy the salmon, that even fish ladders wouldn't save them, that the fry would get the "bends" going down through the turbines, we scoffed." But the controversy over salmon grew, taken up by interest groups with far more power than the Indians. By the mid-1960s it would dwarf any other river issue. Soon another alarm was clanging: the massive irrigation on the high slope above the river was beginning to erode the bluffs and cause them to slide toward the river. To understand the outrage this caused northwest environmentalists, we have to imagine agribusiness perched on the edge of the Grand Canyon starting to send mud down its banks.

If we put decreasing salmon runs and increasing pesticides aside—large set-asides— the impact of the early irrigators on the ecology of the Priest Rapids valley seems to have been much less stressful than in other regions, or in later times. Because the land was not free, and the water delivery marginal, the early boom never became a huge rush. The native flora and fauna outside the orchards, except for the degraded bunchgrass, thrived.

The human groups in the valley also got along with each other reasonably well, for the irrigators the proof being that the ditch master on the Hanford ditch did not carry a shotgun. The remaining Wanapum were harassed little and harassed others less yet. The valley was spared one more problem of larger districts. Due to its isolation, few migrant workers made it their stopping place, and the rigid class structure of overlord orchardists and indigent migrant workers never developed as it did in nearby districts like Wenatchee. Such an evolution would surely have changed the ambience.

The Shaw/Wheeler family itself, for its times, should get high scores for ecological sensitivity. They didn't kill the natural inhabitants of the desert except for the flies, and sometimes the rattlesnakes on the bluffs. Helen comments that though no one living near the orchards had been killed by rattlers, they knew of a bluff family that lost two children to them. They valued the desert flora even though they planted their own flower gardens. They didn't use poison on "varmints". A sort of poor co-existence was managed with insect pests on the crops, but not with the codling moth. They used methods to fight it that were against their instincts and their own safety, and the moth won. How long they and the other small orchardists could have maintained their humble co-existence in the valley we can't know. When the Depression hit, cutting back all their resources, there was no more money for fertilizer, much less mechanization, and further expansion in acreage was out. But of course the big dams would eventually come.

The orchardists' own survival, not that of the natural world, was their daily concern. As the market kept shrinking, and wage work simply disappeared, the growers of the late 1920s turned more to their only outside support, the Extension Agent. His mantra was unvaried: Diversify, diversify. Frank was his ardent disciple. If the times had been different Frank's (now full time) horticulture experiments would eventually have paid off in the best varieties for the area's climate and soil, for withstanding the rigors of shipping, the insects, and for consumer delight. Despite a very reduced household budget, he was still a regular customer of a tree nursery just down the river at Richland. He must have been their most unusual client. Margaret comments on this passion of her father and her mother's attempts to curb it:

> Tending trees, not the business of farming, was my father's love. My mother, I believe, did not think him a good farmer. He did not make money at it. Machinery, generally the pumping plant or the sprayer, was constantly needing repair. My father, although very manual, was anything but mechanical. This I know: he was expert at picking out the best kinds of trees, grapes and melons, and there was little in nature he loved as much as a tree. He was successful in growing tons of first class fruit that found its way to the Seattle market. But my mother was right—by the time the [bills] were paid, the financial rewards to the farmer were slight or non-existent.

If Jeanie actually blamed their financial failures on Frank's experiments, she wasn't being logical, for we have seen that her own mother, who forsook experiments, staying with the original Winesap apples, couldn't turn a profit either. The larger spreads who produced more, borrowed more, and ended frequently in bankruptcy. And though it was inefficient for Frank to bypass a plow for a hoe, Margaret comments:

> I suspect Dad derived a great deal of pleasure from hand-cultivating around the nectarines, the almond trees which finally bore, and all the varieties of peach he tried from Carman to Elberta to Salway....Nor were the small fruits omitted. He had everything from gooseberries and blackberries through currants and strawberries. On the east slope of the hill were four

kinds of grapes. It seemed that as much as the flavor
and texture of the fruit, the appearance delighted him.
He was always bringing in for dinner a [new fruit
variety] inviting us to share in their exquisite shapes,
colors, and fragrance.

Frank may have carried his diversification to an extreme with eighteen
varieties of apples, and a similar approach to other crops. He saw that with
few exceptions, his neighbors, no matter what they did, stayed marginal
regardless, and apparently thought that if he were going to sink all his
resources and energy into this work, he would have fun at it. Donald
comments that Jeanie's frustration with this was partly because it fell on her
to figure out how to pack the harvest from a single experimental tree so that
it could go as a commercial shipment. The only possibility was an "extra
fancy" custom pack, for a specialized retail market. But though it wasn't
typical business, Donald says that Schroeder, their broker's agent, never
turned down a custom-pack box from them. He must have had special
outlets for these offbeat varieties. Since Frank was never refused, he was
encouraged the more, and his gratitude toward Schroeder grew.
Meanwhile, the experiments added zest to the family meals as they
wondered what their father would bring to dinner that day. [1]

Donald defends his father on the issue of diversification:

You had to constantly be looking for new fruits and
new varieties to find something for the market,
something not overproduced. From a monetary
standpoint, strawberries were still one of the most
successful crops we raised. What drove us to get out of it
[again] was the weeding. I was seven the year of the
second strawberry investment, and a lot of that weeding
fell to me, not just my older siblings.

Bing cherries were an early crop that turned out well. But even then, something that seemed perfect could fail for you. One time it was gooseberries. We found out they could grow at White Bluffs and there was a shortage. Aha! We raised gooseberries and got a decent price. But before long the word came down from County Extension, "Gooseberries are carrying pine rust (or some other evergreen pest). Destroy all your gooseberries!" So we did.

Another time we saw an opportunity in apricots. Not many people were growing them and we had wonderful cots for family use. So we put in a small orchard of apricots. By the time we were getting a good crop, the rush was over. We had the cots, nobody wanted them. We got 2 1/4 cents a pound. One year I remember Dad leased ten extra acres and planted it all to navy beans. That must have been an attempt to get practical. The crop was successful, but he never did it again—either the price was poor or it wasn't interesting enough. As my sister says, fruit was his passion.

Grapes, once regarded as a great promise for the valley, had their own history of disappointment. When asked how Prohibition affected the grape growers, Donald's response speaks for the overall state of the fruit market:

Prohibition? It had virtually no effect on valley grape growers. We never could get a good price for grapes anyway; it never rose over two cents a pound. So by Prohibition no one was even trying to market grapes any more. We just had them for home use. One year we

349

even tried making raisins from our Thompson Seedless. They turned out wonderful, except for one thing—each raisin had a tiny stem attached to it, and we had no idea how to get those off mechanically, so we couldn't sell them. Sun Maid had a secret we didn't have.

Donald had his own special incident regarding moonshiners:

I never told this story before, but there was an itinerant dentist that for years stopped by each summer to get his truck load of grapes. He picked them himself, paying us 2.5 cents, and making no secret about what he would do with them. But I hated the grapes even at that inflated price. For that long tedious labor banking them with a hoe each fall, his 2 1/2 cents just wasn't worth it. One summer, about 1928, knowing that hoeing time would be coming round again soon, when the dentist arrived I told him that we were out of the business. Oh, he was mad, how could I do such a thing! But it was true, no more grape sales. I had decided to let them all die, simply by not watering them.

Donald admits to rebelling only this one time against his Herculean list of chores. "He didn't kill *all* the grapes," Helen comments, "we always had plenty for the family." He doesn't remember any argument with his father over it later. Perhaps, just as Frank didn't like to butcher, it was easier for him to let his son kill his grapes.

In the long agricultural depression that followed World War I, government studies of the Pacific Northwest found that the only crop market that did not fall below cost of production was dairy. The Shaws had been wise to stick to dairy as a balance to their five acres of Winesaps.

Ten years later, during the Great Depression, a Washington State

College study of farming in Benton County found it, unsurprisingly, still doing poorly, with orchardists again the worst off. But farms most diversified were showing the least loss. Going into soft fruit should have been the right move if there were any market at all, but by then Americans weren't buying much, certainly not fruit.

Diversification had its supporters and detractors along a continuum. Some of the more conservative farmers, like the Shaws, started with a particular activity and stayed with it no matter what. At the other extreme were farmers like Wib Morford who shifted crops constantly to catch the developing markets. It wasn't realistic to do that with fruit trees. Donald says that his father didn't lecture on the virtues of experimentation, he just did it, and won respect as a horticulturist, with growers often coming to him for his suggestions. Though Jeanie complained about the extra work it gave her, she was no doubt proud of the results and the recognition.

Diversification had other values besides finding the best markets. Beating California to the earliest market meant finding a variety that ripened one week earlier than another. Diversifying was also a way to cut losses from late frosts. Since efforts with smudge pots and orchard heaters usually didn't work, the answer was to have several varieties of a fruit that blossomed on different days. But as the trouble from imported pests continued to grow, the search for fruits and varieties most resistant to them turned out to be the most urgent reason of all for diversification.

Frank's experimentation went beyond plants at times. Chickens were another interest, though never a commercial one. Everyone had chickens, but Frank's, of course, were more than ordinary chickens. Though he had many kinds—the chicken yard was always colorful—he favored two breeds, Indian game chickens, from India originally, and bantams. They were the most beautiful, but were also were hardy and good foragers. The bantam chickens were really too small to be practical, but were so gorgeous, as pretty as pheasants, that they were forgiven. Frank didn't like his pretty chickens cooped up, he liked them running about, so a game cock with long spurs that could defend his harem against hawks and other predators was valuable. His brother Nat did a spin-off business shipping game chicken fertilized eggs. Some men in the valley fought the game cocks as a gambling pastime, but it is not surprising that Frank never did. Any fighting his cock did was with him, and he had scars on his legs from its long spurs to show. Free-ranging chickens meant great fun for children, too, searching out the nests, but meant there was always a mess on the shaded front porch. Helen says this was the sort of thing that Frank and Jane Shaw had differences over, the children had giggles over, and we can imagine Jeanie caught in the middle.

Ducks, geese, and turkeys were all tried by Frank and rejected in favor of the beautiful and prolific game chickens. Goats were also rejected as too troublesome although Rose raised them later. One aborted plan behind raising Ribbon's two colts was to sell them, in a valley needing a better line of horses. Priest Rapids families increasingly tried everything as fruit failed, from raising horses and pigs to growing melons, sweet potatoes, hops, mint, sorghum, peanuts, and later, sugar beets. The 1925 Grape Festival at Kennewick displayed close to one hundred different crops.

The Wheelers, by 1930 full time non-profit farmers, still had their other major goal to attend to—their four children yet without their college degrees. Now there was no extra cash at all, not even the ten dollar bill Frank used to stick in a letter. But they had learned ways to get around this. When Donald was about to be a senior at White Bluffs High, they recalled the advantage of graduation from a city high school, and he traveled to Seattle for his senior year. Since Marian was already filling the extra space at Margaret's, he turned to the Eagle's "house for indigent boys" and washed dishes for his room and board. He was able to get the advanced math course he needed at Queen Anne High while Margaret crammed French into him on the weekends. Donald's history teacher, a politically liberal woman, was so impressed with his accumulated knowledge and his ability to express it that she on occasion turned the incredulous class over to him and sat back to enjoy his lectures. Like his father, his shyness and patched overalls didn't stop articulate lecturing. He graduated in December and was back at the farm in time to help with the spring spraying. Soon the news came that he had won an alumni scholarship to cover his tuition at Reed. Of course it would be Reed. His parents were able to find housing for him with a professor who already knew his brother and sister, and were glad to welcome another Wheeler.

But how would Donald get to Portland? To get home from Seattle to White Buffs, he had been forced to hitch a ride on a freight car, his first experience with hoboing. Margaret had given him her last car token to get him down to the freight yards. He told his parents it wasn't dangerous, that the conductors didn't mind college boys riding the freight cars, and that others had been with him, which was true, but he had skirted around some of the risky details. Now to get to Portland he and a White Bluffs buddy concocted another daring adventure. His friend had a new outboard motor he couldn't pay for that he needed to return to the dealer in Portland and get a promised refund. He also had an old skiff he was willing to abandon when they reached their destination.

Going down river wasn't dangerous until they reached Umatilla Rapids, a stretch they had never seen. Of course they could beach the skiff if the rapids looked too wild, but they were sure they could make it and did. Donald called his worried parents—they had given him fifteen cents—when they got past the Rapids, leaving his only other shirt in the phone booth. He arrived at college almost threadbare but soon won the respect of his classmates and professors.

The fall of 1931 started off very well with Marian and Donald at college, George and Eleanor at graduate school, Margaret enjoying marriage and the cultural life of Seattle, and Frank at home with Jeanie where he belonged. But soon an unexpected disaster struck, this time not human but mechanical. The apple-washing machine fiasco is an example of how much precision was demanded for orchardry, and how a small error could have monstrous results. And once more the whole trouble started with the codling moth.

Washing apples before packing them had become the law of the land about 1920. A fatality had occurred somewhere that was blamed on the toxic spray that all commercial apples were subjected to. Prior to 1920 packers had been required merely to wear cotton gloves and wipe each apple well before wrapping it. Now, with the new washing regulation, another chore was added to the grower's process. The Extension Agent came around to give demonstrations, and Donald remembers being shown how to put the apples in a dilute hydrochloric acid bath and wash each one by hand to remove most of the spray residue. This fussy extra process went on for some years; someone had to find a more efficient way. Donald tells what happened:

> Someone developed an apple-washing machine, a
> great labor saver. In spring of 1930 the folks decided to
> purchase a second-hand one and try out the new
> technology. However, the Depression had arrived and
> the folks got such a poor price for their early fruit that
> they were unable to make payments on the washer. It
> was taken back by its owners before they could even try
> it out. Wib Morford, a man excellent at putting things
> together, decided to construct a copy of the washer,
> and the next fall they were back in business, they

thought. At one point my mother suggested they should wash some of the apples by hand so that they could compare lots later as to the effect of the two methods. But the men overrode her, and all the apples were put through the washer.

Later that fall they received an alarmed message from Schroeder, their broker, who by then had all their apples in storage at Seattle. Grandma's were not in cold storage, though, because he had run out of room (everyone was holding their apples, hoping for a price raise) so he was watching hers carefully. One day when he opened a box for inspection, he discovered that a number of the apples were spoiling. He checked another box. It was all right. Another box—spoilage. He was perplexed. He opened some of the Wheeler boxes in the cold storage. Spoilage.

In shock, everyone decided it had to be the apple-washing machine as it was the only thing we were doing differently. But why were only some boxes spoiling? Later, after a lot of debate, we concluded that the apples that were lower down in the tank were under just enough water pressure that the acid bath was forced into them through the calyx, while the ones farther up survived fine.

The folks were in a real fix and I felt terrible because I had just started classes and I couldn't leave to go help them. They would have to separate out and repack the good apples. The spoilage turned out to be about twenty percent—all of their profit margin, were there any to be had. In the end, Schroeder himself repacked grandma's boxes without charge. Wib, later joined by Rose, went to Seattle to repack the rest while Mother watched their children.

The apple crop had been exceptional that year, hardly a blemish on them according to a letter from Mother. Now what was left sold for a dollar a box. I think it was the worst single disaster of our farming. I tried to write about it later, and I couldn't. I just collapsed, thinking about it.

The battle with the codling moth intensified. By 1936 the Wheelers, Jane Shaw and many others would make the tough decision to pull out their remaining apple trees. Jane's apple trees were the first trees that had been planted at Mayflower Farm by her and her husband. Helen, who was there to witness the destruction, says, "It was one of the saddest events to happen to Grandma. She cried as each tree went down." Donald adds, "I was in Europe and they didn't even tell me. They knew how I'd feel." There was nothing left in an apple tree but sentiment, and of that there was plenty, but one couldn't sell it. From then on the destruction was easier. The Wheelers would pull out one crop after another, each time to replace it with something new to entice the public, yet not entice the pests, each year with a shred of hope.

The only good side to the apple washing disaster was that it gave Rose her chance to go to Seattle, not just to repack apples, but for medical treatment she needed. Frank and Jeanie watched her children. She took her portfolio of drawings with her, and Marian arranged for her to meet the Northwest artist Ziegler. He was impressed enough to offer her free lessons. Wib returned to the farm when the apples were packed, but Rose stayed in Seattle six months turning out sketches. Then her husband called her home.

The Wheelers urged her to return for more lessons, but the wife and mother was needed. Rose's art career was again postponed, but not forgotten.

That spring the Wheelers came up with another idea to give Jeanie a change from farming and to make money as well. Donald says it originally came from him to be seized on by his father. At Reed he had received a gloomy letter from his mother—she wrote him every week—and it disturbed him that he, George and Maion off at school having a fine time, and here was his steadfast mother feeling so defeated. If this letter had been in Jeanie's own collection she would no doubt have destroyed it as she did her other "whiny" ones:

> We are canning 12 qts of meat tonight. It is a job I loathe. How I would like to live in town where there is just housework and sewing, not this everlasting fussing with meat and butter and outdoor work. We could have swam in milk for the same value in money as the hay—besides all the work. Well, I was only 24 when we bought this ranch but that was plenty old enough to know better. My mother always told me about the futility and the hard work but at that time apple growers were just doing fine—and we thought to have an independent old age. Ha! Ha! Daddy said today he guessed we'd starve when we were old if it wasn't for the children.... Marian says she hates to see the time go by, learning something every day. So with three in college and a fourth pursuing the cultural life we ought to be satisfied. Some record for hard times.
>
> ...It is time to put on the lime sulfur—heaven knows how we will manage. Roberts has put on a man in Wib's place at $40 a month, board himself, and has five

children. Of course the farmers can't help it. It's all
they can afford. Well, 'scuse me if I seem doleful. I have
to work it out of my system once in a while—and your
shoulders are broad and your years young.

Lots of love, Mother

Donald's brainstorm for his tired mother was that the Wheelers should
rent a large place near the Reed campus that Jeanie would run as a
boarding house for students and enjoy the culture of Portland. Several
exchanges of letters went back and forth, with all of the family giving their
advice. George finally torpedoed the idea. He feared that his little brother
would inevitably be pulled into helping out at the boarding house and be
drawn away from his studies. He was probably right, says Donald, as Jeanie
wouldn't be able to do the whole thing alone. Donald was dependent on his
alumni scholarship, which required top grades. Other serious questions soon
arose: supplies, licenses, how one collected rent from broke students, and just
how much a person netted from these operations. Although students were
still trying to go to college, few of them could pay their bills at their boarding
houses.

The older Wheeler youth were more practical than their father, and
Donald says he ended up embarrassed. Though Frank kept bringing up
boarding houses and similar notions, all with the idea to get Jeanie into an
interesting and paying project, none of them materialized. In an earlier
brainstorm he had even thought of Jeanie starting a women's clothing store
in White Bluffs, and had ordered samples sent from New York via his sister.
But she collected bargain clothing with no appeal for White Bluffs women
who, even if isolated, knew what was in style. The main person to benefit
from the unusual surfeit of clothing was Marian, who looked great modeling
it, a jealous little Helen observed. "I guess we'll have to keep that one,"
Frank would say, again and again. Few sold and Jeanie quietly put the rest

away.

Just how much Jeanie herself felt she needed these new "business" challenges no letter reveals. She kept packing fruit and that spring wrote to Donald, "There were tears in Daddy's eyes over your good grades....Our children are our lives now when material blessings fail to develop." We recall Helen's words, "There was nothing, nothing the folks wouldn't try to make that farm a success." But the new circumstances stopped them. In the 1930s all the experiments didn't really matter as no crop was going to find a market, nor was any little business going to make a profit.

18

HUNKERING DOWN

"It is the Era of the Great Garbage Can."
Frank Wheeler, letter to his son, 1931

BY LATE 1930, U.S. farmers were advised that there was not just overproduction, but extreme overproduction in a country where thousands, soon to be millions, were going hungry. The masses couldn't buy milk, let alone fruit. The long-denied Depression was now official in the Northwest. Farmers were advised to start using as much of their own products as possible, rather than trying to sell on the crowded market. But for years the Wheelers and others had been doing just that when their prices made it little sense to ship. Yet, the imbalance between production and market grew worse, as few farmers would take the risk of reducing their own harvest.

The "soldier-settlers" with their young orchards would be among the families to suffer first and most. Encouraged by the state, they had started farming at the worst possible time, and though some had trees now bearing, they had years of accumulated debt. Most of them had concentrated on apples, the popular, conservative crop. Reierson, the mercantile owner at White Bluffs, comments in the *Family Histories* that if more of them had heeded what the County Agent said about diversifying, they might have survived. But statistics from the State College reveal there was no major movement away from apples in the county, and that by 1932 soft fruit growers were doing no better. Nor was anything. Alfalfa, so popular in the valley, having sold for $35 a ton during the war, now dropped to as low as $2.50. Benton County wheat that sold at $1.29 a bushel in 1929 plummeted to $.20 by 1932, while a sheep worth $8.92 in 1930 was worth $3.40 by 1932. Farmers began to slaughter livestock that they couldn't afford to feed over the winter, even at the low feed prices, and couldn't bear to watch starve.

Washington apples piled up in storage, as the growers elected to store them as long as they dared, hoping for better prices. In 1930 the valley apple crop was, to nobody's good, a big one. The White Bluffs Cold Storage, with a capacity of thirty (railroad) carloads of apples and pears, could take no more. Unsold soft fruit and berries didn't pile up, they simply rotted. Livestock prices were the lowest since 1909, said the Kennewick *Courier Report*, yet production in cattle, hogs and sheep increased as irrigators did try to diversify. When fur prices crashed even the bounty on predators was canceled, and trapping a coyote no longer put a meal on the table unless one were driven to eat it.

While prices for the valley produce dropped, very few of their costs of production did. Gasoline actually went up, and railroad and power companies offered no new mercy. Retail food prices at local stores eventually would drop from one-half to two-thirds, but since the irrigators tended to buy only staples, this was not a large part of their outlay. Their big purchases were fertilizer, seed, spray and box materials, gas, repairs, and family needs other than food. By 1932, the State College reported Benton county farmers' average annual net profit at $27, with fruit growers the worst off of all. From the consumer perspective, the housewife in Seattle with a few cents in her pocket was likely to buy milk for children, and chicken and a few vegetables for a big soup, rather than a box of cherries or apricots to munch, delicious as they might be. [1]

The small farmers were better off than city dwellers even so, for at least they could grow much of their food. And it would turn out that the smallest were better off than neighboring large ranchers who were carrying more debt. Before long many valley families that had survived the 1920s found that they were losing their places after all. As mortgagers took back farms and equipment, they took over the farmers' burdens. Bank examiners forced collections by small banks in communities like White Bluffs where the local banker went to the same church and was neighbor to his borrowers. When farmers couldn't cover their debts, small local banks couldn't cover theirs. The Richland bank closed in 1930 after twenty years service, the White Bluffs bank in 1932. One large irrigator commented that the bank closure was when his family really felt the Depression, but by then most families had no savings left in it. Benton County itself was in trouble when people couldn't pay their property taxes. It was forced to cut back on teaching positions and road maintenance. The struggling water companies went into crisis when their stockholders couldn't pay their water bills. They could hardly turn their own water off.

Helen and Donald recall the increase in empty farmhouses scattered through the valley, surrounded by withered orchards and dried hayfields. Trees and grapevines that didn't get watered could die in only a year, alfalfa sooner than that. Some of the places foreclosed had fine orchards next to the nicest homes. These families had borrowed to create this comfortable level of living and the Depression caught them. Donald says, "We were quite surprised that some families who had seemed to be doing well went under, while others managed." One day, Helen saw that certain children were no longer in school; families were simply gone. Several contributors to the *Family Histories* share how their families were forced to give up, and unlike Annie Greenwood, were not glad.

There was less opportunity now to "work out" for extra cash. Some local men like Wib Morford continued to labor at the larger farms and others became migrant workers themselves, going to the next district to harvest wheat or potatoes. But mainly now it was a question of who could keep their costs down, and who had the least debt. And fruit still had to be picked, even if it couldn't be sold, or the orchards would be left a mess. The families who had good pickers or packers could still earn a little at the larger places, and this was how the Wheelers brought cash into the house. Trying to get around the freight and express charges, sometimes men would collect a truck load of produce, find the gas and tires required, and drive to a desert town to peddle their fruit direct. Donald tells of joining in with the Walkers to haul a load of tomatoes to Othello and selling them all door to door. But there was trouble with the old truck, and the price of gas and ferry, and he never tried it again. However, the adventurous Walkers kept the option in mind.

Other farmers acquired a seine net and managed to seine a few illegal sets of salmon from the Horn of the Yakima before they were reported and the net seized. No one was charged, simply warned. Reierson accepted apple trees cut up for stove wood as barter for groceries. Youth away at high school or college would have been forced to drop out had they depended on funds from home. But the students had long since assumed that, aside from packages of food, they were on their own. College was a far better place to be than job hunting.

The economic plagues of the Depression exaggerated the farming risks from nature that people faced every year. Unlike prices, which they counted on to be practically always poor, farmers never knew what to expect from nature. Now negative forces that had nothing to do with the national economy also attacked. Valley winters of both 1929 and 30 were extremely cold, causing winter kill to many soft fruit trees. In 1931 the weather stayed warm all winter, causing the trees to bud out early in a false spring, to be followed by an April killing frost. That year the Wheelers suffered even more than their neighbors, for that was the terrible year of the faulty apple washer. The next year brought more late frosts. The most important advantage the valley farmers had over the rest of the Northwest, their very early spring, was lost in the years of late frosts.

Now families fleeing the Dustbowl disaster in the Great Plains made their way west in their gasping Model Ts and ended up begging for jobs as pickers in Eastern Washington as well as California. Though most went to the famous Wenatchee or Yakima valleys, if they by chance took the wrong road into the Priest Rapids valley they found little reason to stay. Before the Depression was over, 460,000 would migrate to the Northwest, some as pickers, some to work on the big dam projects that were to be (at last) authorized.

Washington itself didn't escape the drought across the West. Similar conditions that had plagued the plateau in 1910-15 returned, driving out remaining wheat farmers. Eventually over half of the Franklin County farms across the river were foreclosed or abandoned. Dried-up farms to the southwest of White Bluffs were probably the source of dust storms worse than the orchardists had seen in years. The drought also caused the worst range fires in decades. The Extension Agent was busy throughout the valley lecturing about about soil protection. Jeanie wrote her children about their own dustbowl of 1931, determined to end with optimism, however feeble:

> ...We are enjoying the most hectic, weird blizzard of
> a dust storm that ever blew its devastating way across
> this valley. Started at noon yesterday, with an eerie
> light, and pretty soon clouds of dust high in the air,
> while down below it was still calm. But not for long, and
> it is still going strong, 30 hours later. Rose and I shoveled

out her living room this morning but it is as bad tonight.
So far our fruit is safe, but heaven knows what'll
happen when the wind quits....The orchard so far looks
fine, full of bloom.

With the market so poor, every cruel blow struck harder. The local paper reported that codling moth invasions of 1932 were double that of 1931 and combined forces with increased troops of strawberry root weevil and peach tree borer. Number of sprayings (and cost) increased again. The next spring an asparagus pest descended. In the mid-1930s the jack rabbits reached the peak of their cycle, and raced through the orchards and alfalfa fields, chewing up everything in their path. A rabbit drive, the first in years, brought out every man except, probably, Frank Wheeler. A year later an expanded predator drive was ordered: death to all coyotes, magpies, gophers, rattlesnakes, crows and hawks. For some men, frustrations could be briefly relieved; you couldn't kill "market forces", but you could blow a magpie to bits. The next year the dust storms increased again, and that enemy was almost as invincible as the market.

Despite the cities being no haven to turn to, the White Bluffs population dropped from 672 in 1930 to 501 in 1940, a loss of one-third. Yet, the Polk directory of 1935 found that of the 166 private householders who had been in White Bluffs in 1913, when promise for the district was at a peak, about seventy were still there. This was enough to maintain a stable, supportive community with a sense of its history. Those farmers that remained were spared the most miserable suffering of rural people. They were not croppers or tenants to be driven off land that couldn't turn a profit, nor were they single crop farmers, such as cotton or corn growers, who had to purchase everything else. Because hordes of Dustbowlers didn't arrive in the valley, their level of humanity to the totally destitute was not tested.

The sad litany of the valley troubles during the 1930s would be almost too much to believe were we not already familiar with worse tales from the Dust Bowl. We also have Helen's perspective to balance it. She was the one Wheeler youth still at home, and she was a great observer of the household and social scene. She assures us that despair did not rule in White Bluffs during those hard times. There was less tension at home with everyone on the losing team together. Frank was unable to buy fertilizer; probably his wealthy neighbors, the Roberts, were in the same fix. He may have had some consolation of an abstract form that, just as he suspected, capitalism didn't work.

More important to Helen, the river and the bluffs were still there to entice adventure. "When we didn't have gas, we still had the boat and horse. And that was all you needed to hunt rattlesnakes, or a pole, line and hook, and a little skill to go fishing." One year at June highwater time, Rose, restless as always with her farm wife role, convinced her husband Wib that they should shoot Priest Rapids on a driftwood raft with the other whitewater men. Helen and Marian then decided they would go along at least part way. Jeanie, assigned to care for Rose's children, protested that no mother had a right to take such chances, but was unconvincing. A group of six went up by truck as far as Coyote Rapids, then hiked up to Priest Rapids to make up the log raft.

Rose came down over Priest Rapids on the raft with Donald, Wib and one other man. The others walked back as far as Coyote Rapids, then joined them for the last wild ride to arrive in White Bluffs with another fine raft of logs to show off. Rose was the first woman, at least in that generation, to go over Priest Rapids. Again she had proved, as she had by swimming the Columbia, that if men could do it women could too. (Some of Frank's feminism had rubbed off there too.) Homesteading women of two generations earlier would have commented, "We did all that and more!" Years later some of the logs and squared timbers they captured became a house for Donald on adjacent river property he purchased.

Helen frankly loved having her father unemployed and at home, being the horticulturist he had always wanted to be. Wib Morford took on the maintenance of the Willowbank family garden as his specialty, assuring that they always had plenty to eat, even if they did crave more meat. Jeanie kept refashioning old clothes so that Helen would have something "new" to wear to high school. She was welcome always to invite in friends. She spent much time with her grandmother and with Rose's children, time she always enjoyed. Things were not so bright in some homes; she remembers a dinner she was invited to consisting of mashed potatoes and fudge.

Benton County and many others teetered on the edge of bankruptcy. This was in part due to Northern Pacific refusing to pay its property taxes, arguing that the land was now worth nothing. The counties finally won a partial victory, but it was years before they got payment. Yet the communities of Hanford and White Bluffs, though much shrunken, did not crumble and blow away. The civic boosters kept promoting the valley as a place to live happily if not extravagantly. Some years the annual County Fair was canceled but the Grange continued its dances. Though the women's fund raisers may have been skimpy in their takes, for their productions Helen gives them high grades. Based on her later experience as high school teacher, she believes the quality of her schooling stayed quite acceptable, with required classes continuing. The *Family Histories* paint a similar picture for twin town Hanford.

The Wheelers were more worried for their children in the cities than for themselves. Donald was secure at Reed, and George and Eleanor on their skimpy fellowships at U. of Chicago, but Margaret, Torvald, and Marian managed to stay just a step above "relief", part of the vast numbers who were not quite indigent. County Relief, made up of a combination of private charity and county funds, was for the disabled and helpless only. The urban counties couldn't begin to fill the need for work projects for the unemployed, nor could they provide enough soup kitchens.

Now Willowbank Farm, and no doubt many others, found their food shipments vital to their city dwelling relatives. When the Wheelers were able to get a box free on board one of their fruit shipments, it was Margaret's job to pick it up and distribute it. She had other connections. Torvald's brother was a ship captain who could bring them "surplus" items, and they knew a green grocer who gave them wilted vegetables at his back door. But the challenge lost its flavor as the months of empty pockets dragged on.

Unlike the Midwest where the farmers were soon the most radicalized group, it was in the cities of the coast where protests began. In 1930 the leftwing organized mass marches of protest in Seattle and other major cities. Mainly such demonstrations were peaceful, but in March in Seattle and two other cities they were broken up by charging police with tear gas.

Margaret wrote her parents:

> ...In a few minutes I'm trotting down to meet the
> kids and go to a meeting. The police will probably let
> loose the tear gas and stink bombs as they did on May 1.
> The bread line here is something ghastly already.
> Marian expects daily to be canned. The price of
> furniture and clothes is way down but who can buy
> them, while food is up. I hope you are getting a good
> price for your fruit.

This is the only mention by Margaret of the demonstrations and other radical political activity that surrounded her. She was working her barter system, and as a newly-wed trying to keep her husband's morale up. Being very much her father's daughter, she probably yearned to be right on the front lines of the unemployed demonstrations with one part of her. But she had married a man who, although willing to talk politics a little or even go to a socialist meeting to pass an evening, wasn't about to join in a march that was likely to be tear-gassed.

She had the instinct to know that romance could not endure fear or boredom, and that Torvald had to stay calm and busy to be happy. He occupied his frequent unemployed days making furniture from scrap for their home, landscaping, and gardening—all things they could enjoy together. Whenever they could, they all went dancing or to a concert. Tor joined the Seattle Opera chorus, hoping to become a professional radio singer and earn money. He wrote a sea story that was published in *True Magazine*, but couldn't produce a follow-up. Whenever Marian could, she took another art course. Margaret expanded her cooking arts as she continued her house parties for best friends. They went to the old Wheeler camp at Longbranch, and Tor built a log cabin. Neither of them focused on their worries in letters to White Bluffs, in fact Tor's letters sound as if life were practically perfect. He believed a job would come up any day. Margaret wrote to her folks to stop fretting about college for Marian. "What Marian wants more than anything is marriage, a home of her own, and a family."

The Wheelers urged them to come to White Bluffs, and of course Margaret yearned to, but wrote, "Are we coming? I think not. The other day the doctor bill arrived. We've paid the hospital $123, but we don't see any family in sight right now." Rose then wrote, asking them to come to the farm "to help", knowing they would need an excuse, and offered to send the gas money. (We wonder where she got it.) Though Margaret loved the farm, and knew there was enough food for everyone there, she wrote, "He'd be no earthly use on a farm, he knows nothing about it...It would be not so good to use your money to go home on a pleasure trip; but if you truly are not feeling well and need me, home I'll hop." She was not telling the true story. Tor liked to work, and anyone could learn to clear irrigation ditches. But she observed that when she went to visit his relatives, the men drank all afternoon and talked about their fishing boats while the women cooked and served. She knew that Tor would soon find a buddy to share some homebrew with, and she couldn't bear her folks witnessing this.

Sometime during the early Depression the Danielsons lost their home, then going from one rental to another, three in the next seven years. Both of them enjoyed creating a home and garden, and having to pack up and start over again and again had to be dismal. But they kept their letters cheerful and energetic, focusing on gratitude for the food shipments.

At White Bluffs the irrigators and valley boosters knew they must hold onto their population whatever the twists of the economy. They had accomplished many civic improvements, but not much with the struggling and critical water systems. In 1929, the courts heard a lawsuit by the remaining two hundred HICP/Black Rock water users claiming that the receiver had not kept up the maintenance, nor paid the county taxes owed. They asked to take over the system. The court found in favor of the users and ordered them to activate a water district so that they could legally purchase the system. The water users created Priest Rapids Irrigation District (PRID). Donald Wheeler says that they feared that if they did not purchase the system, Pacific Power and Light might, and would then raise the rates, and worse, would feel no ethical obligation to provide water to farms so far in arrears, that is, if history had any bearing. PRID protested the sale—how could they purchase anything? The result was the judge approved an auction instead.

Black Rock owed $45,000 in court and receiver costs and $60,000 in county taxes. It was a poor time to be taking over such debts. Dale Wilkinson, as secretary of PRID, tells in his memoirs what steps they took, looking for cash. Milwaukee Road was the other large concern with an interest in the valley. Between the two companies, PPL and the Milwaukee, PRID felt they could trust the railroad more; it had rescued them in 1913. After negotiations, the Milwaukee agreed to a loan of $125,000. An auction was finally held in February, 1931. Donald Wheeler wrote his sister about the excitement, and the worry that PPL "that has no soul" would come in with a bid:

> ...The people were some of them almost in a panic...The sale was held at one o'clock yesterday (21st) in the court house in Yakima. They say mobs of people were milling around on the steps. There was a rumor around that the Milwaukee might take a hand. The P.P.&L. man was there to bid; if no one else showed up the valley was in a bad way. Well, the Milwaukee came through.
>
> I suppose the properties will be turned over to the district as soon as they can clear away enough red tape to hold the bond election. We expect to see things go ahead in the valley now. With a sure water supply, cheap, it will be twice as good as Yakima or Wenatchee.
>
> I don't really believe there was any real danger of the system being junked; the Milwaukee could not afford to lose the valley. The Road has been managed by jackasses or it would have stepped in and settled the business years ago, and the valley would have become an important feeder...

PRID, with the Milwaukee's loan, and the only bidder, took the bid for $45,000. The taxes owed were forgiven. That left it only $15,000 for

needed system repairs, for the Road never came up with more than
$60,000. By then it was facing even worse times with everyone else. Fruit
shipping to Europe, a big market, had stopped. Yet, owning the Ditch system
was an important step forward, for finally the people who really cared
about it were in charge of its future.

Across the country, farmers who were used to enduring cycles of
economic hardship had lost patience by 1932. Unlike some of the city
unemployed who blamed themselves for not finding work, farmers
remembered that only a few years before the government had been
encouraging people out of the cities and into agriculture. These innocents
were now their hard-up neighbors. But the farmers were not unemployed.
They believed they were doing what they were supposed to be doing, feeding
the world, and doing it well. They considered themselves the backbone of the
country. Farmers in parts of the Midwest turned radical, but though
Benton County farmers did not engage in such actions as penny auctions or
boycotts, or turn over milk trucks, the Grange increased its lobbying for
federal help to farmers. Several of the orchardists, Win Shaw among them,
traveled to a hearing by the Board of Public Works at Kennewick to testify
on unfair power rates. They won something significant, as three companies,
including PPL, were ordered to reduce their power rates for irrigating and
spraying uses by twenty-five percent, with a reduction for household use as
well. No longer would it be so easy for the large corporations to simply take
whatever they could. PPL wouldn't go down meekly however. Through a
series of stalling moves, it was years before the rate decreases actually went
into effect.

PRID, trying to produce its own power, had multiple problems from the
start. It could sell its excess power to PPL at only dump rates. It lowered its
yearly maintenance charges slightly, but could not make much change with
only $15,000 to work with. Forty-seven users tried to sue the new district for

what they felt HIPC/Black Rock owed them over the years in lost profits, charging Black Rock had conspired with other corporations to get out of its obligations to the farmers. They lost this case but also petitioned and, after some horsetrading, were granted permission not to join the new district. Perhaps these growers were so weary of all the trouble with HIPC, they could not trust another association. In any case it was quite a financial loss to PRID. It would be five more years, 1936, before a New Deal state government would finally provide support by agreeing to take over the PRID bonds, and advancing it $25,000 from a revolving fund. A state involving itself in a struggling water district—that was something new.

With all the lawsuits, and development attempts, the valley was never a bucolic place, for all its virtues. However, most of the turmoil circulated around the booster associations' efforts and the water issues. Frank Wheeler seems to have avoided this type of activity, even after he was in White Bluffs full time. For one, he was not on the HIPC system, but as we have seen, he hated meetings and most of this struggle took place at meetings dominated by the "businessmen". More and more he chose simply to enjoy his horticulture, family, and hospitality.

"Whenever you need to come home, you are welcome," the Wheelers wrote their children regularly. Marian, when she was finally laid off, arrived to help with the pruning, drive the spray wagon for her father, and later babysit for Rose, so Rose could work in the packing house. But the heat of the valley was still too much for Marian in the summer. She returned to Seattle and job-hunting. Though the other Wheeler siblings came home only in summer, they all knew that they did have a haven to flee to and a place at the table for as long as they wished.

Frank and Jeanie kept the food shipments to the city up for the entire duration of the Depression, making the difference between a poor and a healthy diet for their offspring, and allowing the parents a sense of real usefulness. In return, Margaret or Marian tried to fill orders for the Wheelers for medicines, staples, yard goods, and shoes, often walking miles to do so when they had no bus fare. So much bartering required they keep the phones connected, but more than once they were cut off, and other times no one could find pennies for postage. Trips across the mountains were from east to west, for medical reasons only. Margaret wrote home, telling her parents a little more of the truth of their situation:

> ...As to coming to White Bluffs, we may have to very shortly. Only I don't think you realize if we leave this place, we leave here forever. We are staying here on sufferance now, because we have no place else to go. If we leave, Mrs. E. will probably move in. We have loads of furniture, etc. we'd have to arrange to store....We had better stay here as long as we can. Some people say it will be months before she could dispossess us. But the point I'm making is that we can't go to visit you any more. If we go we stay. And how would that work out? I would just as soon stay and fight eviction for a while.

The Depression took its toll in many ways besides loss of income, farms, and homes, the small dramas getting lost in the horrors reported in the dailies. One incident from the Wheeler memories and letters can serve as a sample. Though the valley had heretofore been all they could ask in a healthy environment, during the 1930s unmet medical needs grew to crisis level. Both Frank and Jeanie were miserable from abscessed teeth they couldn't afford to have fixed for so many years. Finally the only solution, they felt, was to have them all pulled, and get dentures. One early spring in the mid-1930s Frank privately decided he would bypass purchasing the annual spray materials, gave Jeanie the money he had, and insisted she be first to go to a Seattle dentist. Once she was there, she found out from whence he had gotten the funds, and immediately wrote: "I think you ought to get the lime-sulfur on, there won't be an apple fit to ship otherwise. I still have the $10 Donald sent me...and you can use that too if necessary, instead of me giving it to the dentist."

Universal health insurance had been dropped out of the Social Security bill and the modest image of Jeanie, waiting in Seattle for weeks for new funds to be raised for her dentures, can represent the cost of that defeat. Helen remembers that when the teeth arrived they didn't fit or look right at all, and she had to send them back for a redo. Margaret wrote, "It's sad to see our beautiful and social mother sitting home in the cultural center of Seattle, as she won't be seen out in public with no teeth." This was about as personal a hurt as Jeanie suffered from the Depression.

What Jeanie didn't know was just how bad Frank's teeth were. The phone was turned off, and she hadn't heard from home. She asked Helen, also on the coast, to catch a ride to White Bluffs if she could. Helen arrived at the farm to find them in a fix:

> There was no fire in the house (it was February) and both Dad and Grandma so sick in bed with flu they couldn't bother. It was unheard of. I got a fire going, made them tea, then Grandma told me to go down and check on Rose and Wib. The adults there, too, were both in bed with the flu and no fire. The house was full of hungry kids. I never felt so useful in my life, getting the two households back on their feet and functioning in a few days, except for Dad, whose teeth were poisoning him—all their cash had gone with Mom for her teeth. I managed to arrange a ride back to Seattle with him. I think they were able to barter some produce to a dentist.

Sometimes the "make-do" incidents were not so gloomy. When it was time for Donald, George and Eleanor to return to college after the summer break, the same problem arose as before: no one had the train fare. Donald came up with a plan his parents were not thrilled with, but he argued them down. Didn't he know the river if anyone did? He and a friend built a log raft as they had so often, though this time they had no skiff to tie alongside for emergency exit. George and Eleanor also climbed aboard and the four set off down river. The Chicago-bound travelers were dropped off at the Pasco bridge to flag the train, and the boys continued downstream. When they reached Umatilla Rapids, they saw they were too early; the river was still too low. They were wise enough to see that no passage was possible, not even for Ulysses, and beached the raft. Donald caught a ride on into Portland, back again in academia he loved.

Frank had always urged his children to travel, but with no intention that they risk their lives for it. All through college, and even to the World's Fair, Donald would continue to ride the rails, and sometimes the blinds on the passenger cars, which conductors did not tolerate. It meant hopping the train while it was in motion. He says he continued to lie to his parents about the safety of his pursuits. "I had to. If they had known, and something had happened to me, they never would have forgiven themselves."

When Donald was a junior, it was Helen's turn for college. She, like George, had graduated early. Not yet sixteen, she was too young for college her parents felt, and as with George, that gave them one more year to find resources. "But I was determined I was going to Reed", she says. "After I had visited Margaret there as a five-year-old, nothing short of a deluge could have kept me out." The family came up with a good substitute, pooling enough funds to send both her and Jeanie to Chicago— to George and Eleanor and the World's Fair, Helen staying on for the year. Back home again and a year older, she received the Cerf scholarship that George had passed to Donald, who had increased it to $300 for her. She, like the others, would work for her board and room. But it wasn't enough. Then came a surprise, a gift of funds from a friend of George who had worked at the farm one summer. His gift was enough to assure her first year at Reed. At this point there was dissension, showing just how tight things were:

> My parents asked me if Marian could have the gift money for school, since she had been forced to drop out. I considered and said no. Marian had had years of art courses. I had been dreaming of Reed since I could remember; the friend had intended the money for me. If I let it go, when would another chance come? I hadn't seen any cash around the house for years. They accepted it."

Helen went off to Reed and became the fourth Wheeler to graduate from there. Like her brothers and sister, she loved the whole experience, especially venerating the professors. As for campus social life, helped along by brother Donald's contacts, it quickly turned to romance, then to marriage to Millard Hastay when she was about to be a junior. The newlyweds devised a plan that has worked for many couples. He put her through to her degree in English and teaching certificate. She then went out to teach at a rural Oregon school that accepted married women, and financed him through to his degree in Economics. Donald meanwhile had graduated in Political Economy, and was chosen as a Rhodes Scholar, one of two from Washington that year. With all these economists in the family, surely someone could figure out how to make a living, if not save the country.

Many valley youth of the Depression did not end up in college or other training, or like Marian, soon dropped out to find work. Some married, bravely beginning families. Rose, once the most adventurous young woman on the river, stayed home. Yet, she had said she wanted a large family and now she had three, soon to be four, then five children. She knew there was no way a poor farm girl could have a profession, adventure, and family, all three. She taught her children to swim and ride and read to them from *The Jungle Books, Robin Hood*, and Ernest Thompson Seton's *Rolf in the Woods*. She told them about Kamiakin and glorified the Native American past on the very ground where Wib's melons now grew. At least that one time she came over Priest Rapids on the log raft. Years later, her children grown, she would arrive at a campus to enroll again in art classes. 2

The number of valley youth who continued to attend college during the difficult 1920s and 30s seems remarkable. At least five families in the valley had three or more students from that generation finish. The proportion of women graduates, in particular, is impressive. In the *Family Histories* nineteen White Bluffs women and ten Hanford women report having earned degrees, most in teaching, two in nursing. Two earned Master degrees. Almost every other woman that responded reported having gone to business college for at least some courses. Of the men, eleven from White Bluffs and eight from Hanford reported earning Bachelor degrees, with teaching, engineering, and economics the most popular. Three men earned Master degrees or equivalent, and two from each town earned PhDs, while two became lawyers. When Margaret surveyed families who had been residents in 1915, she similarly found they had produced many degreed men and women. One person listed "business". Only a third of the men who responded were farming. Many parents must have seen the sad future for small farming and did not push their offspring in the traditional way to "take over for us". But this academic inclination can't be just a reflection of the economy. It must also speak to the intellectually stimulating climate of the two tiny hamlets.

For the Wheelers, the counter movement back to the city had begun as soon as they had succeeded in moving to the country. Though the farm continued to be the family's spiritual base, once their youth left, none except Rose ever lived year round again at White Bluffs. It probably seemed strange to the parents that their adventure had turned out that way. If so, they had company as more and more young people left the farms of America.

19

NEW MYTHS FOR OLD

"We were all for the big dams then; we scoffed at the biology prof."
Donald Niven Wheeler, 2001

NOVEMBER, 1932. Priest Rapids valley people crowded into the homes with radios to hear Franklin Delano Roosevelt sweep the country. In Benton County, people who had deserted the Republicans to vote Farmer-Labor in 1924 had deserted their party again. Anything had to be better than what they had endured for a decade. Jeanie Wheeler had switched from Socialist to Democrat registration so she could vote for FDR. In doing so, she lost her small stipend on the local election board. "I told you you'd lose your job," Frank teased, this at a time when every penny counted. As for him, he couldn't trust a leader from the ruling class and stuck with Norman Thomas, but it was all right with him that Jeanie made her own choice. When he saw the whole county, and indeed the whole country, had switched, even such a skeptic must have felt a change in the desert wind.

Yet before Roosevelt could take the oath of office, the family were slammed by their worst blow yet. A one-car accident on New Year's eve left Margaret with a severely broken back. Torvald, the driver, unable to see in the rain through broken windshield wipers, had crashed into a concrete wall. The doctors could not say if she would walk again, and all of the family's emotional energy went to dealing with their fright and grief. For months Margaret was in King County hospital, waiting for a miracle. Torvald, with a broken collar bone, was healed before long. In the meantime they had lost their car, their housing, and the piano they had started making payments on. By April he found a short term job rigging ships and a place for them to live. Jeanie came to take care of Margaret, discharged but bedridden. Eight months after the accident, and one patiently hand-crocheted bedspread later, Margaret was walking again. Her fusion of three vertebrae, by a visiting doctor who had never performed one but wanted to try, had succeeded. She went shopping in her back brace and made plans for paying her doctor bills, as usual, with bartered produce from the farm. Once again her family saw her as their model of courage, but she never talked about what went through her mind during those long months of waiting and crocheting.

The world was looking better all around as the federal government began massive public works projects in the Northwest. In the Priest Rapids valley, PWA projects included road improvements, ditch repairs, a high school replacement for Hanford, and community hall upgrades. Frank was not hired on any of them but that was understandable: he was in his sixties. More serious to him, he saw the same favoritism in hiring practices by the county that left some of the most needy families out. Meanwhile Roosevelt promoted many experiments to relieve farmers, including making the terms of loans and refinancing easier, thus saving families from foreclosure. He planned relocation of farm families to better growing districts. Another early New Deal effort of specific interest was the purchase of 9.4 million lbs. of apples for free distribution. At least the White Bluffs Cold Storage would have space for the new harvest. Soil conservation programs, already in force, were intensified. But Priest Rapids farmers, even though they were paid for their conservation efforts, soon saw the conundrum: just as before, every workshop intending to make them more scientific would increase production and thus add to the farm products surplus.

If the country could not increase its markets, it needed a strategy to support farmers while creating scarcities, the odd solution of subsidies we still have today. Under the new subsidy program, three million farmers nationwide agreed, for pay, to cut production. Some refused, saying it was morally wrong to do such things as kill all their piglets immediately instead of raising them to be sold, then killed. As for the fruit farmers, they couldn't take their trees out of production, and would kill them only as a last desperate act before they killed themselves. A tree, unlike a pig, was meant to die when it was old. Nor could orchardists let the fruit fall on the ground to create a rotting mess.

In some districts fruit was picked and dumped. In others it was distributed to the needy. But apples, which unlike wheat could be stored little more than a year, soon overflowed the cold storages again. Some valley growers did take potatoes out of production. But since there was continual shifting of one truck crop for another during those years, it is difficult now to say whether it was due to government advice and subsidy later or the grower's own instinct for what could sell. We earlier mentioned Frank Wheeler's even trying boring beans one year, while Wib Morford tried sweet potatoes Despite Roosevelt's personal sympathies for the small farmers, few of his experiments helped them much. Corporate farms were the ones that benefited from the subsidies, while the strategy of reducing production raised market prices very little. Tenant farmers in some areas were evicted illegally when the lands they tilled were taken out of production by the owner. Others abandoned ruined land to join the mass of rural people drifting to the Far West. Once more large dam promoters dusted off their argument to save displaced farmers through opening more Western land to irrigation. But now people knew that meant huge dams, huge reservoirs. This time the country's leadership listened, and the Priest Rapids valley was amazed to hear that the largest PWA project in the entire country would soon begin, not at Priest Rapids, but upriver at Grand Coulee. No matter, after over twenty-five years of talk, the valley would finally have its great dam and be electrified as well. Meanwhile the project meant a lot of jobs.

The Wheeler family benefited directly from the New Deal in other ways. First George, then Marian, then Margaret were hired on real jobs—George in labor administration in Washington D.C., Marian at one of the Seattle day care centers for working families, and Margaret, still in a back brace, in the new profession of social work. Before long Donald would be in D.C. as well. Margaret's position put her right on the front line of the relief programs. She earned $75 a month climbing tenements to interview applicants for relief and for public works labor. Her impression was that the men weren't "...all leaning on their shovels as rumored. The great majority want desperately to work." Her husband, after all, was one of them, daily trudging from shop to shop, in the end forced to straight commission work as a marine paint salesman. On the fishing docks he finally found appreciation of his talents, winning customers, some of them his relatives, by talking shop in Norwegian.

The Priest Rapids valley did not see dramatic changes from the New Deal, rather they were gradual incremental improvements. By 1934, partly through PWA and partly through the victory on Northern Pacific's property taxes, Benton County was again solvent. It was able to restart the school health program and immunizations, refill some teaching positions, and give pay increases. In 1936 the government began purchasing Benton County produce for its new federal surplus food distribution program.

Thirty-eight million apples and four million pears, as well as dry peas and wheat, left the stuffed warehouses. But again the farmers' market rose little. There was no simple fix, for price controls to protect consumers hurt farmers.

When a system of public assistance started in Benton County that same year, half of the people serviced were senior citizens, settlers of the first and second decades, often with no children left to care for them, still trying to operate small orchards. Though Frank and Jeanie Wheeler had lost his bricklaying income, their children were now mainly self-sufficient, and they didn't have the desperate need for relief that some families had. However, Jane Shaw shared the plight of many if not most of the older settlers. As a widow, she had continued to maintain her orchard with the help of the Wheelers, but it was losing money like all of the others. Now in her mid-seventies, she was scarcely able to do much of the work herself, but it was a matter of pride to her to hold onto a sense of independence. Jane needed resources of her own, at least to be able to knit and sew for grandchildren. But for years the Wheelers had had no cash to share with her for even such practical items as yarn or yard goods. Her sons apparently thought the Wheelers were responsible for her, since she had been their partner. The Wheelers agreed that they should be able to feed and clothe her, and did, but had no cash to share.

Jane's public assistance checks of about $25 a month started arriving, to her great relief, but the benefit was short-lived. Helen remembers:

> Grandma was soon cut off when a caseworker
> noted that she was receiving a magazine, *Comfort*, that
> cost a dollar a year. 'If you can afford this, you don't
> need welfare!' was the comment. Grandma never got
> her payments restored. We never knew who had
> reported her and for what reason. It was just one more

blow to a woman who didn't deserve it."

Obviously the seniors' eligibility for assistance was strict, if not partisan, and meager indeed.

The beginning of the hard-won Social Security program was an insult to small farmers when they were not included. Jeanie Wheeler saw a way around it. She had saved, along with all her other paper collections that her children deplored, her years of packing shed pay stubs, and thus was able to prove eligibility. We can picture her triumphantly climbing down from the attic, waving the precious slips of paper at Frank. But others had no such history at hand. To Frank, the social security program was a disgraceful compromise in other ways. Universal social security and a universal health system were what was needed, not payroll taxes. But once again the fear of socialism was creating backlash, and the longer FDR stayed in office the more the New Dealers fought a conservative trend.

The Wheelers' frustration over how to care properly for Jane as she aged was balanced by good news for the family. Margaret, after trying for so long, was pregnant. She planned to continue work as long as she could, but Frank, worried for her, urged the couple once more to come to White Bluffs:

> You ought to come home, plan to when things are
> slack....You are a long way from the end of your
> resources. What you need now is more vacation, build
> up. You both have good cards to play, but why not rest
> on your oars. I think you picked up faster than you ever
> did [after her accident] and that is the one job you need
> right now and it is coming to the lovely time of the year.
> I want Tor to come very much...try it till October
> anyhow and Ill have Big Boy so busy he will think it is a
> weekend. We all worked for this place for years, lets use

it for a few months anyhow. Its hokey to thrash around
in any city like a short-tailed bull in a swarm of gnats.
Come together or come how you must.

What more could Frank say? But again, they did not come for more
than a brief visit. Margaret gave birth to a healthy daughter just after the
New Year, 1936, and with Torvald working part-time, took eight months
off to enjoy motherhood. She wrote pages every day in her journal about her
baby's development and neglected her entertaining and tutoring.

The Wheelers always considered their daughter's recovery and ability to
bear a child as one of the miracles of their history. They did not know yet
that she was a candidate for rheumatoid arthritis, just that she had
"rheumatism", as her father did. But though she refused to let this slow her
down, Torvald was not faring so well. Despite all of her efforts to keep him
feeling useful, humiliation from years of unemployment crippled his spirit,
and alcohol became his medication. He didn't have a strong philosophy like
the Wheelers' bred into him since childhood to explain what was happening
to the country. The failure was personal. While his wife was busier and
busier, he was begging for sales. Drinking with customers led to gambling,
and despite the baby and finally managing to buy another home, the
Danielsons were in few years divorced. Both Helen and Marian thought of
Tor in later years as a symbol of what the Depression had done to so many
men. "He was a great guy, with a wonderful sense of humor, full of energy.
He always tried to find work or stay busy." says Marian. "There was nothing
wrong with him at all, and the Depression just ruined him." Helen agrees,
"Everyone in the family loved him. The Depression just pulled the pegs out
from under him."

Almost at the same time Margaret's baby was born came George and
Eleanor's first. Marian decided it was time to take steps as well. Who could
tell if normal times would ever come again? After eight years, she and her

fiance had not been able to put together funds to rent a place, much less own one. That year she broke off their long engagement and married Armistead Coleman, a commercial artist she met at the opera. Her new engagement and marriage rivaled Margaret's for speed. The couple moved to Washington D.C. where he had contacts and family, and her brothers were both living. Starting a home and family on the salary of a commercial artist meant that times would not be easier, but she was right on the edge of the art world that she loved.

Frank and Jeanie now had three children far away in the East, and Helen and her husband in California. George had purchased a family farm in Virginia, but it was commuter's farm, a place for raising children while he worked in D.C. Rose seemed to be the only Wheeler child who would be truly farming, and that heavily subsidized by Wib's off-farm wages. The Wheelers had planned on their farm as a way to at least be independent in their old age and no burden on their children. They had a short time left to realize this, and the New Deal had not yet proven to be a permanent cure to the economy. But now the Wheelers found a renewed role for Willowbank Farm when Margaret began to send her girl to her parents for her summers. Before long George's and then Donald's toddlers would start coming from the East for summer visits. The cycle of childhood adventures on the river was happily born again. For the grandparents, the greatest value now was providing a country place for the fourth generation on the farm. With the river, lush garden, and orchard performing for the extended family's pleasure, and ample time to enjoy babies and toddlers, the price of a peach was almost irrelevant.

Jane Shaw, however, was now failing, and like many of the original settlers in their eighties required constant care and would soon be gone. Those with no family to care for them, or too difficult to care for, were forced to go to the State or County hospitals. Jane was among them when she became senile and too dangerous for the Wheelers to care for. "Margaret and I made them do it," says Helen. "but it was terrible for Mom." The obituaries in the district paper were sadder than they should have been, for it seemed that not only a generation but a unique way of life in the valley was passing with the original orchardists. No one knew that worse times were coming, but Jane and the older settlers were spared them.

The most interesting New Deal experiment in White Bluffs didn't last long, and probably wasn't intended to, but is a fond memory for Helen. "The Canning Coop was the best part of the New Deal for us, a wonderful project that should have become permanent." In 1936-37 several Eastern Washington communities received state loans to initiate local canneries. About ten families, including the Wheelers and Morfords, joined the White Bluffs Canning Coop, which soon was known for its excellent tree and vine-ripened canned products. It sold to nearby communities and as far away as Seattle. The members also did much canning for their own households, about half of their effort, Helen believes. Although the members mainly processed apricots, peaches, and tomatoes, they also experimented with vegetables and meat, and later with frozen fruit, an innovation being introduced by the Extension Service.

Wib Morford was sent off for training to be the coop bookkeeper, but for the rest of the members it was definitely a learn-as-you-go project of small farmers trying to run a marketing business. It lasted just three years, its short life partly due to lack of quality control, such as carelessness in processing. Donald believes not enough training had taken place. "In one instance, Mother, who understood the importance of consistency, was not listened to by some of the crew who were shorting the sugar. An inspector coming through rejected an entire batch, causing a fight among the coop members as they sought to blame each other." A shortage of tin cans as the new war in Europe expanded was another problem. Wib, who was not only the bookkeeper but the vice-president, told his family he believed the coop was a victim of sabotage as well. A new outside manager was brought in to promote expansion, pushing the coop into more products and equipment purchases before they were ready, causing it to fall into the red. Wib and other members came to believe it was a deliberate effort to undermine the coop, and that the new manager was an agent of the big canning companies.

In 1940 the coop folded, to the regret of its members and everyone else who had gained the benefits. The larger Richland coop, employing up to 120 people at peak, lasted longer but in the end, according to local opinion, was outdone by the corporate canners. When the canning corporations decided it was time, they could systematically undersell the coops through sheer volume until they drove them out. This was the history of small coops earlier, and would continue to be. Whether the suspicion of sabotage at White Bluffs was true or not, the two communities' similar conclusions about the role of the big canners shows how the small farmers viewed them. By 1940, with new European shortages, the market was pulling out of its slump, and many of the New Deal experiments were activities that the business world regarded as no more than temporary options.

More lasting, important improvements through PWA came to the valley. The new road work may not have looked like much —a paved cross-state highway was still a few years in the future—but each year a few more miles were graveled and oiled. The little patches added up until finally, with the opening of the South Pass across the Cascades, a trucking route clear to Portland was available. Its impact was far more than better road conditions, for it meant the monopoly of the railroad on freighting was over. Federal funding and technology had won a battle the farmers never could. Not only was faster, cheaper shipping assured, but the powerful fruit brokers in Seattle now had competition from Portland.

During the same period of New Deal priming, the power plant at Priest

Rapids, now under the new water district, PRID, was upgraded so that it no longer had to buy power from PPL, was actually able to sell surplus power, and water rates actually went down. Deteriorated ditches were repaired. PRID vowed it would be able to water more acreage of desert land as soon as customers appeared.

Far more wide-reaching was the dam project at Grand Coulee. In 1933 Congress finally passed the legislation for the Bonneville Dam construction on the lower Columbia, the same year that it approved the Tennessee Valley Authority. Two years later it approved the Grand Coulee project, and began planning for several other dam sites. After decades of the government refusing to sponsor expensive irrigation and public power projects, the switch in policy was fueled by Roosevelt's sympathy for farmers, but also the urgent need to put people to work. Recruitment flyers once more flooded the country to call people to the Washington desert, but this time not to farm. The news brought as many as 8,000 workers to the Coulee site, mostly men under thirty from desperate areas of the Midwest and South. The wages were good at a dollar an hour when road work was below fifty cents.

Though so close at hand, few of the valley men signed onto the Coulee project. If they did hitch a ride up the river to take a look, they were treated with the shock of the largest construction project ever to date attempted, but also to the degrading conditions of a boom town of barracks, shanties, and honkytonks. Woody Guthrie's famous promotional ballads for the dam had little to do with the life of the laborers. Blaine Harden, who grew up there as the child of a welder on the dam, describes Coulee City as "the cesspool of the New Deal, the Sodom and Gomorrah of the engineered west", where people competed to put as much down their throats as flowed down the Columbia. Probably it was no different than any huge construction camp of confined laborers. It was not only a social cesspool, it was dangerous work; over seventy men lost their lives on the project. Yet few then questioned its long-range value. This giant dam, along with the one at Bonneville and their high voltage tie-ins, would change the face of the Northwest even more than the new highways, and massive irrigation would be part of it.

Engineers calculated that the Columbia contained forty percent of the potential hydroelectric power in the country. It was more than enough to water a section of Eastern Washington desert larger than all its current irrigation districts combined, and, just as in 1906, was planned to encourage the unemployed of the cities back to the country. The settlers at White Bluffs must have wondered if they had been simply thirty years too early. To prevent corporate farming from seizing the opportunity, the Bureau of Reclamation ruled that the acreage an individual family could farm in the Columbia Basin Project would stay at the current 160 acres allowed on its other projects. Social visionaries again added their voices. Lewis Mumford, like an echo of John Wesley Powell two generations before him, argued that electricity could transform rural society to a modern Jeffersonian democracy, free of wood chopping and water hauling, but that social planning had to be part of it. Though Mumford may not have realized it, the living model, with ample problems but surviving, was just down the river from the great dam.

Frank Wheeler believed that electrification was essential to cure the malaise of the countryside, but he was skeptical that it could happen:

> (Month?)1936...I see Roosevelt has peeled off his shirt
> and is ready even before election, or because of, to go to
> bed with the Power Trust, calling a conference to
> prevent duplication or farther extension of TVA into
> financial competition. He is a complete and absolute
> pottie and his second term will be a delight to monopoly
> and a menace and goose egg to every worker and

liberal.

This time, at least in this aspect, Frank was wrong. The Bonneville Power Administration would be extended. The huge Coulee Dam would be followed by more big dams, and more, as long as there was desert to be watered. The planners and engineers had all the work they needed for decades, and the negative side of all the river harnessing—and some social critics did question bringing great populations into an arid region—was for the time submerged.

It is difficult now for us, having witnessed the negative effects of big dams, to appreciate what all this meant to rural people then. Looking beyond the Washington desert to the nation as a whole, social analysts agree that the one sweeping and permanent change wrought by the New Deal for farmers was through the Rural Electrification Administration. The Wheelers had been fortunate in having enjoyed electric power in their home for years, but in 1935, only twelve and a half percent of U.S. farm households had electric power; six years later, over thirty-five percent did, most of it due to big dams. [1]

After years of stagnation, the valley people were ready to move. Benton County PUD in 1937 voted to float a bond to enable delivery of power throughout the county, estimating it would cost the consumers twenty-five percent less than the current price. The much lower rates would give small irrigators a chance finally to succeed. The changes promised were too late to help much the generation that Wheelers belonged to, now in their sixties. It would be up to their children and the remaining soldier-settlers to seize the new opportunities. If the Wheeler sons had been at home, all of this news would have excited them. But they were far away in Washington D.C. busy with their own challenging jobs and raising families, reading about it in the newspapers and their parents' letters. The news did arouse the interest of outsiders, and for the first time since the irrigators had arrived, a large private development corporation proposed to bring 3,000 new acres into production near White Bluffs.

Donald Wheeler believes that all the small farmers of Priest Rapids valley of that day really needed was the improvements to the diversion dam at the rapids, not Grand Coulee and its offspring. But now they were a small piece of a huge technological revolution to include most of the Columbia Basin. This was what corporate farming was waiting in the wings for, and it did not intend to let the 160 acre-per-farm rule stand in its way. Before long the pressure to do away with this rule would inevitably succeed. The Columbia Basin today is not the home of the small irrigators of whom Powell dreamed, but of agribusiness holdings, some of which serve only as tax writeoffs for millionaires.[1]

The electrification of Eastern Washington was not without other losses, and not surprisingly, it was the Indians who again sacrificed. The irreplaceable loss, after Celilo Falls, was the Kettle Falls fishery, for unlike Bonneville, no ladders were built into Coulee Dam. The tribes of the region lost their prime fishery and filed suit for losses. (Almost sixty years later they would settle for fifty-three million and annual payments of fifteen million.) But in the 1940s, Indians and biologists had no strength against the sentiment that now surged for more big dams. Frank Wheeler sympathized with the Indians he knew, but though we have no letters from him on this issue, he probably didn't see how the loss of their fisheries at certain spots could be important enough to stop rural electrification for all. He understood farming, not fish, and in that he represented most of the valley. We recall Donald's words, "We were all for the big dams then." And that included his father.

With many New Deal measures in place, money circulating better, and unemployment down, Roosevelt was pressured to close down many of the

PWA programs and all of the direct relief programs, the argument being that people could now find work. Marian Wheeler returned to Seattle from a trip to the farm and found that her nursery school job had disappeared. She wrote home, "No explanation or apology—the funds were simply withdrawn and the nursery schools all over the state abandoned." Contrary to optimists' hopes, as soon as the flow of federal funding to projects stopped, the country slipped down its sinkhole again. Work projects had to be reintroduced.

The "Second New Deal" programs didn't succeed as well as the first time around. Although production was up and unemployment was down, consumers were not purchasing enough apples, or anything else. Leery of recent history, they were putting more into savings, and speculation had become a dirty word. Change more fundamental, greater even than great dams, was needed. While the government was still struggling with the answers, an evil vision had unfolded in Europe.

Donald saw it as he finished his studies at Oxford and left for Paris for a year of courses at the Sorbonne. He would soon be joined by a classmate from Reed, Mary Lukes, and then married. In Paris, for the first time in his life, he experienced true political fear as France was pulled left and right. He found it dangerous to speak, as first Mussolini, then Franco and Hitler shouted their answers to the economic dilemma. American leftwingers of every stripe, though they argued amongst themselves routinely, saw what happened in Spain as a warning to the world. Frank didn't need persuading, writing Margaret ":..I never was a pacifist. We need an armed alert working class. Even the old slavers of colonial days knew that, even if it was a danger to them." But though he saw what Hitler represented, he perceived the situation in Europe as caused in part by his own country. His words reflect perspectives more common today regarding the influence of multi-national conglomerates on world events:

...This country was founded on the pure extract of slavery in its most leprous form. Still trying to whitewash it. We are near a rocky headland with an old tin can and a shoestring for an anchor. The truth is, Europe is in an uproar today because of the invasion by Amer-British bankers and their use of tools like Hitler. The bastard Toryism of US is the most indecent in history...The situation is lots worse than most people realize.

The "situation lots worse" would be alarming soon.

The return of the Depression in the U.S. left the vulnerable fruit growers befuddled. The problems of Europe beyond them, they left them to Frank Wheeler to stew over and turned their attention to their own beast again. Again, the commission house was causing the growers outrage. This time the problem was in the grading practices. Traditionally the growers did their own grading as they packed, and stamped the boxes accordingly, along with an I.D. number for the orchard. From time to time an unannounced inspector came through the packing sheds to check on grading accuracy. Now a rumor started that one or more of the brokers—Schroeder, of the Walter Bowen Company was mentioned—might be guilty of cheating on grades and prices after the fruit arrived in Seattle.

Donald believes that people had hostile feelings still simmering from 1923 when the commission rate had gone from ten to fifteen percent. Now some growers suspected that the fruit they graded at the packing house (and were being paid for that grade), was being sold at a higher grade in Seattle, with someone pocketing the difference. Margaret was asked by her folks to go down to the Seattle warehouse and check on certain identifiable boxes and see at what grade they were being sold. A letter from her to the Wheelers indicates that she was sure they were right, that boxes they had graded and been paid for as "fancy" were being sold as "extra fancy".

Jeanie Wheeler was convinced, as were other growers, that their broker Schroeder was cheating them. Frank was not. He considered Schroeder more than a business associate and refused to think he would deliberately pull such a scam, after being a guest in their house for years whenever he came to town. He had received too many favors from Schroeder. How could this same man be cheating them? Donald had no opinion on this; he, George, and Marian were far away. Helen, who was on the scene more, says that at the time she believed her mother was right. Another possibility was that Schroeder, or someone, was changing the grade, but didn't consider this as cheating, just "business". But to Frank that could never be acceptable.

In any case, it was at least an accusation that quite a few families came to accept. About 1938, when the market had been rock bottom for almost ten years, two of the energetic Walker boys, now men, came up with a bold plan to overcome the monopoly of the commission houses and the railroads. Now that the valley had somewhat decent roads, and a link to cross-state highways, the growers were no longer captive to the railroad. Why should they be captive to the wholesale houses either, the Walkers argued. It was a breakthrough into a new kind of marketing, with the supposed skimming giving them the excuse they needed. They proposed to use their own truck and operate an unlicensed illegal (drive-by-night, no headlights) operation, delivering fruit straight to retail outlets they would arrange. Their neighbors could pay them instead of the railroad, at half the price, then by-pass the broker's fee as well. A new generation with new ideas.

The Walker men found plenty of takers, but though the word was soon out that the families were faring better with this double by-pass, Helen says that the Wheelers did not take part for the first season or two, despite their precarious financial condition. Frank was holding out and paying for it. A letter to Donald in May, 1939 showed what a box they and the other growers were in. Frank enclosed the monthly power bill for $51.50 and a statement indicating that they were $1093 in arrears to PPL, obviously needing Donald's help. Averaged out, it appears that they were about three years behind on power bills. Ten years of virtually no income, yet the Wheelers had on the surface managed to keep out of serious debt. Now the truth was revealed. PPL eventually would put a lien on the farm, and probably on several more in the same condition.

A year or so into their venture, the Walkers came to visit the Wheelers. The market was improving. "You Wheelers had better get in on the deal," was their message. Helen remembers that Jeanie decided they had waited long enough and they should join in, but Frank resisted. If anyone had complained about the railroad and the commission house it had been Frank, but now he was in a quandary. He still refused to believe the accusations against Schroeder, and to join the Walkers' venture secrecy was required. He would have to go behind the man's back, and that ran against his grain. Yet, he couldn't tell him either, and get his neighbors in trouble. The Wheelers argued. Helen says, "It was the only time I ever heard Dad curse at Mom. 'Woman, you don't know a damn thing about it,' he said, and walked out of the room and went down in the orchard." The feeling left in the room was wrenching. Helen watched her mother complete a deal with the Walkers, and Frank said no more on the topic. He had tried everything to keep his farm alive, and these young men, in turn, were now trying everything.

The Wheelers paid a price for the trucking venture. Schroeder found out about the insurrection and that the Wheelers had finally joined it. He may have heard a garbled story, but didn't feel obliged to extend the usual credit the next spring for spray materials—either that or Frank couldn't ask him to. And though the depression of prices wasn't over, inflation had entered the equation. Frank had to find his spray loan elsewhere. He wrote Donald:

> "...Furthermore the [storage warehouses] are now in combination to raise the price on boxes from 5 1/2 cents to 8 cents/box. Its like them both. I cant do anything but keep these trees alive this year...the warehouse turned me down for credit for spray materials, and by the time I had a loan approved through the Grange, it was too late to get the lime-sulfur spray onto the peach trees."

Donald was upset to be getting the news so late from a father who didn't want to come begging. He decided it was time for him to think more about the future of the farm.

Before the following spring Jeanie did what she had to. She sat down with Schroeder, they ironed out their grievance, and their credit was restored. Donald realized his aging father needed more assistance with the place, and there were few able-bodied men in the valley to call on. Wib Morford was nearby, but working full time for a large ranch, also for the coop, and managing the family garden. Most younger men were gone to defense industries. In 1940 Don purchased a portion of Willowbank acreage from his parents, allowing them some operating cash, and planted a new orchard of 300 apricot trees. He and his wife Mary then decided they would go further than that. For Donald, the magic place of his youth was still alive, and with two toddlers now, they saw the same virtues in the valley for a family that his parents had. They were able to purchase the abandoned Brice place just north of his parents. Donald says that they got "a very good deal...about $2000." It was a long commute from Washington D.C., but their idea was to spend as much time as they could each summer at White

Bluffs developing the farm, the old dream resurrected. Donald meanwhile saw that his parents got more of the help they needed to continue.

No sooner did the market shudder with a little life than White Bluffs started to look attractive again. One day in 1939 the Wheelers noticed they had new neighbors; a fourth wave of settlers had arrived. But unlike the early settlers, they were experienced: third generation Mormon irrigators from Cash Junction, Utah, who could look at the situation and know exactly what they were getting into. They had studied potential locations for their new colony from Texas to Western Washington and had chosen White Bluffs. Helen remembers that about twenty families, perhaps more, moved into many of the abandoned houses and farms left by the soldier-setters and others who had been defeated, or had retired, and began resurrecting the dried-up fields and orchards. They were not a vanguard of corporate farmers/absentee owners, but people who would join the community in every way.

Helen Wheeler recalls that the survivors in the valley were delighted to welcome new settlers with young families. They helped to help ease the personal loss in the departure of so many neighbors and friends. New population was important economically too, for the boosters were still continuing to promote their district. For Helen and her peers, oblivious of Mormon agribusiness elsewhere, and indifferent to their internal bureaucracy and theology, the new neighbors were a great addition to the social scene. She remembers that even though the Mormons were something new and different for the valley:

> I never heard a word against them, religious or
> otherwise. Our Presbyterian church had closed from
> lack of members, so Grandma started going to the
> LDS, which had moved into an empty building near us.

> She stayed Presbyterian, but they were very welcoming
> to her and everyone, and they were good neighbors.
> They offered social events for the whole community.
> Some of the teens went to the LDS dances and started
> dating. Rollin, [Rose's son], began going there as a boy
> and eventually joined them.

For the Wheelers, the Mormons may even have provided some balance to the domination of the Freemasons in town, and they gave new life to the Grange.

The timing of new energy for the valley was perfect. As war ripped apart Europe creating shortages, the U.S. economy charged ahead. Though there were long years of misery in store across the ocean, the abandoned fields of White Bluffs were again greening, some of them with a new crop, sugar beets, and little rows of twigs again burst forth blossoms in spring where skeletons had stood. For the next few years, the growers who joined the Walker enterprise also did well; in comparison to earlier years, they did very well. In fact, if one kept one's eyes trained close to the ground, and ignored history, everything was better. The Farm Security Administration was again promoting cheap U.S. lands under the "Food For Freedom" plan. Beleaguered Europe needed American produce; yes, America needed more farmers.

Donald and Mary did not bail out the Wheeler farm alone. In the Priest Rapids valley, as everywhere in America, military/defense orders, more than the New Deal was ever able, brought the Depression to an end. Willowbank Farm and its neighbors sent off boxes of fruit to a once again healthy market. Orchardry as a profession seemed almost sane again, but the Wheelers wondered for a second time if there had to be a war for them to make a decent living. During the agricultural depression, all normal development had halted for twenty years, making it impossible to say with assurance whether small-scale irrigation had succeeded or failed in the valley. Now, with a war market coming on, no fair evaluation was possible again. All the surviving farmers in the valley could say with certainty was that their beloved community had new health and that public power was at last coming.

The United States entered World War II. Along with the calls to the military, a national recruitment for defense workers hit the valley, and flyers were again fluttering in the wind, but this time urging people to the city, and to steady jobs, serving one's country in the fight against fascism. Aluminum prospectors began exploration of the valley, and Frank recalled the early developers' flyers that had extolled the vast potential for Columbia Basin industry, how its power could be turned to defense when needed. They had owned a crystal ball.

The government's plans for Grand Coulee Dam changed. Its last concrete was poured six months after the attack on Pearl Harbor. The dam workers went home, and the demand for its power quickly switched from rural electrification and irrigation to aluminum production for aircraft. Seattle's new aircraft industry and other aluminum manufacturing created the biggest and longest economic boost the Northwest had seen. It would be ten years before water was pumped up into the dry coulee to make the holding lake for irrigation.

When the war production was over, the public power movement had become too popular to stop. Roosevelt was gone, but his words were famous: "We are going to see with our own eyes electricity made so cheap it will become a standard article of use not only for manufacture but for every home." It would come true for Washington, but it would be coastal industries that provided the push. At first the government's plan was that Bonneville Power Administration would wholesale cheap power to private retailers like PPL. The public power advocates objected that the consumers needed the same break, that prices should be held at cost all the way to the householders. The power trust screamed "socialism!" The State Grange had fought for public power for too long to put up with this tactic. In 1935 it brought a friendly suit to test the constitutionality of public power and won.

The war market would again be temporary, but the cheap, ample, and subsidized public power coming on line was not. But it did not mean, after all, a permanent victory for the small farmers, for even cheap hydroelectric power couldn't change history in their favor. Frank, in the end, was right about the future for farming. Despite all the great changes to the countryside, the end of the small, sustaining family orchard was only a generation away. Though the argument for the federal reclamation projects was the encouragement of small farming, the main rural beneficiaries of subsidized power would be the new corporate farms of hundreds, even thousands of acres coming to Eastern Washington and the rest of the West. By the 1960s the small orchards and truck farms would begin to disappear. As dams multiplied, salmon runs would disappear. David Sohappy, a Wanampum child perched in his father's dugout while young Donald Wheeler watched the seasonal salmon spearing, would dedicate his days to saving Indian fishing rights.

In 1941 Rose and Wib Morford said goodbye to White Bluffs. They, with their five children, were among the many young couples who left for work in the wartime shipyards of Seattle. Margaret was already managing a Travelers' Aid office there, and they would stay for a while at her house, then at the Wheeler camp at Longbranch, Washington. They would become permanent coastal dwellers and develop a family farm, "a stump ranch", with a superb garden near Gig Harbor, Washington.

In 1942, the Priest Rapids valley crops were excellent, and so was the market. The community was in top health. In March of 1943 came letters of eviction.

20

ENTER THE SERPENT

"...the US constructs a worse than pagan System of Exploitation of every productive thing for a few, the same old piffle of tariffs, armies, race hatreds, and all..."

Frank, writing to his daughter Margaret

IN FEBRUARY OF 1943 Frank and Jeanie Wheeler were alone at Willowbank Farm. It was the quiet season after pruning and before spraying began. They waited for a most beautiful time in White Bluffs as one type of tree after another would burst forth in pastel clouds. The songbirds would soon return, then the multicolored carpet of wildflowers across the desert. This year, however, the farm had an air of melancholy, for Jane Shaw had recently died at eighty-four. Both of the partners who had planted the first trees were now gone. George, Donald, Marian and their families were still in the East, Helen and her husband in California. The U.S. had been at war in the Pacific for over a year, and Margaret and the Morfords were working in defense industries in Seattle. The Wheelers missed the footsteps and laughter of their Morford grandchildren that had grown up right next door. Jeanie, though relieved from worry for her mother, was still feeling the loss of her as she went about the activities they had shared, reflecting on how the successes of Mayflower and Willowbank

Farms had been possible in good part because of Jane.

The economy was the best it had ever been in the Priest Rapids valley since that first decade when the steamers ran the river, and it had all seemed so promising. The wartime market was strong, and the crops were lush. Power, transportation, and water systems were improving enough that small orchardists thought they might have a real living if the market could hold. They had years of catch up to do.

Aside from the eternal problems of farming, the Wheelers' own problems were much different from the early years of building the farm and raising children. Their worst problems in recent years had been how to care for Jane and how to find farm laborers, with the young people gone to the military or defense work or college. They badly missed their children. They had moved too far, and their visits were too limited. But these were the common problems of older parents, and especially rural parents, who saw their offspring scatter and were left to care for their own aging parents.

Frank was lucky to find a neighbor who, with his youngest son not yet drafted, was building up a small place and looking for extra work. J.V. Grisham and Walter worked out perfectly. Grisham was a man with a wide array of skills. He not only helped with the pruning and spraying, he did extensive carpentry repairs to the Shaw house, including building an addition for a modern bathroom that Helen's husband would plumb.

White Bluffs was in another transition stage. Many of the Wheeler neighbors were widows, widowers and aged bachelors. Eventually their farms would go to young families who could take advantage of all the New Deal technology. Unless they were the children or grandchildren of settlers, they might never know the story of the earlier struggles. Still, families could not be sure what the end of this war would bring. Would some of the absent young people, like Rose and Wib Morford, turn their faces homeward in a new "back to the country" movement? It was possible; it had happened before. Meanwhile the young Mormon families in the valley were set to do well with a real highway system and a vastly improved water district coming on line.

The Wheeler children had not entirely deserted. At least one, usually more, came every summer with their spouse and children, and they expected to come regularly and help more when gas rationing ended and crowding on trains abated. Three years earlier Donald and his wife Mary had hired Wib to begin a large two-story log house with concrete basement on the Brice place they had purchased. The logs and sawed timbers had been collected from the river and stockpiled for years. The original homestead era schoolhouse on the place also contributed timbers. In a variation on how Frank and Jeanie had started out, Donald would work for salary most of the year, and he and his family would spend as much time as they could farming at White Bluffs, but without the stress of long separations that Frank and Jeanie had endured. To avoid that, they would have to hire much work done, and the plan was that Grisham would help there too.

Grisham wrote regularly in detail to Donald to tell him what he had accomplished at Willowbank Farm, and what still needed to be done. In spring of 1942, however, Don had received a letter of apology from him that he had not carried out all his usual tasks. Now all three of his sons had been drafted, and his wife required hospitalization. Grisham felt forced to go to Pasco to work for the higher wages now available. He was concerned that the renovations and routine upkeep on Willowbank Farm had fallen behind:

> Well, the trees are in bloom and the cots look fine.
> The peaches don't look so good. I pruned all of them
> and they are in bad shape, lots of deadwood...I pruned
> your young cot orchard and the raspberries also. The
> places need a lot of work...it's too much for your dad to

do, and it will cost considerable as you can't be here to do it yourself...Tell me what to do about it and please don't misunderstand me because I hate to see you waste money for pumping etc.

It was not all Grisham's fault that the work didn't get done. The previous winter the Wheelers, after thirty-nine years, had taken a long trip, their first vacation together. They rode the train east, and visited around to their transplanted children, and got acquainted with new grandchildren. They found themselves at home in the old role of baby tending. They toured the highlights of Washington D.C. and stayed at George and Eleanor's commuter farm in Virginia.

Frank had tried to put his own farm work out of his mind, knowing that it was in Grisham's hands. Even in neglect, the orchard, for once, could be profitable. Then they got his letter of apology. But the Wheelers had known for a long time that nothing ever worked out just as it should with farming. They came home to face the seasonal spring work, and did what they could, knowing they would soon to be joined by grandchildren, then the usual summer crowd with many hands to help. The market was fine; the river was wonderful as ever. They were together.

But on March 6, 1943, without warning, every resident of White Bluffs and Hanford and adjacent areas received a letter from the U.S. Department of Defense:

Dear Sir or Madam:

You are advised that on February 23, 1942, the United States of America instituted the above proceeding to acquire certain real properties by condemnation, including lands apparently owned or occupied by you....I enclose a copy of such order, which will serve to advise you that the United States was on

such date given the right immediately to take possession
of such property.

A portion of the attached legal notice read:

> "...property described in the petition for
> condemnation is being acquired in time of war for
> military, naval or other war purposes...as provided in
> Title II Section 201 of "Second War Powers Act, 1942,
> Public Law #507, 77th Congress, March 27, 1942...".

The condemned land included almost 200,000 acres around White
Bluffs and Hanford, a wide swath on the west bank of the river, from
Wahluke village to Richland, and a strip along the east bank. The area
nearest the towns was to be vacated by May 31, while those in a border area
farther out would have a little more time. A following letter told them to
send the abstract or title for their place, by return mail if possible.

The Wheelers stared at their orders in disbelief. They and their
neighbors had a little less than three months to give up their homes,
businesses, orchards and fields, and move out. Sanger quotes Annette
Heriford, from a Valley family, "It was a terrible shock. I can't describe it.
It was unbelievable. The only thing that made it credible to us was because
of the war. Our town had been chosen for the war effort. We were so
patriotic. Although we could go along with that idea, it was still a terrible
blow."

The residents could not dream what the project was. Since it was top
secret, Frank deduced it was to produce a deadly weapon, some kind of
poison gas. But why couldn't it be a temporary move until the war was over,
people wondered, and why did the project have to be in their perfect
farming area? They knew they could not possibly get fair compensation.

Jeanie wrote to their U.S. Senator Bone, asking him why some
uninhabited land out in the desert, of which there was plenty, couldn't be

used for the project? On April 13, they received a reply from him that gave no answers:

> "So far none of us have been able to learn the exact purpose of the acquisition, the Department shrouding it in mystery...I can assure you my protest to the Department over this matter was vigorous. I wish I had the authority to compel the appraisal of lands at a value reflecting what my correspondence seems to indicate to be the real value. In a great war such as this..."

and he ended with bleak consolation.

An Eastern Washington real estate man, Marc Miller, later wrote in his contribution to the *Family Histories* that it was he who was hired by the Army and who put General Groves onto the idea of the Priest Rapids valley for the mysterious project. (He had earlier had success finding the White Bluffs site for the Mormons.) Miller recalls flying over Eastern Washington with the team, going over their site requirements, and realizing he knew just where to point them. We wonder how soon he realized what a train of events he had put in motion. He says he suffered for it later.

Why their valley was chosen was soon clear to the settlers: the abundance of water, the available railroad link, and ironically, the new power available from Bonneville and Grand Coulee dams, the victory they had finally achieved. Perhaps the government had even found needed minerals nearby. Whatever "it" was, it took a lot a space, and it had to be isolated from any center of population, so they would be moved out, hundreds of families, some there for four, even five decades. Years later the Army revealed that it had looked over the entire country for a site for the project and believed White Bluffs-Hanford "the only place in the country that could match the requirements for a desirable site." The Army couldn't see one problem to dissuade them. The project code name became "Site W".

Bewilderment grew to anguish as public meetings were held at both towns to make the decision and the process clear and inarguable. The citizens learned that all public buildings and businesses would be torn down along with the houses, and the orchards uprooted or left to die. They would be compensated of course. Families were ordered not to talk about it, and especially not to write to the men on military duty as it could demoralize them to hear they had no home to come back to.

One meeting was not enough for people to truly understand. More meetings caused more anger as it sank in that the removal was permanent. Just like the Indians, they wouldn't be coming back. But this time every single person would go; no little band of Wanapums would be left to quietly camp along the banks at their old spots. Even the graves—177 at White Bluffs—would, like the Indian graves at the dam, be dug up and moved. White Bluffs and Hanford would be wiped from the face of the earth.

The growers begged to be allowed to harvest the year's crops to raise funds they would need to make this major change, but they were told that was impossible. Only the asparagus and strawberries would be ready in time. What was to become of them, then, to be leaving in June with little or no income from harvest? What if they refused to meet the deadline? When would their payment from the government come? The government was not pleased with the patriotic response. To be sure that everyone got the message, on April 1, the Coyote Rapids pumping plant was seized and the water from the Ditch cut off.

Parker writes that some of the residents who were on the coast working in the war industries had never received the notice and came home for a visit to find to find they no longer had a house. Their personal belongings had been removed and piled somewhere. Some of them didn't stay the night; they turned around and drove away, unable to think. In May the Wheelers wrote their attorney, Lloyd Wiehl, of the old homesteading family, "The appraisers still have not arrived, and we are expected to vacate by May 31. What can we do?" All he could tell them, at that point, was to be sure to get a receipt from the government before they left. He would do better later.

The appraisers did arrive at last, and rushed through the places ignoring everything but the orchards and main domiciles. Animals, equipment, outbuildings, and any land not planted were passed over with a blink. They ignored people's attempts to point out value to them. The Wheelers had by then accepted the seizure of their property, as had everyone else, as a criminal injustice they could do nothing about. Now they had to endure the rudeness and ignorance of the appraisers. "What's that old barn over there?" one asked of Donald Wheeler's new home almost completed. Another appraiser commented, "You should be glad to get out of this godforsaken place." Now the residents were insulted as well as grief-stricken.

No one could tell the families when their money, whatever it amounted to, would arrive. How could they go anywhere? Not everyone was as fortunate as the Wheelers, with children saying their parents could stay with them. Dupont, the construction contractor, offered jobs building the project site, and some men felt they had no choice but to take them. Some saw nothing wrong with this, considering that they had no other way to make a living, while others who refused those jobs called them traitors. Jeanie wrote Margaret, "There are 800 men working at Hanford. Vern gets $80-90 a week. If only Daddy were five years younger. We just miss the good income on every hand." She could feel better about that later, when they knew what the plant produced, that he had not laid his hand to it.

Some former settlers-turned project workers were allowed to stay awhile in their houses and pay rent to the government. If their places still had water access they were paid to care for the orchards, spraying and irrigating. However, when it came time to pick and pack the fruit, they were not allowed to. Instead, prisoners of war were brought in. This caused more pain, as the prisoners, most of whom knew nothing about harvesting fruit, marched into the orchards to get the cherries, apricots, peaches and pears out of the trees anyway they could. The orchardists wrote in *Family Histories* how they couldn't bear to watch, couldn't understand why they were not allowed to harvest right and earn a little cash. The Wheelers and others close to town were spared this last scene; their trees were bulldozed first.

When the residents got their appraisals, their disdain and sadness exploded again to fury. The Wheeler/Shaw place, now forty acres with three houses, barns, wells, over twenty acres of producing orchard, pasture and vineyard, an irrigation system supplying several other families, and many feet of water front, was appraised at $1500. The others fared no better. Annette Heriford remembered, "They appraised my father's thirty acres [near Hanford] at $1700...the pump and well alone had cost us $1900 plus the concrete pipe..." Sanger interviewed Lloyd Wiehl about the appraisals, "What they did, they brought in the Federal Land Bank people from clear out of the state...They didn't understand the valley or fruit, they didn't think much of the valley, and they brought in terribly low appraisals. Highway robbery!" Other settlers comment that one reason for the low appraisals was that the Soldier-Settler Project had been so unsuccessful from the State's viewpoint.

Salvaged Wheeler letters from this period are few; the time Jeanie normally took to store letters safely was impossible now. People knew they shouldn't be discussing the project, whatever it was. A letter from Margaret merely says, "Thanks for the wonderful asparagus....Maybe the girls [Morford children, now in Seattle] will be out of school in time to help you pack." One comment from Jeanie to Donald does reveal her feelings. "The huge gravel digger is busy in the upper corner of your place. Aren't you happy to know it's the best gravel in the valley?"

Dupont brought in thousands from across the country, just as the men had come for Coulee Dam. One government photographer remembered that new hires by the bus load turned around to leave as soon as they experienced their first dust storm. The Garden was reverting rapidly.

Frank wrote a plaintive note to each of his children, "If you want to see this place again, you had better get over here." Helen was the only one allowed time off from her job. Civilians had second priority on the jammed buses and trains of the coast, but somehow she begged and pushed her way through the crowds of soldiers up to White Bluffs, just in time to see the bulldozer at work in their orchard. As the catskinner knocked down their fence, Frank and Jeanie rushed out, "You're letting our cows out! What do you think you're doing?" He yelled back, "That's my business!" Later he called to Jeanie, "What's the name of that river over there?" Incredulous, she snapped back, "That's my business!" and turned away before she broke down. Helen was the only one of the six children to see the place before it was gone, and says, "I've never gotten over that scene. I many times wished I had not come."

The valley families decided they would not accept the appraisals. Though they had differing opinions about how long the current strong fruit market could last, or about the future for small farming, for years they had been hearing from both private and government experts of how valuable their land was for other development beyond farming. Donald's wife Mary wrote for the family to Washington D.C.: What about the advertised great industrial potential of the valley? What about the anticipated great city? Now this same land was suddenly worth nothing. They didn't have to be Rhodes Scholars to know that great profits were being made by war industries such as Dupont. Though the residents, including the Wheelers this time, supported their country going to war, they knew there had to be funds to pay families decently for taking away their life work and their children's inheritance.

R. Reierson, the owner of the White Bluffs mercantile and also in charge of civil defense for the region, writes in *Family Histories* that he was one of those who promoted the idea that the appraisers could be sued. More meetings took place, this time without the government men. Almost every family decided to sue and hired an attorney. Lloyd Wiehl was a good choice; if anyone knew the valley it was Wiehl. Reierson says that three test cases were presented in court. One won an increase from $6,500 to $30,000; the second and third doubled their awards. The residents won all of the first eighteen suits to go to court. The government, observing how things were going, decided to settle on all of the remaining suits. Wiehl wrote later:

> Charles Powell, later a federal judge from
> Kennewick, and I got together and we took most of
> those land cases to court and the verdicts were so much
> over the appraisals....We settled nearly all the cases out
> of court....So we later went to court over the crops.
> Some of the crops, in court, brought more than what
> they had appraised the land for. One year's crop.

Miller, who had shown the valley to the Army, says that he took a lot of criticism for his earlier role, left the government job, and as an independent appraiser who did know the valley was able to help the families win much better compensation. Wiehl was successful in getting the Wheelers' amount raised twice, from $1650 to $3700, finally to $6500, including Donald's place. The increase was mainly due to a new appraisal of the crops.

At Donald's place, the appraisers found, oddly, "no evidence of crops". Donald sighs: "The 300 new apricot trees had been girdled by jack rabbits the winter before when everyone was gone. We lost them all. It could be a hard place." Due to the war, there had not been enough able-bodied men left in the valley to organize a traditional rabbit drive. Only a thin curtain, not even a wall, kept Nature from seizing back its own.

After the attorney fees, most settlers netted over twice the original offer. Later the shareholders in the Priest Rapids Water District who used the Ditch brought suit for the value of the excess power now generated by the diversion dam. They won $50 per acre per shareholder.

When it was time to move, the government gave assistance. Each family was allowed one trip with a large truck to their destination. The Wheelers were headed for Seattle where they planned to stay at Margaret's for a time. One cow and the horse, Molly, so much a part of the family that they couldn't be left behind, would go to Rose and Wib's new place at Gig Harbor. When the truck driver arrived on June 10th, he had brought his wife along to keep him company. What he was thinking of, to have filled up needed space in the truck this way, was a mystery, but added one more insult in the long list. After loading animals and belongings into the truck, Jeanie took up the only space left in the cab. On Frank's last trip out of White Bluffs, he rode across the mountains with his horse and cow, huddled in a quilt on top of his household goods. The cold and stress left him sick for weeks at Margaret's. Then the worst of it was over for the Wheelers.

Very soon the desert reclaimed the abandoned farms. A worker at the new project complained that a wind came up every afternoon at four, and by July the sand in the main street of Hanford was a foot deep. The alfalfa disappeared. The fruit trees left standing became skeletons. Bulldozers buried the remains of the houses and other buildings, fences, wells, everything deep in the sand. The government didn't want people to think of coming back to salvage anything, or to see what had been their homes.

The settlers scattered to wait for their funds. Frank and Jeanie Wheeler traveled between their children in the East while they waited a year and thought about a place to roost. Their letters to Margaret were still about everything except White Bluffs. Jeanie broke her reserve once:

> Daddy and I are glad to be here to help the boys
> and Marian, but we so desperately miss a home of our
> own. Not long ago Daddy said mournfully, 'A few years
> ago we were the people, and now the children are the
> ones doing the real work.' Of course it's part of the
> normal picture of easing into old age, but what isn't
> normal was the violent uprooting from our home and
> the scene of our children's growing up. We are glad to
> be busy so as to ease the pain, but now long to settle
> down.

They were at George's place in Virginia when their settlement arrived. "Do you want to stay here with us or get a place of your own?" their son asked. They didn't hesitate; they would be heading back west, back home. Jeanie had kept up her correspondence with several of her old neighbors, knew their spiritual suffering, and wanted to be near them. The *Family Histories* mention in several places that the move hastened the death of elders, one settler naming five widows that were gone within the year. For the remaining soldier-settlers, a younger group, and some already on temporary relocation to the war industries, or for the young men off at war, moving might have been easier. Perhaps it was easiest for the Mormons who had been there a short time, were mainly young, and would find it less difficult to form or join a new community elsewhere.

When the former White Bluffs teacher, Mary Powell Harris, interviewed resettled farmers years later, most commented that they were now "doing all right", that they had more than they ever had at White Bluffs. Many were the younger people who had grown up during the Depression, and were just climbing out of it when they were evicted. In a monetary sense they did "have more" now, but one wonders how they felt about the loss of community and surroundings, and how the changes had turned out for their parents. The older people didn't have the strength to start new farms, and their compensation was not enough to buy into working farms. In the end, most of them settled in small homes in the farming towns of eastern Washington. With their friends and neighbors scattered to the winds, social supports along with them, they would have a lot of time on their hands and meager livings.[1]

Frank Wheeler was seventy and Jeanie sixty-one when they left White Bluffs, too young to completely retire, too old to start a new commercial farm—not on the final net figure of $4500, Donald having given his share to Rose. "She had ended up the worst off." But Frank and Jeanie had great human resources to call on, and, it turned out, were among the most fortunate of the evicted. In November of 1945 they found themselves once more with catalogs in hand, writing up an order for a small family orchard, flowering shrubs, seeds, and bulbs. They chose a whole range of fruits, berries, nuts, and shrubs they thought could thrive in their new location, back where they had started, west of the mountains. They named their new place "Eden's Bower."

The day they mailed off their order was the beginning of a new life that they could not have grasped alone. The Wheelers got their new chance through a three-acre place on Bainbridge Island, the summer home of Donald's wife's Lukes family. The house needed gradual renovation, but it was large enough to contain many visiting grandchildren. A fir forest bordered their place, and an excellent clamming and swimming beach was just down the hill. The island was quiet, rural, yet convenient, with a system of buses, a post office and small general store only a half mile away. They could ride the ferry into the city. It was a coastal retirement version of White Bluffs, with no profit-loss books for Jeanie to brood over. Before long, Frank had a flock of chickens of all varieties, including free-running bantams that dug in Jeanie's seeded flower beds. Despite them, Jeanie carried her passion to the ultimate and developed one of the largest, most admired informal flower gardens on the island. Her only regret was that so many of her old neighbors didn't have such an opportunity.

Frank found small bricklaying jobs in the community, and now enjoyed the work. He rarely talked about anything to do with desert irrigation or the struggles of commercial farming, or what happened at White Bluffs, even after the war was over. He lambasted Truman in letters, but it was not specifically for the eviction, one time ending with a familiar theme: "It is simply amazing how devoted to wealth and cowardice we are in this country. I think myself it is largely the fruit of black slavery." The dilemma of the arid west, the dangers of pesticides, the increasing destruction of nature—these were all to become huge themes for Frank's children in the next decade. It was as if Frank wanted to put the past behind him and live in the present, and his children apparently felt the same way, for it was over twenty years before Margaret, then the others, began to write about White Bluffs. Jeanie, forever the resilient soul, kept continuous contact with her "Old Town" friends, made new friends, and saw that Frank went to church and to Grange with her.

Though in the here and now Jeanie and Frank were together, doing what they enjoyed, we can't know how much they reflected on all the years they had spent apart from each other for the sake of that orchard, or on the uses it had in the end served. Jeanie had never been, despite all her letter writing, one to share her deepest feelings with the world. Frank, though at one time quite the opposite, in his old age became a quiet man. Later, though Jeanie and the rest of the family could talk about the eviction, he became more and more silent.

After the eviction, the mysterious project area became a forbidden and guarded land, with Hanford a temporary top secret city of many thousand construction workers. Later Richland would be a permanent city of technicians. On August 6, 1945, the evicted residents who read the Richland paper, *The Villager*, saw the headline: "It's Atomic Bombs...President Truman releases the secret of Hanford Product." Their beloved lands and river had been used to manufacture plutonium for the bomb that destroyed Nagasaki and 70,000 people.

The Priest Rapids valley settlers stayed in contact through the annual White Bluffs/Hanford settlers' picnic at Kennewick or Prosser, later Richland. It was an event that many, like Wib Morford and his son Rollin, would never miss. Others refused to go, while others, like Helen and Donald Wheeler finally were able to bear attending and were glad they did. Jeanie in much later years enjoyed the accolades she got when she was the oldest person at the reunions. The younger crowd who attended talked about the new lives they were building. But like all people who have suffered a diaspora, mostly the settlers talked about the natural beauty of their lost homeland and the created beauty of their farms, community, and lives they had left behind. Through all this, they nursed their bitterness. Then slowly, over the decades, it eased its grip on their spirits.

In later years the security of the area around the town sites was loosened and a pilgrimage by special bus was allowed for the people attending the annual picnic. The bravest took the offer, Annette Heriford of Hanford among them. She would become for years the major organizer of the annual event. Each year the settlers-turned-pilgrims park their cars under the poplars that still line the river bank by the town sites and walk about, searching for signs of their former lives. Almost nothing can be seen of the towns, of the farms only rows of dead trees. But the slough is still a good place for a picnic, just as Jeanie and Frank would have spread it on a summer weekend. A few fish hide along the bank in this strangely wild stretch that is now known as the Hanford Reach. The pilgrims meander for an hour or so along the riverbank, stare out at the bluffs, sift the sand for pieces of a house or fence, and let memories run through them as the river swirls past.

In the 1969 one of the Wheeler grandchildren ran into a man who told her that his job as a youth was to accompany his father across the river to what had been White Bluffs.

> We used to run horses on the east bank, and we'd go
> across the river by boat where we weren't supposed to
> be, and we'd saw up those dead fruit trees, then bring
> them across and haul them home, sell them for
> firewood. All those dead fruit trees. We used to wonder
> about the people that had lived there, that pretty place
> by the island.

MEASURING EDEN

"We used to wonder about the people that had lived there..."
An unnamed woodcutter from the east bank, 1950s

MANY DESERTS IN THE WEST have had water applied to them to produce world class fruit. The Priest Rapids valley is important for history not for its fine fruit but for the small irrigators' success in creating a real-life agrarian community close to what John Wesley Powell and Horace Greeley had dreamed of. White Bluffs was idea given breath thirty-seven years, while its populace, arriving as strangers to each other and to irrigation, learned not only to grow fruit but community.

What they achieved was by no means predictable. Only a few social theorists concerned themselves with the character of the communities that would evolve as water remade desert lands. And of those, some argued it could create small democracies, others feared water system-based autocracies. The technology involved was controversial from the start, with tentacles pulling at it from other tangled issues of Indian treaty rights, urban poverty and unemployment, railroad interests, western lands speculation, world markets, energy development, labor reform, and the generally chaotic economic health of the country. Though few of the 1906-07 settlers may have known it, the Priest Rapids valley drama was influenced by every one of these issues. Economic, social, and political issues first brought the settlers to the valley, then weighted their fortunes as farmers, then forced an early exit.

While all the arguments over western lands simmered and even boiled, two world wars and an extended depression of twenty years (1921-1941) played havoc with the fruit market. After the first few years, the Priest Rapids growers never experienced a "normal" market. They experienced only the extremes of war markets and depression. The New Deal years finally brought the public power that the small irrigators had been fighting for, and an east-west trucking route broke the railroad's monopoly. But before the effects on orchardry could be truly known, that is, over a full economic cycle, they were all evicted. They would never know if their dreams of wealth were only dreams, but the broader history is clear. Once the government gave the green light to large dam and reservoir construction in the West, corporate farming found loopholes to override the slim protections for small landholders and very soon won the field.

The Wheeler family, who have as individuals provided most of the testimony for this book, arrived in the valley with an unusual background, even for that diverse crowd. Yet after a few years' residence they were hardly exceptional at all in what happened to them and how they saw it. If we can trust what the other settlers report in the *Family Histories*, the Wheelers turn out to be a generally reliable voice on the desert irrigation adventure—its successes and failures.

"Dad should have known better" was Donald's final remark on the whole venture. This was at a family get-together including two of his siblings in 2000. Marian and Helen were indignant, declaring that their father chose the perfect place to raise a family. But Donald didn't dispute that. He knew what his parents had accomplished as much as anyone. He was speaking as a political economist of the risks already known regarding small scale farming. How could irrigation make it that much different? Frank did know better with one side of his mind, of course. He, like his neighbors, simply wanted a chance at that life for himself and his family. Who knows how many of his neighbors went against their own psyches' whispered warnings?

If we accept that small scale irrigation was bound to fail in the West, and that if the Priest Rapids valley orchardists hadn't been evicted they could have bought time for only one generation more, we should at least look at the years that White Bluffs did exist and measure its success. We should not measure narrowly in profits and losses, but as broadly as the history herein told.

The settlers of 1906 and most that came later arrived with limited resources, expecting to build from scratch. For half of their tenure, American agriculture was in severe depression and only after the early-1930s did federal social programs begin to fill in the gaps. Until then, the tiny local post office and the military draft were what people knew of the federal government. Outside of what the county and state could provide—very little beyond roads and schools—local volunteers expected to do whatever needed doing for a community. In White Bluffs, from all accounts, they excelled.

The *Family Histories* and the Wheelers' own memories are admittedly colored by nostalgia for the golden years of childhood. However, Parker's straightforward summaries of weekly newspaper items, and the letters from the Wheelers' collection confirm that even in the worst years, with the exception of a TB epidemic, White Bluffs was a remarkably healthy place, physically and socially, to live. Youth left the schools ready to compete in colleges and on jobs. The residents practiced social tolerance and harmony to such extent that a family as atypical as the Wheelers were widely included. If the town didn't quite reach the level of Athenian democracy, according to all accounts it came closer than most. And women voted. Hanford lost more population but in other ways seems its twin.

We should also measure the value of the individual lives in this human-wrought Eden. Looking at the four partners, as a perspective from which to look at all the residents, we can say that the life in the valley was good for a wide variety of personalities and needs.

George Shaw can stand for many of the older settlers who had the simplest sort of requirements for a good life and found them at White Bluffs, more than he would have as an aging logger west of the mountains. He had everything he needed, once they were in a real house. He had no children to support. George didn't live to see the Depression but we can imagine him making do, especially with his well organized wife, and his daughter to care for him in his old age. He was surrounded by his beloved animals, many descendants, and an amused community for his yarning. George had an advantage most of the farmers did not have in the startup years—a partner pumping in funds. He must have had hopes for irrigation at the start, but soon realized that farming was farming, good only for people who didn't expect a fortune, and that irrigated farming was too much work for the rewards. But he soon figured out how to make the best of it.

Jane Shaw had broader expectations and sacrificed more than George physically and spiritually to build the two farms and the White Bluffs community. She can represent the many activist farming women who reached out beyond their homes to make the community as special as it was, and to recognize the worth of each member. As for her more personal goals, she worked very hard, but she was no longer taking in washing as she had at Hoquiam. Her boarding house was popular, her gifts usually appreciated. Her lameness, a setback for an active woman, she had to endure. Jane put up with the pettiness of a village and enjoyed the camaraderie of it as she probably would have anywhere. Here she lived only a stone's throw from her devoted daughter and six interesting grandchildren she could watch grow up. Only in her last two or three years could she feel less productive than she wished; she had fulfilled her side of the partnership. As for the settlers' chances to succeed in greening the desert, she would have commented that the fate of this garden, just like the first, was in God's hands. Many of the valley's older generation would have agreed with her.

Evaluating the life in the valley for Frank and Jeanie Wheeler is more complex. White Bluffs, for Frank, was an escape from the physical, political, and spiritual corruption of Tacoma. He hoped also for escape from heavy and boring physical labor; his trees would never bore him. He didn't expect to form a utopia or a socialist enclave, just to be part of a healthy, supportive community, and to have more time with family. He gave up any chance for labor organizing when he moved to the desert, but he had never been a real organizer; he was by nature a preacher. In White Bluffs he still got his word in. As a lover of natural beauty, he was totally pleased with the valley.

Although Frank probably never heard of the Myth of the Garden in so many words, he knew well the various pressures on Congress for desert development. For him, the victory of the small-scale irrigation movement, not just the success of his own farm, was important. He found out that without public power the irrigators weren't going to get far. Finally, all he could do was to keep a community pump going. The continuing failure of the valley to succeed economically except in wartimes had to be depressing to him. Yet, as he would remark to Margaret in several contexts about gathering riches on this earth, "Why be disappointed..."

Even though Frank was unique in political philosophy for the community, and he was gone from the valley more than other farmers, most of his outcomes were like the other growers with large families. He soon saw

424

that to survive they had to expand, and that brought new difficulties. But his health suffered more from the bricklaying, work he would have been stuck with in any case, than it did from the orchard. As a working man, he never would have gotten to see the gardens of England or the vineyards of Italy. Though he wasn't able to travel, through his farm he earned himself the best "vacations", and eventual semi-retirement that a tree lover could imagine. Meanwhile he had provided the healthy home for his wife and children that he had dreamed of. Frank was like many of the farmers who, for the sake of their families and their own peace of mind, stayed at White Bluffs long after they realized they would never tear up their mortgages.

We know that Jeanie, like Frank, loved the natural world of the valley. She, like him, cared about the overall welfare of the community and small farmers in general, not just her own family's wellbeing. For her especially, the family's activism through the popular Grange lodge was an important means to fight off despair when everything went wrong with farming. Though the Grange didn't win enough fights, the members did at least have a voice and a tie to a national movement. At Grange the Wheelers could find agreement with neighbors on immediate issues that bridged the blank stares some of Frank's rarer ideas encountered.

If anyone wanted the farm to do more than just skin by it was Jeanie, and on her worst days we know from one letter that she at times regretted the whole venture. Most of the growers felt the same yearning for a taste of wealth, and probably had the same regrets at times. Most of them had children to prepare for the world, and the valley wasn't cooperating financially. But on the other hand the valley was everything else they had hoped for. Through Jeanie's, Jane's and others' creativity and devotion they had built an exceptionally supportive community. Their elders were provided a fairly secure old age, their children were safe, and even their education was not much slighted. Jeanie can represent all the women who worked so hard, oft_____ ___ ____ __ ___ simple demands of running a house__old and raising children __th __ _____ces, along much of the labor of their own farms, and then going out to the mad ru__ of the packing house_. She can represent all those women who loved the desert and river enough to stay.

Probably more than most of the valley women, Jeanie missed the culture of larger towns. On the other hand, her integration into the White Bluffs community, like her mother's, gave much sense of personal and social value. Often raising children was frustrating for her, but staying in Tacoma wouldn't have made rearing six easy. Some valley women not as strong as she ended up with chronic ailments. Yet their lives were heaven compared to the lives of prairie-farming women. As they looked back in the *Family Histories*, the Priest Rapids valley farmers, men and women, did not complain about the work but about the market, and about the lack of recognition for their quality fruit.

For many residents, not just the Wheelers, education for their children was even more important than economic comfort, and having them graduate from college surely balanced some of the disappointments they felt. That so many valley families somehow encouraged, if not supported, their children through college is one more tribute to the quality of people they were and the quality of the community and schools they built at Hanford and White Bluffs.

Probably not every grower loved his trees as much as Frank did, nor did every woman drink up such pleasure from her flower garden as Jeanie, but from the observations in the *Family Histories* we learn that among the valley residents there was a widespread recognition of the beauty of their surroundings. The river and its bluffs first seduced the settlers, then they fell in love with their own created orchards and gardens. Sandstorms aside, they were daily offered a bouquet of pleasure for all the senses that made up for too much work and too many dinners of boiled beans.

The special goal that Frank and Jeanie had the most trouble achieving was to have more time together. Frank would have spent more time farming and less bricklaying if Jeanie had agreed to it. She simply knew more about their day to day needs and bills than Frank did. But he, just as much as she, wanted a rich life for their children, so he kept on working until the Great Depression, blessedly, gave them their out. By 1943, their last farming year, Frank and Jeanie could truly say they had achieved as much of their personal goals as human beings could expect. As for the other irrigators, if we can believe their children, that was true for many of them.

The six Wheeler siblings, regardless of their individual memories and interpretations of the White Bluffs experience, all agreed that it taught them a great deal, maybe all they needed to know, about work, living with nature, family enterprise, community, courage, and loyalty. By the time they themselves retired, they had finished their urban experiences and were all living back in the country again, growing a few fruit trees and fine gardens. They all carried the town of White Bluffs in their hearts and involved themselves in their community and in public service wherever they lived. Forty years is not much time in human history, but it is enough for a community to establish its character and embed itself in its citizens.

The future of the orchards, the town, the Priest Rapids valley as a whole—that history was cut off. But we can predict the outcomes, had it not been. A generation later, driving through the gigantic Columbia Basin Project just to the northeast, we can travel for miles and not see an inhabited residence, much less human beings working in the orchards and fields, much less yet children playing. We see miles of uniform, flourishing, industrialized orchards and vineyards, systematically watered by great ditches, with the owners and their seasonal crews living elsewhere. No doubt they are worrying about the market. Their children are home playing video games, or cruising, looking for something to fill their evening. The promised cities never materialized, and it is just as well. Instead we have agribusiness and the still problematic nuclear plant close-by, but also the hard-won Hanford Reach National Monument where the original environment of the river, valley, and bluffs is preserved, one hopes, for eternity.[1]

When we evaluate those early, small irrigation experiments in the Priest Rapids valley, we need to remember that the "greatest good for the greatest number" was the Grange philosophy. It was not about efficiency but about quality of life. Modern agribusiness demonstrates that the way to run an irrigated farm for profit is large scale, not small. Of course the early agrarian promoters knew that, but were after something else. The settlers leapt at the chance. Many people would again today, even if they, like Frank should "know better".

Controversy over today's huge irrigation projects ranges further. Critics like Donald Worster believe that the idea of watering arid desert, the hydraulic vision of progress, was wrong from the start. The Bureau of Reclamation, as the unsurpassed monster bureaucracy, was little concerned about long-range social and environmental costs. He points out that developing the desert made sense only for land speculators like the railroads when we already had so much land with adequate rainfall in the East, Southeast and Pacific Coast. Farmers in those regions that needed help were underserved due to the emphasis on developing the arid West. (It is not clear where western mining and its water needs fits into his argument).

Wallace Stegner talks about the water needs of today's huge desert cities like Phoenix and Los Angeles and a dozen more, and asks us to examine what their ever-growing water demand has done to the Colorado River, and is doing now to the aquifer. He, too, questions whether we should ever have allowed the watering of the West and the building of huge cities in the desert. As for the Columbia/Snake, Blaine Harden, Richard White, and Alice Outwater ask if we needed to turn those great rivers into an industrial canal with over fifty dams, the nemesis of the salmon runs? Did we truly need the Columbia Basin Project with the huge government subsidies it requires? But today's irrigators in turn comment, "These people don't understand where their food comes from." Possibly none of these commentators ever observed a community like White Bluffs; they would be hard-pressed to find one today.

Mark Fiege takes the more positive view, that we have learned from our errors, and that the irrigated landscape is not a degraded one but a hybridized one where successful arid land orchard communities eventually form a partnership with nature—the Agrarians' original dream. If so, where are these communities? Perhaps in tiny pockets, careful not to advertise, between the vast holdings of agribusiness, golf courses, and mall parking lots.

What would Frank Wheeler have to say about these arguments? All the economic and environmental dilemmas of today sweep away the dreams and agonies of small irrigators of one hundred years ago, betting their lives on what was soon, if not already, an anachronism. But there is something in that Priest Rapids history that needs to be held onto. Given that we can't recreate a successful small-farming scene for any significant number, there is another part of the White Bluffs experience that can be salvaged for today. The times were simpler than today, and White Bluffs never more than a village, but surely the community built there, vital and healthy, still attracting new people when it was forced to close, has messages for us. Powell may have been right, that by being bonded to an essential water system requiring honesty, cooperation, and sacrifice in order to function, the settlers would learn to build and maintain a viable, generous community. There is sense in that. But there is more at work in this story. The other magic ingredient has to be that White Bluffs was located not just at any random spot of irrigated desert, but in such magnificent surroundings. The Columbia and its bluffs attracted three groups of people—the Indians, the homesteaders, and the irrigators—all of whom saw the beauty, not just the livelihood, and watched it nurture the energy and imagination of their children.

AFTERWARD

"And I behold once more
My old familiar haunts, here the blue river,
the same blue wonder that my infant eye
admired."

from *The River*
—Ralph Waldo Emerson

I WAS LIVING ON the Yukon River one winter when I was surprised to receive two boxes from my aunt Helen Hastay. They contained packets of letters belonging to her family, who had lived on that other great western river, the Columbia, starting in 1907. Curious as to why she had sent them, I picked up a letter and started to read. It was from Frank Wheeler, her father and my grandfather, and it turned out that most of them were. I was intrigued by his uninhibited metaphorical style and bold ideas—one of which had taken him to the Columbia—and I decided the best service I could do for family history was to put the letters on disk. But that meant dating them, for many envelopes or cancellations were missing, and the inside dates typically said only "Monday", or "Wednesday". The post went fast in those days. I had other intriguing puzzles to solve from the contents, and before I knew it, I was hooked.

My grandfather, a brick mason, was often away from home on jobs. His letters were first drafts, whatever had been on his mind as he slapped mud on bricks. My grandmother saved every one, thus reminding herself that this so absent spouse and father was indeed the intriguing man who had courted her, not just the guy who sent home the bacon. She had tried to store them by year, along with others, even a few of her own that had been returned to her for safekeeping, as people did in those days. These were ordinary people, not expecting to be published, so they must have assumed their children would want to know their history. Some of the years were missing in the packets; others held a stream of weekly messages.

A big puzzle for me was why my grandfather, a journeyman with a decent income and home and a growing flock of toddlers, decided that his family and his wife's parents, all coastal people, should become partners in desert farming. As I read, a rich story, richer than I had ever heard from family anecdotes, unfolded like a crazy quilt with questions I needed answered to carry out my simple recording task. I started thinking about a book after I dug out a manuscript by my mother, never finished, that described their desert community, and another that told about her grandparents. With ever more questions, I traveled down to Washington to interview my surviving aunts and uncle several times.

I knew nothing about the turn of the century irrigation craze that had swept the West after Great Plains dry farming was destroyed by drought years. I turned to western historians, scientists, and naturalists for this piece of the puzzle. Martha Parker's book on the Priest Rapids valley solved many dating problems. Then my aunt found me a copy of *Family Histories* of the White Bluffs-Hanford Pioneers Association, compiled in 1981. I was encouraged to discover how much Parker, my family, and the other descendants agreed on the important events, issues, and values in the lives of the fruit growers of the Priest Rapids valley. White Bluffs, it turned out, was a special community for many people, not just my own family. At one point, my uncle Donald Wheeler, said, "If you want to write about the place you really need to refresh your memories. Go to the annual pioneers' picnic with us this summer." I agreed.

I had some strong recollections to build on, like my last visit to White Bluffs in 1942, age six, riding across the desert from Yakima in a small stage. My escort chosen for the trip was Ellis John, an ex-con. Of course I didn't know his history; he was just a nice old man, one of the few Wheeler's neighbors I remember besides Clara Barrett, my grandmother's best friend. I can still picture my uncle Donald's log house, never to be finished, and feel the cool dark fragrance of the packing shed, and the relief of the screened porch with beds where we children slept, or dropped midday, exhausted from the blazing sun.

The vast desert and river world is what has stayed with me most. I recall sailing and learning to swim in the slough between my family's place and Barrett's Island, and one long trek up the outside of their island, my mother with us, cordeling that famous rowboat the *Ho Eliza* to a spot for seining whitefish. And of course I remember the wonderful family horse, Molly, who I learned to ride, and the coyotes singing on the bluffs in the evenings. Many picnics at the slough roll into one, but the summer I was five I had an infected foot from a sliver and had to sit on the bank with a potato poultice, the object of little pity from my dog-paddling cousins. I had plenty of time to study the natural world. After the startling view of the river and great bluffs across, what lingers most powerfully from that summer are the smells: the blackcap patch, the apricot tree in the back yard, the sweet odor of mulberries all over the ground by the picnic area, the willows in the swale, the riverbank itself, sagebrush and the citronella mosquito repellent we laid on for evening—they all bring White Bluffs back to me.

During the midday heat we little kids were ordered to stay in the shade, but city girl that I was, at first I didn't understand the implications. I went out to the orchard barefoot in the morning to play in the stream of the irrigation ditch under the trees. When the temperature started to rise. I saw I was trapped there, without the straw hat I was supposed to be wearing. There was no crossing the now scorching sand in my unhardened feet. I was in for a long day of it, I thought. But at noon here came an angel of mercy out of the peach trees, in overalls and straw hat, carrying a hoe. "What's the matter, lamby?" said my grandfather, and lifted me up on his shoulders. A perfect snapshot of Frank Wheeler, I now know.

In late July, 1999, I drove with my uncle, Donald and his daughter to the annual pioneers' picnic at Richland. I had my permission approved to enter the still-closed Hanford Works. On the morning of the scheduled caravan, I tied on my straw hat and steeled myself for an overwhelming sun. Instead, I was blessed by a day that never went over 85. We loaded bottles of water and drove up the river across sagebrush barrens. We were too late in the year for the wild flower bloom, but later I discovered to my pleasure that many of the desert flowers also thrive on the high rocky hills north of Nome, Alaska, where I live. The sage, rabbit brush and greasewood were all strange and wonderful to me and full of hazy memories. As we went upriver, the bluffs loomed closer and closer to the east bank until by the time we reached Hanford and drove down to the river, they shot up from a narrow stretch of benchland and were shocking in their golden rise above the blue-green water. I was entranced.

From Hanford onward upriver, the scene was not all beauty. We passed through rows of blackened stumps in fields of asparagus gone wild. A few sites of farmhouses were recognizable from the circled skeletons of shade trees that had once sheltered them. Arriving at the townsite of "Out Town" White Bluffs we found nothing remaining but a sign and the small concrete bank structure. We drove a mile farther down to the ferry landing at the "Old Town" site, its concrete ramp still ending in the river. Here we saw living trees, descendants of the original poplars, and parked in their shade. Across from us were the great bluffs again, but at this point they were gleaming creamy white with gray striations. The current swirled past the tip of Barrett's Island, green with willow. All the shapes and colors and smells of the natural world were as my six-year-old senses had stored them, and that thrilled me. I felt as if I had stepped into a holy place; I know I was not alone in that.

The site of the Wheeler place is a short distance up the river reached by a sand road. My uncle and I walked along it to where the orchard and houses had been. He pointed out the site of the Shaw house, now indistinguishable in the sagebrush. Down closer to the river, greenery takes over to partially hide piles of blackened tree skeletons I didn't want to see. The swale where they tethered the cows is now a park of high willows, rye grass and locust trees. Mule deer came out of the shade to stare at us, then ambled off. A porcupine watched us from a willow. We came to the site of the house the Wheelers had lived in after the tents, but there was nothing left, I thought. Then I spied a small piece of shingle, my prized souvenir of the trip. I was quite overcome.

I thought the black locusts were all second growth until I saw a wire embedded high up in one of the tallest. It was a surviving original tree, and it turned out there were several, still watered by the river, now at least sixty years old, probably more. Through the tangle of wild roses and rye on the bank was the green slough where I learned to swim, and Barrett's Island where we picnicked that last summer of 1942, all so familiar. There is no real beach anymore as the controlled flow of the river doesn't rise up in the spring to scour off the bank. Across the tip of the island and the blue of the main channel, the bluffs shimmered, but my uncle showed me where erosion from irrigation on the plateau is scarring them. He waded through the willow brush to the bank to point out the ruins of the Wheeler pumphouse he had helped build, turned cockeyed where the evicters' bulldozer left it fifty-seven years before. I took a picture of him standing on it, then left him to be by himself and walked slowly back down the trail to rejoin my cousin. My dried bouquet and my piece of shingle are more pleasing for me than the results of my poor photography work. I knew I needed to return another year for better pictures, though there is no way to capture the magic of the bluffs. For a long time I simply stared out across the river.

All of the caravanners converged at noon at the ferry landing. They were in a somber mood. It would soon get too hot, they said, so we should go back. I wanted to stay, but couldn't argue. On the way back we stopped so I could take a picture of a section of the Hanford Works that is just upriver from White Bluffs. At the bend, its ominous gray angles with smoke drifting upward loomed over the brush, badly at odds with the magic scene. "That's it?" It was hard not to start raving. But my companions had been on this pilgrimage many times. "That's it." said my uncle, "That's it."

I had started with a typing job and ended up with a rich history covering four decades of a particular family, with its own ideas of what constituted the good life, and a perspective on the community they helped form at White Bluffs. The story evolved also into an up-close view on a technology that became a cause, then a definition of the West. The Shaws' and Wheelers' story tells how that played out for thirty-seven years in a real community on the greatest western river. For me, the best recognition possible for those years is that the Hanford Reach is now a National Monument, and a magnificent section of the Columbia's natural world that they lived in and loved is now preserved for everyone. It is up to everyone to see that it endures.

NOTES

Chapter 1.

    1. A sample of what Frank Wheeler has to say in his unfinished memoirs:

> "The Chamber of Commerce had forced the
> exchange of location for the city hall to a rotten one. The
> city was swindled out of its teeth by the patriots, so as to
> provide a good site for the Chamber, who then proceeded
> to fleece the city on its building...Tacoma seemed destined
> to get a bad start. The woolen mill and Exposition
> building, finally the Hotel itself burned—all incendiary no
> doubt, as there was never a word said, and the Land Co.
> owned the controlling if not entire stock."

    2. The full text of the 1910 brochure, and later similar ones, is found in Martha Parker's book. Courtesy of Harry Anderson.

Chapter 2.

    1. George Shaw's long 1904 letter to his daughter Jeanie on the birth of her first child, the only letter by George we have, is worth quoting in entirety, since he was so reserved aside from his yarning. It shows a man far from inarticulate. The comment, "I hope if she should live..." was not just sentimental, as the Shaws had lost their youngest child.

> My Dear Daughter Jean,
> Your very kind letter came to me all right and I was
> never more pleased to hear from anyone. I am so glad
> you have gone through all this and that you are getting

along so nicely and then I think you have such a sweet little baby girl, I can hardly wait I want to see her so badly. I hope she keeps well and grows, and I hope if she should live that she will be so much company and comfort to you and Frank, as you yourself have been to us. I expect you will spoil her and just as soon as she is large enough I shall expect to have her with us part of the time.

My Jean, it does not seem long since I came home from the woods and when I went into the room where your mother was she lifted up the covers and there I saw my first born. You were a wee little thing and I can see you yet as I write these lines—only two days old. I thought you were the most precious little bit of humanity I had ever seen and now so soon it seems you have one of your own. Well I would like to go through the same again, Yes, I wish your mother had the strength but it will be best for us to pass it up to the younger people to raise the babies. But those were the happiest days I ever knew although we were poor and had to work hard. I was at home most of the time and it gave me sort of a contented feeling to sit by your mother and see you helping yourself to the dinner.

Well my Dear Daughter, you certainly know some of the joys of married life as well as some of the pains. I am thankfull the good lord gave you strength to go through with it all. And that you will soon be strong again. I want to say this to both of you, do not be in a hurry for the next,

perhaps you will think I am meddling with something
that is not my business, but there has been too many poor
little mothers that did not have the chance to recover
from the shock of the first one before they had it all to
go over with again. Well, I hope this finds you all well
and I know you are happy so may God bless you and
keep you is the sincere wish of your loving father.

GW Shaw ps Kiss the baby for me. G

2. This excerpt from Frank's memoirs shows that he knew all about the practice of dummy entrymen.

There was a determined effort to do the Indians out
of their land and run them out—murder or any means
was just right. More, the lumber company sent anyone
out to take up land, gave them 500 or 1000 and supplies
for a fake title as openly and respectably as an other biz.
It is said 1000 men were shot in the woods in the harbor
country, and Iv no doubt it was grossly underestimated,
after the big thieves got what they went after. And when
they did not, they were ready to kick the props out.

3. In reading the oral histories of other families who were swept up in Washington's desert land boom, we find that many of them had reasons similar to the Shaws and Wheelers. In the *Family Histories for Hanford and White Bluffs, Washington*, health concerns are mentioned frequently. Another large group included venturesome types who habitually moved about the West. Some of these were small business people who saw opportunity in new communities needing services, others were laborers going from district to district trying to find a way out of unemployment. Some were bachelors, others had families and were just above the poverty level; they hoped to find jobs as farm managers for absentee owners, or as simple

tenants, and arrived with everything they owned, creeping across the sand road in wagons. But other boomers were retired people with savings, yearning for the idealized rural life. Some even arrived with their own train cars full of supplies.

4. Donald Wheeler, the fifth Wheeler sibling, who died in 2002, was our best informant on the early technical problems of the HIPC, other water companies, and related irrigation issues in the valley.

5. The first Mayflower Farm orchard order made was to Sunnyside Nursery, dated February 1907, so we know that the Shaws arrived not long after this. The order reveals Frank's early passion for diversity. For the family orchard: One each of apple trees—Bismark, Winter Banana, Gravenstein, Early Harvest, Jonathan, Barley Sweet, Bellifleur, Wagener, Whitney Crab, Wisner's Desert; of apricots, one each—Red Astraham, Moor Park; one nectarine. Total: $6.26.

For the commercial orchard: apple: Winesap—109, Jonathan—133, Winter Banana—2, Transparent—34, Delicious—21; cherry: Bing—14, Lambert—3, Royal Ann—2; pear: Bartlett—38, D'Anjou—22; peach: Elberta—108, Red Bird—6, Carman—8, Lemon Cling—3, Salway—6; apricot: Triumph—8; prune: 4; nectarine—1. (No prices on second part of order).

6. Helen Wheeler Hastay recalls these wild flowers from the 1930s: wild rose, violet, sage pink, bluebell, yellow bell, scarlet mallow, red begonia, saffron flame cactus, brown-eyed Susan, iris, chicory, wild onion, yucca, larkspur, balsam root, mullein, mustard, aster, and along the river, wild rose. Ida Burch from "In-B-Tween", between White Bluffs and Hanford, lists much the same and adds sego lilies, evening primrose, and wild wall flower. She says the wild begonia was a dock. All of these are mentioned by author Ron Taylor except the sage pink, begonia, chicory, and mullein. These may have been local names for flowers he does mention. There was

only one kind of cactus, the prickly pear. Someone gave its blossom a fancier name—saffron flame.

Chapter 3

1.A.J. Splawn was one of the few historians who wrote extensively about the area during this period, much from his own experiences as a cattleman in the late 1800s and also from research and personal interviews. In his biography of Kamiakin, he states that this foremost leader of the Yakimas and other dissenting tribes was a progressive, and that prior to the Yakima War, he had been an experimental irrigator, returning to it after peace was declared.

Kamiakin was for some time blamed for the suffering and deaths on both sides for his refusal to give up Indian lands. But Splawn and others later saw his resistance, at the very end of the "Indian Wars", as helping to bring to U.S. public attention the injustice of the treaties, just as did the later suffering of Chief Joseph's Nez Perce band. Splawn may also have helped, through his effort to understand Kamiakin and others, to move Indian policy in a more intelligent and humane direction.

2. Lists of the homesteaders in the valley pre-1906 are provided by *As Told by the Pioneers* and by Mary Powell Harris, who taught school from 1922-24 at White Bluffs. Some locals criticized her book for relying too much on gossip; nonetheless it is valuable for its record of the early families. She says much of the early history of the county was lost in a Yakima courthouse fire, but lists these names as being prominent among the Priest Rapids valley homesteaders before the boom of 1906-7, starting from the earliest, with some leaving before others arrived: Williams, Kent, Terrill, Filey, Gable, Parker, Pitt, Brice; followed by Borden, Craig, Wright, Muir, McGlothlen, Cord, Koppen, Crawford, Ogg, Hoffman, and Allards; then Meek, Wiehl, Helsom, and finally Barrett in 1904.

Many of these early families were still in the White Bluffs area in 1913, listed in the phone book or mentioned elsewhere: Allard, Barrett, Borden, Brice, Cord, Craig, Helsom, Hoffman, Koppen, Meek, McGlothlen, Wiehl, and Wright. In the 1920s Cord, Helsom, Wiehl, Wright, Allard, Borden, Meek, Koppen, and McGlothlen were still there. Then the ranks thin. From the 1930s Helen Wheeler recalls the only Allards, Barretts, Bordens, Helsoms, Koppens, and Wiehls, and but knows there were several "old family" women by other married names too.

Pitts Island was sold to Barretts in 1904 and became Barrett's Island. Hay Island where Pitts cut eighty tons of hay one summer, had been used by the Indians earlier for a winter pasture. It became Locke's Island. Lockes, unlike the others listed, dry-farmed on the Wahluke Slope and used the island only as a summer recreation spot.

Chapter 4

1. Martha Parker lists some prices the valley growers got for their produce in April, 1908: Strawberries-$4 to $5 a crate; alfalfa hay-$9 a ton; oats grain- $32 a ton; potatoes-.90/cwt; eggs-.15/doz; creamery butter-.45/lb; poultry-$6-7/doz.

2. The name of the young bull was "Illahee Stokes Pogis". For those who like literary mysteries, who named him —Frank, Jeanie, George, Jane, or Margaret? Illahee was a Chinook Jargon work meaning "the land", without doubt taken from an Indian language. "Stokes Pogis" was the name of the town where the church, the source of Gray's famous poem, "Elegy in a Country Churchyard" was located. Margaret has to be included in the list, as any eighth grader in those days had read it.

Chapter 5

1. All of our newspaper quotes were collected by Martha Parker.

2. From the Metsker map of White Bluffs-Hanford area, pre-1943.

Chapter 6

1. Martha Parker reports that the suit was filed by K.W. Shafford. In 1909 in another water rights case, J.T. Woody won a case on appeal to the State Supreme Court against the Benton Water Co. at Richland for selling him land that was supposedly irrigable by gravity flow but turned out to be *above* their canal. The higher court had reversed a lower court , (quoted by Parker p. 155) "No rogue should enjoy his ill-gotten plunder just because his victim is by chance a fool."

Mary Powell Harris has an entire chapter of her book dedicated to court cases in the district over water rights, bankruptcies, and receiverships, mainly concerning HIPC and its successors.

2. The phenomenon of "pooling" is described by Donald Wheeler:

> The gradient in a river forms a succession of pools, and between the pools are rapids. When the river is flooding, the pool rise above the rapids is slight because the momentum of the rapids at flood pulls it away. Below the rapids the river flattens out for a while. Because there are fewer rapids and less pull there, this pool rises a lot. When the lower pool rises it subtracts from the hydraulic power available, as it is the size of the drop that makes the power. At low water, the reverse happens: the pool below the rapids is low, there is more drop and hence more power.
>
> This pooling effect is the same at dams, and has been known since ancient times, but was not taken into account adequately when the diversion dam was planned. It did not store water with the result that in the Priest Rapids Valley and in all orchard districts depending on diversion dams, the time they needed the most power to pump the water was in May and June when there was the least power being generated. The control of flow was at the farms'

measuring boxes.

3. The lobbying for a real dam continually hit obstacles. In 1915 efforts were halted when a group of affected landholders demanded a higher price for water rights than the dam investors were willing to pay. The dispute went to court, but the landholders won. It was appealed; they won again. Interest in the dam waned. In 1923 it revived, but this time the huge Oregon gillnet fleet on Lower Columbia objected. They saw the salmon runs declining and wanted no dams at all. Despite this, in 1925 the government issued a license to the Washington Irrigation and Development Co. (backed by General Electric) to start dam construction, and gave them six years to complete it. But General Electric soon found it must have better proof that power sales would make an adequate profit. In 1927, the fishermen were still protesting, and G.E. was granted a two year delay for multiple reasons. But soon the Depression put everything on hold until the New Deal.

Chapter 8

1. The particularly "activist women" that Helen remembers through either the Ladies Aid or the Women's Club were: Barge, Brisco, Fanning, Houk, Keal, Kincaid, Koppen, Leander, McFee, McMurray, O'Larey, Taylor, Thum, Tromanhauser, Sutherland, Wheeler, and later arrivals Holecek and Mikol. Some of them were in both groups.

2. A sample monthly balance sheet of 1927 from the White Bluffs Women's Club showing some of their activities, submitted by Jeanie Wheeler, Sec/Treas.

3/19 Balance: $90.65

Receipts: [These included fund raising activities they put on, such as serving dinners at events.

Dues $33, Cemetery $57, Relief $17, Garden party $191.21, Bake Sale

$15, Gifts, general $28.50, Dinner $8.10, Concert $50.05, misc. $6.85 Total $498.06

Disbursements: Dues (state/national) $13.15, Flood Relief $11.60, Local relief $16.42, Library $32.77, Cemetery $130.23, Other Civic work $32.05, Disabled Vets $3, Children's Home $5.00, Conventions $15, Operations $9.35, Dinner (Chapter) $10.90, Concert (Ms. Rowland) $25, Flowers $4, Girl Reserves $10.65, Garden Party $59.51, Misc. $7.58 Total: $388.50

Chapter 9

1. They had paid off the original mortgage of $2500 in 1912, but immediately remortgaged to the same company for $1337 and received their certificate for 20 shares in the White Bluffs Water Co. In 1915, through Niven's loan they paid off in full, the deed was conveyed, and they owed only him.

The decision to buy the Hensley tract meant that funds went to this first instead of toward the loan with Niven. What happened next tells the farmers' circumstances even before the Depression officially arrived. Neither the Shaws nor Wheelers were able to make payments on the principle of the Niven loan. They made only annual interest payments to him for years, of $40 or $50 each. During the Depression, when Frank no longer worked for wages, neither family was able to pay even that. Niven let it go. There is a friendly letter from him letting them know that he is suffering financially too, but he doesn't push them. The loans were finally paid off in the early 1940s by Donald, now working, and his wife Mary. Niven had written Donald about the situation.

Chapter 10

1. The list of flowers in Jeanie's garden at the "Green House", as remembered by Helen: marigold, hollyhock, nicotinia, clarkia, delphinium, larkspur, columbine, bachelor button, poppy, snap dragon, foxglove,

Canterbury bell, portulaca, cosmos, aster, daisy, chrysanthemum, daffodil, iris, gladiola. (She started most of these each year from seeds or bulbs.) Jane Shaw's perennial garden: Virginia Creeper (covering the porch) rose, lilac, spyria, wigelia, quince, clematis, mint, flowering almond and several others of the shrubby sort. The perennials listed in Jane's garden were also in Jeanie's.

Chapter 11

1. Donald and Helen recall their typical home medicine cabinet supply:, flax seed, castor oil and milk of magnesia (for digestion), epsom salts (for aching feet and soaking infections), teething syrup (in those days sometimes containing laudanum, but Helen says theirs didn't), aspirin, baking soda, rubbing alcohol, iodine, camphor oil (for steaming and hot compresses for chest and throat infections), golden seal (an antifungal, and for canker sores), boric acid (for eyes) zinc oxide and witch hazel (for skin irritations), citronella (mosquito protection), sulfur candles (for fumigating bedbugs), and finally, "spirits" (except during Prohibition, for colds and flu). The school gave cod liver oil, and iodine tablets to prevent goiter.

Other drugs available through a doctor included quinine, arsenic and mercury to combat infection, and chloral hydrate, opium, and morphine to ease symptoms or pain.

Chapter 13

1. From the May 10, 1923 recruitment brochure from the State of Washington Dept. of Conservation and Development's White Bluffs-Hanford Settlement project, as collected by Martha Parker:

> ...Each town has a modern water system, electric lights,
> good business houses, newspaper, moving picture theatre,
> etc. There are fraternal organizations and the class of
> citizenry is good; there are no Orientals, and the
> American Legion Post of the valley, now in its third year

of 100% membership, declares there shall be none....

Fred Weil is listed on the title page as the "Colonization Agent and Chairman, American Legion Land Settlement Committee". Parker says that the Priest Rapids Valley Legion Post was formed in 1921, with Fred Weil as its Commander. Weil got mixed reviews. Harris says that he was charismatic and a good fund-raiser, but some people thought he was inclined to sharp practices. "It depended on whether he was getting something for you that you wanted."

2. Parker gives more details: In addition to the house the settler would receive a small barn and poultry house, fencing that he would install, a pump, and irrigation pipe. He would not receive seed, plants, livestock or machinery, but other reasonable, low interest loans could be made for some of this. For example, he could acquire by government loan, with no down payment and six percent interest, four milk cows, and could keep their offspring.

Chapter 16

1. Donald adds, "Though the C grades and culls mainly weren't sold, we had plenty of uses for them. We ate them, fed them to livestock, and made cider. Eventually it turned to vinegar and we had a great many uses for that too. We pickled all kinds of fruits, tomatoes, and vegetables.

Chapter 17

1. By the 1930s, as recalled by Helen and Donald, their father had grown at least these varieties, and others they don't recall :

Apples: Winesaps, Jonathans, Transparents, White Winter Pear Maine, Delicious, Golden Delicious, Baldwin, Hubbertson Nonesuch, King David ....(and more, total 18)

Pears: Bartlett, D'Anjou, Bosc, Seckle

Cherries: Bing, Lambert, Olivet, Royal Ann, English Morello (pie cherry)

Peaches: Mayflower, Carman, Early Crawford, Elberta, Red Haven, Salway, Hale

Apricots: Tilton, Moor Park

Plums: Greengage, Damson

Grapes: Thompson Seedless, Flame Tokay, Black Prince, Delaware, Concord, and Niagara

Berries: strawberries, dewberries, gooseberries, blackcaps, Himalaya blackberries

Melons: cantaloupes, watermelons, cucumbers

Alfalfa

Navy beans (tried one year)

The family garden included: beans, cabbage, carrots, corn, peas, leaf lettuce, melons, onions, potatoes, squash, tomatoes. Wib Morford experimented with sweet potatoes and peanuts and grew especially fine melons. Asparagus was in the orchard. An almond tree was included with the other "family orchard" trees.

As for the other growers, already by 1923 the valley not only shipped its crops of the early years including asparagus, alfalfa, grapes, strawberries, onions, potatoes, apples, and honey, but now shipped as well: hops, sunflower, corn, poultry, hogs, sheep, filberts, sorghum, oats, barley, tobacco, sweet potatoes, melons, peanuts, sugar beets, and a wide variety of berries and soft fruit. The County Extension office stated that just about anything could be grown in the valley. Yet the most popular crop remained apples.

Chapter 18.

1. Two years into the Depression, the Farm Management Dept. at Wash. State College found that the average Benton County farm was only 23.8 acres. It was still a district of small farming. They averaged 11.4 acres in alfalfa, 5.2 in orchard, 3 in potatoes, 2.7 in grains, and .6 in asparagus. Berries and grapes no longer made the top list. As for livestock, they

averaged 4.4 cows, 3 hogs and 174 poultry. Some large poultry and alfalfa raisers were skewing the average. The average annual gross income declared was apples: $1160, dairy: $401, poultry: $207, soft fruit: $172, other livestock: $161, potatoes: $92, asparagus: $72, and other non-farm sources: $219. Obviously apples were still king, with dairy and poultry significant. The average net income that year was $28. It is the same picture as Jane Shaw's receipts (see Chpt 16) for a few years earlier.

Yet, with all its problems, Benton County was one of the top producers nationwide, based on production figures collected by Schuddakopf in 1972 from the 1930 U.S. Census. Benton County, with its small population, ranked 65th in the nation's counties for total production of fruits and vegetables, with principal crop being apples. Its overall county ranking for some specific crops: asparagus—21st, apricots—37th, apples—42nd, pears—46th.

Some of Jeanie's saved receipts from Walter Bowen Co. for 26 days in 1931 tell what had happened to the already fragile fruit market. Gross is the sale price, net is their amount after freight and commission house cuts but before other expenses. Compare these to the figures from Jane Shaw's sales to her coop in 1926-27 (chapter 16).

> 7/15--10 boxes peaches and pears: gross 8.00, net 4.49
> 7/16--15 boxes peaches and pears: gross 13.50, net 8.77
> 7/18--21 boxes peaches and pears: gross 15.25, net 8.75
> 7/21--26 boxes peaches: gross 22.00, net 13.50
> 7/22--5 boxes peaches: gross 3.75, net 2.10
> 7/23--10 boxes peaches: gross 7.30, net 4.00
> 7/30--27 boxes of pears, nectarines and peaches :
> gross 29.45, net 18.75
> 7/31--8 boxes pears: gross 4.00, net .40
> 8/8--9 boxes peaches: gross 9.00, net 5.76

8/11--20 boxes peaches: gross 21.30, net 14.10

8/12 <u>Net total for 26 days: $107.47</u>

(Costs of boxing materials, spray , fertilizer, water, and labor not included.)

In 1932 Jeanie wrote to Donald, "We should cut down all the apple trees." They were apparently doing no better on the market and were increasing trouble due to the codling moth. But it would be eight more years before they could bring themselves to destroy them.

2. The Wheelers' college experiences didn't end with their Reed degrees. Margaret, after achieving all but the thesis for a Master in Social Work and working for twenty years in that field, went back for a M.A. in French in 1960 and taught French an Oregon high school until she retired. George was a researcher in agricultural economics for over twenty years at a University in Prague, then returned to the U.S. and taught at Washington State University and Franconia College until he retired. Helen was a homemaker while her husband taught at W.S.U., in later years taught high school English in Pullman until retirement. Rose in her late forties completed several art courses, then earned a degree in nursing and worked in geriatrics at a Tacoma hospital until her retirement. Donald's achievement of a PhD would wait thirty-nine years. He spent eighteen years in dairy farming, finally to return to Oxford to finish his degree. He taught at Franconia College, then at the University of Manitoba until retirement. Marian did not return to college but did much art work out of her own home, specializing in Victorian dolls. After retirement Helen joined Marian and Rose in their art activity, taking up watercolor. All of the Wheeler siblings chose country places in western Washington for their retirement, complete with gardens and small orchards.

Chapter 19

1. Following Grand Coulee, in 1954 the Bonneville Power Administration completed McNary Dam. The much-prophesied Priest

Rapids Dam finally went up in 1956. That was the head of navigation. The dam at the Dalles was complete in 1957. By 1970 there were twenty-six federally funded dams on the Columbia, with vast new areas opened up to irrigation. The Bureau of Reclamation's Columbia Basin Project would be the largest irrigation project in square miles in the country. Many more dams were privately built in Washington. Again agencies allowed developers to ignore the law. Outwater says, "Despite state laws requiring fish ladders at dams, by 1940 eight unladdered dams had been built on the Yakima River alone."

Just as the irrigation lobby had dreamed, the desert was intensely productive. The costs to the nation were significant. Outwater states that "The forty-year Columbia River Project amounted to a 96.7 percent public subsidy...In the end, by 1991 the Bureau [of Reclamation] would have spent 18 million in capital outlay for diversion dams, reservoirs, canals, pipelines, pumping plants, etc." Meanwhile the Bonneville Administration, had serious fiscal problems due in part to its subsidized rates, in part to overexpansion, in part to faulty estimates of costs in developing nuclear plants. That story has been covered extensively by Blaine Harden, Richard White and many others.

Chapter 20

1. The desert kept its hold on the evicted families. At the 1947 reunion for White Bluffs and Hanford, those attending listed these desert towns as their new locations: Tri-City area—44; Yakima area—48; Grandview/Sunnyside/Prosser area—48; Wenatchee—6; other Eastern Washington small towns combined, about 40. Seattle/Tacoma area claimed 25 and Spokane 10.

Chapter 21

1. After the war ended, the nuclear plant became a gigantic problem for not just the region but the country. Closing it down did not end this, for

gradually the massive amount of careless dumping of radioactive and other toxic wastes came to public light. After over seven years of intensive cleanup, with a calculated fifty-five million gallons of radioactive waste in underground tanks, over a third of which are leaking, it is acknowledged by the government to be one of the most toxic places on earth. Cleanup continues.

By the late 1960s another threat to the river, its riparian borders, and its flora and fauna occurred when the bluffs began sloughing, causing landslides. In one incident this practically closed the eastside stream by Locke's Island. Scientists proposed that it was caused by irrigation on the Wahluke Slope. By 1997 they estimated that the water table had risen 400-500 feet in some locations and that five million acre feet of water were stored in the ground adjacent the bluffs. (See under Sources, "Irrigation's Role Debated as White Bluffs Slide Away." *Tri-City Herald* Nov. 12, 2000.)

There are many ironies in the successful fight for the Hanford Reach National Momument. By 1998 the mid-Columbia was regarded as number one of "most endangered rivers" by environmentalists. But the involved county administrations and many area farmers did not want a protected areas set-aside. They argued that the land should pass from the nuclear energy works back to private enterprise. It was too valuable not to be farmed (and taxed); furthermore, it had been taken from farmers in 1943 and should be returned to farmers. Indian tribes asked that at least a portion be returned to them for their management as a cultural area, for it was, after all, really their land. Biologists, however, argued that it was a uniquely biologically diverse area of shrub-steppe land, practically gone from Washington, and that the "wild" twenty miles of the Reach could not be properly protected unless under government control. It was the only place on the river where Chinook salmon could spawn naturally, though their success was being threatened by the sloughing of the bluffs.

Other supporters of the Monument concept pointed out that the area could not be farmed without irrigation, that the available water was already delegated, and that the government was not likely to invest in more expansion of the already overgrown Columbia Basin Project. The argument seemed to have circled once again: did we really need more farming? The Hanford Reach won its National Monument status. Most people appreciate the Reach for what it now is—a rare stretch of almost wild American river and unique shrub-steppe, teeming with wildlife, and accessible for recreation and meditation. Most will not realize that it was brought to us through the destruction of one society after another.

SOURCES USED

Bard, J.C. and J.B. Cox. "Euro-American Resettlement of the Hanford Site (1805-1943)".
  Hanford Cultural and Historical Resources Program, Dept. of Energy. Richland:
  Updated website, 2004. A summary history of the Hanford-White Bluffs area
  during the time of the homesteaders and orchardist, followed by a discussion of
  whether it is valuable to do an archaeological study of the townsites and farms.

Brown, John A. and Robert Ruby. *Half-Sun on the Columbia: A Biography
  of Chief Moses*. Norman, OK: U. of Oklahoma Press, 1965. Chief
  Moses' efforts to hold onto land along the middle Columbia has
  parallels to that of the Chiefs Sohappy and Smoholla of the
  Wanapum tribe.

Cahill, Tim. "A Lethal Dose of Salvation." *Outside Magazine* June 1999.
  A look at the toxic waste problems at the Hanford Nuclear Plant.

Clark, Robert. *River of the West: A Chronicle of the Columbia.* New York:
  St. Martin's Press, 1995. Clark has a chapter on the efforts of
  David Sohappy Sr. in the 1950s to hold onto fishing rights along the
  lower river.

Collette, Carlotta. "A Visit With the River People of the Hanford Reach."
  High Country News Dec. 8 1997. A reporter talks with Rex Buck,
  Wanapum, and others about the designation of the Hanford Reach as a
  wildlife refuge.

Coleman, Marian Wheeler. Personal interviews. All comments by Marian Coleman,

Coleman, Marian Wheeler. Personal interviews. All comments by Marian Coleman, the fourth Wheeler child, are from interviews in 1998-2000.

"Collected Letters and Papers of the F.M. Wheelers of White Bluffs" Unpublished, in possession of the author. This includes all of the letters of the Wheelers and Shaws quoted here.

"Collected Letters and Papers of Wheeler/Lukes Families", unpub. files. This collection is now in the archives at the Univ. of Washington library under "Donald Niven Wheeler".

Connelly, Joe. "Babbitt vows Protection for Hanford Reach." *Seattle Post Intelligencer* May 16, 2000. Tells of the fight to protect the Hanford Reach as a national monument.

"Family Histories for Hanford and White Bluffs, Washington." Richland Washington: White Bluffs-Hanford Pioneer Association, Hanford Science Center, Compiled 1981. This collection of personal histories was written by the settlers from 1906 onward.

Fiege, Mark. *Irrigated Eden: The Making of an Agricultural Landscape in the American West.* Seattle: U of W Press, 1999. Fiege bases his study on Idaho desert projects. He takes a positive view of modern day irrigation and its potential to exist in harmony with nature.

Gerber, Michelle S. *On the Homefront: The Cold War Legacy of the Hanford Nuclear Site.* Lincoln: U. of Nebraska Press, 1992. Gerber has a chapter on the environment and communities that the project supplanted.

Greenwood, Annie Pike. *We Sagebrush Folks.* Moscow: U. of Idaho Press, 1939, rp. 1988. Greenwood's personal account of a woman's life on an irrigated Idaho wheat ranch contemporary with the Priest Rapids settlement adds breadth to the picture of small irrigator families.

Harden, Blaine. *A River Lost: The Life and Death of the Columbia.* N.Y: W.W. Norton, 1996. A journalist travels downstream in the 1990s and observes the social and environmental issues that emerged along the Columbia as an "industrialized canal".

Harris, Mary Powell. *Goodbye White Bluffs*. Yakima: Franklin Press, 1972. One of the few books written about the pre-1943 White Bluffs farming town, it is valuable for its interviews of the homesteaders during her stay in 1920-22, and for its chapter about the water struggles.

Hastay, Helen Wheeler. "Jeanie Shaw Wheeler: A Biographical Sketch". unpub. ms. 1997. Helen, the sixth Wheeler child, and her brother Donald were the two living Wheelers who contributed most to this history.

_____. "Memoirs". Unpub. Manuscript, 1998.

_____. Personal interviews, 1997-2002.

Helland, Maurice. *They Knew Our Valley*. Yakima: M. Helland, 1975. Helland tells the story of how the town of Yakima was moved to benefit the railroad, a gambit repeated at White Bluffs.

Home Physician and Guide to Health. Eds: Evans, Newton; Percy Magan and George Thomason. Mountain View, Cal: Pacific Press Pub., 1923. This reference is typical of the texts families used in the absence of health professionals.

"Irrigation's Role Debated as White Bluffs Slide Away." *Tri-City Herald*. Nov. 12, 2000. Describes the problems of sloughing of the bluffs caused by irrigation on the plateau.

Jeffrey, Julie Roy. *Frontier Women: The Trans-Mississippi West, 1840-1880*. NY: Hill and Wang, 1979. The real life of the women, based on first-hand accounts—journals, letters, and interviews—is interesting to compare with the lives of White Bluffs women.

Kirk, Ruth and Carmela Alexander. *Exploring Washington's Past: A Road Guide to History*. Seattle: U. of Wash. Press, 1991, rev. 1995. A capsuled White Bluffs history.

Koppen, Jennie. *Excerpts from the Diary of Jennie (Crawford) Koppen 1995-1898, Wahluke, Washington.* Richland: The Hanford Science Center, 1979. An early pioneer family just above White Bluffs.

Lage, Laura Tice. *Sagebrush Homesteads.* Pullman: Wash. State U. Press, 1999 rp. The Tice family history tells of the struggles of dry-farming homesteaders up on the Columbia plateau near Othello, pre-WWI.

Lichatowich, Jim. *Salmon Without Rivers: A History of the Pacific Salmon Crisis.* Wash. D.C.: Island Press, 1999. A well-documented history of the salmon crisis adds another perspective on the damming of the Columbia River.

Meinig, D.W. *The Great Columbian Plain.* Seattle: Univ. Wash. Press, 1968. A geography of the region that illuminates the challenges of farming on the edge of arrable land.

Metsker Map. "The White Bluffs-Hanford Area Before 1943." Tacoma: Wash. State Historical Society. n.d.

McWhorter, Lucullus. *The Crime Against the Yakimas.* Republic Printing, No. Yakima, 1913. An account of how the fishing sites and treaty lands suitable for agriculture at the Yakima reservation gradually fell into the hands of non-Natives.

Morford, Rollin Wheeler. Personal interviews and letters to author,1997-2001.The son of Rose Wheeler Morford, Rollin was at White Bluffs most of the time until he was fourteen.

Mullins, William H. *The Depression and the Urban West Coast, 1929-1933.* Bloomington: Indiana U. Press, 1991. A coverage of the economic and social problems that the Wheeler siblings faced in Seattle, 1929-41.

Nisbet, Jack. *Singing Grass, Burning Sage: Discovering Washington's Shrub-Steppe.* A Nature Conservancy of Washington Book. Graphic Arts Center Publishing, n.d. This book about the lands, flora and fauna within the Hanford Reach contains beautiful photos of the natural shrub-steppe and some history of its degradation.

O'Connor, Georgianna and Karen Wieda. *Northwest Arid Lands: An Introduction to the Columbia Basin Shrub-Steppe.* Batelle Press, 2001.Valuable for its description of the terrain, flora, and fauna the irrigators encountered.

Outwater, Alice. *Water.* New York: Harper Collins, 1996. Contains a chapter on the demise of the anadromous fish stock of the east coast and another on the effects of damming along the Columbia and Snake.

Parker, Martha Berry. *Tales of Richland, White Bluffs & Hanford 1805-1943.* Fairfield, WA: Ye Galleon Press, 1986. Parker's collection of dated newspaper stories and photographs, along with interviews of area pioneers, was essential to this history for providing correct dates and sequences of events mentioned by settlers, 1906-1943, and for the history of the fruit market, the water companies and railroad spur.

Raban, Jonathan. *Bad Land: An American Romance.* New York: Random House, 1996. The tragic story of western dry-farming is valuable for placing the early 1900s irrigation craze in perspective.

Roueche, Marjorie. "What About the White Bluffs Townsite?" *Shrub-Steppe Ecology Series,* Columbia School District, n.d. A capsule history of the townsite.

"Sex, Salmon, Secrecy." Reel Moon Media, Belfair, WA. A film documentary about releases of toxic waste into the river at the Hanford Nuclear Plant in 1999.

Sanger, S.L. *Working on the Bomb: An Oral History of WWII Hanford.* Portland: Portland St. U Press, 1995. Included are interviews with the workers who first went in 1943 to build the Hanford Works, and an interview with Frank Buck, Wanapum of Priest Rapids.

Schlick, Mary Dodds. *Columbia River Basketry.* Seattle: Univ. of Washington Press, 1994. This study contains many good photographs of Columbian River region Indians as well as of their basketry.

Schuddakopf, Margaret Jean Wheeler. "Family Sketches." Unpub. ms, 1980. These unpublished manuscripts are one of the main sources for this history. The oldest child of the Wheelers, she was the first of them to live full time, 1912, at White Bluffs.

_____"What Happened at White Bluffs". Unpub. ms, 1970. Schuddakopf completed a draft of a social history in 1968, then put it aside. She was working on it again when she died in 1980; much of its information is included here.

Schuster, Helen. *The Yakima: A Critical Bibliography*. Bloomington: Indiana U. Press, 1982. Lists publications regarding the Yakama tribe.

Schwantes, Carlos. *The Pacific Northwest: An Interpretive History*. Lincoln: U. of Nebraska Press, 1989. A valuable look at the socioeconomic scene and radical politics of the Northwest during the time of this story.

Shannon, David. *The Great Depression*. Englewood Cliffs, N.J.: Prentice Hall, 1960. He includes a chapter about the effects of the Depression on the rural Northwest.

Smith, Henry Nash. *Virgin Land: The American West as Symbol and Myth*. New York: Random House, 1950. The Myth of the Garden, and how it was promoted, is integral to understanding the fascination that the irrigation movement had for turn of century middle-class Americans.

Splawn, A.J. *Ka-mi-akin, Last Hero of the Yakimas*. 2nd ed. Portland: Bineford & Mort, 1944 (1st ed. 1917). Kamiakin looms large in the history of this region. He was an early irrigator, a warrior, and a refuser, never going to the reservation. Splawn also describes the early years of the cattlemen, of which he was one, in Eastern Washington.

Stegner, Wallace. *Where the Bluebird Sings to the Lemonade Springs: Living and Writing in the West*. New York: Random House, 1992. Stegner talks about the uses and misuses of the arid West, focusing especially on the large projects of the Bureau of Reclamation.

Stiffler, Lisa. "A Bittersweet Reunion at Hanford". *Seattle Post Intelligencer,* August 9, 2001. Reporter reviews the history of the eviction as she visits with the settlers and their descendants at the annual picnic.

Taylor, Ronald J. *Sagebrush Country: A Wildflower Sanctuary.* Missoula: Mountain Press Pub., 1992. The wildflowers admired by the Shaws and Wheelers are shown and described here.

United States Works Project Administration. *Told by the Pioneers.* 3 v. Federal Writers Project for State of Washington, 1936-38. These accounts include some from early homesteaders along the mid-Columbia.

Waller, O.L. "Irrigation in the State of Washington" U.S. Dept. of Agriculture, Wash. Gov. Printing Office. June, 1909. One of the documents promoting desert irrigation projects.

Watkins, Marilyn T. *Rural Democracy: Family Farmers and Politics in Western Washington, 1890-1925.* Ithaca: Cornell U. Press, 1995. It is interesting to compare what was taking place in Western Washington rural areas during the years that the Grange was the voice of the farmers on the east side.

Watkins, T.H. *The Great Depression: America in the 1930s.* New York: Little, Brown and Co.,1993. The chapters referring to rural areas and to farmers' troubles nationwide add a broad perspective.

Wheeler, Donald Niven. *The Collected Works.* Portland: Linda M. Elias, 1995. Dr. Wheeler, the sixth Wheeler child, grew up in White Bluffs to become a professor of political economy. Includes essays on topics related to orchardry at White Bluffs.

_____. Personal interviews and letters, 1997-2001. Donald was my foremost direct informant on the socioeconomic issues of the valley from 1920 until 1936.

Wheeler, George S. "Memoirs". Unpub. ms., 1988. All comments from George are from this document, in possession of his son, Frank Wheeler. The third

Wheeler child, an agricultural economist and professor, he was unfortunately not alive for interviews.

White Bluffs Spokesman, 1907?-1934. This weekly newspaper was in operation during almost all of the time of the orchard years, owned and operated by the O'Larey family after 1910..

White, Richard. *The Organic Machine*. New York: Hill and Wang, 1995. An illuminating account on the transformation of the Columbia from its natural to its present day state.

Wilkinson, Dale. "Memoirs". Unpub. ms. that includes his years at White Bluffs as a telephone company owner and town activist, from 1911-1943.

Winther, Oscar. *The Great Northwest: A History.* NY: Knopf, 1947. He Includes a the chapter on the early navigation on the lower Columbia and the wars for control between the railroad and steamship companies that affected White Bluffs.

Worster, Donald. *Rivers of Empire:Water, Aridity, and the Growth of the American West.* New York: Pantheon Books, 1995. Worster is one of the strongest critics of the irrigation movement, and its inappropriate altering of the western desert, and especially of the role of the Bureau of Reclamation in allowing small irrigation, against regulation, to be overtaken by agribusiness.

Zwinger, Susan. *The Hanford Reach: A Land of Contrasts.* Univ. of Arizona Press, 2004. A description of the unique natural world of the Hanford Reach with its healthy, protected population of indigenous flora and fauna of shrub-steppe lands, now rare in the Northwest.

PHOTO AND MAP CREDITS

We are grateful to the following for providing or allowing us to use these photographs and illustrations:

Marion Wheeler Burns: A10, cover photo:Rose Wheeler with peach harvest, 1914

Dept. of Energy ORP, Richland: C5-Street scene, New Town, White Bluffs

East Benton County Historical Society: C6-Oasis Saloon, White Bluffs

Helen Hastay and Marion Wheeler Burns: A1, 3, 4, 5, 6, 7, 8, B2,3, 5, 6, 7, 9, 10, 11, 14; C1, 2, 3, 4, 5, 9, 12, 13, 14, 15, 16.

Marthiel O'Larey: B7-Priest Rapids Power Plant pre-1943; C9-Neighbor Boys with Truck; C11-Swimmers at White Bluffs Ferry Landing

Martha Parker: A2-Hand-drawn map of White Bluffs-Hanford area, pre-1943

Rich Steele: back cover photo of Hanford Reach

Yakima Valley Regional Library: B1-Wanapum Lodges

YakimaValley Musuem: A9 - Apple Orchard in Bloom; B3-White Bluffs Ferry; B11-Work Party in Orchard; B12-Spray Crew; C8-Apples

INDEX

ABOUT THE AUTHOR

Nancy Mendenhall grew up on Puget Sound in
Washington and spent her childhood summers until
1943 at her grandparents' Willowbank Farm just
north of the White Bluffs townsite. She earned a
Masters in English from Western Washington University in 1968. An Alaska resident since 1961, she
taught in the public schools, then for the University
of Alaska Fairbanks, retiring as campus director at
Nome. Commercial and subsistence salmon fishing
has been a favorite summer occupation. Mendenhall
published *Beachlines: a Pocket History of Nome* in 1997.
From 1996-1999 she coordinated a three year
Rockefeller Foundation oral history project for the
Nome area. She is currently preparing an updated
second edition of *Beachlines.*